S0-BRJ-807

82/1/9 Purchased at Waldenbooks, Meadow
Glen Mall; Medford, MA _____ 3.99

m.g.o.

World Futures

THE GREAT DEBATE

World Futures

THE GREAT DEBATE

edited by *Christopher Freeman*
and Marie Jahoda

UNIVERSE BOOKS

New York

82/1/9 Purchased at Waldenbooks, Meadow Glen
Mall, Medford ___ 3.99

Published in the United States of America in 1978 by Universe Books
381 Park Avenue South, New York, N.Y. 10016

© Copyright 1978 Science Policy Research Unit, University of Sussex, England

All rights reserved. No part of this publication may be reproduced, stored in a
retrieval system, or transmitted, in any form or by any means, electronic, mechanical, photocopying, recording, or otherwise, without the prior permission of the
publishers.

Library of Congress Catalog Card Number: 78-57544
ISBN 0-87663-328-9

Printed in the United States of America

Contents

Contents

Acknowledgements

Much of the work on which this book is based has been made possible by a grant from the Social Science Research Council and by two Leverhulme Trust fellowships in support of a programme of studies on social and technological alternatives for the future at the Science Policy Research Unit, University of Sussex.

Under these sponsorships an interdisciplinary core group has previously contributed to the field of forecasting in several other books: *Thinking About the Future*, H. S. D. Cole *et al.* (eds.) contained a critique of Meadows' well-known *Limits to Growth; The Art of Anticipation*, S. Encel *et al.* (eds.) examined the values and methods in forecasting; *Global Simulation Models*, J. A. Clark and H. S. D. Cole, was a detailed critique of the first generation of world models and of computer simulation in particular, and *The Poverty of Prediction*, Ian Miles, discussed the contribution of social scientists, particularly those involved in the social indicator movement, to forecasting.

The present book is our first attempt to go beyond critical, methodological and historical studies into forecasting proper. Like its predecessors it is the result of teamwork, including the contributions of members of the Science Policy Research Unit who do not belong to the core group. The attribution of authorship in such teamwork is inevitably difficult. No individual is solely responsible for the merits or defects of any one chapter. After the presentation of a first draft, intensive discussions within the Unit led to a second draft, sometimes but not always produced by the original author. Further discussions repeated this process so that in the end it became virtually impossible to say who had contributed which idea or formulation. Within the team, however, each individual clearly carries responsibility for specific issues raised in this book, has done the hard groundwork and continues to be involved with the same problems. Several contributors felt that individuals should not be identified as 'authors' of chapters in this book. Others argued that both credit and responsibility in intellectual endeavours are better assigned to persons than to a collectivity; their view prevailed in the end.

With so prolonged a team effort the selection of editors presents a comparable dilemma. In addition to the core group involved in the project other members of the Science Policy Research Unit performed the editorial task of commenting on drafts of chapters and the tenor of the whole book; in doing so they have not only improved an individual's work but added ideas of

Acknowledgements

their own. In one sense then, all of the following have performed editorial functions: John Chesshire, John Clark, Sam Cole, Charles Cooper, Christopher Freeman, Jay Gershuny, John Gribbin, Amilcar Herrera, Marie Jahoda, Mick McLean, Pauline Marstrand, Ian Miles, Geoffrey Oldham, Robert Otto, Bill Page, Keith Pavitt and Howard Rush.

When the time came to pull the material together a group of five, given full power by all authors, shared the considerable remaining editorial task. They were Sam Cole, Christopher Freeman, Marie Jahoda, Ian Miles and Keith Pavitt. In spite of quite radical changes introduced in the text for the sake of coherence of the volume, all authors could accept the result of the editorial efforts. If only two of this editorial group were finally selected as the editors, this has more to do with their overall responsibility and with the convenience and traditions of book production than with any special role in the editorial team.

Before the five editors tackled their final task they had the benefit of comment and advice from a number of experts who read through an earlier draft, and whose specific contributions to the improvement of various chapters are acknowledged in their place. But two of them must be singled out: Dr George Ray of the National Institute for Economic and Social Research and Professor Dudley Seers of the Institute of Development Studies who have taken the trouble of going with a fine toothcomb over many of the chapters. Their critical comments were invaluable.

Finally, we want to thank the supporting staff at the Science Policy Research Unit who gave us such competent help. In particular Vivien Johnson who checked the bibliographies, and Melanie Hempleman and Hazel Robards, who not only typed and re-typed with great efficiency, but called us to order when our efforts at improving the text, a task that is in principle unending, threatened to become so in practice.

The editors

Introduction

CHAPTER 1

Introduction

Marie Jahoda

This book is a contribution to the debate about the future of humanity within the next half century or so. Even though this debate has in the last decade been conducted largely by natural and social scientists, it is far from 'academic' in the derogatory connotation of this term. The future concerns everybody; and to the extent that disciplined thought about it has any purpose, the result of studies of the future may inform policies that affect everybody not only tomorrow but today. That is why this book has been written not just for our colleagues and students in universities, but in the hope that it will be read by concerned members of the public in general.

When scientists enter this debate they deal with a topic different from their customary concerns to which they apply experimental designs, rules of scientific evidence, precision and prediction. For however important these canons of procedure remain within a limited aspect of studies concerning the future, there is only *one* thing certain about it: the human future is in principle unknowable – it cannot be predicted. Imagination and intuition actually play a greater role in the work of scientists than is normally acknowledged. But even so there remains one feature peculiar to studies of the future and different from other scientific work. Ordinarily the scientist's creative invention leads to predictions that can be checked here and now. Imagination and intuition in research bearing on the shape of things to come cannot be tested in the present. Only when the future has become the present will we know it.

Does this mean that there is after all not much difference between scientific forecasts and science fiction? The question is less rhetorical than one would like it to be, but there are a few systematic differences: forecasting by scientists is based on the knowable present and an understanding of some factors that made it what it is; it relates the current to the future state of affairs by identifying where policies could commit the future in the direction of one out of several possibilities. While it is probably beyond the power of the human mind to spell out all the consequences of a current policy decision,

1

some of its implications can be suggested. Above all, scientific forecasting
should remain deliberately within the realm of the possible, as we can now
conceive it.

Even though this distinguishes science fiction from forecasting in theory,
the lines are less clearly drawn in practice. An imaginative writer like H. G.
Wells suggested decades ago in *The Shape of Things to Come* that the future
'has given the world occupation without servitude and leisure without
boredom . . . We can arrange to take a turn with the meteorological
observers in the upper atmosphere or tune our lungs for a spell in the deep sea
galleries below the rafts of Atlantis.' His image of the future matches the
vision of some systematic forecasters from the Soviet Union and the United
States when they speak of a future in which tourist trips to the moon will be
available or in which Americans will have to learn to avoid boredom.

At the other extreme, the apocalyptic prediction of the end of the world, a
consistent theme in human imagination since the days of the Bible, is
matched by forecasters concerned with the world's current population
problem:

> Mankind itself may stand on the brink of extinction; in its death throes it
> could take with it most of the other passengers of Spaceship Earth. No
> geological event in a billion years – not the emergence of mighty mountain
> ranges, nor the submergence of entire subcontinents, nor the occurrence of
> periodic glacial ages – has posed a threat to terrestrial life comparable to
> that of human overpopulation.
>
> [The Ehrlichs, 1970, Introduction]

These juxtapositions demonstrate that imagination, values and
speculation do indeed enter all thinking about the future, whether offered as
science or as fiction. It is certainly not a foregone conclusion that fiction
writers are always less correct than systematic forecasters. After all, it was
Harold Nicholson who in his novel *Public Faces* foresaw the atom bomb,
while Rutherford, having split the atom, did not think that this great
scientific achievement would have practical consequences.

The moral of this story is that systematic forecasting cannot compete with
the untrammelled imagination of a fertile mind that predicts correctly a
major single event; no one will hold against Nicholson other occurrences he
described that have not come to pass. Science fiction broadens the horizon of
systematic forecasters, but it can never replace it. Forecasting as conceived in
this book cannot predict history to come; it is limited to the identification of
possible futures and of problems that might have to be faced on the way to
such futures.

If this lesson in humility needs to be hammered in further, a thought
experiment suggested to us by Dr. George Ray clinches the point. Let us
assume, he suggested, that we started this book in the year 1900, though
equipped with the methods for forecasting of the 1970s. In that relatively
peaceful and placid period would we have foreseen the First World War?

After all, it is always difficult to forecast the *first* of anything. Would we have guessed the coming to power of the Communist Party in Russia? A year before the Revolution Lenin said he did not expect to see it in his lifetime.

What conceivable chance would we have had of foreseeing the rise of Nazi power in Germany, not just the outbreak of the Second World War but the attack of Japan on the U.S.A., the outcome of the war and – perhaps the most surprising thing of all – the rapid economic recovery of the losers, Germany and Japan?

In the last twenty-five years there has been no new world war. But would we have forecast this in 1950 in the midst of the Cold War? The U.K.'s Labour government had just announced a rearmament programme that was to increase the resources devoted to military expenditure by some fifty per cent over three years. Under those conditions, if we had forecast that over the next twenty-five years the Cold War would gradually merge into a period of détente, we would have been dismissed as incurable optimists. Who would have dared to predict then that the greatest military power the world had ever known would lose the Vietnam War, into which it had poured tens of thousands of lives as well as equipment worth billions of dollars?

We would have failed not only with regard to such major political events. Few could possibly have expected in 1900 (and in some of the cases randomly listed below not even in 1925) that in seventy-five (fifty) years' time

— there would be anything like an E.E.C.;
— there would be radio and television receivers in almost every household;
— 1½–2 million people in 'domestic service' would simply disappear from the scene;
— household work would be mechanised to the extent of today;
— entirely new, never-heard-of materials would be in common use, such as plastics, man-made fibres and synthetic rubber;
— air transport would link the whole world with frequent services;
— something like a United Nations would exist and consist of some 150 or more *independent* nations;
— there would be no colonial empires left;
— the almighty pound sterling would be where it is;
— man would have landed on the moon;
— or Hiroshima and Nagasaki would be destroyed by atom bombs.

Such realisation of the limits of forecasting imposes an obligation on us to use all conceivable caution in presenting our work and indicating what degree of confidence we have in various statements and why. The purpose of this introduction is to describe in a broad perspective the scope and limitations of our approach to forecasting, to explain – and justify where possible – underlying assumptions and to give the reader an overview of where in the sequence of the text we concentrate on specific issues.

The historical context in which we live inevitably determines the starting point of our work, as it does that of others. In the current debate the following facts and arguments have been used, in addition to the danger of nuclear war, to explain the widespread unease about what the future may hold:

(1) The developed world, including industrialised communist countries, has experienced an unprecedented rate of economic growth in the third quarter of the twentieth century; it is argued that growth based on the assumption of ever-expanding individual consumer demands is wasteful, has ever-increasing human and physical costs, and leads inevitably to the degradation of the environment and a lower quality of life.

(2) It is argued that economic growth cannot be sustained in future, given the physical demands that it will place on a finite world. Sometimes this argument is used to justify the continuance of present patterns of poverty in the world, and sometimes to justify redistribution.

(3) The futures debate has been influenced by the many concrete manifestations of the growing determination and power of countries outside the rich industrialised areas to intervene in and change the pattern of world-wide economic relations.

Not all participants in the current debate about the future have argued in terms of all three points, and of course they have also raised many others. We have learned much from their efforts, even where we disagree with their conclusions. This is why Part I is largely devoted to the work of others. Chapter 2 reviews some of their contributions over the past decade. This may help the reader, as it has helped us, to locate what follows in this wide-ranging debate. Our belief that this debate matters rests on a conviction that rational argument is one, though not the only factor influencing the way individuals, groups and governments view the future and take action accordingly.

Chapter 3 analyses the methods and assumptions of other contributors to the forecasting debate and introduces one major characteristic of our approach that has guided our forecasts: the establishment of four distinct profiles that define possible alternative world situations in half a century or so. These profiles are combinations of two dichotomised variables that are in the centre of the current unease: rate of economic growth and level of international inequalities. Assumptions about the size of the future world population are identical in all four profiles. One of these profiles – the combination of high growth with a significant reduction in international inequality – constitutes our *a priori* preference for the world to come. This choice is based on values, not on facts. This is one reason why we have used all four profiles throughout the book: by comparison with three others we can demonstrate why we consider this to be the profile worth striving for. Another reason has already been discussed: we do not believe that the future can be predicted. All that can seriously be done is to examine the problems and benefits to be expected from a series of alternative possibilities for the world's future. Such an examination is performed in Part II, which presents three issues of fundamental importance for the future. These issues have been the central concern of many other participants in the world futures debate, and we agree with them that supplies of food, energy and materials are critical for any global forecast.

Chapter 4 deals with the questions of food and agriculture; chapter 5 discusses the problems posed by the question of whether energy supply can meet an ever-growing demand; chapter 6 examines from the same point of view a number of non-renewable resources, largely metals. In each one of these three basic sectors of the world economy the role of technology is crucial. As chapter 2 will show, the arguments of Malthus have been taken up in a new form by many of the most influential contributors to the world future debate. Both they and their critics recognise quite clearly that whether or not population will outstrip resources depends not only on demographic trends, but also on the rate, direction and continuity of technical change. Working, as we do, in a research unit whose primary concern is with policies for science and technology, we see as one of our main contributions the clarification of this issue in the debate. This is why chapter 7 follows the discussion of sectors with particular emphasis on policies for the application, development and transfer of technology.

Inevitably, Part II touches on many issues besides the assessment of the four profiles in relation to each sector. Each of the chapters already discusses social, economic, political and international mechanisms that regulate now or might regulate in the future the workings of the economy. It is not in absolute physical shortages or in environmental disaster, these chapters conclude, that the world faces the most serious dangers, but rather in the necessary and far-reaching changes in these social mechanisms. Part III is devoted to a discussion of these matters.

Futurologists are not the only group of researchers who have made statements about the probable course of events or about major mechanisms in the global socio-economic system that may shape its future. Above all, economists have for centuries striven to understand and predict development. Accordingly, Part III begins in chapter 8 with an effort to come to grips with economic theories that have specified mechanisms that either drive the world system as it functions now, or could do so in the future. We have distinguished, as other analysts have also done, three main types of economic theory: neoclassical, Keynesian and Marxist. While there is some overlap in their diagnosis, each of them concentrates on different mechanisms and prospects for change.

Whilst economic theory is probably the most articulate and clearly formulated, it would be impossible to consider it in isolation from the other social sciences, or from the values, interests and assumptions that permeate all discussion of social and economic policies. Our analysis suggested that the three main schools of economic thought were closely related to similar schools in sociology and political science, and all were bound up with attitudes to social change that could broadly be described as 'conservative', 'reformist' and 'radical'. We designate these as three 'worldviews'. These classifications are crude and over-simplified, and do less than justice to all the subtle varieties of individual theorists and their followers. They should be seen simply as a device for structuring an extremely complex set of problems and indicating very broadly the way in which theories and values interact with forecasts about the future and related policy prescriptions.

Some forecasters fear or advocate a future that is different from these three: they believe that the predicaments are not manageable within either a conservative or a reformist or a socialist world but that totalitarian reactionary and fascist political solutions will prevail. The danger of revolts from the extreme right cannot be denied in the light of recent history and the contemporary world scene. The reason why this is not represented among the theoretical approaches is that we could not discover in the literature a systematic theoretical exposition suitable for our purposes.

The identification of social values in the worldviews has had another asset for the anticipation of possible futures: it allowed us to put some flesh on the bare skeletons of the four profiles. There is, of course, in every one of them scope for widely varying qualities of life, depending on the values that will prevail. Chapter 9 spells this out in the construction of twelve scenarios, looking at each profile from the point of view of each worldview. As a result it can indicate in broad perspective aspects of the quality of life that might be experienced in each scenario.

Prospects for social change depend, however, for every one of the scenarios on the largest question that looms ahead: can global war be avoided? Chapter 10 discusses this overwhelmingly important issue, inevitably ending the substantive part of this volume on a frightening note.

Finally, we attempt in chapter 11 to pull together what we believe we have achieved in this volume. We believe that the framework of ideas, which holds all chapters together, demonstrates both the possibility and the need for forecasting; we have shown that our method of analysis reveals formidable dangers and difficulties ahead; but above all we have convinced ourselves, as we hope to convince the reader, that a desirable future is at least in the realm of the possible, if the right social, technological and political choices are made.

PART I

Points of View in the Futures Debate

CHAPTER 2

The Global Futures Debate 1965–1976

*Sam Cole**

INTRODUCTION

In the last few years a series of long-term global forecasts has caught the attention of the media and the public. Many have called for dramatic new thinking about the possibilities for the long-term future, and for a re-orientation of present trends in world development. The purpose of this chapter and the next is to compare the content and prescriptions of some of these forecasts, to set out some of the assumptions upon which they are based, and to distil from such comparison whatever guidance they have to offer for our own approach to thinking about the future.

Since this book is concerned with long-term alternatives for development, and in particular the availability of natural resources of all kinds, we shall first examine forecasts in terms of global ecological constraints. We shall not be comprehensive, but shall try to show a wide range of views, and to give some idea of the recent debate about them. The authors considered and their major work are listed in Table 2.1. Most of them have had much publicity, some have achieved notoriety, and some are believed to have an influence on government policies.

The futures debate of the last decade has taken place against a background of rapidly changing national and world affairs. The late 1960s and early 1970s was a period of economic growth slipping into recession and inflation. Problems of alienation and environment became major issues, reflecting for some people a more general disillusion with industrial society. Many people argue that there has been a shift in the global balance of power. The humiliation of the United States in South East Asia, and the successful attempt by the OPEC group of countries to reverse terms of trade for a major commodity have added weight to calls for a new international economic

*I am indebted to Jay Gershuny and Ian Miles for help with this chapter.

TABLE 2.1   *Major Authors Considered*

Kahn and Wiener	USA	(1967)	*The Year 2000 – A Framework for Speculation on the Next Thirty-Three Years*
Spengler	USA	(1966)	'The Economist and the Population Question'
Ehrlich	USA	(1970)	*Population, Resources, Environment – Issues in Human Ecology*
Forrester	USA	(1971)	*World Dynamics*
Meadows *et al.*	USA	(1972)	*The Limits to Growth* – A report for the Club of Rome's Project on the Predicament of Mankind
Heilbroner	USA	(1974) (1976)	*An Inquiry into the Human Prospect Business Civilisation in Decline*
Dumont	France	(1974)	*Utopia or Else*
Schumacher	UK	(1973)	*Small is Beautiful – A Study of Economics as if People Mattered*
Mesarovic and Pestel	USA/W. Ger.	(1974)	*Mankind at the Turning Point* – The Second Report to the Club of Rome
Leontief *et al.*	USA	(1976)	*The Future of the World Economy*
Kaya *et al.*	Japan	(1974)	'Global Constraints and A New Vision for Development'
Herrera *et al.* (Bariloche Foundation)	Argentina	(1976)	*Catastrophe or New Society?*
Tinbergen	Netherlands	(1976)	*Reshaping the International Order (RIO) – A Report to the Club of Rome*
Modrzhinskaya and Stephanyan	USSR	(1973)	*The Future of Society – A Critique of Modern Bourgeois Philosophical and Socio-Political Conceptions*
Kosolapov	USSR	(1976)	*Mankind and the Year 2000*
Kahn, Brown and Martel	USA	(1976)	*The Next 200 Years*
Galtung	Norway	(1977)	*Self-Reliance: Concepts, Theory and Rationale*

order. Forecasters have certainly been influenced by these events, but it is far less clear in what way their prognoses have influenced the course of affairs.

During the decade there have also been important international conferences on a range of global issues, several of which are under the auspices of the United Nations: the Human Environment (UNEP, Stockholm, 1972), Population (U.N., Bucharest, 1974), Food and Agriculture (F.A.O., Rome, 1975), the North–South Conference for International Economic Cooperation (Paris, 1975), the Habitat Conference on Human Settlements (Vancouver, 1976), the Conference on the Law of the

Sea (U.N., New York, 1976) and Trade and Development (UNCTAD IV, Nairobi, 1976). The topics of these conferences in fact indicate the major agenda of the futures debate. Most futures studies have something to say about each of these issues, although the focus of the debate has shifted systematically and parallels these conferences.

Several forecasters, such as the Hudson Institute, have had direct access to, and are employed by, government. One group, the Club of Rome, has even included cabinet ministers among its membership, and has brought together leaders including heads of state from several nations to discuss long-term issues. The extent to which these discussions have extended the horizons of their day-to-day actions is debatable. Other forecasters, such as Paul Ehrlich, have gained spectacular coverage by the media, and the sales of works such as *The Limits to Growth* reached several million in more than a dozen languages.

Many modern forecasts are variations or extensions of the Malthusian view that there is a tendency for population to outstrip food supply. Works such as *The Limits to Growth* and the writing of Robert Heilbroner and the Ehrlichs take this view. Many other forecasters, notably Herman Kahn and his colleagues, most Soviet writers and the Latin American Bariloche group, claim explicitly to be non-Malthusian. However, they do forecast or speculate about an end to demographic and economic growth. Underlying the prognoses and the suggestions about change there are often very different socio-political views and very different assumptions about the nature of physical resource constraints and technological change.

One new aspect of the world futures debate is the application of computer models to the analysis of global trends. Several of the authors we discuss have constructed world models, arguing that the complex and interacting nature of the modern world makes such a device for analysis essential. But there is controversy about this; we hope to identify in our discussion how and where the models have made a specific contribution to the debate about the future.

Each of the current views of the future that we present has its precursor in the nineteenth century or before. The humanist view of the prospect for improvement in human nature and social structures goes back at least to Thomas More and Francis Bacon. The technological optimist's view is aptly summed up by Charles Babbage, the progenitor of the modern computer: '. . . the dominion of mind over the material world advances with an ever accelerating force.' Babbage's views (in 1832) have a familiar ring. He sees technology not merely as a means for expanding production, but as a creative response to future problems. He foresees, for example, an energy crisis – '. . . power is not without limit and the coal mines of the world may be ultimately exhausted' – and proposes some strikingly modern-sounding technological solutions: tide power for driving machinery, geothermal energy, the liquification of natural gas. The pessimistic neo-Malthusian outlook and its critique have strong nineteenth-century counterparts. The comparison of the first edition of Malthus' *Essay on Population* with *The Limits to Growth* is a familiar one.

For the present, however, we shall consider only contemporary works on the future, presenting them in more or less their original order of publication and indicating where appropriate more recent modifications in the views expressed by their authors. Table 2.2 summarises forecasts by the different authors, showing their general opinions about the nature and causes of present trends, their opinions about Malthusian constraints in food, energy and raw materials (including environmental and technological factors) and finally their prescriptions for policy and the likelihood of these being implemented or successful.

Table 2.2

	FORECAST	(a) OUTLOOK	(b) DIAGNOSIS
1.	KAHN/WIENER	Qualified optimism - continued upward trend - era of political stability - but 'islands of wealth in a sea of poverty'	Step-wise progression to world-wide post-industrial society - change and continuity of the multifold trend
2.	SPENGLER	Current prospect for poor countries definitely Malthusian - income gap grows	Economic size facilitates growth - seek optimum population - 'technology, prudence and reason'
3.	EHRLICHS	World is already over-developed - ecological collapse possible - living standards in poor countries likely to fall	Population control essential - theoretical limit to poor countries development - bring into line with resource realities - individual attitude change is the key
4.	FORRESTER	'Overshoot and collapse' of world system through resource shortage	Industrialisation is more dangerous than population - urgent task is to face issues - 'hard choices must be made' - low level inegalitarian equilibrium
5.	MEADOWS	Limits reached in next 100 years	Only safe way is to slow down - population growth is greatest impediment to redistribution - must achieve equilibrium or face overshoot and collapse
6.	DUMONT	With present trends inequalities today will remain indefinitely and give rise to serious revolt	Distribution of population is the basic cause of injustice - stop the population explosion - solution through economic adjustment - continued confrontation and struggle
7.	SCHUMACHER	The world will face environmental degradation, energy shortage and reduced quality of life unless we mend our ways	Essential problem facing mankind is the choice of scale of technology and organisations - redirect R&D to eliminate giantism, complexity and violence

Table 2.2 (cont.)

FORECAST	(a) OUTLOOK	(b) DIAGNOSIS
8. HEILBRONER	Grim Malthusian outcome in poor countries - worldwide totalitarianism or anarchy	Only major disaster will slow the pace of growth - danger that 'Malthusian checks' will be offset - central issue is to deal with the environment - may be possible to ease long-term adjustments
9. MESAROVIC/ PESTEL	Developing world crisis - regional resource catastrophes could spread worldwide and paralyse future orderly development	Survival of world system is in question - need technological restraint with social, institutional and life-style reforms
10. BARILOCHE FOUNDATION	Catastrophe is an every day reality in poor countries - extreme economic difficulty predicted in Asia and Africa by 2000	Scarcity is not due to physical limits - population growth is not the major factor - must achieve basic needs in poor countries but without help this will not happen in a reasonable time
11. KAYA	Developing countries could run into an impasse	Alleviating poverty is greatest problem today - advanced nations must take steps to reform structure of industry - new type of international division of industry
12. LEONTIEF	Second Development Decade strategy does not provide for sufficiently rapid closing of income gap between developing and developed countries - gap would not diminish by the year 2000	Significant changes in economic relations between developed and developing countries - high growth rates in poor countries coupled with slightly lower rates in rich countries are needed
13. MODRZHINSKAYA	Refute neo-Malthusian theories - socialist post-industrial society conjectured	Prosperity is limited by social structure (especially capitalism) not by technical possibilities or financial resources
14. KOSOLAPOV	The next quarter century promises to be turbulent and dynamic - finally society will become a global association of people	The future today is being moulded in the struggle for communism, with the world revolutionary process and the scientific and technological revolution going on simultaneously

Table 2.2 (cont.)

FORECAST	(a) OUTLOOK	(b) DIAGNOSIS
15. TINBERGEN	World becoming increasingly complex politically - cornucopia of growth turning into Pandora's box - Third World turning from defence to defiance - no sane person could seriously envisage a world in which the world's poor live like today's affluent minority	Rich and poor **have** unparalleled problems which cannot be solved independently - dependency relationships of Third World must be reduced - equitable order requires changes in the distribution of power - political changes have not been reflected in institutions
16. KAHN/BROWN/ MARTEL (1976)	Things are going rather well - 6:1 chance that all serious long-term problems will be successfully dealt with in due course - super industrial society to emerge in late 20th and early 21st Century	Roughly 100-200 years from now world population and economic growth will level off in a more or less natural and comfortable way - closing of the gap will not occur soon

(c) MALTHUSIAN CONSTRAINTS

	FORECAST	FOOD	MATERIALS	ENERGY
1.	KAHN/WIENER	Food technology limits possible within a few centuries	Little reason for concern	Long-run prospect of cheap and inexhaustible energy - several hundred possible sources
2.	SPENGLER	Yields could increase 300% - without population growth gap could be bridged in 50 years	Long-run availability depends on energy supplies - current mineral resources last only decades	Prospects better than for non-fuel minerals but depends on having 'safe' nuclear fusion
3.	EHRLICHS	Limits of production are nearly reached - surplus in proximity to starvation	Hardly reason for optimism - even abundant energy will not help	Energy availability does not place limits except via thermal pollution
4.	FORRESTER	Physical limits cause collapse of populations	At current rates and exponential growth 250 years supply - because of trade whole world faces simultaneous collapse much sooner	Not mentioned - included with other natural resources
5.	MEADOWS	Physical and social limits force collapse of agriculture in 100 years - 'law of increasing costs'	250 years supply only - collapse in 50 years through physical shortage and exponential growth	Needs ultimately adequately supplied by nuclear power
6.	DUMONT	Agricultural production limited - optimistic claims are dubious	'Limits' data used in argument	Nuclear power is dangerous but necessary

Table 2.2 (cont.)

(c) MALTHUSIAN CONSTRAINTS (cont.)

	FORECAST	FOOD	MATERIALS	ENERGY
7.	SCHUMACHER	In principle possible to produce enough through sound ecological practice - supplies endangered by 'callous' instrumental view	Theoretically finite but no crunch imminent	Optimistic about substitution - lack of realism about most discussion of energy prospects
8.	HEILBRONER	Needs of poor countries surpass ecological possibilities	Problems of mining energy and waste are gigantic	Staggering increase in demand by poor countries - failure to find new sources will postpone thermal collapse
9.	MESAROVIC/ PESTEL	Possibilities for expansion of production are in rich countries	Inexhaustibility cannot be taken for granted	Nuclear power is a 'Faustian bargain' - use solar power
10.	BARILOCHE FOUNDATION	Scarcity of poor countries not attributable to physical limits	Minerals are extracted at decreasing social cost	Fossil fuels depleted in next 100 years - nuclear fusion power is 'inexhaustible'
11.	KAYA	Agriculture is not a satisfactory basis for continued development	Vast quantities of metal resources in earth's crust will not be exhausted in the near future	Growing demand for energy threatens to precipitate a temporary energy crisis
12.	LEONTIEF	Dramatic developments bring new land into production and double or treble yields	Tremendous growth in consumption - not a problem of absolute scarcity - problem is how to exploit more costly reserves	Coal is relatively plentiful even under conservative estimates
13.	MODRZHINS- KAYA	Reject inevitability of growing food shortage - can turn deserts into 'flowering orchards'	Raw materials shortage is illusory	Energy shortage fears unfounded - fusion is inexhaustible
14.	KOSOLAPOV	By 2000 progress of plant genetics and selection will have boosted crop yields severalfold	No constraints - increasing use of synthetics based on biological principles	Mankind is on the threshold of momentous changes in global energy supplies
15.	TINBERGEN	Generally agreed all of the most suitable land is in production - humble wheatsheaf destined to become a powerful weapon of economic warfare	Fears about exhaustion may well be exaggerated - oceans' sources are potentially enormous	Energy (and water) are major resource problems - problem is to develop new sources of clean energy
16.	KAHN/BROWN/ MARTEL (1976)	Not in any reasonable sense limited by physical resources - allocate resources to agriculture technology - world likely to be better fed 100 years from now	Alarm seems genuinely misplaced - even with factor of 60 increase in demand would reject the notion that world could run out of resources	Energy costs are likely to continue historic downward trend indefinitely

Table 2.2 (cont.)

(c) MALTHUSIAN CONSTRAINTS (cont.)

FORECAST	ENVIRONMENT	TECHNOLOGY	POPULATION
1. KAHN/WIENER	Environment could be degraded but new techniques can preserve it	New technology developing at an increasing rate - even 'far out' predictions can materialise by the year 2000	Exponential growth but developing countries may escape the 'population trap'
2. SPENGLER	Danger of destabilising 'natural equilibrium'	Improvements will ease 'external pressures' but in poor countries resource problems are greater than technology capacity to counteract them	The greatest threat - up to 50 billion by 2100 - control will not happen automatically
3. EHRLICHS	Environment cannot stand world industrialisation	Technological optimism is based on ignorance	Planet already over-populated - drastic rise in death rate
4. FORRESTER	Pollution brings collapse in 50 years as thresholds are passed	Technical success in one area leads to problems in another	Maximum about 7 billion - stable level 4 billion
5. MEADOWS	Exponential cost of pollution control cannot be met	Optimism about 'cost free' technology is not justified - blocks to technical progress	Collapse at about 16 billion - population could level off at about 8 billion
6. DUMONT	Pollution is ultimately the limiting factor	Modern technology is wasteful	4 billion in 1975 is already too high
7. SCHUMACHER	Increasing damage - need to humanise and ennoble man's wider habitat	Too large, as it grows it requires increasing proportion of maintenance	Population only a contributory, not major factor, to world problems
8. HEILBRONER	Rapidly moving to the ecological limit - thermal collapse a major threat	Pollution-free technologies are essential - abandon industrial mode of production	20 billion by 2050 - 6.5 billion with sufficient coercion - main checks are famine and disease
9. MESAROVIC/PESTEL	Need to exist harmoniously with nature or nature will react against man	Exponential growth assumed	8-12 billion by 2100
10. BARILOCHE FOUNDATION	Increasing economy does not necessarily mean increasing pollution	Technology grows faster than consumption - if poor countries had technology production would outstrip population	Highest 14 billion in 2050, lowest 10 billion size depends on satisfaction of basic needs
11. KAYA	Thermal limit between 20 and 300 times present level of energy consumption	Relatively high capital intensive types of industry could be transferred	Growth rate depends on per capita income

Table 2.2 (cont.)

(c) MALTHUSIAN CONSTRAINTS (cont.)

FORECAST	ENVIRONMENT	TECHNOLOGY	POPULATION
12. LEONTIEF	Technologically pollution is a manageable problem - economic costs high but not unmanageable	By the year 2000 developed countries other than the USA will use the 1970 technologies of North America - other countries will move in this direction	Extremely steep rise in population - UN estimates used average about 10 billion
13. MODRZHINS-KAYA	Could be serious but can achieve planned reconstruction of the entire surface of the planet - true conquest of nature	Can revolutionise the whole process of social production within 20-30 years	Population growth depends on social development
14. KOSOLAPOV	'Ecologise' technology; science based interaction between man and nature	Create scientific and technological base for any degree of prosperity in the world	Average lifespan will be 100 years by 2000
15. TINBERGEN	Life support systems are under unprecedented attack from urbanisation, industrialisation and our lifestyles	Technologies can be developed that will help solve problems - exploitation, extraction, substitution and environmental degradation - greatest gap between industrial and Third World countries is in scientific and technical R&D	Population growth defies easy generalisation - 7 billion by 2000 - 12-20 by 2100 - reduction cannot be achieved without development
16. KAHN/BROWN /MARTEL (1976)	Technologically and economically feasible to maintain environment at an acceptable cost	World-wide technological unity - a decade or two of technological crises and solutions - technology easily transferred to poor countries	Population growth will cease at about 7.5 to 30 billion - to slow need economic development

(d) PRESCRIPTION

FORECAST	ECONOMIC	INSTITUTIONS	MORAL
1. KAHN/WIENER	More growth the better	Violence is a mechanism of change - existing institutions should make use of it (when it occurs) - but above all protect freedom of choice	No requirement for human nature to change - the best may be the enemy of the good
2. SPENGLER	Economic penalties to control population, urbanisation etc. - high rate of saving	Not discussed	'Prudence and reason' - irresponsibility of fostering sub-marginal man
3. EHRLICHS	Low level economy in rich countries - de-development plus 20% aid to poor countries - semi-development in poor countries	Social and political reforms essential - but there is no time to destroy existing institutions	Dramatic and rapid changes - adapt conserving ethic

Table 2.2 (cont.)

(d) Prescriptions

FORECAST	ECONOMIC	INSTITUTIONS	MORAL
4. FORRESTER	Efforts to indus- trialise in poor countries are 'unwise' - wealthy nations must move back a generation	Need for international arbitration	Can traditions become compatible with equilibrium?
5. MEADOWS	Stop industrial and population growth	Create a totally new form of human society	Equilibrium requires great moral resources
6. DUMONT	Semi-austerity in rich nations - 5% aid - industrial capacity used for poor countries	Decentralised national planning supervised by world bodies	Return to the simple life - peasant ethic of austerity and dignity - new morals and new faith
7. SCHUMACHER	Move from economic rationality to humanist economics	Smaller human-scale institutions	Achieve dominance of human values over the machine
8. HEILBRONER	Short-term redistribu- tion - long-term frugality - transfers will not solve problems	Authoritarian govern- ment - unprecedented levels of public con- trol required	Cannot have power without obedience
9. MESAROVIC/ PESTEL	Organic growth - coordinated global economic cooperation - 5% investment aid to poor countries	'Globalism'	Conservationist global ethic and harmony with nature
10. BARILOCHE FOUNDATION	New patterns of socialist development world-wide (possibly 2% aid)	Fundamental socio- political reform	End the ideology of growth
11. KAYA	Mistake to look for development based on agriculture or mining - optimal division of labour needed in manufac- turing industry	Autarky and self- sufficiency are unrealistic policies	Not discussed
12. LEONTIEF	High investment and a brisk expansion of international trade - significant changes in world economic order	Far-reaching changes of social, political and institutional character in poor countries	Not discussed
13. MODRZHINSKAYA	End capitalist and imperialist patterns of growth	World-wide socialist reform	Create truly human and highly moral relations between people of all nations
14. KOSOLAPOV	World-wide system of economic relations by 2000	Continued debate in international relations	Total abolition of all traces of social oppression and human inequality

Table 2.2 (cont.)

(d) Prescriptions

FORECAST	ECONOMIC	INSTITUTIONS	MORAL
15. TINBERGEN	Promote quality rather than quantity - industrial and Third World countries make use of comparative advantages - emphasise labour-intensive methods in Third World	Cooperative global and multilateral solutions - reconcile interests of transnational firms and Third World countries	Poor countries should reject aspiration for Western style of life - preoccupation with growth is morally and ethically corrupting - shift from a war to a peace mentality
16. KAHN/BROWN/ MARTEL (1976)	Task ahead is for America and developed countries to help poor countries to exploit the income gap	Critical but multipolar, partly competitive, mostly global and technological economy - vital institutional reforms	Should encourage the evolution of American values in certain directions - must learn how to spread their wealth without becoming satiated - income gap not necessarily tragic or immoral

FORECAST	(e) CAN MAN CHANGE THE WORLD?	FORECAST	(e) CAN MAN CHANGE THE WORLD?
1. KAHN/WIENER	Man is developing tremendous power to change his own environment. Even so there is 'good reason to discount changes through choice'	10. BARILOCHE FOUNDATION	The future is a direct result of human action
2. SPENGLER	Conditional optimism that change is possible - the number of economists is growing faster than the world's population	11. KAYA	Not discussed
		12. LEONTIEF	Not discussed
3. EHRLICHS	Change possible but prepare for the worst		
4. FORRESTER	Social systems are insensitive to policy changes	13. MODRZHINSKAYA	Scientific and technological progress make it possible for man to feel increasingly confident
5. MEADOWS	Cause for hope - difficult but not impossible	14. KOSOLAPOV	By consciously and continuously deciding what to do man is giving effect to his predestination as a creator
6. DUMONT	People will not grasp the danger unless personally affected		
7. SCHUMACHER	Fear and despondency and paralytic reaction prevent people from doing anything	15. TINBERGEN	Governments inherently underestimate their people - in time of crisis people will accept changes in behaviour
8. HEILBRONER	Impassioned polemics against growth are futile - small ability to engineer change	16. KAHN/BROWN/ MARTEL (1976)	Only rarely is a choice available - attitudes that create a resistance to economic growth can impede the resolution of current problems and deepen the malaise they predict
9. MESAROVIC/ PESTEL	Political willpower and action will only come when consequences are obvious		

FUTURES OF CONTINUED GROWTH — A WESTERN VIEW

Until the end of the 1960s, the most popular forecasts of the postwar period reflected a desire for economic growth and a certain technological optimism, expressed by writers such as Arthur C. Clarke (1964), Colin Clarke (1970), Buckminster Fuller (1972), and by Herman Kahn himself.

We start our review with the best-known of the futurologists – Herman Kahn. We return later to his most recent book and the way in which his views have been influenced by the intervening futures debate.* In *The Year 2000 – A Framework for Speculation on the Next Thirty-Three Years*, published in 1967, Herman Kahn and his co-author Anthony Wiener 'sketch out constraints on social choice'. Before this in 1960, through a book entitled *On Thermonuclear War*, Kahn had aroused both fear and respect from many quarters for thinking about the unthinkable in relation to atomic weapons.

In *The Year 2000* the authors emphasised problems rather than solutions but, compared with others whom we consider later, Kahn and Wiener perceived relatively few major problems. 'The most crucial issue of our study is that economic trends will proceed more or less smoothly through the next thirty years and beyond', and 'capacities for and commitment to economic development and control over our external and internal environment are increasingly seeming without foreseeable limit' (p. 116). Contrary to the fears of some other authors, Kahn and Wiener argue the 'quite plausible' view that 'despite much current anxiety about thermonuclear war generally we are entering a period of general political and economic stability at least so far as the frontiers and economies of most of the old nations are concerned' (p. 128). In the main, therefore, in *The Year 2000* and later works, Kahn and his various colleagues see the world entering *la belle époque*.

The Year 2000 describes a set of 'plausible', fairly detailed, alternative 'scenarios' of the future. A variety of global politico-economic situations is considered, ranging from fast growing 'development orientated integrated worlds', to less appealing 'destruction dominated worlds culminating in all-out nuclear war', culled from Kahn's writing *On Thermonuclear War*. Kahn and Wiener's original work is now over ten years old, and its 'dated' nature has already become evident in some of the detailed predictions. *The Year 2000* did not predict such international and domestic political issues as the ecological movement, the oil crisis or the 1970s' recession.

The idea of scenarios as employed in the book is to outline possible mechanisms whereby these varied but 'hypothetical' futures might occur. In *The Year 2000* these are centred around a so-called 'surprise free' or 'standard world', which is obtained by projecting a set of 'multifold trends'. These forecasts are based on the idea that 'the basic trends of Western society, most of which can be traced back to the twelfth or eleventh centuries, can be seen as

---

*In this chapter page references refer to the first named book for each author.

part of a common, complex trend of interacting elements' (p. 6). Kahn and Wiener pay considerable attention to justifying these trends and the underlying idea of 'continuity' in world affairs, although they caution that any day may witness some 'historic turning point'.

The numerical projections are, in fact, largely exponential extrapolations of recent economic and demographic trends with modest growth rate adjustments to account for the peculiarities of particular nations. Because of the model of development they use, developing nations are assumed to follow the stages of growth of already industrialised nations. Although their 'surprise free' projections in *The Year 2000* give a world in which all societies become more wealthy, notwithstanding changes in the relative international economic pecking order, it is essentially a picture of the world *status quo* maintained. It is also a world in which Western technology and Western social forms are adopted by developing nations.

Like other authors who see levels of economic development beyond those that industrial societies have already attained as desirable, Kahn and Wiener tend to concentrate on what this life might be like. They provide a number of illustrations, almost entirely confined to the U.S.A. 'The upper middle classes' in the America of the year 2000 might 'in many ways be emulating the life style of the landed gentry of the previous century, such as emphasising education, travel, cultural values, expensive residencies, lavish entertainments, and a mannered and cultivated style of life' (p. 207).

Kahn and Wiener's book has the reputation of being technologically optimistic. Through a list of 'very likely' technical innovations they indicate further the kind of benefits that economic growth as it is currently proceeding is likely to bring; for example, 'general and substantial increases in life expectancy, postponement of ageing and limited rejuvenation' and, more exotically, 'physically non-harmful methods of over-indulging'. They list a range of devices that 'most people would consider as (largely) unambiguous examples of progress or human benefit' (p. 52). They observe that their 'optimistic' projections derive from the increased rate at which new technology is being developed (p. 122).

Despite fabulously high income levels and the achievement of 'post-industrial society' by several major powers, Kahn and Wiener foresee large variations of income. Except for the 'voluntary poor', most 'relatively poor' people would be 'amply subsidised'. They dub even this society as 'alienation amid affluence' (p. 193). Unlike some other authors, Kahn and Wiener see much alienation as essentially containable and unlikely to bring about major social changes.

When we come to consider Kahn and Wiener's discussion of possibilities for world economic and institutional reform, the nature of their optimism is again made clear. They observe that although many violent scenarios are 'realistic', few people believe that anything but peaceful scenarios (natural revolution, aided evolution and negotiation) can be 'used to play an important role in reforming the system'. Yet, 'it is the mechanisms of low-level violence of crises and small wars that are most likely to be involved in systematic change'. These will occur, they say, whether we like it or not, and we should be prepared to exploit these mechanisms of transition. Repeating the thinking of *On Thermonuclear War*, they argue that it might be better to accept a greater amount of 'low-level violence' in order to 'deal better with high levels of violence' (p. 385). The issues of distribution, they say, 'provide one reason for believing that a world government could only be created out of war or crisis – an emergency that provided an appropriate combination of the motivations of fear and opportunity' (p. 382).

The threat of war seems, in the opinion of Kahn and Wiener, to be confined largely to the developing nations. The disparity between the rich and poor worlds, even if it gives rise to radical political movements, 'probably does not imply any serious confrontation in the twentieth century, for the underdeveloped countries even in concert are unlikely to possess the resources . . . to wage serious military campaigns against one or more developed countries' (p. 365). A picture of 'international anarchy . . . ignores entirely the self-regulative mechanisms and rules of behaviour that can arise and be maintained in informal organisations' (p. 363).

Throughout the book, Kahn and Wiener are less certain about the fate of poorer nations: 'Whether satisfaction in their absolute progress or envy and resentment of increasing discrepancies between rich and poor will be the dominant reaction of the people of the less developed world, depends of course on many economic, political and cultural factors.' While the improvements in living standards compared with their parents will be clear to many people, 'the increasing discrepancies between their lives and those of the industrialised societies will be brought inescapably to the attention of even the most primitive and isolated communities by cheap and improved worldwide communication and transportation' (p. 142). There can, they say, 'be little doubt that problems of development constitute a serious economic and moral concern' (p. 364).

Despite their reputed optimism about technological change, Kahn and Wiener point out that more 'controversial issues' are raised by the arrival of some of the technical innovations that they list as very likely before the year 2000. These are issues of 'accelerated nuclear proliferation; of loss of privacy; of excessive governmental and/or private power over individuals; of dangerously vulnerable, deceptive and dependable over-centralisation; of decisions becoming necessary that are too large, complex, important, uncertain or comprehensive to be left to mere mortals whether private or public; of new capabilities that are so inherently dangerous that they are likely to be disastrously abused; of too rapid or cataclysmic change for smooth adjustment and so on' (p. 116).

Indeed, in some scenarios in *The Year 2000*, Kahn and Wiener briefly point to the dangers that are central to the neo-Malthusian authors to be discussed next: 'Finally we question whether man's unremitting Faustian striving may ultimately remake his natural conditions – environmental, social and psychological – so far as to begin to dehumanise himself or to degrade his political or ecological situation in some very costly or irrevocable manner' (p. 117). Once more we see the less optimistic side of Kahn and Wiener's forecasts. Even though they hint at the very things that concern authors such as the Ehrlichs, Meadows and Heilbroner, and indeed often appear to be describing the *same* futures as these authors, they simply refuse to be overawed by the magnitude of the problems posed. The standards Kahn and Wiener set for the resolution of major problems are surely lower than those of other futurists, and so their pessimism about achieving them is also less.

Despite their numerous caveats, Kahn and Wiener's work gives the impression of inevitability about the underlying trends they describe. In addition to theories of 'continuity', there is an impressive display of facts and figures and the whole document is backed up by the reputation of the Hudson Institute. As Marien has observed (*Futurist*, 1973), 'for better or worse Herman Kahn heads nearly everyone's list of futurists and *The Year 2000* tops nearly everyone's list of contemporary professional books on the future'. According to Wiener, the work reflects a 'more or less Western capitalist ideology'. Soviet commentators, for example Arab-Ogly, view Kahn's work as a 'premeditated attempt to influence public opinion rather than a serious attempt at prediction' (1975). Indeed Western commentators too, such as Shonfield and de Jouvenel, have shared this opinion. Dumont, an author we consider later, sees Kahn's brand of optimism and inevitability as 'semi-lunatic'! True or not, as Marien points out, Kahn warrants very serious consideration – 'the Hudson Institute view of the future has actually influenced both government and corporate policy in the United States and presumably will continue to do so'.

CHALLENGES TO GROWTH — THE MALTHUSIAN SPECTRE

During the late 1960s the concern about rising populations and environmental deterioration increased. The neo-Malthusian prospect, outlined by Julian Huxley at the United Nations as early as 1948, was repeated by several authors. In direct contrast to Kahn's *la belle époque* or the works of Marxist writers, they give the impression that the world is rushing blindly towards catastrophe. There will be an inevitable clash between exponential population growth and a finite environment. Like Malthus himself, they often place great emphasis on the need for moral reform, and their views about the nature of the crisis, and the ways to avoid it, inevitably reflect their underlying political and economic values.

An influential restatement of the Malthusian position was given by the American economist Joseph Spengler in his 1965 presidential address to the American Economic Association, in a paper entitled 'The Economist and the Population Question'. In more recent work, but without serious modification of his original thesis, Spengler has extended his analysis and data base. In the book *Population Change, Modernisation and Welfare* (1974) he provides a more detailed theoretical justification of the modern Malthusian position.*

Spengler's projections and recommendations are directs particularly at the poor countries and indicate to him a long-run prospect that is 'definitely Malthusian'. 'Population cannot cross the boundaries imposed by physical limits'. In setting out the reasons for the failure of Malthus' projections, Spengler, in contrast to Kahn, emphasises that poor nations lack the same opportunities to repeat the historic development of the rich countries. Even if aid were given, without skills and without capital there is little chance of it being used properly, since these countries have not yet reached the conditions for economic 'take-off' (p. 19).

In Spengler's view, economic measures such as carefully designed taxes on population and on wasteful consumption would serve to correct Malthusian trends. Strict population control and 'prudence' are the key. One dollar spent on population control is worth a hundred spent on aid (p. 16). If only population growth could be brought under control, other problems could be solved, and economic growth would proceed. What is needed is a restructuring of 'relevant penalty–reward structures' and of the 'motivational milieu' in developing countries. Rapid increases in urban employment would permit application of labour-saving agricultural methods. High personal investment and advanced technologies introduced from abroad but adapted to local needs are central to his economic strategy. At the international level he advocates restructuring of international exchange rates to encourage trade in raw materials and agricultural products. Spengler sees many of the same barriers to advancement as Kahn and Wiener, but he is considerably less hopeful that they can be overcome. Nevertheless, he does not appear to be as pessimistic as other authors (such as Heilbroner), whose population and resource assumptions are very similar.

*The contrast with the population debate of the 1930s is interesting (see Pohlman, 1973). Spengler has in fact been active in the debate about population since the early 1930s when he was concerned with under-population in industrial nations rather than over-population in the developing nations. In *The Birth Rate — Potential Dynamite* (1932) Spengler observes that . . . 'Among the white peoples living in countries where industrialisation has made its greatest advances . . . at present not enough children are being born to replace the existing population. Only in the agricultural white nations, among the Asiatic peoples and in Egypt do we find a high birth rate and a steady increase in the population . . .. Will the birth rate continue to decline? Will the swarming peoples of Latin America, Africa and the Orient crush the low-birth rate nations?' To combat this decline Spengler argued, 'let the state offer to pay to couples whatever wage is necessary to induce these couples to undertake the work of producing, rearing and educating the desired number of children'.

Eco-catastrophe

Compared with some other neo-Malthusian authors, Spengler's pessimism about the future is restrained. With the publications of Anne and Paul Ehrlich the idea of eco-catastrophe was born. Passionate television appearances made Paul Ehrlich for a time a focal point of a strong environmental movement. In their book *Population, Resources, Environment* published in 1970 and in their more popularised works *The Population Bomb* (1971) and *How to be a Survivor* (1971), the Ehrlichs argue that the world is *already* over-populated and, in the industrial countries at least, 'over-developed' in terms of the world's ecological resources. In their view the eco-system is already in jeopardy, and for ecological reasons the planet simply cannot stand the kind of industrialisation imagined by Kahn or even Spengler (p. 62). Unlike Kahn and Wiener's book, which concentrates much more on case studies of possible *future* situations, the Ehrlichs detail a large number of areas in the recent past in which things have gone wrong, and use these to exemplify specific objections to various 'optimistic' schemes that have been proposed.

The Ehrlichs consider it possible that the 'capacity of the planet to support human life has already been permanently impaired'. 'Spaceship Earth' is now filled to capacity or beyond and is running out of control (p. 3). As population growth especially continues there is the possibility of lethal plagues, nuclear war . . . even driving the human race to extinction (p. 332). The kind of technological optimism expounded by Kahn and Wiener is based on ignorance about environmental and other issues.

For the Ehrlichs, 'de-development' of the industrial regions rather than growth is needed. Taking a radically different view from Kahn and Wiener, the Ehrlichs propose that in the 'over-developed countries' economic growth rates should be reversed in order to 'bring our economic system (especially patterns of consumption) into line with the realities of ecology and the world resource situation' (p. 323). The Ehrlichs summarise their view of the current situation as follows: 'By making the fundamental error of basing our standard of progress on expansion of the GNP, we have created a vast industrial complex and great mental, moral and aesthetic poverty. Our cities are disaster areas, our air is often unbreathable, our people increasingly regimented and our spirit increasingly dominatable' (p. 304). There must be a massive campaign to de-develop the United States: 'Once the United States has clearly started on the path of cleaning up its own mess it can then turn its attention to the problems of the development of the other developed countries; population control and ecologically feasible semi-development of the under-developed countries' (p. 323).

Opponents of economic growth such as the Ehrlichs are not criticising only the Western model of development; they explicitly include the Soviet Union's aspirations for development: 'A major cause of humanity's current plight . . . lies not in the economic differences between the super powers . . . but in the economic attitudes that they have in common' (p. 279). Dramatic measures must be taken to effect some level of redistribution of the wealth of the world, and they advocate 'unprecedented aid'; the figure mentioned is twenty per cent of rich nations' GNP over a fifteen-year period (p. 302). But unlike Kahn and Spengler, the pattern of development cannot be a Western 'consumist' one. They observe that the 'most impressive of the many reasons why under-developed countries cannot and should not be industrialised along the developed country lines' are the environmental ones of pollution and thermal limits. Most pressing is 'ecologically sensible agricultural development. . . . that is for semi-development' (p. 300). 'They must design a low consumption economy of stability and in which there is a much more equitable distribution of wealth than in the present one' (p. 323). In the Ehrlichs' view, even if the measures advocated by Spengler could be introduced, the environment would not be capable of supporting them.

The difference between the measures advocated by the Ehrlichs and those advocated by Spengler lies largely in their emphasis on governmental and collective moral reform towards a conservationist ethic. For the Ehrlichs, 'the basic solutions involve dramatic and rapid changes in human attitudes, especially those relating to productive behaviour, economic growth, technology, the environment and conflict resolution' (p. 322). Religion, the conservation movement, education, the legal system, must all be used to bring about changes. 'The world cannot in its present critical state be saved by merely tearing down old institutions even if rational plans existed. We simply do not have the time. Either we will succeed by bending old institutions or we will succumb to disaster' (p. 324).

Despite their plea for massive redistribution, the Ehrlichs often appear to be overawed by the magnitude of their own prescriptions. Indeed, their position is frequently ambiguous: 'For some very poor nations there may already be no hope.' In their more pessimistic passages the Ehrlichs advise us to 'prepare for the worst' and suggest that a policy of 'triage' may be called for. This involves writing off all nations that are felt to be beyond 'realistic help'; those that belong to the tragic category that is 'so far behind in the population–food game that there is no hope that our food aid could see them through to self-sufficiency'. The Ehrlichs say India might be a candidate for triage, and that if experts who advocate it are right 'this would be preferable to thoughtless dispersal of limited food reserves without regard for their long range effects' (p. 310). Thus, the Ehrlichs consider the extreme alternatives: altruism and despair. Frightened by their own image of the world, they retreat into despair.

The Limits to Growth

Those who were not convinced by detailed documentation of the state of the environment and the earth's limited potential in the Ehrlichs' book might well have been moved by an even more dramatic Malthusian prediction issuing from a computer: world population growth and industrialisation in the face of finite natural resources would bring about starvation, ecological disaster and an abrupt decline of population. Ignoring Kahn and Wiener's region by region extrapolation, this was the message of Jay Forrester in *World Dynamics* (1971). Forrester's computer model essentially described five interlinked 'global sub-systems': population, natural resources, capital, agricultural and pollution. The fact that it came from a computer made Forrester's a dramatic and original forecast. His authoritative-looking graphical output made front page reading in the international press. Surprisingly, however, virtually no empirical evidence was given to substantiate the numbers he had inserted in his model (Cole, Freeman, Pavitt and Jahoda, 1973).

The book contained an important idea, which was expressed by earlier Malthusian authors such as the Ehrlichs but not spelt out so clearly – that of the mutually reinforcing nature of events. Forrester's claim is that attempts to solve one problem will only exacerbate another. For example, attempts at population control would be inherently self-defeating since the consequent rise in living standards would promote industrialisation and this, he argues, is ecologically even more disturbing than population growth (p. 11). By the same token, attempts to improve diet by improved agricultural technology would be defeated for precisely the reasons indicated by Malthus. Forrester dubs this decline 'overshoot and collapse'. Only a package of population, resource and environmental policies directed towards some kind of equilibrium society would suffice, for even the most optimistic expectations for technology do not permit continuing growth. We may now be living in the 'golden age'. It may be unwise for poor countries to attempt to industrialise, and the rich–poor gap may well be closed by an unwilling fall in the living standards of industrial nations (p. 12). Redistribution apart, Forrester shares a view with the Ehrlichs: 'the wealthy nations must move back a generation in the production of material wealth.' Without this, international strife over environmental rights could pull average world-wide standards back a century.

Forrester poses the question, 'what will happen when the resource supplying countries begin to withhold resources because they foresee the day when their own demand will require the available supplies? Pressures from impending shortages are already appearing . . . will a new era of international conflict grow out of pressures from resource shortage?' (p. 70). Elsewhere (Laszlo, 1973) he has suggested that 'the present accelerating pace of international trade is a device to allow growth to continue until the entire world simultaneously approaches shortages of all traded goods'. This interdependence is used as a partial justification for the global averaging used in the *World Dynamics* model, but it is also used to support some arguments for 'triage'. To avoid being affected by collapse in the least able poor nations, industrialised countries should as far as possible disassociate themselves economically and politically from them.

Forrester's criticisms of 'contemporary capitalism' are certainly less ambiguous than the Ehrlichs'. His specific recommendations for action oppose the more altruistic of the measures advocated by the Ehrlichs. Forrester would consider their proposals on aid quite unrealistic. He argues instead that humanitarian impulses, as embodied in health services, food aid or attempts at industrialisation, are counterproductive (p. 124). Elsewhere he repeats his assertion that 'development aid is a disservice to most countries because it attempts to establish a non-sustainable future' (*Futurist*, 1976). He advocates the reversal of such policies in order to bring about 'rising pressures' by rising populations. Forrester argues that attempts to solve problems of physical shortage arising from Malthusian limits by technology only without paying attention to population increase would merely 'transfer the pressures to the social area, resulting in such symptoms as loss of confidence in government, kidnappings, aircraft hijackings, revolutions and war'. 'By solving the problem of physical limits without controlling population and industrial growth, we essentially say we will accept major atomic war as a solution to the growth problem; when put that way I doubt that it is a good trade.' He argues that we should 'equalise pressures' – 'tolerate some hunger, some energy shortage and some revolutions'. Only with 'effective arbitration', presumably through international regulation, can war and violence over resources be averted (p. 125). He excuses the lack of discussion of these issues: 'Only broad aspects of the world system are discussed here, not the difficulties of implementing the changes that will be necessary if the present course of human events is to be altered' (p. ix).

Forrester's computerised intervention in the debate gave significant impetus to the Malthusian cause, being cited, for example, in 'Blueprint for Survival' (*The Ecologist*, 1972), a document insisting on the need for the United Kingdom to set course for equilibrium and to halve its population. In more recent articles (e.g. *Futurist*, 1976) Forrester has modified his original position to some extent, preferring to assert that the world is currently passing through the turning point in its logistic growth, and so could be heading towards the equilibrium state, rather than into 'overshoot and collapse'.

Forrester's appearance in the world futures debate was stimulated by an international group of businessmen, civil servants, academics and (more recently) politicians – the Club of Rome. This group was, and still is, concerned to bring to the attention of the world's leaders the nature of the so-called 'World Problematique' (i.e. the interrelated issues of population growth, environment and moral decline), and has sponsored several of the studies described in this review. Its members hit on the idea of using a computer to advertise their cause. In the words of their spokesman and chief executive Aurelio Peccei, 'What we needed was a vehicle to move the hearts and minds of men out of their ingrained habits' (Gillette, 1972). Despite its impact, Forrester's *World Dynamics* was originally intended as an exploratory venture in this direction.

Under the auspices of the Club of Rome, Forrester's model was developed further by Dennis Meadows and his team of system dynamicists. The result was that Forrester's impressionistic and starkly Malthusian forecast was almost immediately 'confirmed' by this apparently more authoritative and more widely publicised study, *The Limits to Growth*. Unlike Forrester, the Meadows' team initially express some concern in *The Limits to Growth* about world regional differences and demonstrate by simple extrapolation that present trends in population and GNP for particular nations lead to a phenomenally large income gap between rich and poor.

Using a more elaborate version of Forrester's computer model, but still with variables globally averaged, the authors of *The Limits to Growth* conclude that 'if the present growth trends in world population, industrial-isation, pollution, food production and resource depletion continue unchanged, limits to growth on the planet will be reached some time within the next one hundred years. The most probable result will be a rather sudden and uncontrollable decline in both population and industrial capacity within the next one hundred years' (p. 23). In fact, the current trends lead to a collapse of the world economy and of world population *before* the year 2000. Surprisingly, the assumed growth rate of the world economy in the model up to the point of collapse seems considerably higher than Kahn's forecasts or extrapolations.

The Meadows remark that in their model 'discontinuous events such as wars and epidemics' have been ignored. These would bring an end to growth 'even sooner' than the model actually indicates, and so the model is, in fact, 'biased to allow growth to continue longer than it probably can in the real world' (p. 126). The Meadows' team are more emphatic than Forrester about the need for urgency in tackling the 'World Problematique'. To delay thirty years makes the problem insoluble even with the solutions they suggest.

The principal difference from Forrester's results lies in the greater stress placed on the need for 'ecological and economic stability'. In this state, as with Forrester, world population and capital would be deliberately held constant at something less than twice the present levels. The Meadows stress the urgency of the present predicament; like the Ehrlichs they view an end to growth as something to strive for. They argue that income redistribution is more likely in this new 'equilibrium' society, but with the Malthusian sting that redistribution becomes 'social suicide' if populations get too large and the 'average amount' available is not enough to maintain life (p. 178).

The Meadows' team have almost nothing to say about what should or might happen to poor nations relative to the rich nations under the policy of no growth. 'There is, of course, no assurance that humanity's moral resources would be sufficient to solve the problem of income redistribution even in an equilibrium state' (p. 179). However, they say, there is 'even less assurance' in the present state of growth. Even so, they cite without comment and with apparent approval the seemingly contradictory remark that 'the stationary state would make fewer demands on our environmental resources, but much greater demands on our moral resources' (p. 179).

The Meadows are at pains to distinguish an 'equilibrium' society from a 'stationary', unchanging society. An equilibrium with zero population or capital growth would not be seen as an 'end to human development'. Technological change would permit increased consumption. 'The possibilities within an equilibrium state are almost endless', although it would require some sacrifices. They are as unforthcoming as Forrester about how this state would be achieved. At their most explicit they speak in *The Limits to Growth* of global society and 'controlled, orderly transition from growth to global equilibrium' (p. 184), of 'managing' the transition (p. 180), 'if the world's people decide to strive . . .' towards this goal (p. 24).

Equilibrium would require trading of certain human freedoms such as 'producing unlimited numbers of children or consuming uncontrolled amounts of resources, for other freedoms such as relief from pollution and crowding and the threat of collapse of the world system' (p. 179). Elsewhere Meadows is reported as giving some idea of what he means by coordinated management: 'really outstanding companies . . . tend to have small leadership, maybe one guy, able to diffuse throughout the organisation a concept of goals and values. He pushes these down, not decisions. He guides people in a fashion much more co-ordinated than you would have with central planning. We have the capability to achieve that' (Rothschild, 1975).

For many people the debate about the future is the *Limits to Growth* debate. The use of the computer, big interdisciplinary research teams and evangelical television presentations helped to reinforce ideas already set out by Ehrlich, Spengler and others. Much as Kahn, *The Limits to Growth* has been a stimulus for other forecasters, some also sponsored by the Club of Rome. Despite their efforts to publicise the dramatic nature and urgency of the prescriptions of *The Limits to Growth* (Gillette, 1972), the Club of Rome prefer to view the work as a first hesitant step towards a new understanding of our world (King, 1974).

The Culmination of Despair

The most fatalistic of the present-day Malthusians is Robert Heilbroner. In his works 'The Human Prospect'* and 'Growth and Survival' he accepts with

---

*The version of 'The Human Prospect' cited here appeared originally in the *New York Review of Books* (Jan. 1974). It was later published with some modification as a book. 'Growth and Survival' originally appeared in *Foreign Affairs* (1972) as a review of *The Limits to Growth*. Heilbroner's conclusions about an end to growth in the industrialised world are a far cry from his writings of the early 1960s. In *The Making of Economic Society* (1962) he considers that there is 'every reason to believe that the present trend of technological advance will be maintained . . . By 1980 or by the year 2000 — a work week of 30 hours or even 20 hours is by no means unimaginable'. (p. 234).

some qualification the basic resource-limited future of *The Limits to Growth*: 'Under any and all assumptions, one irrefutable conclusion remains. The industrial growth process, so central to economic and social life of capitalism and Western socialism alike, will be forced to slow down, in all likelihood within a generation or two, and will probably have to give way to decline thereafter' (p. 32). Like the Ehrlichs and Meadows, Heilbroner argues that environmental constraints and the enormous population growth in poor countries will drive beyond present misery to a 'grim Malthusian outcome', but he rejects the viability of their 'solutions' and goes beyond them to describe the mechanisms of social and economic breakdown and societies' attempts to survive these disasters. He is 'more sanguine' about possibilities for technological change than the Meadows and sees polemics against economic growth as futile; 'only a major disaster will slow the pace of growth'. He argues that there is no hope of meeting the challenges of the future without paying a 'fearful price'.

In his descriptions of future conditions in poor countries Heilbroner provides a stark contrast to Kahn's visions of the post-industrial society. 'The descent of large portions of the under-developed world into a condition of steadily worsening social disorder, marked by shorter life expectancies, further stunting of physical and mental capacities, political apathy intermingled with riots and pillaging when crops fail . . . ruled by dictatorial governments serving the interests of a small economic and military upper class and presiding over the rotting countryside with mixed resignation, indifference, and despair. This condition could continue for a considerable period, effectively removing these areas from the concern of the rest of the world, and consigning the billions of their inhabitants to a human state comparable to that which we now glimpse in the worst regions of India or Pakistan.' The 'intolerable social strains' that resource shortages will bring are thus made quite explicit (p. 23).

Because of the increasing rich–poor gap, 'nuclear blackmail and wars of redistribution' must be anticipated. But he expresses doubt whether even the wealth of the industrial nations could solve the food problems of the poor. 'We are entering a period in which rapid population growth, the presence of obliterative weapons and dwindling resources will bring international tension to dangerous levels for an extended period' (p. 32).

Heilbroner describes the kind of institutions required to bring the escalating effects of environmental constraints under control. He argues that many of the 'economic and social problems lie outside the accustomed instruments of policy making' (p. 21). In fact, he says, 'only two outcomes are imaginable' – anarchy or totalitarianism (p. 23). Nevertheless, preferring totalitarianism to anarchy, Heilbroner suggests the occurence of quite dramatic institutional changes. Only authoritarian regimes are likely to be able to cope with problems arising from the central environmental issues of the future: 'To solve the problems of pollution . . . assuredly the extension of public control far beyond anything experienced in the West, socialist or capitalist . . .' is needed. 'If the issue for mankind is survival, such governments [capable of rallying obedience far more effectively than would be possible in a democratic setting] may be unavoidable, even necessary' (p. 31). This advocacy of 'strong government', which he says appears to play into the hands of those who applaud 'orderliness of authoritarian or dictatorial government', is justified because the 'weakest part' of the humanitarian outlook is that it is unable and unwilling to come to grips with certain 'obdurate human characteristics'. Current institutions have failed and there is a loss of confidence in industrial societies, geared to material improvement, which have 'failed to satisfy the human spirit' (p. 22).

Heilbroner's major concern is how to cope with inevitable economic decline. Although in the longer term he looks to the same kind of changes in values as other Malthusian authors, he feels obliged to distinguish between 'temporary' and 'longer term' solutions. To meet the challenge he foresees, Heilbroner rebuffs 'appeals to our collective foresight, such as the exhortations of the Club of Rome' or the 'Blueprint for Survival' (1972). He says the 'challenge to survival still lies sufficiently far in the future, and the inertial momentum of the present industrial order is still so great that no substantial voluntary diminution of growth, much less a planned reorganisation of society, is today even remotely imaginable' (p. 33).

In his most recent work. *Business Civilisation in Decline* (1976), Heilbroner again emphasises that 'the unavoidable curtailment of growth thus threatens the viability of capitalism by removing the primary source of the profits' (i.e. expansion) (p. 108). Not only Western society is threatened; 'the curtailment of the future must bear on every form of civilisation. . . . most important by far is apt to be the growing tension between poor nations and rich ones' (p. 106).

LIVING WITH LIMITS

Other authors have also taken the thesis set out by Meadows *et al.* as a point of departure for their own discussion. René Dumont, with his book *Utopia or Else* . . . (1974), is quite typical of authors who for many years have been concerned with the plight of poor countries, and he uses the opportunity of debate about world-wide development and possible ecological disaster to restate his position. E. F. Schumacher, similarly, uses the futures debate to further his own critique of present patterns of development. Dumont rejects Kahn's 'unthinking optimism', and accepts much of *The Limits to Growth*. He concludes that there is no possibility of poor countries reaching the standards of living realised in the United States: 'the rich countries' hopes of surviving rest solely on the continued poverty of the rest of mankind' (p. 14). Like the Ehrlichs, Dumont is exceedingly critical of the wasteful consumption in rich countries, which, he says, can only continue to take place at the expense of the poor. Ultimately this situation 'will incite these nations to launch a series of dangerous revolts' (p. 6). 'By the time the under-developed nations are eventually in a position to build up their own heavy industries from their own resources they will already have been robbed of their best minerals and oils. This will mean they can never become even remotely competitive and their expansion will be dreadfully restricted.' He castigates 'Western profligacy' and insists that rich countries should direct their production to helping less-developed nations. In view of their high levels of consumption, he sees a major task as reducing population growth in rich countries (p. 66). Armaments and the private motor car must be abolished. Dumont points out that his diet of austerity for rich nations does 'not in any way imply that production should be brought to a halt'. Rich countries must expect to manufacture increasing amounts of industrial equipment and provide increasing quantities of fertiliser, at least until the developing countries can provide for themselves.

Although Dumont accepts the importance of aid and other assistance from rich to poor nations (the figure mentioned is five per cent of rich country incomes), he insists that rich countries should cease to 'burden' and 'dominate' poor countries; thus aid must be *given*. But most important in Dumont's scheme is that poor countries should achieve independence; as a first stage, agricultural independence.

Dumont considers that 'Revolts are inevitable in dominated countries' (p. 81). He believes that 'this new world is not and never will be a rational structure; it will be an arena of confrontation and struggle' (p. 97). 'A common front on behalf of the condemned people of this earth' with the 'dual aim of less inequality and improved chances of survival' should operate on a world scale (p. 141). However, poor nations should 'put their faith in a neutralist, non-aligned foreign policy' (p. 83). Nevertheless, he sees ultimate institutional cooperation at a world level.

Schumacher shares many sympathies with Dumont, particularly concerning the situation of poor nations and the underlying themes of *The Limits to Growth*. But while he views Herman Kahn type optimists as 'the blind leading the blind', he is equally unsympathetic to the 'doom watching pessimists' and especially to Heilbroner (*Futurist*, 1974). In *Small is Beautiful* (1973) Schumacher describes in some detail his concern with the nature of modern technology. It is too large, and as it grows it requires more and more simply for its own maintenance: 'The most striking thing about modern industry is that it requires so much and accomplishes so little' (p. 97).

According to Schumacher, a principal reason why in many parts of the world the poor are becoming poorer is the 'negative demonstration effect' of modern technology. The established processes of foreign aid, which cause sophisticated technologies to be introduced into unsophisticated environments, are counterproductive. The essential problem facing mankind, he says, is the choice of scale. Although somewhat less pessimistic about resource limitations than many authors, Schumacher argues that growth must stop. In any case, there is little evidence, he argues, that growth is conducive to world peace. 'Only by reduction in needs can one promote a genuine reduction in those tensions which are ultimate causes of strife and war' (*Futurist*, 1974).

THE 'SECOND GENERATION' MODELS

Although *The Limits to Growth* computer models and the world-wide publicity they received provided a powerful stimulus to the futures debate, both the techniques and the underlying theories were subjected to strong criticism. On the technical level the shortcomings of the models and the unreality of many of the aggregative assumptions were exposed. As a result a 'second generation' of models attempted to eradicate some of the more obvious weaknesses and errors. At the same time, others attempted to use the technique of computer simulation modelling for very different purposes and came up with conclusions diametrically opposed to those of *The Limits to Growth*.

The new models all attempt to tackle the question of international trade and, with the exception of the Latin American model, they all explore futures in which global development is fostered largely by expanded international trade. Unlike *The Limits to Growth* these world models treat the world as a set of interacting regions.

Strategy for Survival

Mankind at the Turning Point by Mihajlo Mesarovic and Eduard Pestel (1974a) outlines the content of a global computer model far grander than that of the Meadows' team. The original Forrester model had only 40 equations, the Meadows model had 200, but that of Mesarovic and Pestel is claimed to have 100,000 (p. 34). Like *The Limits to Growth* this model received considerable support and publicity from the Club of Rome. The major theme is the interconnectedness of world events and the need for global solutions. It also emphasises the possibility of impending disaster and reflects the 'conviction that the world will have to face a cluster of crises of unprecedented type and magnitude which might very well appear before the end of the century and possibly more overwhelming thereafter in ever faster succession' (Mesarovic and Pestel, 1974b).

Mesarovic and Pestel are more concerned than the authors of *The Limits to Growth* with the questions of income redistribution on a global scale. Although they pay homage to the long-term problems arising from resource and environmental constraints and particularly the potential dangers arising from the 'Faustian bargain' of nuclear power, they are also less pessimistic than the Meadows team about global resources. They merely declare that 'long-term availability cannot be taken for granted' and that 'now the world is again approaching an era of scarcity' (p. 85).

Their so-called 'Strategy for Survival' model assumes (contrary to *The Limits to Growth*) that some effective population policies will be introduced. Even with a slowing down of population growth, and without setting severe resource constraints, a widening gap between rich and poor worlds is predicted, most seriously for the region they describe as South and South East Asia, which would lead to 'collapses' at a regional level 'possibly long before the middle of the next century' (p. 122).

Mesarovic and Pestel argue that in the 'emerging world system' there is the 'world-wide dependence on a common stock of raw materials, problems in providing energy, and food supply, sharing of the common physical environment on land, sea and air . . .'. This creates a high level of interdependence, which causes a 'disturbance' of the normal states of affairs in any part of the world to spread quickly elsewhere (p. 18).

Like Heilbroner and Schumacher they see the widening rich–poor gap threatening world political stability. International political polarisation with the threat of nuclear war, in their opinion, 'makes closing the gap a question of the survival of the world system as such'. They observe that 'desperadoes' and 'nuclear blackmail' will 'paralyse further orderly development' (p. 69). 'For each region its turn would come in due time.' Like Forrester, they see the possibility of progressive collapse across regions. The oil and food crises should not be viewed as temporary; they are early manifestations of a long-term global development crisis.

Mesarovic and Pestel argue that since the problems of the world are inter-related they require a 'global approach'. There is 'no more urgent task than to guide the world system to a path of organic growth' (p. 196). The closest they come to a definition of this is 'functional inter-dependence between constituent parts in the sense that none of them is self-contained but rather has to fulfil a role assigned through historical evolution' (p. 5). 'Co-ordinated global cooperation' is its most important facet – it would, for example, avoid the possibility that 'undesirable growth of any one part [of the system] threatens not only that part but the whole as well'. But unlike Forrester, who sees trade as a mechanism for encouraging global collapse, Mesarovic and Pestel see it as essential to build up the export potential of poor countries and especially South Asia, for the solution of the world food problems. Attempts at self-sufficiency are likely to lead to 'disastrous results'.

In economic terms, Mesarovic and Pestel envisage a 'world-wide diversification of industry leading to a true global economic system'. 'Balanced development' in all regions would take account not only of national conditions (factors of production) but, just as important, of long-term, world-wide interests. It is essential to build up the economic base of poor countries;

apart from food commodities, only investment aid that provides the right
kind of 'intermediate technology' (p. 66) should be given to developing
regions. They estimate the cost of aid if an attempt were made to reach the
income targets suggested by the Tinbergen Committee for the Second United
Nations Development Decade. This would reduce average income
differentials with rich countries to a maximum of 5 to 1 for the poorer regions
such as Tropical Africa and Southern Asia, and to about 3 to 1 for Latin
America (Codoni, 1974).

The economic transfers required would, they argue, not be possible with
prevailing international economic arrangements. They call for social and
institutional reforms and repeatedly emphasise that in 'the urgent quest for
peace' evolution through cooperation rather than confrontation is essential.
It would *not*, they emphasise, involve 'globalism' in the sense that favours
uniformity; not 'a monolithic world system, one language, one structure, one
government, etc.' Like the Meadows, they do not attempt to spell out in detail
what it would involve, only what it would foster, namely, 'world consciousness'. They do not make global Malthusian resource assumptions and, surprisingly given their exhortations about the 'oncoming age of scarcity'
(p. 147), the world growth rates implied by Mesarovic and Pestel's computer
results are much closer to those of Kahn and Wiener than to those of
Meadows and Forrester. Thus, with 'domino effect' collapses averted, these
authors appear to foresee relatively high economic growth for some time to
come.

The United Nations World Input–Output Model

The world input–output model constructed by Nobel Laureate Wassily
Leontief forms part of the United Nations study on the impact of prospective
environmental issues and policies on the international development strategy
initiated in 1973. The objective of the study was to investigate the inter-
relationships between future economic growth and environmental issues:
'One question specifically asked by the study was whether the existing and
other development targets were consistent with resource availability and geographic distribution' and whether 'to the extent that some resources are
limited . . . desired growth rates [should] be modified' (Leontief *et al.*, 1976
p. 3). But, unlike *The Limits to Growth*, the United Nations model is concerned more with the closing of the income gap between rich and poor
countries than with the possibilities of world economic growth.

According to the authors, a scenario based on current trends 'turns out to
be rather pessimistic' (p. 72). Furthermore, scenarios based on the recommendations for the Second United Nations Development Decade do not
provide for a sufficiently rapid closing of the gap, when population increases
are taken into account. Instead, the authors examine the implications of

scenarios in which the growth rates are set to reduce the income gap between poor and rich countries by about half by the year 2000, from the present average of 12 to 1 to 7 to 1.

The model is claimed to provide detailed results by region and by sector of the 'conditions of growth' needed to achieve these targets. The results appear to contradict those of *The Limits to Growth*. The authors argue that 'mineral resource endowment is generally adequate to support world economic development at relatively high rates, but that these resources will probably become more expensive to extract, as the century moves towards its conclusion' (p. 25). On questions of environmental pollution they are more optimistic: 'though pollution is a grave problem for humanity it is a technologically manageable problem' (pp. 31, 49). They estimate that the costs of control are in the region of 1.5 to 2 per cent of gross domestic product.

The study concludes that 'No insurmountable barriers exist within this century to accelerated development of the developing regions ... the principal limits to sustained economic growth and accelerated development are political, social and institutional in character' (p. 48). However, no prescription is given in the work for these changes. The implications of the assumptions about technology in the model are not discussed either, except for a brief mention of need for redistribution. Thus, the limits to growth imposed by mineral resources, agriculture and environment can be overcome. But the achievement of targets is dependent on significant changes in current economic relations between the rich and poor nations. The study stresses the need for a 'steady increase' in investment in poor countries: 'Accelerated development is only possible under the condition that from 30 to 35% and in some cases up to 40% of their gross product is used for capital investment' (p. 49). The study discusses what restructuring of developing country economies might be needed: 'Accelerated development in developing regions would lead to a continuous and significant share in the developing regions' world gross product and industrial production' (p. 50). Growth in developing countries would therefore in part come through a 'brisk expansion' of international trade. In this context they emphasise the importance of reducing the balance of payments deficit of developing countries. This would be done by stabilising commodity markets, stimulating export of manufactures from the developing countries and increasing financial transfers (p. 51).

Global Constraints and a New Vision for Development*

Like other global modelling studies, 'A New Vision for Development' is a reaction to *The Limits to Growth*. The Japanese work team of the Club of

---

*The most easily accessible English translation available is in the journal *Technological Forecasting and Social Change*, Vol. 6, Nos. 3 and 4, 1974.

Rome, led by Yoichi Kaya, argue for an international order based on a modified international division of labour, which would provide for both the immediate problems of poor nations and their longer-term development needs. 'The approaching limits of our earth however compete for our attention with another equally, if not more serious problem, the poverty and inadequate economic growth rate of the developing nations. In these nations of Asia, Africa, and Central and South America, where over half the world's people live, development is made extremely difficult by rapid population growth, chronic malnutrition and often by an unstable political order' (p. 277). The authors continue: 'Furthermore, if we look some distance into the future we can easily see that the developing nations will run into another impasse when their manufactured goods begin to compete with those of the advanced nations in the world market.'

They set out to devise a 'New Plan for Development' based on a world-wide redistribution of industry to help the developing nations (p. 371). They calculate the pattern of investment world-wide that would lead to a maximum rate of increase in poor nations' gross products. The authors argue that their industrial redistribution plan is 'actually a form of indirect foreign aid whereby the advanced countries co-operate to facilitate the development of the less wealthy nations' (p. 386). The Japanese work team suggest a 'new type of international division of industry . . . light industry should be promoted in Asia, and agricultural industry in Middle and South America as well as in North America and Oceania' (p. 279). In addition, 'relatively high capital effective types of industry could be, with suitable restrictions, transferred from the advanced to the developing nations' (p. 278).

Redistribution of industry is seen as especially important because, the authors argue, 'if economic self-sufficiency should be overly emphasised then only the regions with adequate natural resources would actually attain this goal' (p. 385). The idea of 'encouraging self-development through expansion of agriculture and mining industries comes from a mistakenly exaggerated idea of the richness of natural resources in the developing nations' (p. 372). They are, thus, against isolationist strategies such as those suggested by some authors and conclude that a policy of economic self-sufficiency is unfavourable, for if each nation should strive to maintain self-sufficiency the plan would be largely ineffective. This plan would impose sacrifices especially on Japan and Western Europe among the developed nations, and on all of the developing nations (p. 386).

Beyond Underdevelopment and Dependence — Basic Needs

For the Latin American Bariloche group, led by Amilcar Herrera, current trends clearly lead to a widening gap between rich and poor nations. The catastrophe predicted by 'some models in vogue' (an oblique reference to *The*

Limits to Growth) is already a reality for much of mankind. It is not necessary to wait a hundred years to perceive it, nor to build a model to show it. Global aggregation and focusing on relatively distant issues causes attention to be drawn from more pressing and important problems.

The Bariloche team, like Mesarovic and Pestel, concern themselves with world-wide redistribution, but they also place great emphasis on redistribution *within* regions. While they emphasise the need to account for ecological limits, they take a 'non-Malthusian' stance and argue that present-day Malthusians only support the interests of rich countries. In their opinion socio-political factors rather than the resource limitations – stressed, for example, by Forrester and Dumont – stop backward societies developing in the same fashion as the presently developed nations. Resources will not be exhausted in a 'historically significant time-scale'.

Like Dumont, however, they believe that the consumption patterns of populations in rich countries and the cities in poor nations are irrational and destructive. They share both the Ehrlichs' and Heilbroner's view that the ideology of growth is strongly built into Western forms of capitalism and socialism. Indeed, pollution and environmental deterioration arising from this could provoke ecological collapse. Bariloche see the widening rich–poor gap and destructive patterns of consumption as having socio-political origins. The result of failing to rectify these obstacles to development could be 'almost as catastrophic as any Malthusian scarcity'. According to Bariloche the problem for the Third World countries 'consists essentially of finding new principles such as "eco-development" to avoid dangers which now confront industrialised countries'.

Their model describes a world society in which consumption is divided evenly within four regions: Latin America, Asia, Africa and the rich world. Using the model, the authors claim to demonstrate the material viability of an 'ideal' society. They demonstrate how each of the major world regions can develop to a maximum, non-ecologically-destructive level. Where this differs dramatically from *The Limits to Growth* equilibrium state is that it would be 'an egalitarian society, at both the national and international levels . . .[with] . . . inalienable rights regarding the satisfaction of basic needs – nutrition, housing, health – that are essential for complete and active participation . . .' (Herrera *et al.*, 1976, p. 25). The model is designed around this concept.

Unlike most other modellers, the Bariloche group stresses the importance of 'autarky'. The satisfaction of the basic needs is achieved in all regions with the use of almost exclusively local economic resources. This does not exclude trade, which remains at about the current proportion of regional product. Each world region is treated as an economic unit, which 'pre-supposes total collaboration between the countries forming it' (p. 44). Differences between socialist and capitalist countries are not made explicit in the mathematical model (p. 43) and all countries are assumed to 'follow the same policy after 1980'.

The Latin American team thus appear to be examining quite a different international economic order from that proposed elsewhere. The authors argue that basic needs can be met within thirty years, except for Asia where the 'food sector fails'. The solution advocated by the authors is an effective population policy and the use of non-conventional foodstuffs. They examine a scenario that assumes 'international solidarity' and that the developed region devotes two per cent of income to aid exclusively Africa and Asia, a scenario not dissimilar to that advocated by Mesarovic and Pestel. For Africa this does not affect the time period within which basic needs are satisfied, and for Asia it makes 'very little difference' (p. 101). Assuming that the present distribution of income is maintained does, however, appear to have a much greater impact on the results: 'At the very best [it] delays the goals of a liberated humanity, free from suffering and misery, by at least two generations. It also implies need to devote between three and five times more material resources to the achievement of the desired objective, thus multiplying the pressure on the environment' (p. 106).

The significant contributions of the Bariloche model therefore are the concept of 'basic needs' (which now appears to be rapidly entering the vocabulary of international organisations; I.L.O., 1977), and the demonstration that an egalitarian society requires far fewer resources to satisfy basic needs than does an inegalitarian one. The assumptions about trade are, however, formally and quantitatively little different from those of Mesarovic and Pestel or Leontief.

In *Self Reliance: Concepts, Theory and Rationale* (1977),* Johan Galtung has presented many political and social ideas similar to those used in the Bariloche study. He argues that the spread of Western thought through culture and science, of socio-economic practice through capitalism, and of military-political practice through colonialism has meant that the 'world-encompassing centre–periphery formation [is] built as a program into Western civilisation' (p. 1). He argues that the Third World cannot become self-reliant by imitating the First and Second Worlds. The hierarchical interactions of the present structure of the world economy must be broken up, and replaced instead by cooperation between countries in the same socio-economic position. He is in favour not of anarchy, of the world divided into small, local communities, but of a world where more power, initiative and higher levels of needs-satisfaction are found at what is now the periphery.

Self-reliance takes the form of using local factors – local creativity, raw materials, land and capital, which too often the centre has drained away (p. 5). Galtung argues (p. 19) that there is a problem in delineating self-reliant regions; it should be sought at many levels, local, national or collective (sub-regional, regional or Third World) but, if this does not work, some type of 'limited co-operation' with the developed countries might be sought. Self-

*Our commentary is based on a draft.

reliant countries must be able to produce for basic needs, so that food dependency, in particular, cannot be used as a weapon in a crisis. Galtung also suggests (p. 15) that a self-reliant country would better be able to withstand military pressure, since, because of its localised structure, it could offer paramilitary and guerilla-type resistance, as well as non-military forms of resistance, even after an occupation has taken place. Because of the inevitable external pressure that Galtung considers would be placed on poor countries, he argues that self-reliance as a doctrine is more in the field of 'psychopolitics' than in the field of economics.

The International Order

The most recent of the published studies sponsored by the Club of Rome is entitled *Reshaping the International Order* (RIO). The project team, which includes many members of the Club of Rome, was led by Nobel Laureate Jan Tinbergen, who also chaired the 'Tinbergen Committee' (see Codoni, 1974), which was responsible for the national development targets advocated for the U.N. Second Development Decade (and considered in the Mesarovic and Pestel and the Leontief studies). The RIO report was 'promoted' by the results of the U.N. General Assembly Sixth Special Session, 1974, to work towards the establishment of a new international economic order (Tinbergen, 1976, p. 4). With this study the Club of Rome appears to be refining a position hinted at in the study by Mesarovic and Pestel, and the Club of Rome's 'World Problematique'.

According to the Tinbergen study, Vietnam, OPEC, inflation, economic instability, growing alienation and threats to basic values, all engendered by pressures to consume more, make it clear that the 'cornucopia of economic growth' is turning into a 'Pandora's Box' (p. 12). In Tinbergen's view a 'sudden and historically important change' took place in 1973 when the OPEC initiative took the Third World from 'deference to defiance' (p. 13). Consequently, he argues, the world's problems have increased substantively, and the world has become more complex politically, with the appearance of many new powers of importance and strength in the neutral and third worlds (p. 43). The rich and poor have unparalleled problems that cannot be solved independently (p. 21).

On physical resources the authors appear less pessimistic than either of the two other major Club of Rome studies, *The Limits to Growth* and *Mankind at the Turning Point*: 'Fears expressed in recent years concerning the exhaustion of natural resources may well be exaggerated' (p. 37). Although technologies can be developed that will help solve problems of exploitation, extraction, substitution and environmental degradation, failure to recognise that maldistribution is an important aspect of the 'environmental crisis' might prove 'disastrous for all' (p. 33).

The authors call for a new international order in which 'a life of dignity and well-being becomes an inalienable right of all' (p. 4). But they say any new world order cannot be based on an exclusive philosophy of economic growth and material riches. In fact, poor countries should reject the aspiration for a Western style of life: 'no sane person could seriously envisage a world in which the world's poor live like today's affluent minority . . . to believe it is possible is an illusion, to attempt to construct it would be madness' (p. 74). Thus, although the book argues that resource constraints are apparently less severe than Mesarovic and Pestel fear, economic growth possibilities are in fact more limited.

Unlike the other Club of Rome projects considered so far, the RIO study does not employ a computer model, but goes well beyond their previous analysis of economic, technological and institutional factors. Tinbergen argues that, although in the post-war period political realities have changed, these have not been reflected sufficiently in international institutions. An equitable order entails changes in the distribution of power (p. 105). Like Dumont, the Bariloche team and Galtung he argues that dependency relationships of poor countries must be reduced through 'new-style self-reliant development' – they should exercise full sovereignty over the exploitation of their own resources and play a larger part in their processing (p. 179).

The industrial countries are vulnerable to the collective pressures of the poor, whose greatest power is in their solidarity (p. 37). There should be greater collective bargaining through the United Nations, more resource cartels and more trade between the Third World countries themselves (p. 180). But, by the same token, the 'humble wheatsheaf' could be destined to become a powerful weapon of economic warfare against the Third World countries (p. 31) unless they achieve greater self-sufficiency in basic foods (p. 179).

In Tinbergen's view, both industrial and poor countries must develop the industries in which they have a comparative advantage, and not attempt to protect inefficient industries (p. 112). On this point his argument bears similarities to the Japanese Club of Rome study on the international division of labour. The greatest disparity between industrial and poor countries is in the field of scientific research and development. Because multinational firms excel in both technological and marketing knowledge, a major problem is to reconcile the interests of 'transnationals' in security of investment with the independence and development objectives of developing countries (p. 40). As matters stand, international firms tend to accentuate rather than reduce income inequalities in poor societies (p. 4). Tinbergen hints at the threat posed by the 'sky-rocketing' expenditure on armaments (p. 76) which employs, he says, almost half the world's scientific and technological man-power. The problem is not simply to shift from a war to peace economy, 'but from a war to a peace mentality' (p. 26).

SOVIET VIEWS OF GROWTH

Soviet futures literature is often highly critical of Western 'bourgeois futurology'. Marxist writers are especially cynical about Kahn's efforts, but neo-Malthusian writers are similarly denounced.

Most Soviet futures literature spells out in considerable detail the marxist theory that forms the basic framework for thinking about the development of society. Western futures literature, in contrast, usually leaves the underlying theory implicit or, as in the case of Kahn and Wiener, constructs a theoretical position based on long-standing 'multifold trends'. However, like Kahn, the society of the future envisaged by the Soviet authors is claimed to be non-utopian – it is the result of a 'natural-historical' transition from capitalism.

It is evident that the Eastern European debate about the future responds to the debate in the West – about environmental issues for example – although it is less clear where the various nuances within the Soviet debate arise. According to Modrzhinskaya (1973) the catastrophes viewed by neo-Malthusian authors are seen merely as the material manifestations of a basic, essentially political problem: the whole course of social development shows us that imperialism alone is guilty of the fact that the mass of the population in the Asian, African and Latin American countries is forced to live in poverty. The downfall of the capitalist system is needed; notions of post-industrial social improvement are mere reformism: 'the future under capitalism can only be gloomy'. Thus, Modrzhinskaya quotes Lenin in advocating whole-hearted 'development of the revolutionary movement . . . in every country without exception' (p. 346). However, there may be some catastrophes and setbacks as intimated through another quotation from Lenin: 'It is undialectical, unscientific and theoretically wrong to regard the course of world history as smooth and always in a forward direction, without occasional gigantic leaps back' (p. 260). But these are essentially only incidents on the road to socialism.

In the main, Soviet forecasters do not make detailed global forecasts of the kind described here for other authors. Like Kahn and Wiener, Modrzhinskaya sees the main line of progress as economic growth. Citing Lenin, she states 'Marxists regard the development of productive forces as the main and supreme criterion of progress' (p. 257).

Although Modrzhinskaya's estimates of *current* known reserves of raw materials and energy are very similar to those used by the Meadows' team and other Malthusians, her faith in mankind's ingenuity to extend these resources is far greater: 'Over the last twenty to thirty years the pace of scientific and technological development has acquired quite exceptional hitherto unprecedented proportions, and it is difficult to imagine with what tremendous speed man's propects for mastering the forces of nature will develop in the future' (p. 336).

Modrzhinskaya has total confidence in the scientific and technological revolution: 'Soviet scientists . . . categorically reject all theories of future energy shortage and raw materials shortage' (p. 315). The basis for the long-term energy forecast is the exploitation of nuclear technologies: 'simple calculations show that there is enough deuterium as a fuel on earth to last for hundreds of millions of years'. With limitless energy come limitless resources: 'All in all, the earth's crust for 16 kilometres below the surface contains trillions (10^{17-18}) of tons of different metals. This makes it difficult even to envisage a level of production at which mankind would begin to experience a shortage of metals' (p. 317) In agricultural production man will be equally successful, eventually 'turning the deserts into flowering orchards' (p. 332). Modrzhinskaya argues that scientists now recognise the dangers posed by environmental factors, and sets out future tasks ranging from the transformation of the deserts to the damming of the Bering Strait in order to conquer the Arctic permafrost.

V. Kosolapov* timetables the progress of science and technology in his book *Mankind and the Year 2000* (1976). Like Modrzhinskaya he believes that technology will be 'ecologised' and will, wherever possible, improve the ecological equilibrium (p. 208). There are many similarities with Kahn and Wiener in the breakthroughs he expects: by the turn of the century land transport will travel at 500 km/hour and passenger aircraft at 12-15,000 km/hour; by 2030 rail transport will be established on the moon (p. 179); construction technology will have developed from the application in 1970 of the mass-produced composite materials to the use of 'biological principles in the manufacture of materials' (p. 161); nuclear, cybernetic and automated technologies will be applied in all areas of development; by the end of the twentieth century there will have been a tenfold increase in the level of scientific research. Economically viable weather control techniques will be available for individual areas and atomic power stations will be the main suppliers of electricity (p. 210).

The lifestyles that these technological breakthroughs will provide are described by Modrzhinskaya. For the Soviet Union, she says, there will be 'a considerable rise in the material and cultural standards of the whole people' (p. 352). Towns will be planned so that the 'majority of inhabitants will have to walk only 100 to 150 metres (2-7 minutes) from their flat to work, school and the shops . . .' (p. 328). In some towns, people will live in 'ultra-high blocks of 200–300 storeys and higher . . . to leave more room for sun, greenery, fresh air and water'. Kosolapov expands on this view of the future. Housework will be fully automated by the year 1990, and by 2005 tourist trips to the moon will be in operation (p. 211). Most industries are expected to become highly or totally automated: transport will be operated, as a rule,

*The work of this author appears to be based on the preliminary findings of the long-range development plan covering the period 1976–90 set up in 1972 by the Central Committee of the CPSU and the USSR Council of Ministers (p. 44).

without direct human participation, with the help of electronic devices such as automatic pilots and autodrivers.

Despite the similarity to Kahn and Wiener in the degree of technological optimism displayed and similarities in the lifestyles described, the Soviet writers' future is more strongly normative. We are told the progress of knowledge 'is creating a totally real scientific and technological basis for producing any degree of prosperity for *all* people in the world'. A major 'prospective achievement of a socialist world order' would be 'truly human, highly moral relations between peoples and nations, total abolition of all forms and traces of social oppression and social inequality'. But Modrzhinskaya argues, 'it is impossible to switch distribution according to needs if there is no full abundance' (p. 358).

Thus, in Eastern European authors' views, changes in technology would bring about social reforms. As a Rumanian forecaster, Manescu, explains: 'the gap between high and low incomes, between the earnings of the various social categories will grow smaller as a result of the process of social homogenization, of training and qualification, of gradual disappearance of the essential differences between physical and intellectual work' (Nicolescu, 1974, p. 28).

Ultimately, the aim of the society would be a transformation into a 'creative collective engaged predominantly in mental work' (Kosolapov, 1976, p. 211). Here, again, there is a difference in emphasis between the futures posed by Kahn and those of Soviet authors. In Kahn's world, 'intellectuals' may achieve little satisfaction; in Kosalapov's world, cultural life is centred on educational activities and scientific achievements of all kinds. By 1983 advanced countries will spend up to 8–10 per cent of income on education; by 2020 this figure would rise to 10–13 per cent. In this respect, the future presented by the Soviet authors resembles Bell's (1974) post-industrial society more than the populist version put forward by Kahn and Wiener.

Similarly, Kosolapov claims that by the year 2000 international agreements would 'guarantee a stable living standard for everyone on the basis of the advance in the level of production' (p. 211). Progress will be limited not by scientific and technological possibilities, nor by labour and financial resources, but by the social structure, in particular the contradictions of the capitalist system, the danger of wars and colonialism. Indeed, most of the Third World countries given by Kahn as examples of 'successful' development would be counted by Modrzhinskaya as 'colonies' still dominated by the capitalist world.

Although all Eastern European forecasters take a marxist perspective as the basis for their forecasting activities, there are differences in emphasis. Kosolapov appears to take a less conflict-ridden view of the future of international relations, although still arguing for the transformation of capitalist societies and the disappearance of colonialist and racialist regimes. In his view the next decades will be marked by a continued détente in international relations. Global measures will be implemented first to limit the arms race and then to reduce armaments. The production of nuclear weapons will be dis- continued. Of the saving in military spending, 'a considerable part' will be channelled in aid to Third World countries (p. 208). By the year 2000 'national economies will become integral parts of a world-wide system of economic relations'. It must be assumed that Kosolapov means that trade will be fully internationalised – 'finally the future society will develop into a global association of people engaged in creative labour' (p. 209).

THE FULL CIRCLE

This review began with a summary of Kahn and Wiener's book *The Year 2000* (1967). Much of the influential futures literature that has emerged in the intervening decade has been very critical of Kahn's approach as over-com- placent in terms of both overall possibilities for growth and its distribution. Kahn has responded to the neo-Malthusians in a highly critical manner. Like other authors, however, over the years he has modified his position.

His latest book, *The Next 200 Years* (1976), written with Brown and Martel, is presented so as to counteract the pessimism of the neo- Malthusians. Disasters, they say, are not impossible but 'any limits to growth are more likely to arise from psychological, cultural or social limits to demand, or from incompetency, bad luck and/or monopolistic practices inter- fering with supply rather than from fundamental physical limits on available resources' (p. 181). Further, far from being despondent about the situation of the poor nations, Kahn and his colleagues assert: 'Prospects are good and getting better for the coping nations, . . . [some] developing countries . . . will help drive the world's economic growth in the twenty first century. For the non-coping nations the immediate prospects are not good, but our projection is that over the long-term they will gradually join the ranks of the coping nations' (p. 213). Indeed, they argue, 'without growth the disparities among nations so regretted today would probably never be overcome' (p. 9).

The basic 'theory' underlying the predictions of *The Year 2000* was that of continuity of the 'long-term multifold trend' and exponential extrapolation (to 2020) of economic and demographic trends. In *The Next 200 Years* the idea of the multifold trend is retained, at least to explain cultural and political tendencies in the world at large (p. 180). For economic and demographic trends the theory is modified more dramatically: 'The basic assumption underlying our 400 year earth-centred scenario is that the rates of world population and economic growth are now close to their historic highs and will soon begin to slow until finally, roughly 100–200 years from now, they will level off in a more or less natural and comfortable way' (p. 26). 'In much the same way that the agricultural revolution spread round the world, the

Industrial Revolution has been spreading and causing a permanent change in the quality of human life. However, instead of lasting 10,000 years, this second diffusion process is likely to be largely completed within a total span of about 400 years or roughly by the late twenty second century' (p. 20). The slowing of growth rates will already be apparent by the year 2000: 'Barring extreme mismanagement or bad luck, the period 1976–85 should be characterised by the highest average rate of world economic growth in history, perhaps 6%, although by 1985 or soon thereafter the slowdown of the upper half of the distorted S-shaped curve should begin to be felt' (p. 188). Kahn and his colleagues are at pains to stress therefore that 'a reduced level of *demand* rather than inadequate supply will drive the transition' (p. 50).

In *The Next 200 Years* the authors are far more thorough in their analysis of natural resources and technological possibilities (p. 85). *The Year 2000* led to Dumont's (almost correct) rebuke that he could find only one mention of agriculture in the whole volume.* In *The Next 200 Years* the authors attempt to demonstrate in some detail that there is not *one*, but several plausible technological routes that would satisfy expected demand for food, raw materials and energy whilst preserving a satisfactory environment.

Despite the long-term tendency for demand to decline at the higher levels of income, the authors observe that for a long time to come poverty will remain. The 'relatively successful portion (about half) of the Third World should attain about $2000 per head by the year 2000 and a still desperately poor group, mostly concentrated in the Indian sub-continent but including limited parts of Latin America and Africa . . . could (with reasonable policies) average about $200 per head by the year 2000' (p. 195). 'In particular we believe that large income gaps between nations could persist for centuries, even though there will be some tendency to narrow' (p. 208).

The very existence of this gap offers the greatest hope to developing nations. 'The task ahead for America and for the developed world is to help raise the capacity of these [developing] nations' institutions to exploit the gaps whose very existence can accelerate their growth' (p. 214).

The authors see the United States as responsible for world economic growth, and are not enthusiastic about the activities of zero growth advocates. In complete contrast to the exhortations of Dumont, Heilbroner and especially the Ehrlichs, they say Americans have a duty to be rich. The diffusion of growth is seen by the authors of *The Next 200 Years* as a 'more or less natural and comfortable process' but nevertheless they say 'there are lots of wiggles and reversals in the basic trends' (p. 185). Quoting Kuznets, the authors point out that 'Difficulties and the problems lie in the limited capacity of the institutions of the underdeveloped countries – political, legal,

*Kahn and Wiener remark in *The Year 2000* that they have 'left out such important things as food, agriculture, new non-nuclear power sources, new methods of transportation, new materials and so on' (p. 116).

cultural and economic – to channel activity so as to exploit the advantage of economic backwardness' (p. 214).

Before the end of the century they expect to see internationally 'the end of the post-World War II system politically, economically and financially' (p. 189), leading to a 'unified but multipolar, partially competitive, mostly global and technological economy' (p. 191). This will exhibit 'Increasing worldwide unity in technology, private industry, commercial and financial institutions, but relatively little unity in international legal and political institutions' (p. 192). 'Despite much hostility, [there will be] a continuing, even growing, importance of multinational corporations as innovators and diffusers of economic activity and as engines of rapid growth' (p. 191).

The growth centres will be the United States and Japan especially, but a new developed bloc comprising mainly the Comecon, O.E.C.D. and Persian Gulf nations will emerge (p. 194). The threat of war and direct military intervention seems to be somewhat reduced as compared with Kahn's previous work. 'In comparison with any earlier period the developing nations are relatively safe from military threats by the developed world' (p. 46). Nevertheless, the authors say, 'a war involving the widespread use of nuclear weapons . . . as we contemplate the tasks ahead, . . . is probably the "single biggest danger"' (p. 219).

Their detailed recommendations, they say, 'run counter to the major conclusions of the Club of Rome's second report [Mesarovic and Pestel, 1974a] which emphasises the importance of global interdependence and stresses the necessity of solving problems in a "global context" by "global concerted action". We believe that this goes in exactly the wrong direction, and that the organic interdependence it suggests would ensure that a dislocation anywhere would be a dislocation everywhere. We prefer redundancy, flexibility and a degree of "disconnectedness". If India, for example, goes under we want to be able to save her, not go down with her' (p. 216).

CONCLUSIONS

Thus, the future debate has become vast in scope. It has also become confused in nature. Different authors use the same words to express different ideas, often adapting their language to the jargon of the day: expressions such as 'radical institutional and social change', 'appropriate technology', 'self-reliance', or 'the new international economic order' each encompass a wide range of meanings, depending on who uses them.

To some extent this is inevitable, given the complexity of the problems and the diverse national and disciplinary origins of the participants in the debate. The Bariloche group explicitly take up a stance favourable to the Third World in general, and to Latin America in particular. The report of the Japanese Club of Rome reflects a strong national interest when, for example, it criticises the doctrine of self-sufficiency, or 'American and Australian Monroeism' (Kaya and Suzuki, 1974, p. 386). Throughout the debate Kahn champions the U.S.A. and Modrzhinskaya the U.S.S.R.

Some futures writers have strong commitments to particular disciplines and methods. Ecology has had such a strong influence on neo-Malthusian writers that it has been described as the new 'dismal science'. At the same time, advocacy of systems-analytic methods has on occasions been as evangelical as the policies prescribed. It can be argued that Forrester used the spectacular and controversial results of *World Dynamics* to highlight his own simulation technique, as he did in his earlier *Urban Dynamics* (1969). Forrester, Mesarovic and Pestel and, less forcefully, Leontief, all recommend their own preferred method whilst pointing to the unsatisfactory features of others. Each, in effect, argues that the world is 'extraordinarily complex', that its main tendencies are beyond the comprehension of the unaided human mind. Only a holistic (i.e. integrated) analysis is adequate, and this requires systems models. Meadows links holism to Eastern philosophy and the ecological unity of humanity and nature. High technology methods of analysis are thereby justified on the basis of notions of natural harmony and simplicity.

The inadequacy of empirical data increases the possibilities for arriving at different assertions about trends in one and the same phenomenon. Even where data exist, futures writers have often been very cavalier about empirical evidence.

But whatever the differences, limitations or imperfections in their work, all the futures writers of the past ten years share common concerns very similar to those of the classical economists of the late eighteenth and first half of the nineteenth century. Adam Smith, Thomas Malthus, David Ricardo, John Stuart Mill and Karl Marx each had his personal foibles, and they differed amongst themselves on many fundamental issues. Yet they were all concerned with long-term trends in a modernising and industrialising society; with the possibilities of, and constraints on, economic growth offered by natural resources, investment, population and technical change; with the effects of economic growth on income distribution, patterns of living and the quality of life; and with debate about the appropriate objectives, policies, institutions and structures of power for the changing society.

Like the classical economists, today's futurologists all calculate that world economic growth and population growth must or will eventually stop. But they differ enormously about when and at what level this will or should happen. They also differ about the desirable and feasible distribution of the world's future wealth and about the institutions, political systems and styles of life in a better future world. These differences are fundamental to the debate and their origins can be traced back to differences of opinion in three problem areas: resources and technical change; the desirable political objectives and norms for society; and the economic, social and political processes whereby society evolves and changes. It is to these problem areas that the rest of this book will be devoted.

CHAPTER 3

Assumptions and Methods: Population, Economic Development, Modelling and Technical Change

Sam Cole and Ian Miles

Despite differing values and assumptions the futures writers agree on some things at least. For example, *if* present population and economic trends continue, a widening 'gap' between rich and poor countries is likely in terms of income per head. Most authors offer reasons why these trends should not or cannot continue. They agree that population growth must end eventually, but disagree about what levels of population and incomes might ultimately be possible in the light of resource and environmental constraints, and whether income 'gaps' can be narrowed or closed.

In this chapter we shall examine in greater detail the assumptions made by various authors about population and economic development, and then discuss the assumptions we shall be making ourselves. We shall also explain our reasons for adopting the analytic framework applied in later chapters of this book.

WORLD POPULATION

Most forecasters present a wide range of estimates of trends in world population. Typically, they examine two kinds of question: what will happen if the present trends continue unabated, and what will happen if various measures to slow down population growth are introduced. The most critical assumption in world population forecasting is whether and when what is commonly known as the 'demographic transition' (essentially a change from high to low rates of population growth) will occur in the poor countries. Forecasts vary widely, especially after the year 2000, as a result of differing assumptions about growth rates, possible changes in fertility, and the potential effectiveness of different population policies. As Figure 3.1 shows, forecasts of population in the year 2100 vary by almost an order of magnitude, even though all authors imply some levelling-off is inevitable. Several mechanisms for

51

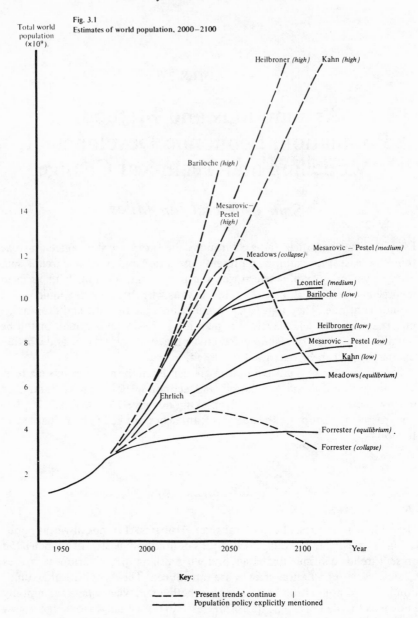

Fig. 3.1
Estimates of world population, 2000–2100

Total world population (×10⁹)

Key:

– – – 'Present trends' continue
——— Population policy explicitly mentioned

bringing about a slowing down of population growth are postulated or advocated. These range from the application of an overt and official population policy (the Ehrlichs, Meadows, Mesarovic and Pestel etc.) to more spontaneous changes in behaviour following on improvements in overall economic well-being (Kahn, Bariloche, Modrzhinskaya).

Spengler, Heilbroner and the Ehrlichs extrapolate current growth rates of population exponentially to the end of the twenty-first century and beyond. The high levels that they foresee are dominated by growth of population in poor countries. But the most dramatic population forecasts, although not the highest, come from *The Limits to Growth* and *World Dynamics* models of the Meadows and Forrester. According to Forrester the 'basic behaviour of the world system' indicates a maximum population of about 5½ billion in the early twenty-first century (1971, p. 9); the Meadows team suggest that the peak will occur at a level of 12×10^9 in the middle of that century (1974, p. 124). In both cases, a catastrophic decline to about half this level follows, with the rate of decline approximately equal to the previous rate of growth. These results do not come from an assumed demographic transition; they represent catastrophes predicted from assumed limitations in the Earth's carrying capacity. The Ehrlichs (1970, p. 245) argue that population growth must be reduced by an effective policy. If this does not bring about decline in world population then a succession of local tragedies, mainly deriving from lack of food, would keep the world's population at what the Ehrlichs refer to as 'the level of the lowest United Nations estimate'.

Some of the extreme estimates are deliberate exaggerations. When Heilbroner speaks of world population in the region of 40 billion, his intention is to show that such a figure is insupportable, and his expectations are evidently much lower; if 'strict population control' were implemented, the minimum figure could be 9 billion.

The Soviet authors pay little attention to population. They simply argue that production can expand faster than population, given conducive social and political arrangements. Kosolapov postulates that because of advances in medicine the average lifespan will be 85 years by 1980, and by the year 2000 it will be 100 years with chemical control of ageing (1976, p. 182).

In *The Year 2000* Kahn and Wiener make a large number of extrapolations of population growth for the world, for regions and selected countries. In their 'standard world' they estimate a world total population of around 6½ billion by the year 2000, of which 5 billion are in the poor countries. They caution that the estimates are 'somewhat arbitrary and the projections from them might easily be wrong' (p.137). They observe (p.151) that 'at some point in the next *few centuries* presumably population itself would have to stabilise, perhaps at a level somewhere between 10 and 50 billion — though this is extremely uncertain and depends on unknown factors such as food and technology' (thus hinting at the possibility of Malthusian limits at higher levels of population). In *The Next 200 Years* this range is narrowed somewhat with lower and upper limits of about 7.5 and 30 billion, and a working figure of 15 billion is used by the authors. The anticipated reduction in the rate of worldwide population growth is, they say, best explained by reference to 'the demographic transition', which they point out is not a hard and fast theory but merely 'a description of historical experience' (pp. 2–32).

Unlike the authors of *The Limits to Growth*, some of the later mathematical modellers have not built a causal model of population growth. The
United Nations modellers under Leontief choose simply to use the 'medium'
and 'low' figures prepared by the Population Division of the United Nations
Secretariat. Figures for the Year 2000 are given: in the 'low' projection the
population of developed and developing regions are 0.7 and 2.3 billions
respectively and in the 'medium' projection the corresponding figures are 1.0
and 2.5 (pp. 122–15). Mesarovic and Pestel construct a population model
that is very detailed, providing estimates for each one-year age-group in ten
world regions, but in which population trends are not dependent on other
variables. They further postulate that a population policy can be implemented and can become effective (1974a, p. 75). Even then, given the present
age structure of regional populations, they forecast an eventual total world
population of somewhere between 8 and 12 billion (p. 187) depending upon
whether the 'equilibrium' population policy that they strongly advocate
becomes effective in 1975 or 1995.

The Japanese and Bariloche models both involve causal assumptions
about demographic change. Kaya's Japanese group use a straightforward
formula that does not take into account age structure, but treats birth and
death rates as functions of gross regional product. The Bariloche model uses
more complex assumptions about the effects of changing socio-economic
factors on life expectancy.

It is clear from comparing these projected population growth rates that any
forecast is likely to contain a wide margin of error. Theories of demographic
growth are controversial and, on past experience of population forecasting,
unreliable. (For a comprehensive survey of demographic theory and its implications for development see Casson, 1976.) Even if we dismiss the 'doomsday'
forecasts, a wide range of population estimates for the year 2100 remains –
between 8 and 30 billions in the works considered here. For the year 2050 the
range is narrower – from about 7 to 14 billion.

More recent forecasters have tended to put forward the 'developmentalist'
view that a levelling-off of population will be achieved only with economic
growth. Even so, a recent study by the Worldwatch Institute (Brown, 1976)
runs counter to many of the forecasts resulting from this perspective, since it
concludes that world population growth has slowed down to such an extent
that the levelling-off point may be at a population size only about twice that
of the present, in other words, at the lower end of the range of figures cited
above.

In the forecasting undertaken in later chapters of this book, we take population trends as an exogenous variable. This is a simplifying assumption,
especially in relation to the future of food and agriculture (Casson, 1976).
However, like other forecasters, we cannot cover everything; our expertise
lies in other areas and we believe that it is in these areas that our contribution
can be most useful.

Also like other forecasters we assume a process of demographic transition

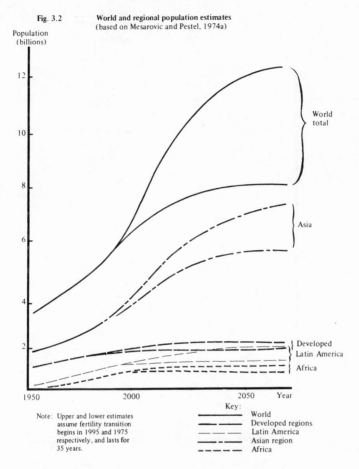

Fig. 3.2   World and regional population estimates
(based on Mesarovic and Pestel, 1974a)

Population
(billions)

Note: Upper and lower estimates
assume fertility transition
begins in 1995 and 1975
respectively, and lasts for
35 years.

Key:
━━━━━ World
━━ ━━ Developed regions
━ ━ ━ Latin America
━ ·━ · Asian region
─ ─ ─ ─ Africa

where birth rates in the poor countries adjust downwards to approach the death rates. The eventual level of world population is very sensitive to the length of time necessary for this adjustment, and professional opinion differs about how long this will be. We assume a relatively wide range of uncertainty about it: that it might take from 20 years to 60 years from 1970. For the sake of convenience we use the population projections of Mesaroviç and Pestel based on assumptions of transition periods from 1970 of 19, 40, and 60 years. These are very similar to those made by Frejka (1973) on the basis of similar assumptions, and they are reproduced in Figure 3.2.

PATTERNS OF WORLD ECONOMIC GROWTH

The world forecasters talk about major 'gaps' in income per head between rich and poor countries of the world. Figure 3.3 indicates the magnitude of

Fig. 3.3.   Examples of economic growth levels (GNP per head (U.S. $)) in rich and poor
countries projected by forecasters on the basis of present trends.

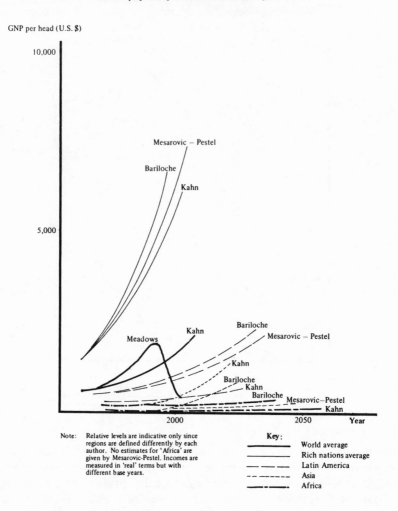

GNP per head (U.S. $)

Note: Relative levels are indicative only since
regions are defined differently by each
author. No estimates for 'Africa' are
given by Mesarovic-Pestel. Incomes are
measured in 'real' terms but with
different base years.

Key:

———————   World average
———————   Rich nations average
— — — —   Latin America
— — —— —   Asia
—— — —— ·   Africa

the gap in various forecasts if present trends were to continue. Authors such
as Dumont, Spengler, the Ehrlichs and Heilbroner, who do not give
quantified forecasts of a widening gap between rich industrial countries and
the rest of the world, remark on its growing magnitude.

A concern with 'gaps' is not the prerogative of futurologists. A considerable literature on this topic stems from development economists. There are
volumes of conference papers with titles like *The Widening Gap* (Ward *et al.*,
1971) and *The Gap Between Rich and Poor Nations* (Ranis, 1972). It has
been pointed out that simply contrasting the GNP per head levels of different
countries provides no adequate indicator of differences in social conditions

or levels of welfare. It might be possible to live better at a lower income (as measured in GNP terms) in one country than in another, and the macro-economic accounts of poorer countries have often been regarded as suspect.

Nevertheless, according to Kuznets (1972) there has been a widening of the gap in income per head between the richest and the poorest countries over the past century. Even in the post-war period the growth rate per head of the industrial nations has been more rapid than that of the poorest countries. There is some evidence that this tendency has been offset more recently, however; some poor countries such as Brazil, Singapore, South Korea and Taiwan have displayed rapid rates of economic growth. As Kuznets points out, the income gap is not mirrored in all aspects of national development: mortality and literacy rates, for example, show some convergence between rich and poor countries.

The problems of how to conceptualise 'gaps' – what groups of nations to compare and what measures to employ – receive little attention in the fore-casting literature; Galtung and Kahn are exceptions here. The more recent modelling efforts do attempt to disaggregate different groups of nations, but they emphasise regional groupings rather than common economic develop-ment patterns and prospects, which might be better related to political systems, levels of population or natural resource endowment. It is almost always taken for granted that the significance of gaps in gross national product per head is self-evident when, as we have seen, this is not always the case.

Some economists have questioned whether the 'gap' is itself of very great importance, arguing that the priority should be increasing social welfare in the poorer countries, instead of engaging in what are seen as invidious com-parisons. Some maintain that with modern technologies major advances in welfare in such fields as health and education are not necessarily dependent on prior economic growth. But the assumption that growth is a condition for improved welfare is widespread, so that the stimulation of high absolute rates of growth in poor countries is considered by many to be crucial. Like Kahn, many economists see continued growth in the industrial nations as a pre-requisite for world development, pointing as evidence to the pre-war braking of growth in parts of the poor world, caused by the sluggishness of the Western economies.

Others believe that 'gaps' can have pernicious effects in their own right, leading, for example, to resentment and unwillingness amongst the leaders of poor countries to cooperate in economic and political agreements, and to dis-satisfaction and unrealistically high aspirations amongst their populations. Attention is also drawn to the imbalance of power associated with economic inequalities, which could prevent the adequate recognition of the interests of poor countries in trade negotiations, and possibly hinder their economic development. A similar point has been made forcefully by proponents of 'dependency' theories (e.g. Furtado, 1964) who argue that poorer countries have been drawn both economically and politically into what is almost a sub-missive posture towards their richer trading partners, and thus have been unable to formulate or pursue development goals corresponding to local needs and conditions. However, these theorists do not regard the quantitative 'gap' in itself as responsible for dependency; it is the interaction of different forms of economic organisation – albeit reflected in different levels of economic growth – that restricts the development of the poor world.

The discussion of 'gaps' occupies a large portion of the futures literature, especially in the work of Dumont and of the more recent modellers, who argue that 'gaps' are threats to world stability and/or are ethically inadmissible. They therefore propose more or less radical changes in the world economic system. Among the non-modelling forecasters only Kahn does not advocate extensive changes. There is great divergence in expectations; on overall growth, Kahn seems to indicate upper limits of world average per head consumption approximately ten times the current *U.S.A.* average, while Forrester and Meadows see at best something like twice the present *world* average being achieved.

It is not always clear from the statements of authors – and especially those who do not use models – what levels of income they have in mind in their 'normative' forecasts (i.e. the futures they would prefer to see). Since rates of growth and ultimate world-wide levels of production are often determined by the assumptions about technological possibilites and ecological constraints, one can gain a rough idea of the possibilities of growth considered desirable. For example, the Ehrlichs believe the world to be *already* over-populated in terms of available resources and consider that less-developed countries' living standards may actually decline; while they may regret this, a decline in the living standards of the industrialised world does not worry them – indeed they seem to regard this as both desirable and necessary.

The model-builders forecast the relative GNP growth rates possible for different world regions if the measures they advocate were implemented. These results are shown in Figure 3.4. As one might expect, given the objectives of the modelling exercises, all models now show a narrowing gap between rich and poor nations. Compared with Figure 3.3, all show the growth rate falling below the historic trend in rich nations and accelerating in poor countries. There are clear differences between the regional growth rates projected by various models. For example, for all regions (except the Asian region) the Japanese model projects the highest growth rates. The Latin American model projects lower growth rates, but a more rapid narrowing of the income gap.

The major variables determining growth rates in the models are levels of investment and technical change. It is surprising to find that the economic growth forecasts of different modellers should be as close as they are, given their very wide range of underlying assumptions about economic and institutional factors. It would seem that similar values of parameters derived

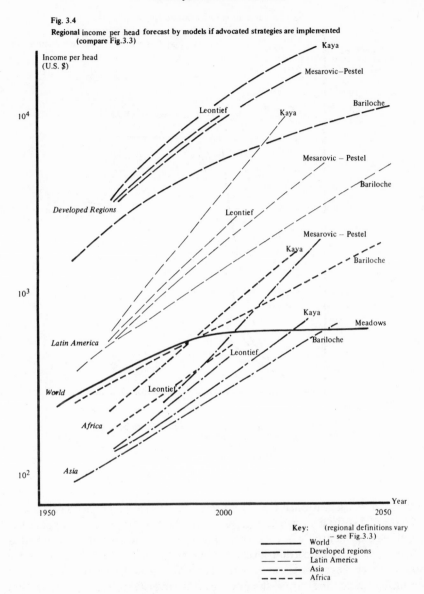

Fig. 3.4

Regional income per head forecast by models if advocated strategies are implemented
(compare Fig.3.3)

Income per head
(U.S. $)

Kaya

Mesarovic–Pestel

Bariloche

Leontief

Kaya

10^4

Mesarovic – Pestel

Bariloche

Developed Regions

Leontief

Mesarovic – Pestel

Kaya

Bariloche

10^3

Kaya

Meadows

Bariloche

Latin America

Leontief

World

Leontief

Africa

10^2

Asia

Year

1950   2000   2050

Key: (regional definitions vary
      – see Fig.3.3)
———— World
— —— — Developed regions
— — — — Latin America
—·—·— Asia
— — — — Africa

from historical analysis (especially rates of technical change) have in some
cases been adjusted to give 'plausible' overall growth rates when the models
are used to forecast (Cole, 1976).

The quantitative levels of growth projected by modellers certainly do not
always correspond to their commentary and recommendations. Mesarovic
and Pestel, for example, strongly emphasise ecological constraints and the

Fig. 3.5   Total world product if prescribed policies are implemented

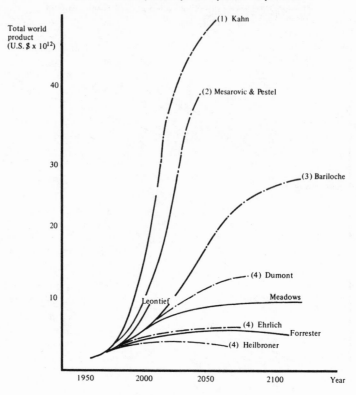

Notes: (1)   Total growth levels off at $50–200 x 10^{12} in 200–300 years
        (2)   No indication of final level
        (3)   Levels off when basic needs are satisfied
        (4)   Indicative only

need for a 'conservationist ethic' yet forecast that income per head can rise by a factor of 5 to 10 in all world regions within the next 50 years, and apparently continue exponentially beyond then. The Bariloche team call for a levelling-off in growth, once certain levels are reached, not for reasons of resource supply, nor because they believe economic growth necessarily implies pollution (in fact they argue the opposite), but in order to avoid potential (but unquantified) environmental hazards.

At this point we may begin to summarise two crucial aspects of the various world forecasts: the growth of total world product and the ways in which it might be distributed between rich and poor countries. Figure 3.5 depicts the *total* economic growth in the world projected by different authors in their 'normative' forecasts (in the case of Kahn the distinction between 'normative' and 'trends continued' is vague, however). Figure 3.6 tries to show how dif-

Figure 3.6   Wealth and distribution in preferred futures

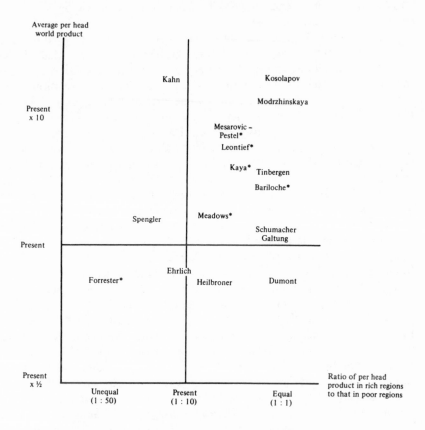

Note: This diagram is a rough indication of the profiles of economic growth considered by authors
to be possible *if* their proposed policy measures were followed. Quantified forecasts are
indicated *; however, all locations are at best approximate, and some authors implicitly or
explicitly admit that a considerable range of uncertainty surrounds their forecasts.

ferent authors see their 'normative' futures in terms of average world income per head *and* its global distribution between rich and poor nations, if the measures they each advocate were implemented.

Mesarovic and Pestel, and the Japanese group, argue for an immediate globally coordinated solution with emphasis both on redistribution of the world's wealth (partly through diversification of industries around the world) and on establishing a new international division of labour. They repeatedly emphasise that cooperation would be in everyone's interest, and that conflict is likely to harm all involved. Kahn believes that such interdependence and reliance on the poor world is likely to run counter even to Mesarovic and Pestel's own objectives for global stability. He prefers developed nations to maintain a certain degree of independence against the possibility of further OPEC-type activities, and argues that if they do this they will be in a better position to help ailing nations.

Dumont, Galtung and the Bariloche group, despite their conflicting opinions on ultimate long-term resource availability, consider that, in the short term, the development of the poor world could be assisted if poorer countries attempted to uncouple themselves from dependent relations with industrial nations – in short, adopted some kind of autarkic or 'self-reliant' strategy. But in the long term, even these authors look toward new international mechanisms for distribution. For Forrester and the Ehrlichs isolation of the very poorest countries would lead to their economic collapse, but they argue that it could prevent the spread of disaster to the rest of the world.

Few non-modelling authors quantify the levels of trade they envisage, and most indicate only that they consider aid should be between one and two per cent of rich countries' GNP; these figures are apparently based on the United Nations recommendations for the First and Second Development Decades. While the world modellers appear to examine a wide spectrum of possible trade and aid arrangements, the assumptions made in their 'normative' forecasts do not always reflect their prescriptive rhetoric (the Ehrlichs are an exception among forecasters in suggesting that advanced nations should devote 20 per cent of their income to developing nations). Although the Bariloche group advocate regional autarky, trade is not actually kept to a minimum in their model. In fact, the assumptions made are similar to those of Leontief and Mesarovic and Pestel, where trade is a major theme, and to those of Kaya's study, where a very high level of trade corresponding to an 'ideal' development-oriented international division of labour is sought. The recommendations made by the Bariloche group for the amount, if not the form, of assistance to poorer nations are similar to those of other writers.

Although in *The Year 2000* Kahn and Wiener do not advocate economic aid from rich to poor countries, they do discuss its economic merits and conclude that 'it is *a priori* possible to achieve a surprising amount of development over a ten to thirty five year span if modest amounts of capital are made available'. But they continue, 'of course it has become increasingly clear that for most of the under-developed nations the limitations have as much to do with in-abilities to absorb capital productively as with unavailability of capital' (p. 253). This argument is repeated in *The Next 200 Years*.

Some of the world models portray divergent patterns of growth for different regions. The nature of these differences for the groups of countries designated as 'Asia' and 'Europe' are shown in Figure 3.7. Strict comparison is hampered because the countries comprising the regions vary from model to model, and the sectoral divisions are not strictly equivalent. In the Bariloche model, for example, economic sectors are designed around the concept of 'basic needs'. Despite this it is obvious that differences in the suggested

Fig. 3.7

Composition of regional economies

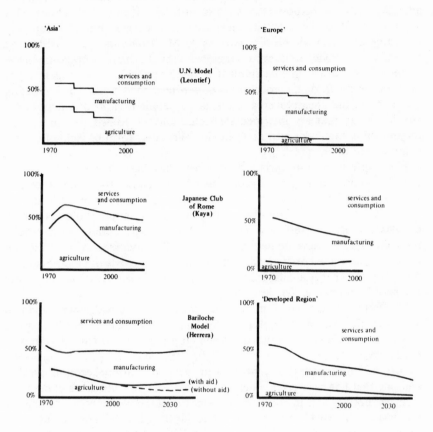

Note: Sectoral divisions are not strictly comparable as different definitions are used in each model. For the Latin American model the 'developed' regions are shown. The results for the U.N. model are calculated for ten-year time periods.

regional patterns of development exist that are in part related to the assumed pattern of trade. Leontief's U.N. model indicates a gradual trend in the composition of regional product of the Asian region towards that of an advanced country. The Japanese model seems to suggest that an immediate rise in agricultural production in the 'Asian' region will be overtaken by a shift towards light manufacturing as agricultural productivity improves; overall the trend is similar to that of the U.N. model and is more pronounced than that in the Bariloche model.

Although several authors comment on the specific technological requirements of developing nations and in particular their need to employ more labour through less capital-intensive methods of production, no explicit account is taken of this in the world models. Only the Bariloche group include the problem formally in their model, but this is seriously hampered by lack of adequate data on the possibilities for substitution of capital by labour. This neglect is hard to reconcile with most authors' comments on the seriousness of unemployment in developing nations. In Mesarovic and Pestel's 'Strategy for Survival' model it is even suggested that the highly capital-intensive methods, which are in fact implied by assumptions in the model, might 'worsen the plight of the poor in the under-developed regions by increasing the ranks of the unemployed and displaced people in large urban areas' (p. 66). They say that an 'intermediate technology' is needed, yet no explicit relationships that take into account this particular form of technology are employed in their model.

The expression 'appropriate technology' has been introduced into the debate by some development economists in preference to the older expression 'intermediate technology'. This is not simply a question of academic pedantry, as the latter term often carried the connotation of old-fashioned, obsolescent and less-efficient technology. The 'appropriate' technologies recommended for development might be equally 'modern' and 'scientific' but better suited to the specific endowment and relative costs of labour, capital, materials and energy available in poor countries. (This issue is taken up more extensively in chapter 7.)

The failure of the world models to deal adequately with unemployment and with the use of technology more 'appropriate' to the needs of poor countries is unfortunate since increased employment is often held out as a major route to redistribution and hence the relief of poverty and malnutrition. This is a question central to any new international economic order, and one that has been given much attention both in the literature of development economics and in some of the recent conferences on restructuring (or preserving) the world economy, in particular the I.L.O.'s 'World Conference on Employment, Income Distribution and Social Progress, and the International Division of Labour' held in Geneva in 1976.

This conference reflected the awareness among economists that maximising the rate of growth of GNP has not always been in harmony with the goal of increasing employment in the poor world. Contrary to many expectations, 'modern' industrialisation has been found not necessarily to increase industrial employment at a rate anywhere close to the rate of growth of population of the country in question – indeed, in some cases there has been an absolute decline in industrial employment (Morawetz, 1974). Many analysts have produced evidence that economic growth itself was not sufficient to put an end to poverty and unemployment, and that many growth-oriented development strategies were counterproductive when evaluated in these terms (e.g. Adelman and Morris, 1973; Little, Scitowsky and Scott, 1970).

The World Employment Conference sought to relate these issues to the development of a new economic order, proposing national development of goals construed in terms of the satisfaction of a set of 'basic needs'. The resemblance of this orientation to the work of the Bariloche group is not coincidental – a version of the Bariloche model was presented at the conference as a starting-point for discussion. The use of this model, which also drew upon the Leontief input–output model to suggest targets for GNP growth and the allocation of production by 1990 and 2000, suggests that the work of world modellers is becoming to some extent respectable within the development debate.

The development strategy proposed by the I.L.O. conference differs from the view that the free market and economic growth are the cornerstones of development, and from the historic 'Russian' pattern of development based on heavy industry. In the development literature we can find prescriptions for the creation of productive employment opportunities by the stimulation of more 'appropriate' production patterns (changing the composition of the economic output, for example, from import-substitution to export, or from luxury items to mass consumption goods, or towards small-scale industries, which tend to be more labour-intensive than large-scale industrial developments). These changes could be promoted through the international economic system by appropriate trade agreements. The results of the I.L.O. conference were largely confined to assurances from individual governments that they would bear 'basic needs' in mind, and to the establishment of some information-gathering services (I.L.O., 1977).

While the problem of world employment and the division of labour has been raised – although hardly at adequate length – in the pages of such journals as *Futures* and *The Futurist*, the attention devoted to them in the world futures debate is meagre. Insufficient studies of anything other than conventional industrial technology have been conducted (see, for example, Morawetz's (1974) review of the economics literature on the relations of industrialisation to employment in poor countries). Thus the Bariloche group, who do try to describe an alternative path of development, are in the end frustrated by inadequate data about other than conventional technologies. It is likewise extremely difficult to assess the theses of Galtung and others about the viability of decentralised, low-technology communities. On the other hand, lack of empirical demonstration is in itself no reason for excluding ideas such as those presented by Galtung from discussions about the future. An important role of futures research – and this should include the building of global models – is to direct attention to the problems that should be studied and discussed.

The Political Context

Some insights into the values and assumptions underlying the positions in the world futures debate can be obtained by considering the political debate over the future world economic system. The various forecasters' quantitative analyses rest on very different perceptions of the current economic relationships between and within the industrialised and developing nations. Galtung and Dumont, for example, see the industrial countries as dependent on poor world raw materials for continued growth, whereas Kahn appears to be arguing quite the reverse – the rich world can now develop quite independently of the poor, while the best hope of development for the poor world lies in the continued expanding prosperity of the rich.

The differences in views about aid and trade mirror a controversy apparent not only in the academic journals of economists but also in the meetings and decisions of the international organisations that influence world trade. Concern with what is perceived to be an inequitable international division of labour and with the development and trade strategies to be employed by under-developed countries has a much longer history than one would gather from a perusal of the forecasting literature. The current debate is prefigured, for example, in the writings of Russian economists of the revolutionary period.

The Bolsheviks initially hoped that the 1917 revolution in Russia would mark the breaking of the 'chain of imperialism' at its weakest point, helping to precipitate communist revolution in the industrial countries of Europe. Bukharin and Preobrazhensky, in outlining their vision of the communist future in 1920, foresaw a socialist international division of labour, in which Russia would supply raw materials to Europe. As hopes for a Western revolution receded, the new Soviet government found itself in a position in some ways similar to that of many newly independent countries – faced with the need to create a modern economy without the option of extracting wealth from overseas colonies of one's own. Bukharin argued that Russia should trade with capitalist nations, producing agricultural goods for the world market and importing industrial equipment. Against this Preobrazhensky, along with Trotsky and his followers, called for rapid industrialisation and for the extraction of a surplus from agriculture, involving the severe restriction of peasants' consumption, so as to increase investment in industry. By the mid-1920s Russia was indeed set on a course of planned industrialisation, and under Stalin the tempo was increased. This industrialisation policy represented a deliberate rejection of the existing international division of labour, which was seen to assign Russia to agricultural labour for Western Europe, itself a military threat to the new regime. Foreign trade, which Preobrazhensky had seen as a drain on surplus and as encouraging unwanted political ties, was cautiously accepted as a means of importing commodities that could not yet be produced domestically.

Similar issues attracted press headlines in 1976 with UNCTAD IV (United Nations Conference on Trade and Development), but it is worth remembering that in the three previous UNCTAD meetings poor countries expressed dissatisfaction with their role in world trade, arguing that the industrial countries unfairly discriminated against their traditional produce and manufactures, that their terms of trade were becoming more unfavourable (i.e. the prices of their imports were rising more rapidly than those of their exports, which, it was argued, was partly a result of technical change), and that unstable commodity prices threatened their economies. International economic organisations like GATT (General Agreement on Tariffs and Trade), the I.M.F. (International Monetary Fund) and the World Bank were, it was argued, primarily operating in the interests of the richer countries.

In a sense, the poorer countries can be seen as being in a similar position to that of revolutionary Russia, but seeking to emulate the Russian experience of growth by a negotiated shift in the world's pattern of industrialisation rather than by following the path of forced 'super-industrialisation' at the expense of the peasant population. (However, policies of import-substitution themselves have tended to impose heavy costs on peasants in these countries.) There are of course many possible reasons for not following the Soviet path – such as international and domestic political constraints and the comparative smallness and resource shortage of most poor countries. Furthermore, the experience of industrialisation in such countries in the post-war world economy has been mixed; even if industrialisation is a necessary basis for development, it does not seem to be a sufficient one. Many countries have found that investment in manufacturing has not brought prosperity or regular employment for the majority. Some poor countries have reduced the proportion of their gross national product in agriculture to levels similar to those of industrial countries in Western Europe, but their condition remains one of under-development. Their governments are hostile to what they often see as a subordinate position in the world economy, which they are assigned by the present international division of labour.

UNCTAD IV brought to the fore issues that had only been dimly visible in the work of the world forecasters (except Tinbergen), although there are clear attempts to grapple with them in the more recent works. Its significance was highlighted by the turbulence of the world economy in the early 1970s, with the food and oil crisis and rapid inflation. Some observers took these events to indicate a qualitative change in the position and strength of the industrialised countries relative to the under-developed world, while others attributed them to change in the relative status of the U.S.A. compared with its main competitors, and yet others saw in them a possible onset of a new world depression. UNCTAD IV was one of a spate of highly charged international meetings that took place within the space of a year. In the autumn of 1975, at a UNIDO (United Nations Industrial Development Organisation) conference in Lima and at the Seventh Special Session of the United Nations, representatives of poor countries argued for a major shift of patterns of world industrialisation: poor countries should treble their share of world industrial production by the year 2000. The 'North–South' Conference for International Economic Cooperation, UNCTAD IV, and the I.L.O. World Employment Conference called for a world development strategy oriented towards increasing employment and eradicating poverty in poor countries.

Before and during these conferences the economic issues were inextricably entangled with political developments. A conference of ministers of foreign affairs of the 'non-aligned nations' meeting in Lima worked on a programme of Third World solidarity and independence, based on increasing bargaining power by forming a council for raw material producers and exporter associations, a fund for establishing buffer stocks of raw materials and poor world primary produce, and a fund for social economic development. The Group of 77, an organisation of over a hundred poor countries, established a permanent secretariat in which some observers detected the makings of a 'poor countries' O.E.C.D'. Apart from the new vigour of these calls for change, a further notable development concerned the divergence in the positions taken by the U.S.A. and the nine European members of the Common Market (E.E.C.). These differences too are to some degree paralleled in the world futures debate of the 1970s.

Several observers of the Seventh Special Session of the U.N. (Barraclough, 1976; Ruggie and Gosovic, 1976) noted that while Western nations stressed the theme of 'interdependence' it was given a markedly different slant by different countries. The U.S.A. and Japan and, to some extent, West Germany argued that the free market system in international trade was basically in the interests of all nations, and that with a few adjustments economic growth would 'trickle down' from rich to poor countries. Kissinger stressed the role of OPEC's action (in increasing oil prices) in upsetting the economic system. Some observers have argued that this was part of a strategy to divide the Third World countries, as was the U.S. desire to keep negotiations restricted to specific resources rather than the terms of trade in general. It is not difficult to relate these U.S. theses to the positions put forward by Kahn and Spengler: their belief that under-developed countries will 'take off' into more rapid growth as they become integrated into the existing world economic system; that these countries' chief hope lies in cooperation with the West rather than with OPEC or the Soviet bloc, for example. We may also draw parallels here with the Japanese futurologists' prescriptions.

At this same U.N. meeting, the countries of the E.E.C. responded in a somewhat more accommodating fashion to the proposals and documents provided by the Group of 77, suggesting that more international planning should characterise the world economy in order, for example, to stabilise commodity prices. However, they jibbed at proposals for redistribution of the world's wealth by major structural change in the economic system, for example international agreements that fixed, rather than merely stabilised, commodity prices. In the world futures literature, this 'European' position finds parallels in recent Club of Rome studies, especially *Mankind at the Turning Point* (Mesarovic and Pestel, 1974a) with its advocacy of 'organic growth' and interdependent development within a revised form of the present international division of labour.

The Group of 77 countries argued that more than a revision of the international order was called for: a new order rather than a new deal within the existing order. This would involve rapid industrialisation in their countries, the improvement of their terms of trade, greater access to the markets of the rich countries, and the regulation of commodity prices. These proposals – which Western governments clearly view with some alarm – resemble the positions advocated in the futures debate by Dumont and the Bariloche group, who propose that, if such transformations are not forthcoming, withdrawal from trade with industrial countries might be necessary. A similar view is held by Galtung and less forcefully by Tinbergen, which seems appropriate, given that the Scandinavian countries and Holland tended to support the Group of 77 at the U.N. Special Session. The Soviet bloc countries maintain a low profile at these meetings, although at UNCTAD IV there were clashes between Russian and Chinese delegates, with the latter accusing the former of imperialistic designs by their support for a 'socialist' international division of labour. It may be significant that the Russian futurologists pay little attention to future international exchanges, and that other commentators from Eastern Europe have expressed dismay that poor countries accuse Eastern and Western countries alike of exploitation (*Soviet News*, 19 October 1976).

PROFILES OF WORLD DEVELOPMENT AND METHODS IN FORECASTING

Assumptions and prescriptions of future world development are heavily influenced by political interests and values. As we have suggested in an earlier book, forecasting can never be value-free, and according to our values the reduction of world economic inequalities should be a major concern of forecasting (Encel *et al.*, 1975). We have identified two central issues in the futures debate: the future rate of economic growth attained by the world economic system and the distribution of this growth between nations. As already argued, such indicators can only approximate our concerns; economic growth need not necessarily mean improved living standards, and international equality levels tell us nothing directly about economic equality within nations. But they are useful approximations and we have already used them to contrast the futures portrayed by different forecasters (Figure 3.6).

The use of these indicators yields four possible 'profiles' of the world's future: a high growth, more equal world, a low growth, more equal world, a high growth, less equal world, and a low growth, less equal world. We shall use these four profiles to guide our explorations of problems of the future: in developing alternative futures for food, energy and materials; in examining how differing political and analytical frameworks perceive the desirability and the feasibility of achieving different patterns of growth; and in exploring future patterns of quality of life, and of military expenditures and weapons development.

Before leaving this résumé of the world futures debate, however, we shall discuss some issues of method in forecasting, and explain why we have rejected the use of computer modelling.

Our approach to forecasting is oriented towards developing descriptive scenarios and bears some similarities to that used by Kahn and Wiener in *The Year 2000*. The alternative futures described in *The Year 2000* are viewed in terms of a theoretical perspective that remains largely implicit but is based on the idea of a long-standing 'multifold trend'. Even with this theory of continuity and change, uncertainties concerning specific combinations of events lead to a very wide range of possible alternatives, although virtually no explicit links are made between their detailed scenarios and the alternative growth rate projections. In *The Next 200 Years* the links are even more tenuous and the range of economic and demographic possibilities (four scenarios are discussed, representing different levels of world growth) is even wider than in *The Year 2000*. In our view, one can make firmer links between economic growth rates and alternative prescriptions and assumptions about ecological, technological and other constraints.

This requires us to be more explicit about the assumptions underlying the various profiles and scenarios that we discuss. Although our choice of growth rates and levels of equality considered in the profiles is to some extent arbitrary, a high growth world is obviously more consistent with optimistic than with pessimistic assumptions about ecological and technological constraints. In most modelling some attempt is made by 'sensitivity analysis' to check how much results change when specific assumptions are varied. In *The Limits to Growth* the underlying model remains unaltered, even though different sets of resource assumptions are made. Similarly, the Bariloche group propound a single theoretical approach, even though alternative assumptions are made about levels of economic assistance to poor nations. In Part II we shall attempt to assess the effect of different assumptions about economic growth, population growth, technological change and the like upon our conclusions. Even more ambitiously our method also tries to take into account 'variations' in the underlying theory; this is the primary purpose of Part III of the book.

Such an approach does not readily lend itself to the use of the major methodological innovation in the recent futures debate: large-scale computer models. For this and a variety of other reasons, we have chosen not to use one ourselves. Although the models present numerical views of the future, they disguise rather than reveal the extent to which their results are dependent on their assumptions and data. As with other forecasts, we have found that results coming out of a model are in part determined by the explicit normative goals set for the models; for example, decline in growth in industrialised countries is seen as desirable on ecological grounds by several authors. Likewise, economic growth in the models is determined by debatable assumptions about resource endowments or diminishing rates of return to investment. Trends are also affected directly and explicitly by the assumed pattern of world trade, and by the choice of investment rates used in the model. In all cases, the outcome of the models concerning physical constraints follows from the input assumptions, without any need for computer runs, so that the models are largely redundant for this purpose.

The results of the models are affected to a more limited degree by their structures. A model that relies on globally averaged levels, as does *The Limits to Growth* model, implies quite drastic assumptions about the distribution of population in relation to production and the nature of world-wide trading patterns. Models recognising regional divisions in the world can achieve closer approximations to reality, although whether nations should be classified into regions according to geography, natural resources or type of social system then emerges as a major issue. Regions are effectively treated in the world models as homogeneous economic units. Thus, the circumstances of particularly poor nations are hidden, as are sectoral difficulties and differences. While nations in close geographical proximity are likely to have mutual interactions, these are not bound to be integrated as several models presuppose. Any form of regionalisation inevitably sets limits on a model and on the range of scenarios that can reasonably be examined.

The models have little to say on the distribution of income within nations. Although most forecasting authors proclaim the need for internal reform – and even argue that the favourable results are contingent upon them – rarely, if at all, do the inputs to the models take any account of them. Only the Bariloche group argue from their model that a major redistribution of income per head would be immensely beneficial to such objectives as the relief of squalor and malnutrition.

Some of the modellers are well aware of these methodological problems. The authors of the U.N. model observe that 'since the system is complex and large, the formulation of specific questions and the interpretation of answers that come out of the computer in the form of figures is a task that has to be approached with great care and circumspection' (Leontief *et al.*, 1976, p. 70). The Japanese team say it is 'rash to give much credence' (Kaya and Suzuki, 1974, p. 379) to the absolute numerical values their model produces. The authors of 'Strategy for Survival' point out that 'the uncertainty in considering such time horizons is tremendous yet unavoidable' (Mesarovic and Pestel, 1974b, p. 18).

Improved data or methods of calculation, disaggregation and calibration cannot finally resolve the difficulties of forecasting. They cannot overcome fundamental questions as to how much the past conditions the future, and how far human actions may reflect or transform this conditioning. The numerical results emerging from a computer analysis are likely to be at best only marginally more reliable than those derived from far less elaborate methods. In general we accept Kahn and Wiener's view in *The Year 2000* that 'it makes little sense . . . to invest in substantially more sophisticated forecasting methods at this time' (p. 133). We would tend to accept Kahn's conclusion that 'the whole procedure' should be taken with 'a grain of salt' (*The Next 200 Years*, p. 133), rather than Mesarovic and Pestel's claim to have 'proven' anything 'by logical and factual analysis' (p. 136).

Our approach is not a technique for 'forecasting the future of the world'. We are trying to develop a method that permits us to integrate specialist contributions, to examine specific policy problems at the regional, national and international levels within a global and long-term context. This does not mean that we can demonstrate precisely how policy choices will affect the long-term future, but it does demonstrate why certain factors ought to be taken into account in considering a wide range of practical policy problems.

CONCLUSIONS AND ASSUMPTIONS ABOUT TECHNICAL CHANGE

From our analysis of the course of the world futures debate and from our own earlier work we have derived four basic 'profiles' as a framework for a discussion of alternative futures. From this debate we have also derived another central issue: the limitation of natural resources in relation to population growth and economic development. As Table 2.2 in chapter 2 has shown, most of those involved in the futures debate have taken up the older concern of Malthus and the classical economists: future food supply. To this ancient concern they have added the future supply of materials and energy. We do not dissent from the general view that the availability of food, materials and energy is fundamental to any global forecast. Indeed in our earlier work on *The Limits to Growth* models we were surprised that the energy sector was not included there, and took up this issue in our own critique (Cole, Freeman, Jahoda and Pavitt, 1973).

Chapter 2 has made it clear that despite the differences in views among the participants in the global futures debate, and despite their very different policy prescriptions, there was agreement on one point: the rate and direction of technical change is crucial to the outcome, whatever global future is desired or predicted. Kahn and his associates devote a large part of *The Year 2000* to a discussion of probable future changes in technology, and the whole of *The Next 200 Years* is based on 'optimistic' arguments about the generation and application of a wide range of new technologies.

At the beginning of the nineteenth century differing views about technical change were also at the heart of the debate on the future. Malthus' predictions were based on the assumptions that agricultural productivity would increase at best arithmetically while demand (due to increased population and economic growth) would enlarge geometrically. With this model, or even with a model that postulates 'outrageously' high fixed levels of productivity, exponentially growing demand will always overtake supply at some point. As Spengler and many others have pointed out, Malthus was wrong largely because he took insufficient account of scientific discovery and the possibilities for technological change and substitution.

In the current debate about the future very diverse ideas about future technological possibilities also operate. Forecasters often share a similar view of the past with regard to changes in resource costs or the environmental impact of industrialisation, but because they choose to place emphasis on different parts of history, or even because they have an approach to life that demands different degrees of caution, their interpretations for the future vary considerably. The difference in prescription between the optimists and the pessimists lies not just in the speed of technical change, but also in its assumed momentum and direction towards certain – often unspecified – goals. Clearly this is one of those crucial questions where political values decisively influence technical assumptions.

Two major questions embodied in these views of future technological change are: what are the mechanisms of change, and how fast can technological change proceed? Few forecasters are at all clear on the first question. Kahn, for example, talks of a process of 'synergism and serendipity' whereby innovations are generated from multivarious origins in an unforeseeable fashion. He illustrates his point for a particular U.S. missile system. Modrzhinskaya too hints at a similar model in speaking of the chemical sciences as a 'treasure trove from . . . which people will derive everything they need . . .'. It is only the mathematical modellers who are obliged to provide a 'formal' theory of technological change, and often they run into problems. Not only do the explicit assumptions in the Meadows' model not fully reflect their commentary but there are a number of internal inconsistencies (Julien and Freeman, in Cole *et al.*, 1973). Furthermore, the assumption of a sudden jump in technological efficiency, which both Meadows and Forrester take in their 'technologically optimistic' runs, has an immediately aggravating effect on the supply/demand balance in their models. The Bariloche group argue that current technology more widely applied is sufficient to achieve the ends they desire. Within their assumption of constant resource costs there is, of course, the further assumption that technological progress will continue at least at the historic rate. Mesarovic and Pestel, in their model, attempt to assess what the historic post-war rate has, in fact, been for different world regions. The results show that for some regions technology seems to be advancing at a faster, and for others at a slower than exponential rate. Furthermore, there are apparent discontinuities.

In fact, all modellers assume that some further technological improvement will occur, although in some sectors diminishing returns will be in evidence. Assumptions about technological change are vital to the results of all the models. The relative growth rates of sectors and regions can be changed considerably by small changes in the assumptions about rates of technical change. This is demonstrated by the Bariloche group when they consider scenarios in which a tendency towards zero technological change is assumed, and also in *The Limits to Growth* model when alternative assumptions are employed (Cole and Curnow, 1973). The 'overshoot and collapse' of *The Limits to Growth* world system is averted if fairly modest assumptions are made about the continuity of technical change in materials and food production and pollution prevention.

In the work of both Kahn and Modrzhinskaya future patterns of working life will be highly automated. Both capitalist and socialist post-industrial societies will seek labour-saving technologies. Poor countries will employ technologies of the currently technologically advanced countries. In *The Next 200 Years*, Kahn considers that it is 'much easier to develop than it used to be'. Although he sees over-population and the lack of institutions capable of absorbing technologies as obstacles to industrialisation, Kahn points to some developing nations as having made 'astonishing progress'. Unlike the earliest industrialising nations, he argues, presently industrialising nations can be helped by the presence of more technologically advanced countries. Unlike the past 'today many kinds of industrial activity and scientific technology are easily transferred' (p. 42). Consequently, Kahn points to world-wide 'technological unity' (p. 192).

Many forecasters, however, speak of alternative technologies, especially when considering the problems of poor nations. Schumacher in *Small is Beautiful* is the most explicit here and devotes considerable attention to what he perceives to be the technological needs of poor countries. His central concept is 'appropriate' technology. He quotes Kaldor speaking in favour of high technological production: 'There is no question from every point of view of the superiority of the latest and more capitalistic technologies', and argues, quite contrary to this as well as to Kahn and Modrzhinskaya, that there is indeed such a question. On the one hand, advanced technologies are unsuited both in their inputs and their outputs to less-developed countries; their materials must be imported and their sophisticated products are mainly suitable for developed country markets. On the other hand, with chronic under- or un-employment in these countries, labour-substituting techniques may be intrinsically undesirable. In poor countries, increase in real production, he suggests, should come from the development of 'intermediate technologies' – small-scale production techniques that take advantage of modern technological knowledge to produce basic consumption items without distorting effects on local economies or social structures.

Tinbergen argues that control of technological development is in many ways more important than economic planning (1976, p. 76). In poor countries emphasis should be placed on labour-intensive rather than capital-intensive technologies, and as far as possible the inventive capacity of local populations should be used (p. 72); at the same time he stresses the importance of their gaining access to the 'vast technological knowledge' of international firms (p. 39).

Those who find the assumption of long-term continuity of technical change over the next thirty to sixty years unacceptable or improbable may look back to classical economics for arguments, attitudes and illustrations to buttress their point of view. It was not only Malthus who was pessimistic about the long-run prospects of the economic system and the possibilities of providing ever higher living standards for the greater part of the world's population. His theory was fairly characteristic of the whole tone and approach of economic analysis and policy-making in the first half of the nineteenth century, and was a central strand of European conservative philosophy.

There are radicals as well as conservatives who are concerned about the food/population balance, and about the much wider issues of environmental conservation and the virtues of ascetic lifestyles. The conservatives can relate to a very old tradition of philosophical and religious thought, and in particular to the long-standing and deep-rooted suspicion of technical change as a Promethean way of solving human problems. Indeed it is Kahn and his associates who are relatively exceptional among conservative-minded futurologists in their enthusiastic endorsement of a very high rate of technical change. The neo-Malthusian tradition can appeal to much deeper springs of European conservative thought and attitudes. Here perhaps the difference between American and European history and traditions is an important factor.

Neo-Malthusian forecasters argue that the carrying capacity of the earth is insufficient to cope with the expected increases in world population and world economic growth. The supply of natural resources will be inadequate and technology is not expected to progress at a rate sufficient to prevent widespread shortages. Some neo-Malthusians, such as the Ehrlichs, argue that modern technology itself is harmful to the extent that it is degrading biologically, thereby reducing the earth's support even further. Other forecasters disagree. Some, like the Bariloche group and Leontief, simply assume that the technology required to reduce pressure on the world's carrying capacity will be forthcoming. Others, like Kahn in *The Next 200 Years*, try to demonstrate in some detail precisely how this will happen. We shall now make our own analyses of this problem in relation to food, energy and some raw materials, and then examine general policies and problems relating to technical change, in chapters 4–7.

Even when they agree about economics, forecasters may disagree about what the desirable future direction of industrialised societies should be – from rampant materialism to a new asceticism. Different views about the future quality of life will be discussed in Part III.

PART II

Critical Issues

CHAPTER 4

Food and Agriculture: When Enough is not Enough – the World Food Paradox

*Pauline K. Marstrand and Howard Rush**

WHAT THE OTHERS SAW

All forecasters discussed in chapter 2 mention food and by implication agriculture, although Kahn and Wiener (1967) in *The Year 2000* were not very explicit about how their enormous population would be fed, nor did Spengler explain how populations would continue to grow without food. Most writing about the future has been pessimistic about food. Ann and Paul Ehrlich (1970) are convinced that poor countries cannot achieve sufficiency without drastic population control or education and that further intensification of food production must produce ecological catastrophe. This view is also expressed by Meadows *et al.* (1972) and Heilbroner (1974).

In *Mankind at the Turning Point*, the second report to the Club of Rome, Mesarovic and Pestel (1974) assumed a rather high basic nutritional requirement, 2200–3000 kilocalories (varying in different regions) and 70 grams protein a day, of which 40 grams would be animal protein. They also assumed that 95 per cent of all available land in South East Asia was already in use and that most of Africa was unusable. The figures for calories and proteins are not themselves unreasonable, if an interesting and varied diet is to be made available for everyone. Nonetheless, they are well above subsistence and greatly in excess of minimum physical requirements, and the assumption that 95 per cent of available land in South East Asia is already in use is among the most pessimistic of available estimates. It seems as though, in writing of the future, forecasters want either to stimulate remedial action by painting the blackest picture possible or have such unbounded faith in the

*Important intellectual and reseach contributions to this chapter were made by William Bingham, John Gribbin and Mick McLean, without whom the work could not have been completed. Thanks are due to Hans Singer and Michael Lipton (IDS, Sussex), Tilo Ulbricht (ARC), Colin Blythe and David Baldock (Earth Resources Research Ltd.) for commenting on an earlier draft, and to Keith Pavitt and Ian Miles for structural alterations that improved the development of the argument.

ability of people to apply technology wisely that they do not consider constraints at all.

The collection by Russian authors, *The Future of Society* (Modrzhinskaya *et al.*, 1973), has little to say about the technical constraints on increased world food production and is optimistic about the prospects once political constraints are removed and economic policies operated with production of food as the main objective. Kosolapov (1976) portrays the next century as brimming with technological advances in agriculture: weather modification and desalination, fertilizers for the ocean bed, the sea supplying a fifth of the world's food requirements, and large-scale factory production of synthetic foods. These forecasts could have come straight from the pen of Herman Kahn. The most apparent differences in technology and mechanisms of change lie in Kahn's emphasis on hydroponics (Kahn *et al.*, 1976) and in the Russians' emphasis on socialism as a prerequisite for these means of meeting the world's food demands.

Dumont in *Utopia or Else* . . . (1974) describes the possibility that a world community, trying to use resources to the best advantage of all, would cease wasteful exploitation, transfer resources from the excessively wealthy to the excessively poor, and achieve a situation in which food production would be sufficient and further growth unnecessary. The Bariloche group set basic minimum requirements for food as for other necessities of life and investigated the physical possibilities for meeting them, as well as alternative policies for so doing.

In the lay and popular scientific press, we find a strong echo of the more gloomy conclusions about the future prospects for feeding the world's growing population. In many ways this is not surprising. Every year our media bring us news of famine, and there seems to be no end in sight to the Food and Agriculture Organisation's (F.A.O.'s) battle against hunger, which has already been fought for thirty years. This widespread belief has recently been reinforced by the concern that the ecological carrying capacity of the planet can barely support existing world populations, let alone those projected for the next century. Food crises are not new; history is littered with accounts of great hungers and famines. The neo-Malthusians argue that the present food crisis is fundamentally a problem of population, and that limits on the world's population are a prerequisite to overcoming it.

The starting points for most of these authors, academic and lay, are the projections of population and demand for food issued by the F.A.O. and the estimates of areas of agricultural land published by the U.S. President's Science Advisory Committee in 1967 and by the U.S. Department of Agriculture. In this chapter we show that there is much more 'slack' in the system than they believe and also that the potential productivity of the world is probably much greater. Using the new UNESCO soil maps of the world and the work on productivity of eco-systems carried out by the International Biological Programme of 1964–75, Buringh and others at the Wageningen

Agricultural University in the Netherlands have calculated maximum possible production for the main regions of the world, and have concluded that even Asia and Africa may have the potential to feed the large populations projected for them. We shall also consider some features of the structure of the systems in many countries that impose bias and constraints on the introduction of measures to realise this productive potential.

ESTIMATING HUNGER

Forecasters predict food crises by dividing total world food supplies by total world populations; however, neither total is known accurately. In 1965, according to W. C. Robinson (in Poleman *et al.*, 1973) the percentages of populations covered by registration in various countries were as follows:

Africa	3%	Oceania	78%
Asia	9%	Europe	100%
Latin America	44%	N. America	100%

It is not very much better today. From these fractions, total populations are then estimated. Even the claimed 100 per cent registration of Europe and North America does not eliminate problems in prediction, as attested by recent downward estimates in Britain. This is not to say that such estimates are useless; they are the best we have and they must be made. It is to say, though, that conclusions based upon them must inevitably be tentative.

Food supply figures are calculated on the basis of food entering markets, with estimates of subsistence food made on the basis of limited surveys. Thousands of the world's poorest people eat food as soon as they harvest it or gather it in the wild. The closer they are to starvation the more this imperfectly accounted component of their diet becomes important.

In their early concern not to underestimate world food requirements, F.A.O. experts assumed that an adequate daily diet would be that necessary to keep the North American 'reference man' healthy and economically functional: 3000 kilocalories including 90 grams of protein. Recognising that consumption patterns were unequal, they then allowed for 20 per cent excess in order to provide enough for those with below average consumption. McLean and Hopkins (1974) have shown that this meant that the basic food 'requirements' estimated in this way were enough to feed four times the populations of some countries.

For most of the 1960s the 'protein gap' was identified as a major problem, despite F.A.O. data showing an overall sufficiency in protein. Field workers were reporting severe cases of kwashiorkor and marasmas, which suggested protein deficiencies. More recently, Payne (1973) and others have demonstrated that these effects arise when, lacking sufficient calorie food, the body instead metabolises protein as an energy source, so that symptoms of protein deficiency are produced. Joy (1973) found that in many Indian villages protein food intake was sufficient and that protein deficiency symptoms appeared when calorie intake was inadequate.

The combined effect of these findings has been that nutritional requirements have been revised downwards to 2354 kilocalories per day. This includes a range of from 820 kilocalories for a female child less than one year old to 3500 for an adolescent male of sixteen. Requirements within a country have to be modified to accord with local conditions, the form in which food is available, normal size and growth rates of people and main activities. It is the different weightings given to these factors that produce some of the disparities between estimates. Growing children, pregnant women and physically active people need more kilocalories with a higher proportion of protein. In consequence of this last point, more food per head than this basic amount would be required than that needed simply to keep them alive if people in developing countries were to be able to become more active and productive. Accepting for the time being the 1971 F.A.O./World Health Organisation (W.H.O.) recommendation that 2354 kilocalories a day is the average requirement for a healthy diet, then in 1970 every person known to be in the world could have had 2420 kilocalories had the known marketed supplies been equally distributed. This figure would obviously be revised upwards if non-cultivated foods were included.

The W.H.O. estimates that 10 million children under five are chronically under-nourished. If these have the usual complement of adults equally under-nourished, then an outside estimate would be sixty million adults – a total of seventy million whose malnutrition is so dire that they are utilising protein reserves (muscles, including heart muscles) as a substrate for metabolic energy release. This is less than two per cent of existing world population, and, disgraceful as it is, is probably less than ever before (Eberstadt, 1976). Other estimates suggest that considerably more people are still sufficiently malnourished to be particularly vulnerable to illness. UNICEF figures cited by Sinha (1976) indicate that there are probably ten times as many people involved when we take this criterion of malnourishment instead of the more stringent criterion of starvation; about 700 million in all.

The efforts of the F.A.O. and others over the last two decades have achieved some success and are worth sustaining. We have argued that physically there is enough food now produced to feed the present world population. However, the number of malnourished and under-nourished people illustrates the inequalities that are masked by statistics of regional agricultural production. The ability of future world populations to feed themselves will depend on many factors. Despite growing demand within their own borders, most developing countries continue to export agricultural products, which provide much of their foreign exchange earnings. Although the growing of export crops may extend to areas that formerly grew subsistence food or staples for the home market, these foreign earnings could enable a country to purchase additional food. However, while the volume of these exports increased by about two per cent *a year* between 1961–3 and 1971–3, their value rose by only three per cent *over the whole period*. These worsening terms of trade mean that although they were producing and selling more, the prices they got were not increasing their ability to buy non-agricultural inputs or additional food. Economic growth rates and the distribution of wealth will play a crucial role in the realisation of the productive potential in poor countries and in their ability to feed adequately even the poorest people. Griffin (1974) describes how land tenure relationships and size of holding determine access to financial and other resources and the terms upon which they can be acquired. Unless governments enforce policies to correct these distributional effects, technologies that successfully increase production may well increase inequalities, even to the extent of reducing the share of food going to the poorest people. The fact that the owners of most of the productive assets, including land, are educated in developed countries, aspire to the amenities of urban life and often themselves live in cities, imparts an urban bias to the strategies for development that they propose. Overcoming this bias requires deliberate discrimination in favour of rural cultivators, and even more, in favour of the rural poor, who are often landless

TABLE 4.1　*Rates of food and population growth by regions (1952–62 and 1962–72)*

	1952–62			1962–72		
	Popu-	*Food Production*		*Popu-*	*Food Production*	
	lation	Total	Per head	*lation*	Total	Per head
			Per cent per year*			
Developed market economies†	1.2	2.5	1.3	1.0	2.4	1.4
Western Europe	0.8	2.9	2.1	0.8	2.2	1.4
North America	1.8	1.9	0.1	1.2	2.4	1.2
Oceania	2.2	3.1	0.9	2.0	2.7	0.7
Eastern Europe and USSR	1.5	4.5	3.0	1.0	3.5	2.5
TOTAL	1.3	3.1	1.8	1.0	2.7	1.7
Developing market economies†	2.4	3.1	0.7	2.5	2.7	0.2
Africa	2.2	2.2	–	2.5	2.7	0.2
Far East	2.3	3.1	0.8	2.5	2.7	0.2
Latin America	2.8	3.2	0.4	2.9	3.1	0.2
Near East	2.6	3.4	0.8	2.8	3.0	0.2
Asian centrally planned economies	1.8	3.2	1.4	1.9	2.6	0.7
TOTAL	2.4	3.1	0.7	2.4	2.7	0.3
WORLD	2.0	3.1	1.1	1.9	2.7	0.8

*Trend rate of growth of food production, compound interest.
†Including countries in other regions not specified.
Source: Aziz (1975).

(Lipton, 1977). There are several physical determinants of potential food supplies; two of the most important are land and climate. We shall consider these to illustrate how social and economic factors intervene to constrain the development that technological change might otherwise make possible.

World food supplies have been increasing steadily, and have not yet been outrun by population growth (see Table 4.1). The F.A.O./W.H.O. (1975) recommended kilocalorie requirement means that each person needs about 500 lbs of grain equivalent a year. On average over the last few years 1300 million tonnes have been marketed, enough to feed about 5 billion people. World population was thought to be 3.88 billion in 1974. Even in 1972, when weather conditions reduced crop yields in all regions of the world, the marketed grain could have provided 632 lbs for every person, more than in 1960, a supposedly plenteous year. In 1960 this could have fed 300 million more people than were thought to exist. By 1973, surplus could have fed 600 million more. Despite evidence to the contrary, however, the myth that world population growth is the *cause* of hunger and that hunger can be substantially relieved by world population restriction is continually being re-created and elaborated.

Since its beginning in 1947 and especially since the introduction of the Indicative World Plan in 1969, the F.A.O. has investigated, catalogued and estimated world food needs, stimulated research into ways of meeting them and expedited aid for projects designed to increase food production. Despite setbacks in irrigation programmes, difficulties with fertilizer and the enormous educational effort involved, production has steadily increased; however, inequalities persist and have even been exacerbated.

Table 4.2 shows the total food grown or imported as a percentage of requirements for 1970. Two surprising things about these figures are that no

TABLE 4.2   *Availability of food as percentage of requirements**

	Calories 1970	Protein 1970
World	101	173
Developed	121	229
Developing	96	147
Asia and E. Asia	93	141
Africa	93	141
Latin America	106	172
Near East	97	147
Centrally planned Asia	88	153

*Note that requirements are here defined in terms of the 1970 estimates of 2354 kilocalories per head per day — a figure since revised downwards.

Source: F.A.O., *The State of Food and Agriculture*, 1970.

region as a whole had insufficient protein and that 'centrally planned Asia' (largely China) had *'available'* only 88 per cent of calorie requirements. Eye witnesses of a wide range of political beliefs report that actual starvation is not evident in China, although in Brazil it is.

In countries barely providing or obtaining enough for their people, so that the poorest literally are starving, it is often the case that those unable to enter the food market subsist by gathering wild and discarded food wherever they can, or by doing numerous services for small payments in kind. In this situation it may make sense for parents to have large families, because they represent more hands as well as more mouths – 'Poor people invest in their sons' (Mandami, 1972). Until the living standards of this section of the population are improved, population control programmes will not willingly be accepted.

Inequalities within and between Countries

Tables 4.3 and 4.4 from Simontov (1976) emphasise the inequalities between countries of the same region and also show how actual consumption of food correlates with income at the lower end of the wealth scale in three famine-prone countries. Table 4.4 indicates the kind of variation within regions that condemns people in the most poorly endowed countries to abject poverty and malnutrition. In Rwanda quite possibly the majority of the population lives in want, but in Haiti and Indonesia the wealthiest people enjoy standards comparable to those in America and Europe.

TABLE 4.3   *Inequalities in consumption within some countries*

Country	Consumption in calories
India	
(Maharastra: 1971)	
Income per head:	
Under 25 Rs/month	1540
Over 75 Rs/month	2990
Tunisia	
(Rural area: 1965–8)	
Total expenditure per head:	
Under 20 Dinars/year	1780
Over 150 Dinars/year	3200
Brazil	
(North-east, urban area, 1966)	
Income per family:	
Under 100 Cruz./year	1240
Over 1200 Cruz./year	4100

Source: F.A.O., *Assessment of the World Food Situation*, (1974).

TABLE 4.4   *Inequalities in consumption within*
geographic regions (average
1964–6)

	Total calories	Animal calories
Africa (average)*	2154	121
Rwanda	1908	53
Senegal	2348	224
Latin America	2470	427
Haiti	1904	94
Uruguay	3039	1262
Asia (average)†	1984	129
Indonesia	1798	45
Singapore	2454	385

*Excluding South Africa and Rhodesia.
†Excluding Japan and China.

Source: F.A.O., *Food and Agricultural Commodity Projections, 1970–1980*, Vol. II (1971).

The rapid rise in world prices stimulated further food production, but it also meant that the proportion of world food going to the richer countries and groups within countries has increased, deepening the world inequalities.

Table 4.5 shows how some regions, Latin America, Eastern Europe and Asia among them, which used to be net exporters of grain, have now become importers. In some this is mainly due to population growth, in some to rising standards of consumption. As far as grain is concerned, Western Europe remained surprisingly constant in its demand over this period, although it was generating a small surplus by 1976. The dominant position of the United States emerges clearly in the post-war years.

As Joy (1973) showed, and as the F.A.O. now accepts (F.A.O., 1974), people starve because they cannot buy the food that is available. It is not

TABLE 4.5   *Changing patterns in the grain trade: net exports and imports (million metric tons)*

Region	1934–38	1948–52	1960	1966	1973*
N. America	+ 5	+23	+39	+59	+91
Latin America	+ 9	+ 1	–	+ 5	– 3
W. Europe	–24	–22	–25	–27	–19
E. Europe & U.S.S.R.	+ 5	not known	0	– 4	–27
Africa	+ 1	0	– 2	– 7	– 5
Asia	+ 2	– 6	–17	–34	–43
Australia, New Zealand	+ 3	+ 3	+ 6	+ 8	+ 6

*Estimated.

Source: *Financial Times*, 5 January 1976, based on U.S. Department of Agriculture data.

TABLE 4.6   *Number of countries with surplus and deficit calorie supply by region*

	1961				1969–71 average			
	Surplus		Deficit		Surplus		Deficit	
	More than 10%	Less than 10%	More than 10%	Less than 10%	More than 10%	Less than 10%	More than 10%	Less than 10%
W. Europe	14	5	–	–	17	2	–	–
N. America	2	–	–	–	2	–	–	–
Oceania	2	–	–	–	2	–	–	–
E. Europe & U.S.S.R.	4	3	–	1	7	–	–	1
Other developed countries	1	2	–	–	2	1	–	–
Total developed regions	23	10	–	1	30	3	–	1
Latin America	5	4	8	8	8	6	4	7
Far East	–	4	7	5	4	4	3	5
Near East	1	1	10	2	1	3	4	6
Africa	–	5	18	14	3	8	12	14
Asian centrally planned economies	–	2	2	–	1	1	1	1
Total developing regions	6	16	45	29	18	22	24	33
WORLD	29	26	45	30	48	25	24	34

Source: F.A.O., *Food and Nutrition*, Vol. 1, No. 1 (1975).

unlicensed procreation that produces poverty and hunger but unequal distribution of wealth, in all its forms. Tragically, while F.A.O. policies and aid over the past three decades have more than doubled food production in, for instance, the Indian sub-continent, they have often simultaneously increased the inequalities. As a result the richer eat more, but the poorest eat less.

An indication of the unevenness of regional distribution is seen in Table 4.6 (Simontov, 1976, based on F.A.O. commodity projections). In Western Europe, North America and Oceania in 1961 there were no countries with a deficit and only five with a surplus of less than ten per cent. In Eastern Europe there was one country with a deficit, but it was less than ten per cent. In Latin America there were five countries with a surplus of more than ten per cent and eight with a deficit of the same magnitude. In Africa none had a surplus above ten per cent, only five any surplus at all, while thirty-two had a deficit.

Table 4.7 condensed from Aziz (1975), who used mainly F.A.O. sources, tabulates some of the countries where food shortages are likely to appear over the next few decades, unless they make very rapid progress either in producing more food or in achieving sufficient economic growth to purchase more on world markets. All those with population growth outstripping growth in food production are vulnerable, but those in which population is growing faster than demand as well are the most at risk, because demand is calculated to include a factor for growth in income per head, and thus

TABLE 4.7   *Growth in population, demand and food production in selected countries*

	Population faster than production Demand slower than production	Demand faster than production Population slower than production	Population and demand both faster than production
Population faster than demand	Dahomey		Chad Somalia Rwanda
Population slower than demand		Mauritania Mozambique Congo Sierra Leone Iran Saudi Arabia Burma India Jamaica	Mali Mauritius Uganda Trinidad and Tobago Algeria Jordan Syrian Arab Republic Yemen Arab Republic Ethiopia Kenya Nigeria Chile Guyana Algeria Iraq Tunisia
Population and demand more or less at same rate			Liberia Zaire Cuba Dominican Republic Haiti Uruguay Nepal Paraguay

Source: Based on Aziz (1975).

increased ability to purchase food. Where population growth is less than growth in demand, at least some of the people are getting wealthier and will be able to purchase food, although those who are not could be relatively, and perhaps absolutely, worse off than today. These countries include some of the oil states, and others, such as Jamaica, where there has been a rapid increase in national wealth recently. Congo and Sierra Leone have growths in food production greater than growth in population, so although growth in demand is increasing, people ought to be eating better. Recent accounts of these countries do not suggest that this is so, possibly because consumption is becoming increasingly uneven. Where population growth and demand are similar the latter is probably caused mainly by the former without much increase in income, in which case food availability will worsen unless more is produced.

Countries in which population is increasing faster than demand for food will need special care by the world community if they are not to suffer serious famine whenever their own production falters or world prices rise. Those in which demand is increasing faster than both population and food production will need policies directed at increasing the ability of the poorest people to obtain their share of the food, otherwise they will be increasingly deprived. In all the countries listed food production will need to be increased in order to decrease dependence on outside supplies.

Although world agriculture is already producing enough to feed everybody, the inequalities within countries and regions and those between countries make it difficult, sometimes impossible, for the poorest people to consume their share. In addition, as richer regions and groups demand more, the falling rate of increase in food production will become more serious. Since it is costly and often politically difficult to distribute food from regions of surplus to regions of need, it is important for developing countries to increase their own food production. The poorest people would benefit directly by having more food for themselves and by being able to sell surpluses. Most developing countries will require efficient agriculture in order to achieve economic development; increasing production from agriculture would reduce their dependence on rich countries and increase the quantity and variety of food available to their own people. Although people can survive in reasonable health on W.H.O. basic requirements, they would like more, as recent events in Poland and China have shown. It is also necessary because there will be a lag between reduction in infant mortality and reduction in family size, so population will continue to increase for at least one to two generations before levelling off.

FUTURE NEEDS IN DEVELOPING COUNTRIES

We have shown that globally there is already enough food for the world's population, and we believe that there is physical potential for producing enough for populations even larger than those projected for the year 2000. There remain, however, two important unanswered questions. Can those countries that because of geographical or other constraints are only just producing enough food now, possibly increase their production rapidly without causing unacceptable degradation of the environment, especially of soil fertility? Can this be done, despite the inequalities of access, so that the poorest people get enough?

The most vulnerable regions have already been identified. They include Latin America, Africa (excluding South Africa), the Middle East and South

TABLE 4.8   Demand for food at two population levels and two levels of food consumption

Year	2000				2030				2050			
Population	High		Low		High		Low		High		Low	
Food k.cals/hd	3000	2354	3000	2354	3000	2354	3000	2354	3000	2354	3000	2354
Latin America GE	19.49	15.29	13.60	10.66	35.75	28.05	16.99	13.34	43.28	33.96	17.46	13.70
%	3.7	2.9	2.5	1.6	2.9	2.4	1.6	1.2	2.4	2.1	1.2	0.9
Main Africa GE	13.30	10.44	10.19	7.99	20.14	15.80	11.61	9.11	22.61	17.74	11.75	9.22
%	3.2	2.4	2.3	1.5	2.3	1.9	1.4	0.9	1.9	1.6	1.0	0.7
North Africa & Middle East GE	7.64	5.99	5.88	4.61	11.93	9.36	6.92	5.43	13.64	10.70	7.01	5.51
%	3.4	2.5	2.5	1.7	2.4	2.0	1.5	1.1	2.0	1.7	1.1	0.8
South & South East Asia GE	67.90	53.28	50.06	39.28	111.98	87.87	59.70	46.85	130.54	102.43	60.75	47.67
%	3.9	3.1	2.9	2.0	2.8	2.4	1.7	1.3	2.3	2.0	1.3	1.0

Key: Population. High natural replacement rate = 1 in 2030
   Low natural replacement rate = 1 in 1989
GE = grain equivalent (millions of tonnes/year)
Base GE = GE of baseline intake (1970 average)
% = growth rate in food consumption per year

$$1 \text{ k.cal/day} \equiv \frac{365}{4 \text{ million}} \text{ tonnes GE}$$

Basic intakes 1970:

	Popn. (millions)	Intake (k.cals/hd)	Base GE
LA	284.75	2529	6.57
MA	252.85	2240	5.168
NA	135.51	2282	2.822
SA	1153.11	2041	21.495

and South East Asia. Table 4.8 projects the demand for food in the years 2000, 2030 and 2050 for our assumed high and low levels of population growth, based on Mesarovic and Pestel (1974). The high projection assumes that the natural replacement rate becomes equal to one in 2030, the low projection that this occurs in 1989. This is combined with two levels of calorie requirement, a 'high' assuming 3000 kilocalories per head per day and a 'low' with 2354 kilocalories. Assuming that 1 k.cal/day $\equiv$ 365/(4 million) tonnes grain equivalent, the food calorie requirements are stated as grain equivalents in millions of tonnes a year. This table shows the annual rate of growth in food supply needed to meet the food requirements of people in these regions in four future situations: high population growth and an average calorie supply of 2354 k.cals per day each – i.e. close to the basic nutritional requirement; high population growth and a 'European' calorie provision of 3000 k.cals a day; low population growth with 2354 k.cals; and low population growth with 3000 k.cals. For instance, if North Africa and the Middle East reach Mesarovic and Pestel's high population by the year 2000 they will require 7.64 million tonnes of grain equivalent a year to provide 3000 k.cals per person, and this will require a 3.4 per cent per year increase in food consumption from 1970. If only 2354 k.cals per head were to be available, then a growth in consumption/availability of 2.5 per cent per year would be required. For the 'worst' case, with high population growth and food consumption of 3000 k.cals a day by the year 2000, all four regions would have to achieve very high rates of growth in food supply to meet the demand – over 3 per cent per year in all cases, and 3.9 per cent per year for South and South East Asia. Although physically possible, these regions will probably not be able to achieve this by the year 2000 without help.

This table also suggests a number of important questions. How sensitive is the future rate of increase of supply to population, to level of nutrition and to time horizons? For all regions the calculations show larger discrepancies of demand between high and low population levels than between high and low calorie levels. Apparently increasing the quality of diet would have less effect than continuing high population growth; alternatively, *reducing* population growth sooner rather than later could have a significant positive effect on levels of food available. Are the projected annual rates of growth in food consumption achievable in the light of previous performance? Comparing Table 4.8 with Table 4.1 we can see that the high population projections would require a higher rate of growth than has historically been achieved in all regions to meet either of the consumption levels. The low population projections, however, would not demand unrealistically high rates of increase in production, even to reach the 3000 k.cal/day consumption level by 2000.

If the downward trend in rate of increase of production indicated in Table 4.1 does not continue, and we assume that the 1962–72 rates are the basis of a future trend, then the following possibilities appear. By the year 2000, with low population growth, Africa and Latin America could achieve 'European' dietary levels. South East Asia could reach minimum levels for all. With high population growth Africa would reach minimum levels for all, Latin America and South East Asia would be in difficulty without food from outside. By 2030 the slower growing population could have a 'Euro diet' world-wide. With high population growth Africa could still achieve a 'European' diet, but Latin America and South East Asia would be at risk of falling below. By 2050 both rates of population growth could enjoy a 'European' diet. We can thus conclude that regulation of world food supply will be important at least for the next thirty years; that South East Asia and Latin America will continue to be the most vulnerable regions; but that even the worst assumptions about increased food production provide for a basic minimum diet for all between 2000 and 2030 and a 'Euro diet' by 2050. The most optimistic assumptions produce a world-wide 'Euro diet' between 2000 and 2030.

FUTURE SOURCES OF FOOD

The Land

Most food is produced on land, with a small but significant and growing contribution from inland waters and the seas. The U.S. President's Science Advisory Committee (P.S.A.C.) suggested that the maximum possible area that could be cropped was 6600 million hectares, of which about half actually had been cultivated at some time and about 1400 million was harvested in any one year. They estimated that 64 per cent of this land lay in Africa, Asia and South America; only 37 per cent was cultivated in those countries. At about the same time the U.S. Department of Agriculture (U.S.D.A.) calculated the total amount of potentially arable land to be 1648 million hectares, of which only about 530 million (32 per cent) was actually in cultivation. F.A.O. investigations found about 1145 million hectares of cultivable land in poor countries, of which about 45 per cent was in use in the late 1960s.

Such reports may be understating the amount of land yet to be brought into cultivation. For example, combined results of better land surveying and the new UNESCO soil maps indicate that only about 75 per cent of cultivable land in South East Asia is at present in use, compared with previous estimates of around 93 per cent. An authoritative recent study is that carried out by Buringh, van Heemst and Staring (1975) at Wageningen, Netherlands. Using the new UNESCO/F.A.O. soil maps of the world and the studies of productivity carried out by the International Biological Programme 1964–75, they estimate that there are 3714 million hectares of suitable land, of which 1900 million could feasibly be irrigated. If 1208 million hectares were irrigated and achieved 65 per cent of maximum possible production in grain equivalents then, taken together, the regions of the world could produce 32,390 million tonnes of grain per year, about 30 times present production, which is, as we have shown, already more than sufficient for minimum requirements, were it equitably distributed.

Lester Brown (1974) and others in various papers have postulated that increasing financial costs of development will preclude much of this land from ever being utilised, an assumption built into the *Limits to Growth* model of Meadows *et al.* (1972), but this has been queried on various grounds. That these costs are unduly pessimistic has been argued by Marstrand and Pavitt (1973), who pointed out that the estimates involved are based on the development costs of large projects. Likewise in unpublished papers, Burnett and Morse (cited by Eberstadt, 1976) have pointed out that costs have not increased since 1870 to the present, and in fact if considered as unit costs, those of labour and capital fell by more than half in that period. It seems probable that the range of these input requirements will vary enormously depending on the level of technology adopted. Developing countries could select from a range of technologies the one that best suits their own endowments of labour and capital, and thus minimise costs. However, social and economic factors place constraints on the choice of technologies. 'Ability to select' implies greater understanding of the available technologies and their consequences than is usually possessed, so that programmes to enable exchange of information between potential providers of technology and actual cultivators will need to be much more substantially supported than has hitherto been the case.

In some of the particularly vulnerable countries the rates at which agriculture would have to be improved to come within sight of these levels of production are too large to be achieved in time. Such countries and regions will require assistance in the form of direct food aid, cash aid, controlled transfer of technology and regional food storage to give them food security while they make the change. It should be made clear that Buringh *et al.* are not talking about maximum economic production, with all the connotations of soil exhaustion that this can entail, but about maximum sustained biological production under best appropriate farming practice. Such a future will require an enormous educative effort directed towards the needs of poor cultivators. They are, however, anticipating much more efficient use of the long growing season in tropical countries to produce more than one harvest a year, and to grow more than one crop at a time (multi- and intercropping). Development of this potential will require a similar research and development effort to that put into European and American agriculture in the eighteenth, nineteenth and twentieth centuries.

In general, investigators agree that only about half the potential area is used. The size of the area differs partly because different assumptions are made about the feasibility of obtaining water. All the estimates show that, apart from competing uses of land, existing world food production could be about doubled without improved technology.

TABLE 4.9   *High yields obtained in practice in real
locations (tonnes/hectare)*

Crop	Yield in practice		Wageningen maximum	
Rice	26	(Philippines)	16.8	(Philippines)
	28.6	(India) irrigated	24.2	
	11	(Kenya)	21.5	
	14.0	(Senegal)	16.9	
	16.2	(Madagascar)	17.7	
Wheat	14.5	(U.S.A.)	15–18	
	5	(Netherlands)	10.5	(intercropping)
	6.2	(Finland)	7.2	

Source: Compiled from information cited in Buringh *et al.*
(1975).

Using the P.S.A.C. or U.S.D.A. estimates of land availability, the maximum population supportable has been considered to range from 7200 million
at existing world averages of nutrition, to Colin Clark's estimate of 157,000
million on a 1967 average Japanese diet (Clark, 1967). The work at
Wageningen, already discussed, indicates that future estimates could be substantially higher than these, taking our now more accurate knowledge of the
productivity of eco-systems into account. The authors point out that
maximum production will never be reached, because of land requirements
for other uses and because a maximum is seldom achieved. Like van Ittersum
(1971), they estimate that 65 per cent of the absolute maximum could be
achieved (communication from Buringh, 10 January 1977). They compare
their estimated maximum yields with the best obtained on the various soils
under experimental farm conditions, and Table 4.9 demonstrates that they
are certainly not wildly unrealistic.

Although it remains a controversial issue, studies of both the amount of
land available and of its productive potential provide evidence that food
production in most developing regions can be physically increased more than
had been generally supposed. We know that there is considerable potential
for increasing the yield obtained by better sowing and harvesting techniques,
better storage and better farming practice. Average yield of rice in
Bangladesh is only 15 per cent of what has been obtained on experimental
stations there, and Roger Revelle (1976) estimated that world yields for most
crops were but fractions of yields that had been obtained by good practice on
land typical for various countries, ranging from one-third for wheat to one-
fifth for rice. Mellanby (1975) provides further supporting evidence from
industrialised countries.

Food yields of the levels shown to be attainable in the work of the
Wageningen group, as well as in other research reviewed above, are far
greater than the pessimistic estimates often quoted. More food could be

produced on existing farmland; there is still at least as much land again that could be farmed, and there is still potential for utilising on a large scale plants and animals that have hitherto not been used on a significant scale.

Other Sources of Protein

These increased yields would satisfy the calorific food needs of the world population. We have already discussed the fact that when these requirements are met few people suffer protein deficiencies. However, in regions where the staple food is roots, low in protein, as is cassava in parts of Africa, there is a risk that the very young, the sick and the old may not be able to eat sufficient volume of food to meet all nutritional needs. At the other end of the scale, refined grains and products made from flour may also lack protein. There remain some food resources that are as yet not fully utilised, and these could provide additional protein for those who need it and variety for others without imposing additional environmental stress, if properly managed.

A growing contribution to world food supplies is made by fishing. J. Bardach (1969) reports that the total fish catch in 1968 was 68 million tons, yielding about 12 million tons of usable protein. He estimates that it could be operated at a sustainable yield of about 200 million tons by 1985, giving about 43 million tons of protein, that is about 28 per cent of present world protein requirements but only about 2 per cent by weight of world supplies. Considerable quantities of plant fertilizers could also be obtained by increasing fish yields.

At present more efficient but less selective methods of catching fish are seriously depleting some important fisheries. Bardach's yield could only be realised if the fishing nations of the world agreed to adopt and operate a controlled policy for fishing. (It is interesting to compare his estimate with that of the Russian futurologist Kosolapov (1976) who forecasts that, by 2010, 20 per cent of the world's food will be supplied from the oceans.) F.A.O. sources quoted in *Facts about Development – 3* (I.D.C., 1975) show that the world catch has in fact fallen off since 1968 (see Figure 4.1).

The sea is only one under-exploited source of protein for human consumption. Table 4.10 taken from J. T. Worgan (1973), summarises some of the less conventional sources of food and their estimated potential. Many of them could be produced by growing micro-organisms on organic wastes, which would in any case have to be treated in some way in order to render them harmless. Starch waste, oil waste and sugar waste are already being used for this purpose. Plant concentrates as a source of protein are described by Pirie (1975). Most of these sources are still in the development stage, but sufficiently far investigated to suggest that considerable potential could be realised if they were seriously exploited.

A further source of protein, the possibilities of which have only begun to be explored, is meat from indigenous wild animals. Wild grazing animals

Critical Issues

Fig. 4.1
World fish catch, 1950–73

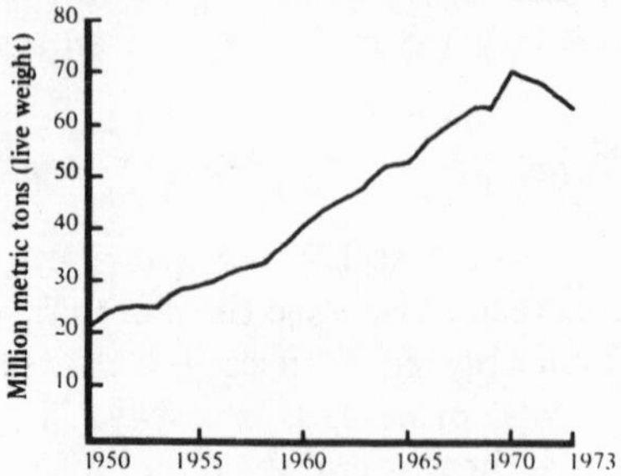

Source: Food and Agriculture Organisation,
cited in International Development Centre
Facts about Development, 3, 1975.

TABLE 4.10   *Unconventional sources of protein*

Source	Estimated potential annual yield of protein ($\times 10^{-3}$, tons)
SCP (hydrocarbon substrates)	23,000
Oilseed protein residues	22,000
Fish protein products (Fish protein concentrate, FPC)	4,800
Plankton (Krill)	2,200
Game meat	500
	(kg/hectare)
Algae	24,800
SCP (carbohydrate substrates)	11,230
Leaf protein	5,000
Fish	800
Other sources: Synthetic amino acids	no
Recovery from wastes	estimates
Plant and animal cell tissue culture	available
Plant growth in controlled environments	

Source: Worgan (1973).

adapted to savannahs, semi-arid regions and steep and relatively inaccessible land suitable for no other agricultural use, require less effort to keep them alive than do the well-known, well-tried and highly specialised domestic farm animals of Europe. Some of these wild animals can survive for several months without drinking water, obtaining moisture by eating succulent plants that are often poisonous to domestic stock. They also represent an insurance against famine, since they do not die suddenly from starvation.

There are some well-known cases of unconventional animals being herded as a source of protein. The Lapps use reindeer, the Tibetans the yak, and the

TABLE 4.11   *Yearlong standing crop (biomass) of domestic livestock and wild ungulates relative to carrying capacity in equivalent East African rangelands*

Type of range	Animals	Yearlong standing crop		Stocking rate relative to carrying capacity
		lb./sq. mile	kg./hectare	
Acacia savannah	Cattle, goats, sheep	11,200–16,000	19.6–28.0	over
Acacia savannah	Wild ungulates	37,400–90,000	65.5–157.6	at or under
Moderately managed grass savannah	Cattle	21,300–32,000	37.3–56.0	at or slightly over
Acacia-conuniphora bushland	Sheep, goats	2,100–8,000	3.7–13.5	at or over
Acacia-conuniphora bushland	Wild ungulates	30,000	52.5	at or under

Source: Talbot *et al.* (1966).

U.S.S.R. has domesticated the eland as a source of meat and milk. It seems likely that the herds of wild grazing animals (e.g. gazelles, wildebeest, eland) in Africa could supply considerable quantities of palatable and nutritious meat. This would call for carefully planned management strategies – the use of aircraft to make animal population counts, the development of the infra-structures of transport, storage and distribution. Hunting activities could be confined to necessary culling; the tourist trade for mainly photographic safaris would not be endangered. Such management of wild animals would be to the advantage of the health of the local people and the environment (Kay, 1970; Skinner, 1973; Stillings, 1973; Talbot *et al.*, 1966; Taylor, undated).

Experiments in South Africa, Uganda and Zimbabwe suggest that it is already economically viable to crop wild animals where a market is assured. The problem is the development of managed cropping systems that can supply meat for local requirements before the natural resources of wild animals are destroyed by other processes of development. In principle, large yields may be sustained from these sources. Table 4.11 indicates the levels of productivity of wild animals that have been established in East Africa. It is apparent that game, even without management inputs of water, fertilizer, etc., can be much more productive than domestic animals. Appropriate management strategies could optimise the use of both wild and domesticated animals to increase the meat protein of Africa by considerable amounts.

TECHNOLOGICAL FIT — THE PROBLEM OF BIAS

So far we have been concerned with increasing food production by extension of agricultural land. Physical factors, such as soil structure and its dependent ability to retain moisture and nutrients, the availability and utilisation of fertilizers and water and the use of energy to augment muscle power, can all be altered by technical means. In this section we consider problems associated with the introduction of technologies to increase production per hectare, per man and per unit of input. These fall into seven broad categories: irrigation, fertilizers, pesticides, machinery, improved varieties, post-harvest handling, and preservation and food processing. Considerable research effort has been devoted to ways of increasing yields in all these categories. However, in evidence to the Parliamentary Select Committee on Overseas Development, the Science Policy Research Unit (G.B. Select Committee, 1976) suggested that most of the research and technological change has not been sufficiently sensitive to the social, economic and environmental implications.

The development of high-yielding varieties of grain is a well-documented example (Poleman *et al.*, 1973; Griffin, 1974). The earlier hybrids required fertilizers and a steady though not actually greater supply of water than many indigenous varieties. In many countries only wealthier landowners could afford to purchase fertilizers and often they controlled the water supply through ownership of wells and pumps. Where such farmers adopted the hybrid varieties, they yielded well, but for poorer farmers without sufficient fertilizer and with unreliable water they could fail altogether. A poor farmer on dry land was safer with a variety of low-yielding strains, at least some of which would produce something, than with one highly demanding variety. Research efforts have not deliberately neglected the poorer farmer, but the problem has been viewed as primarily a shortage of food and has only recently been comprehended as a problem of access to land, water, credit and other necessities to improve yields per hectare. In fact, as Lipton (1977) demonstrates, yields on smaller holdings farmed by the occupier in secure circumstances are usually higher per hectare than on larger holdings. This is also documented elsewhere (Griffin, 1974). These farmers pay attention to details: verges, odd corners, hedges – all are productive.

Far from being attributed to cultural inertia, the failure of many technical innovations to diffuse through developing country agriculture is more often associated with political and economic structures that hinder such diffusion. The traditional practice in many countries of subdividing family plots among the sons creates a large number of small plots, too small to support a family or to produce surplus crops to sell, and too small to provide security for credit to purchase inputs. Farmers may hold their land by arrangements that inhibit them from increasing productivity, as when the rent is based on production in the previous year, or when high yielding land is normally taken by the landowner – if land 'improves', the tenant may lose it. In other circumstances the small and poor farmer and his family are the hired labour for the larger farmers. If all are increasing production the small farmer will have to harvest the increase on the landlord's holding first, or may do it in order to work off debts to wealthier neighbours. He and his family may already be hard put to it to get their own meagre crop in before the grain falls. In parts of Africa there are literally not enough people to gather dung to use as manure or to perform timely harvesting operations if productivity is increased (Makhijani and Poole, 1975). Having produced a surplus beyond his own family requirements a farmer requires either storage against a bad year or a market in which to exchange or sell it and transport in which to reach such a market. He may possess none of these things, or they may be controlled by richer members of the community.

Until these constraints are removed, there is little incentive to produce more. Where they have been removed, as in Taiwan (Griffin, 1974), productivity has increased rapidly and innovation has proceeded apace. In fact, wherever the benefits to poor cultivators are perceived as being short-term, and/or continuing, they will innovate; this has been described for China (Dawson, 1970; Sigurdson, 1975) and the German Democratic Republic (Dunman, 1975). Where the benefits are not so perceived, cultivators will resist innovation, in case it leads to misappropriation of land, to increased obligations to the landowner or to higher risks.

Technological changes in all the seven categories mentioned previously are not only part of the agricultural system. Carruthers (1974) describes how irrigation canal schemes are typically operating only over about 50 per cent of the areas intended; tube wells surveyed by Fazul Haque (1974) were operating at less than 25 per cent of possible time. Lal and Duane (1973) found only 15 per cent of the land area of the Purna project irrigated eight years after construction. It is not enough to finance the introduction of irrigation. Structures must be maintained, operating procedures must be developed and people trained to run them. Most of all, constraining social institutions must be changed.

According to F.A.O. statistics, only 15 per cent of world public expenditure on agricultural research in 1970 was spent in developing countries and only about 20 per cent in 1974. Even if some of the rest was in fact directed at developing country needs, it could not have been playing much part in the training of personnel for those countries.

Apart from manure, green crops and human sewage, all of which require careful management for effective use, fertilizers depend on a chemical industry, and thus may involve foreign exchange. Even if they are produced in the country, transport is still required. Fertilizer production has been badly hit by the rise in oil prices since, over the last fifteen years, so much of it has been based on oil as a feedstock as well as a fuel. Fertilizer is probably the most important single factor in realising the productive potential of agricultural land, since even with irrigation, land will become impoverished without fertilizer. Pest control by chemical means involves similar dependence on already industrialised countries.

Machinery, especially for sowing and harvesting, could make an important contribution, but much of it is inappropriate for semi-arid conditions, apart from the high capital costs involved. Research in advanced countries has produced smaller, lighter and sometimes more robust appliances, but unless marketed with the panache of the multinational tractor giants, market penetration is poor. There is a need to link the experience and technical know-how of indigenous farmers into the R & D systems of poor countries, as described in Encel *et al.* (1975).

Improved varieties of crops adapted to local conditions are beginning to be produced, but research into oilseeds, pulses and tubers has lagged behind wheat and rice. Resources of finance and personnel in the international research institutes are inadequate for the task, and too few of the scientists have practical experience of working under local conditions. Schemes such as that operating from Chieng Mai University (Finfrock and Thoday, 1973), by which farmers take part in breeding experiments and in trying out new husbandry methods, are apparently successful.

Even if more were spent, and more trained people became available, the problem of inequalities would remain so long as problems continued to be viewed from the top down, and solutions imposed without proper understanding of the underlying social causes of the problems. Starting from the level of actual production, the cultivator in the field, and finding out why he does not produce more, would help to direct research efforts towards the constraints operating in poor countries, which are not neccessarily those that had to be overcome in order to release agricultural potential in Europe and America. Storage, transport and food preservation require attention if the increase is not to be wastefully used or even lost altogether.

The adoption of innovation in farming or in any of these sectors requires study by multidisciplinary teams of social and biological scientists as well as engineers, economists, agriculturalists and potential administrators. This is not to say that all agricultural research has ignored social considerations or the needs of the poor. Indeed, such awareness has motivated much of it. However, the social and economic components of technical change need to be considered deliberately and systematically in order to identify incompatibilities, so that adjustments can be made before a socially inappropriate technology is introduced.

Even when a bad technological 'fit' has been clearly identified, its introduction could conceivably still benefit the political groups within a country that would take decisions and control the resources. For instance, expansion of industry over a major part of the most productive land may not harm those responsible for the decisions, but it means increasing imports of food, or decreasing its availability to the poor.

The Role of International Corporations

Researchers are beginning to turn their attention to the effects of 'agribusiness' on agricultural production and technology (Jacoby, 1975;

Kaplinsky *et al.*, 1975; Feder, 1976; Griffin, 1977 and Arroyo, 1977). The role of multinational companies in world agriculture is usually over-shadowed by their activities in connection with other natural resources, especially minerals. However, with interests in food production – in terms of the promotion and sale of fertilizers and farm equipment as well as crop culti-vation and food processing – agri-business is a significant force in agricultural innovation. As Feder (1976) points out, agri-business, whether it is mediated by the World Bank or not, must operate through the social structure that already exists in developing countries. Either it must incor-porate this into its own structures, using local entrepreneurial talent (Austin, 1974), or it must bring in expatriate managers. In both cases these people cannot but identify socially with existing elites, and in the absence of policy to guarantee downward spread of the benefits, the hoped for 'trickle down' effect will be slow to operate and highly selective against the most needy.

Feder quotes the case of chick breeding in Central America. A local, but U.S. educated entrepreneur borrowed $3000 to purchase chicks and feed. Business flourished and he purchased an incubator for $20,000. However, the 'donor' company exporting chicks, feed and incubators also encouraged other operators in the same state. By 1969 there was a glut of eggs. The American partners sold their 50 per cent share to the Central American, who then found that 27 of the 30 farmers supplied had no money to buy chicks and were in debt for food and equipment. The eggs may or may not have been sold in local markets – the profit on the investment went mainly to the American company. Although no detailed analysis has yet been done, there is enough disturbing anecdotal evidence to suggest that multinational companies do not always succeed in achieving a good technological fit for food-producing activities in poor countries.

Large corporations are motivated by the search for steady profit and expanding markets. The ways of achieving these goals are often comple-mentary to national agricultural development programmes and the ob-jectives of international aid agencies – increased productivity and produc-tion. Food is a desirable national product, easing local hardships, reducing the need for imports and potentially increasing exports. However, it is argued by some observers that multinational corporations often take the best land for export crops to the detriment of local food requirements. George (1976) presents many accounts of such processes, including Costa Rica almost doubling its meat exports to the U.S.A. during a period in which its own meat consumption declined by over a quarter, Dominican acreage devoted to sugar cane doubling while food production per person decreased, and more than half the Philippines farmlands being used for export purposes. Arroyo (1977) cites the relationship between increases in the cultivation and export of soya in Brazil and the reduction in rice and beans available for local consumption. These processes directly involve multinational corporations or large national enterprises – in many cases with the cooperation of local elites, despite attempts at resistance by the local farmers and peasantry (George,

1976). The swelling migration to the cities of underdeveloped countries is evidence not necessarily of the attractions of urban living as Kahn (1976) argues, but the forcing of farmers off the land from which they cannot obtain support.

While large plantation agriculture may provide increases in employment and foreign revenue, the production is, for the most part, aimed at the high income consumption market, or as raw materials for export. These benefits must be weighed against the reduction in availability of basic foodstuffs for the poorer segments of the population.

International aid agencies also play a role in fostering the relationship between large corporations and developing agriculture. For example, as a result of the 'protein crisis' in the 1960s and early 1970s, multinational food processing firms were quick to respond to new market opportunities. In late 1971, U.S. aid urged the World Bank to provide 'incentive' grants to private food firms involved in marketing protein food products in Asia, encouraging the production and distribution of low-cost high-protein foods. Additional incentives, including tax reductions and freer imports of capital equipment were taken up by at least fifteen firms. Only one new protein product has appeared on the market (soon withdrawn) since reductions in poverty rather than new products are needed to bridge the so-called 'gap'.

Apart from problems of acceptability of a new food and status connected with using it, all these protein supplements had to be bought. However low the price, people with no money could not have them unless they were distributed by aid programmes. Whether or not similar amounts of money and resources devoted to finding ways in which poor people could feed themselves and/or earn money would have been a better way of relieving malnutrition is a problem that has not been adequately investigated. It is certainly the case that to date the main outlet for novel protein foods has been as health food and cattle concentrate in rich countries and not as diet supplementation for the destitute.

Another formula for increased productivity and production includes direct or indirect vertical integration. Through contract farming or agreements with government agencies private firms can produce incentives for farmers to adopt their advanced technology – in cultivation, storage and transport – and to specialise in one crop. Where the firms involved are international, these technologies have usually been developed for the rich-country market and commercialised there before being transferred abroad. A closed system of research and development that 'allows technological elements to leak out practically by the sole channel of the sale of the finished product' means that those who buy the finished product are forced to use it 'to the ends imposed on them by its nature' (Michalet, 1976).

The requirement to specialise in one crop or product makes the farmers, even if they are richer, very vulnerable to fluctuations on the world market. Sugar, tomatoes, chicks, all have been enthusiastically promoted, rapidly adopted by poor countries, and then subject to gluts and price falls. When this happens the farmers and their families cannot sell the crop, and on its own it cannot provide adequate nutrition.

Big development projects, which make indigenous communities more dependent on the outside world for part of their dietary requirements, and which may remove food-producing land from agriculture, need to be assessed for their effects on the food supplies of the world community of nations as well as upon the country concerned, or its rulers.

Realisation of the maximum productive potential of land on a sustained basis will require investment of effort and money, especially where it involves rapid mobilisation of water resources. Most poor countries do not have sufficient financial resources of their own, and whether or not they receive the necessary assistance in large enough amounts and in time to feed their growing populations will depend on the economic health of the world community.

IF THE CLIMATE CHANGES FOR THE WORSE

The world's climate is always changing (Gribbin, 1978), but we cannot be sure of either the direction or the magnitude of the changes likely to occur in the next few decades. Just when people are becoming aware of the importance of climatic change for food production, the situation has been confused by the addition of human activities as a factor in climatic change. There is ample evidence that the climatic conditions over much of the land area for the first half of this century were exceptionally clement compared with most of the past few hundred years. The cooling trend in the northern hemisphere over the past twenty-five years or so has reduced the length of England's growing season by about ten days (Gribbin and Lamb, in Gribbin, 1978) and may well have contributed to recent agricultural problems in other countries (Bryson, 1974).

Would a return to nineteenth-century conditions in the northern hemisphere be a disaster for world food production? Thompson (1975) points out that cooler summers bring higher yields of both grain and soyabeans in the U.S.A., because of the associated higher rainfall and lower rates of transpiration. The main problem of hemispheric cooling is that it has in the past brought greater variability from year to year and more extremes. Thomas (1957) suggested that if weather were to be as variable from then until 2000 as it was from 1890 to 1955, average yield could be reduced by about three per cent.

Lamb (1972) postulates that changes in atmospheric pressure are causing shifts in the main atmospheric belts surrounding the earth and thus in its climatic belts and that the sub-tropical margins are most adversely affected.

If he is right this could account for the failure of rain in the Sahel and abnormal weather elsewhere. (It may be that it would be wiser to raise productivity in areas likely to be least affected by such shifts.) We are certainly very far from being independent of climate. Records of rainfall in the steppes of the U.S.S.R. between 1900 and the 1940s showed increases in rainfall. Gigantic plans for bringing this land under the plough were drawn up and were implemented after the war. The projected increases in yield have not materialised, and although problems of organisation, motivation and management are apparent, it is also the case that average annual rainfall in the region has declined by about 25 per cent since the 1940s.

Even in the productive American corn belt weather can have devastating effects. In 1974 a cold wet spring delayed sowing. This was followed by torrential rain, which swept away much of the seed when it had been planted. Late summer drought diminished amounts and size of grain, and frost in early autumn interfered with harvesting. The consequent reduction of yield from expected amounts did not cause great hardship to mid-western farmers, and the price of grain rose to over $220 a ton, but similar vulnerability in countries dependent on agriculture for most of their GNP is crippling.

While variability of climate often has serious implications for regional food availability, it need not be allowed to cause major instabilities in world food markets. Surpluses produced by any country should be pooled in an internationally controlled reserve, to exercise the same stabilising effect as the commercially held reserves of Canada and the U.S.A. did until 1972–3. Smaller regional and local reserves, established in situations from which dispersal can be relatively expeditious, could be supplied from the main international reserves.

Where human influence on climate is concerned, the profusion of conflicting theories and the inadequacy of the data have led us to decide to study only alternative futures in which there is no major climatic change. There is as yet no consensus on the likely impact of human activities on the world's weather. The prospect has been raised of a pronounced global warming produced by an envelope of increased carbon dioxide acting like the glass of a greenhouse and trapping heat in the lower layers of the atmosphere (see Broecker, 1975). Its occurrence depends inevitably upon assumptions about the use of fossil fuels. The alternative prospect of anthropogenic climatic doom, that particles spread in the atmosphere by human activities may shield us from the sun's heat and precipitate a new ice age, is equally dependent on assumptions about how the industrial and agricultural activities of man will develop, and as yet there is no certainty that the kind of particles produced in greatest quantities at present do in fact produce a net cooling (see Gribbin, 1975).

Our deliberate decision to ignore climatic change in constructing our profiles of the future seems the least of all evils in the light of the evidence outlined above, although we do take some account of the need for global 'insurance' policies in chapter 7.

PATTERNS OF ECONOMIC GROWTH

The previous discussion concerns average food consumption. What of actual consumption *within* these communities, given that income distribution and access to food is skewed? (McLean and Hopkins, 1974). The F.A.O. has allowed for the effects of this skew in its projections of food demand, and work summarised by Paukert (1973) and that reported by Adelman, Morris and Robinson (1976) suggests that increase in food consumption correlates fairly well with income until about 3000 kilocalories per head a day are being consumed, and that an average income of around $1000 per household is necessary to ensure sufficient for the poorest people. Hopkins, Scolnik and McLean (1975) used this income in their calculations for provision of basic needs, and we have calculated the demands for food that would be generated if these demands were met (Table 4.12). From these calculations it is apparent how important is a more equal distribution of available food supplies, whether through income redistribution or other means.

However, in the following discussion of the four basic profiles of the world's future we concentrate primarily on reduction of disparities between nations, rather than within them.

High Growth with Less Equal Distribution

If economic growth continued at 4 per cent or more a year and no steps were taken to reduce international inequalities, it is probable, on the basis of work reported by Felix Paukert (1973), that the share of the bottom 20 per cent of the population would begin to rise and that of the top 5 per cent to fall at a level of about $500–$1000 per household per year, while the proportion of households in the second and third quintiles would increase. As far as food is concerned, this would mean that a larger proportion of the population would be eating adequately, while inequalities between groups in the variety and quality of food consumed would continue to increase. This would exert increased demand, which if not met within the boundaries of a country, would result in increased demand on world supplies, to the detriment of poorer countries. Countries already developed and some developing countries with oil or other mineral resources might achieve this pattern, with the following tendencies emerging to a greater or lesser degree, depending on cultural factors.

Various small-scale sociological studies suggest that as income increases households at first buy more of their traditional staple foods until they are consuming about 3000 kilocalories per head a day; they then begin to increase the proportion of the animal protein part of it. So one effect of income growth is increased demand for animal protein. This causes increased demand for animal foodstuffs and has repercussions on the world market in grains and pulses. Standardisation of meat products sets a trend away from pasturing towards intensive rearing and thus to waste disposal problems. The

TABLE 4.12 *Projected demand for food*

Continent	'Derived' GDP growth % per annum	Income elasticity of demand	Projected 'demand' 1985		2000		Max. possible GE (million tonnes/yr)
			k.cal/hd	Total (m. tonnes GE/yr)	k.cal/hd	Total (m. tonnes GE/yr)	
Latin America	8.7	0.26	4,169	171	9,903	642	11,106
Africa	9.3	0.48	5,246	168	16,656	738	10,845
Asia East and South East	9.6	0.66	6,021	928	21,765	4,926	14,281

Assumptions: Natural replacement rate → 1 in 2030.
1970 consumption: Latin America   2529 k.cals/hd/day
Africa   2240 k.cals/hd/day
S. & S.E. Asia   2041 k.cals/hd/day

wastes have potential both for further food production and as fuel, but these uses have not often been developed. Makhijani and Poole (1975) in their report to the Ford Foundation on rural energy in developing countries indicate to what extent agricultural wastes are or could be used.

Intensive rearing, processing and marketing of food requires growth in the industry of control for pests, diseases and deterioration during storage. The amounts of energy required for food production would be increased and the demand for all-season availability of food commodities would stimulate processing, packaging, deep-freezing and convenience foods.

People in the upper three quintiles of the income range would probably be larger than their forebears and tend to become overweight. They would live longer, owing to better sanitation and better infant nutrition, and there would be a downward income shift in the pattern of the diseases associated with wealth, described by Blythe (1976): arterio-sclerosis, coronary failure, gut malfunction, obesity, nervous disorders and compulsive dieting, which would stimulate the production of 'cures' for these rather than for the control of infection and prevention of malnutrition.

Meanwhile, as some countries remained or became rich, others would remain poor, and, if there were no deliberate market adjustments or transfer of wealth, would be stimulated by external demand to produce more food for export and more cash crops (coffee, cotton, sugar) on land that might otherwise produce food for home consumption. The income from these activities would accrue unequally and the actual incomes of the lowest two quintiles of the population would remain low and perhaps even decrease relative both to those of the top three and to the levels of prices. Increased dependence on trading partners could result in import of unsuitable goods, including food products. The need for cash income would stimulate migration from rural to urban areas, leading to reduced indigenous food production, increasing dependence on imported food and increased income inequalities.

Such a prospect might correspond to the worst results of policies based on the simplistic application of free market adjustment theories of world economics.

Low Growth with Less Equal Distribution

In rich countries this prospect might be similar to what Britain is now experiencing. It is doubtful whether a low or zero rate of growth arrived at by accident rather than intent could maintain a continuing supply of food at 3000 kilocalories or more per person with a high proportion of animal protein. The size of the groups able to indulge in high living would be reduced. Decreased ability to purchase food from abroad might stimulate home production of food, and possibly better use of grazing, as described by

Mellanby (1975). Inequalities would be increased by unemployment and lowering of income in probably the third and fourth quintiles.

The least developed countries on the other hand might in fact do better for food in a low growth than in a high growth world situation, especially among the lower income quintiles. However, the efforts of the wealthiest to improve their position could result in increased effort to export and thus eventually, reduce availability of food at home. Death from malnutrition and infectious disease would remain high, with an average expectancy of life at birth of 30 or below (P. Abelson, 1975).

Equitable Distribution

Futures tending towards increased equality presuppose policy decisions, based on managerial, humanist or socialist ideas, of what human society could and should be like. To some extent whether the increase in rate of growth is high, low or zero also depends upon deliberate choice. Many European countries have achieved high growth rates since the war and some, particularly the Scandinavian countries, greater equality of incomes. Fairly high rates of growth with a stronger trend towards equality of distribution seem to have been achieved also in the richer countries of Eastern Europe and the U.S.S.R. after acute difficulties in the 1950s. Dunman (1975) has argued that the East European countries appear to be characterised by a slow but steady increase in the amount, quality and variety of food available and a recent increase in the consumption of meat of all kinds. There is a growing processing industry for canned, bottled and packaged foods, some of which are exported. U.S.S.R. and Eastern Europe, having failed to achieve simultaneously both a higher rate of meat production and self-sufficiency in grain, are entering into medium-term importing agreements with the U.S.A. Incomes of food producers are rising in relation to other groups, although they remain considerably lower in all except the G.D.R.

Low Growth with More Equal Distribution

This type of future presupposes either a lifestyle akin to primitive communism or an already high standard of living. The already rich countries could conceivably decide to redistribute income and adopt policies of zero growth and sufficiency. For capitalist countries, with economies linked to others with very different aspirations, this would be difficult, if not impossible and it is unlikely that any will choose it. The U.S.S.R. and Eastern Europe could do it as a group, once they have secured sufficiency and a significantly raised quality of life for the poorest groups of their poorest countries. They may have a problem in obtaining public assent to a decision that any given level of production of food or anything else is sufficient. They would also be affected by their need to survive in a mixed-economy world.

Poor countries that at present have assured sufficiency could conceivably continue with low rates of growth without great hardship, but those with unreliable climate, rapid population growth or inadequate social structure to carry out redistribution will probably not survive far into a low growth future, without acute social problems and worsening levels of nutrition. Altogether it seems unlikely that this future would be chosen *voluntarily*, although this does not rule out the possibility of the world being forced into it.

High Growth Rate with More Equal Distribution

Such a future could occur if the countries that are rich today maintained their current standards or a steady but low rate of increase in economic growth, while the poor countries sustained rapid development combined with policies to redistribute wealth within them. If we accept the assumptions of Hopkins *et al.* (1975) concerning adequate access to food at $1000 per head per year, then Tables 4.13 and 4.14 show that such incomes could be reached for all the continents of the world in under 70 years at growth in GNP of four per cent per year and in under 300 years at one per cent. This is one of the main reasons why we favour a high growth scenario.

According to some extreme proponents of high growth there is no limit to the physical potential for growth, and quantity, quality and variety can go on increasing indefinitely as increasingly desirable technologies are applied to convert raw materials into things required by people. However, there is no doubt that rapid intensification of crop production, with little regard to the maintenance of soil fertility, does eventually lead to soil erosion and loss of fertility, and that ill-designed irrigation on many alluvial soils in semi-arid regions results in salination. But there are areas where continuous cultivation for thousands of years has not resulted in reduced yields, and enough is

TABLE 4.13   *Time to reach average GNP per head of $1000 (1970)*

Continent	GNP/hd 1970* (U.S. $)	Time at growth rate (years) 1%	2.8%	4%
Asia – China	74	259	94	66
Latin America (high)	472	75	27	19
Latin America (low)	403	91	33	23
S. Europe	490	71	26	18
Middle East (oil)	222	150	55	38
Africa – south (med.)	710	34	12	8
Asia – India (med.)	129	204	74	52
Africa (arid)	118	213	77	54
Africa (tropical)	140	196	71	50

*Hopkins, Scolnik and McLean (1975) weighted average by population.

Critical Issues

TABLE 4.14   *Rate of growth in GNP required to reach*
$1000 (1970) in 30, 60 and 80 years

Continent	Rate of growth required (%)		
	Year 2000	2030	2050
Asia – China	9	4.42	3.3
Latin America (high)	2.54	1.25	0.95
Latin America (low)	3.06	1.53	1.13
S. Europe	2.4	1.2	0.90
Middle East (oil)	5.14	2.54	1.91
Africa – south (med.)	1.16	0.58	0.44
Asia – India (med.–low)	7	3.46	2.59
Africa (arid)	7.35	3.64	2.70
Africa (tropical)	6.78	3.33	2.50

known about maintenance of fertility for soils to be managed at optimum, rather than maximum levels of productivity; at the moment most are farmed well below the optimum by methods that still produce deterioration. Salination is under investigation. There may be degrees of vulnerability, which could be classified, and some areas designated for cropping with drought- or salt-resistant crops, or only to be irrigated in exceptionally dry years, thus prolonging their productive life. The valley of the Syr Darya in Uzbekistan has been irrigated since 5000 B.C. and still has only small salt areas, according to Dov Mir in *The Semi-arid World* (1974). An area of 300,000 hectares has been reclaimed by the use of underdraining (Kovda, 1974) since 1956 and a further 180,000 are to be brought into cultivation in the next ten years.

A desirable world future for food would include reduction of waste in production, transport and storage; utilisation of wild animals and plants on a controlled basis; and development of land in Africa and Latin America to enable those continents to produce a surplus. It would also require governmental or international policies to ensure that as development took place the poorest two quintiles of populations became wealthier in relation to the other three even in the early stages, and to protect poorer countries from becoming food colonies of richer ones. Such a future would probably achieve a levelling-off in population growth after about one and a half generations, say 40 years, as people realised that more children would live to adulthood. World population by that time would be between 6007 and 9882 million, according to the estimates of Mesarovic and Pestel, which would be well within world food production capabilities.

Except for those, such as the oil states, which have natural resources in large quantities, poor countries will have to increase their wealth on the basis of agriculture. Agriculture will have to provide not only the bulk of the food to meet indigenous needs, but also often a surplus of food or other crops for processing and/or export. We have seen that in all regions, including Africa and Asia, there is still scope for increasing production from the land, and we have suggested, though not elaborated, the methods whereby this could be done on a sustained-yield basis. This kind of agriculture requires long-term policies, a technically educated workforce, adequate supplies of fertilizer and suitable agricultural equipment, as well as efficient arrangements for storage, marketing and processing. All these things require investment, which cannot always be expected to yield a return in the short run.

Some countries already produce surpluses. Wheat, rice, beef, butter, sugar – all have been stockpiled in the last few years. Storage in the unprocessed state of all except grains is prohibitively expensive. If surplus stocks were donated to a common reserve as part of overseas aid, and if the necessary processing and storage were undertaken by an internationally funded authority, the existing surpluses could be used to stabilise prices and to provide emergency stocks against catastrophe. Particularly vulnerable regions could have smaller stores of suitable foods at nodal distribution points, although the suspicion that the existence of such stocks reduces local food production and encourages small-scale cultivation of low-grade cash crops to purchase non-food commodities requires investigation.

Since North America, Australasia and the E.E.C. are likely to be the main food surplus areas in the next few decades, the responsibility for the composition and size of the food stocks will inevitably rest with them. However, in the future foreseen by Buringh *et al.* (1975) irrigation in much of the arid region of the world will have shifted the balance of agricultural production towards regions with a long growing season, where 2–3 harvests can be obtained on each cultivated area every year. Africa, Australasia, parts of the Middle East and South East Asia will then become the surplus producing areas. The implications of this for the changing pattern of industrial activity are beyond the scope of this chapter, but it is clear that all these regions will have to be urgently concerned with the identification of long-term social and economic objectives and the selection of the best technologies to suit their own requirements in reaching them. The right kind of technical education could well be crucial.

In wartime Britain, equitable distribution as well as higher production were achieved by strong policies, strict legislation and regulation. Some would call this authoritarian, but if such measures are directed at ensuring the spread of the benefits produced by society, then perhaps they are no more so than the regulation of behaviour to prevent theft, fraud and assault.

SUMMARY AND CONCLUSIONS

The main cause of world food problems is *not* physical limits on production, but intra- and international distribution of income; in other words, politics

(Marstrand and Pavitt, 1973). However, given that populations, especially in some of the most under-nourished regions, will rise, and that people's aspirations are generally to eat better, it is necessary to increase production in the future, especially in poorer countries, and to build up international and national stocks.

This increased production will depend on the successful introduction of technical change. Appropriate technical change will require reorientation of R & D towards development of local skills and away from highly centralised and often urban-biased research.

For the next century high rates of economic growth with a more equitable distribution of the resulting wealth are most likely to provide a framework for the achievement of increased agricultural production on the basis of the introduction of new technologies.

While the advanced northern hemisphere countries will be the main producers of surplus food for the next few decades, successful irrigation of land in the semi-arid zones around the tropics will enable full use to be made of the long growing season in these regions. By multi- and intercropping, mulching with organic waste or crops grown to be ploughed in, irrigated land could be kept permanently under crop cover without loss of fertility and with little risk of erosion. Countries in these regions could well be the main food producers by the year 2100.

CHAPTER 5

Some Energy Futures

John Chesshire and Keith Pavitt*

1. The Importance of Energy

Recent contributors to the futures debate recognise the importance of energy for economic growth, and assume that energy demand will continue to increase in future. Heilbroner estimates that raising per capita energy consumption in the poor countries to O.E.C.D. levels would mean a staggering increase by at least twenty to thirty times in these countries. With the exception of Khan *et al.* in *The Next 200 Years*, most other authors are less explicit about future trends in energy demand. However, assumptions about them must have been made by Mesarovic and Pestel, and by Meadows who forecast that all fossil fuel reserves (coal, oil and natural gas) will be depleted in the next 150 to 200 years, and oil in the next 20 to 30 years. Leontief, on the other hand, considers that there is enough coal to sustain future world economic development.

Attitudes towards nuclear energy vary from the unqualified optimism of the Soviet writers about the prospects for thermonuclear fusion, through the qualified support of Dumont and of Mesarovic and Pestel, to the hostility of the Ehrlichs. Many forecasters advocate greater use of solar energy. Assumptions and conclusions about trends in energy demand and about the role of nuclear energy have a strong influence on policy prescriptions, from the materialist optimism of the Soviet writers to the strategies for 'de-development' of the Ehrlichs.

The close association between economic development and energy use is brought out clearly in Table 5.1, which shows the close similarity in world shares of gross national product and of energy consumption in 1965; the

*In addition to our colleagues in the Science Policy Research Unit, we would like to thank the following people for valuable comments on earlier drafts of this chapter: Art Bogers, Robin Cooper, Keith Dawson, Norman Dombey, Jean-Marie Martin, Walter Patterson, George Ray, Adam Sedgwick, Robert Uffen and Brian Wade.

113

114

Critical Issues

TABLE 5.1   *Regional differences in gross national product and in energy consumption*

| Region | Percentage distribution, 1965 | | | Energy consumption per head (tonnes coal equivalent) | |
	World gross national product	World energy consumption	World electricity consumption	1925	1965
North America	33.3	37.3	38.8	6.0	9.5
(of which U.S.A.)	(30.9)	(34.4)	(34.6)	(6.2)	(9.7)
Western Europe	26.1	20.4	24.6	1.8	3.3
Oceania	1.3	1.1	1.5	1.7	3.6
U.S.S.R.	14.0	16.0	15.1	0.2	3.8
Eastern Europe	5.1	6.9	5.1	0.8	3.7
Latin America	4.3	3.6	3.1	0.3	0.8
Middle East	1.1	1.0	0.5	n.a.	n.a.
Japan	5.4	3.4	5.6	0.5	1.9
Communist Asia	3.7	5.9	1.8	0.1	0.4
Other Asia	3.8	2.5	2.1	0.1	0.2
South Africa	0.5	1.0	1.1	0.1	0.3
Other Africa	1.5	0.7	0.7		
WORLD	100.0	100.0	100.0	0.8	1.7

Source: Darmstadter (1971).

increase in energy consumption per head between 1925 and 1965 in all regions of the world; and the large differences between regions in energy consumption per head depending on levels of wealth. Based on 1965 data, Darmstadter found an overall correlation coefficient of 0.9 between GNP per head and primary energy consumption per head (though within wide ranges as Table 5.3 reveals).

Given the economic importance of energy, governments in all countries, including countries with market economies, have had much influence on the development of energy sources and energy technologies, as well as on energy prices and energy use. They have always taken a strong interest in political developments in oil-producing countries. Many have directly and effectively encouraged the formation of national oil companies and, since the Second World War, they have increasingly found themselves dealing directly with the oil-producing countries about oil supplies and oil prices (OPEC was established in 1960). Similarly, government-financed agencies concerned with nuclear technology have diversified from military to civilian applications, or directly pursued the latter. In many countries, coal mining has been partly or fully nationalised, as has the production and distribution of gas and electricity. In all O.E.C.D. countries energy price levels are strongly influenced by taxation and regulation. It is very unlikely that the production and distribution of energy will ever revert to anything resembling a free competitive market, assuming that it ever existed in the past. The commodity is too important, the sources of monopoly power – both national and international – are too great, and the external costs associated with its production and use are too considerable for this ever to be allowed.

As a key commodity, whose consumption increases with economic growth, depletable sources might be used up in the not too distant future. Malthus and Ricardo were very worried about the future supply of food in the nineteenth century. But the possibility of Malthusian constraints is more severe with energy than with food: first, food consumption has been less closely correlated with economic growth than Malthus had thought, which is not yet the case with energy; second, through solar energy and biosynthesis, food is a renewable resource, whereas the main sources of energy today are non-renewable fossil fuels. Large-scale industrialisation has taken place so far almost exclusively on the basis of these fossil fuels.

It is therefore legitimate to ask whether and under what conditions there will be enough fossil fuel to see all the world's population through to industrialisation, and how and where the world will find sufficient energy to sustain high living standards thereafter. Even if the technologies prove to be economically feasible, there are some important problems (or 'external costs') associated with future energy sources. As we shall argue later, the exploitation of shale oil and tar sands could lead to environmental desecration on a very large scale. The large-scale introduction of nuclear energy could create dangers of nuclear proliferation and accidents, given the need for the transportation and storage of radioactive fuels and wastes.

Our concerns are similar to those of Malthus and Ricardo, namely, the implications for possible energy futures of various rates of economic growth in different parts of the world, on the one hand, and of various patterns of technical change and mixes of energy resources, on the other. But we should also mention that, just as the acceptance of Malthus' ideas helped social Darwinists argue that survival of the fittest nations depended on access to vital 'living space', so similar ideas can help justify today the drawing up of battle plans for the invasion of energy-rich areas such as Saudi Arabia. In the past, Malthusian ideas have sometimes offered a convenient cloak under which to hide colonialism. We hope that the reader will, having finished this chapter, be better able to judge whether the same sort of thing is happening today.

2. ENERGY FUTURES

Given our concerns about energy and world economic development, we must inevitably look at least fifty years into the future, since it is unlikely that world population would have stabilised before then, or that the poor countries would have reached the standard of living current in the industrially advanced countries. Over such time horizons our knowledge of the income and price elasticities of demand and of elasticities of substitution amongst different forms of energy is slight. Forecasts representing probable outcomes are, in such conditions of great uncertainty, virtually meaningless. We shall instead be developing 'profiles', representing ranges of possible futures, so that policy implications can be drawn from them. The range of possible profiles is limitless; combining 'high' and 'low' assumptions for just five variables yields thirty-two cases, as in the model developed in the G.B. Department of Energy (1976). Yet the choice of alternatives inevitably involves technical and value judgements, and often arbitrary assumptions about critical variables that can determine the outcome of the whole analysis. Thus, the scenarios recently published by the G.B. Department of Energy all assume relatively high income elasticities of demand for energy over the next twenty to thirty years.

These difficulties and dangers must be kept in mind when reading what follows. Before exploring profiles and policy options for the future, it is necessary to look at past trends in the production and use of energy. This will be done in the next section, and section 4 will examine – inevitably at some length – the prospects and problems of different potential energy sources for the future. Section 5 examines the future scope for energy conservation, and section 6 presents a series of possible future profiles of energy demand. In section 7, we compare these profiles and summarise what we believe are the advantages and disadvantages they offer. In section 8 we discuss the policies required to achieve our preferred profile, and in section 9 we briefly present main policy conclusions.

3. WORLD ENERGY TRENDS: 1900—1974

There is little reason to think that historical trends in energy production and use can or should continue far into the future. But given that we are going to look ahead up to seventy-five years it is important to identify the significant changes in the scale and composition of energy production and use over a period of at least equivalent length.

Table 5.2 summarises the main changes this century. Studies of changes in energy consumption are made suspect because of increasing coverage, changes in efficiencies of use, and changes in exchange rates if monetary

TABLE 5.2   *World trends in the production and consumption of commercial energy, 1900–1974*

Year	Percentage distribution of consumption			World energy consumption (10^9 tce)	Percentage distribution of fuel source			
	Poor countries	U.S.S.R. and E. Europe	Rich market economies		Coal	Oil	Natural gas	Other
1900	2	98		0.76	94	4	1	0
1913	5	95		1.35	92	6	2	0
1929	7	93		1.70	80	15	4	1
1937	7	93		1.80	75	18	6	1
1950	7	18	75	2.50	62	25	9	2
1958	14	22	64	3.76	54	31	14	2
1967	12	24	64	5.68	40	39	18	2
1974	17	23	60	7.97	32	45	21	3

Note: tce = tonnes of coal equivalent.
'Other' includes nuclear, geothermal and hydro-electrical power.
Sources: 1. U.N.E.C.E., *Report to a Symposium on the Future Role of Coal in the National and World Economies* (1970).
2. U.N., *World Energy Supplies 1950–1974* (1976).

variables are used. Nevertheless, it shows that commercial energy consumption increased about tenfold between 1900 and 1974, the rate of
increase being particularly rapid in the period since 1950. The relative importance of the Western market economies in total consumption declined to 60
per cent in 1974, whilst that of Eastern Europe and the U.S.S.R. increased to
23 per cent and that of poor countries to 17 per cent. At the same time, the
relative importance of coal declined steadily from over 90 per cent in 1900 to
32 per cent in 1974, whilst that of oil increased over the same period from 4 to
45 per cent and natural gas from 1 to 21 per cent. The substitution of oil and
natural gas for coal has been particularly rapid since 1950. In poor countries,
the 'non-commercial' fuels such as wood, dung, human and animal power
have been steadily replaced by fossil fuels.

A continuation of past trends for the next seventy-five years would lead to
an annual energy consumption in the year 2050 of about 80×10^9 tonnes coal

TABLE 5.3   *Relations between energy consumption and gross national product in*
industrialised countries

Country	Energy–GNP elasticity coefficient 1925–65	Energy–GNP elasticity coefficient 1950–65	Energy per dollar GNP in kilograms coal equivalent 1965
Belgium/Luxembourg	0.52	0.94	2.59
Canada	1.03	1.13	3.04
France	0.86	1.00	1.57
Italy	1.86	2.16	1.55
Japan	1.12	1.00	1.58
Netherlands	1.29	1.17	2.04
Sweden	1.40	1.59	1.85
Switzerland	1.38	1.64	1.16
U.K.	0.57	0.62	2.66
U.S.A.	0.77	0.81	2.75
U.S.S.R.	1.90	1.25	2.85
West Germany	n.a.	0.76	2.11
Yugoslavia	1.49	1.18	1.64

Note: The energy–GNP elasticity coefficient over a given period is the rate of growth of
primary energy consumption divided by the rate of growth of GNP.
Source: Darmstadter (1971).

equivalent (tce). The gap between the industrialised and the less-developed countries in energy consumption per head would still be considerable; today's poor countries would be consuming about a third of the world's energy, whilst having more than three-quarters of its population. What the sources of energy supply might be is more difficult to determine. The experience of the past seventy-five years suggests that large shifts in energy sources can be envisaged, provided that the alternatives are available.

The main motor of this steady rise in energy consumption has been economic growth, but it is by no means certain that future economic growth in the industrialised countries will require the same rate of growth of energy consumption as in the past. Table 5.3 presents some of Darmstadter's figures (Darmstadter, 1971) of the relations between energy consumption and GNP in selected industrialised countries. It shows that, over the period from 1925 to 1965, there was considerable variation amongst countries in the extra amount of energy associated with each percentage increase in GNP. He reveals that the 'energy requirements' of growth were lower over the period for industrially mature countries, such as Belgium, Germany, the U.K. and the U.S.A., than for later industrialisers such as Canada, Italy, Japan, the Netherlands, Switzerland, Sweden, the U.S.S.R. and Yugoslavia, and suggests that with greater industrial maturity the energy requirements for further growth will further tend to diminish.

Darmstadter also points out that, in 1965, there remained considerable differences between countries in the amount of energy required to generate each dollar of GNP, varying from between 2.7 and 3 kilograms of coal equivalent in Canada, the U.K., the U.S.A. and the U.S.S.R., to between 1.2 and 2 in France, Italy, Japan, the Netherlands, Sweden, Switzerland and Yugoslavia. He suggests three factors to explain these variations: differences in climate, differences in the importance of energy-intensive industries, and differences in the efficiency of energy conversion, depending in large part on the relative shares of coal and oil in consumption – the latter being the more efficient fuel to burn.

Whilst these explanations might be plausible, they are not entirely convincing, especially from the vantage point of 1977. The greater energy requirements of economic growth in the period 1950 to 1965 than in the earlier period in all Western countries, except Japan and the Netherlands (see Table 5.3), is not consistent with the assumption of reduced energy requirements for mature growth. Nor is the comparison of West Germany and Sweden with the U.S.A. in the mid-1970s. The former countries are now as rich and industrialised as the U.S.A., have well developed process industries that use considerable amounts of energy, do not use relatively more oil than the U.S.A., and have somewhat inclement climates. Yet they manage to produce about twice as much GNP as the U.S.A. for each unit of energy consumed.

Two further explanatory factors would complete Darmstadter's analysis and resolve these inconsistencies: energy prices and the growth of the demand for passenger cars at higher levels of income. The greater energy intensity of growth in the period 1950 to 1965 can be explained by both lower real energy prices and the spread of passenger car transport. The greater use of energy for each unit of GNP in such countries as Canada and the U.S.A. can be explained by their relatively lower prices of energy and consequently lower incentive for technical efficiency in energy use.

Thus, future economic growth in the industrialised advanced countries is not pre-ordained to require the same considerable amounts of energy inputs as in the past. Additional energy consumption will depend, amongst other things, on energy prices, energy conversion efficiencies, the size of processing industries and patterns of transport. These conclusions are particularly relevant to our discussion of energy conservation (pp. 137-45) and of profiles of future energy demand (pp. 145-51).

4. FUTURE SOURCES OF ENERGY

Past experience teaches us the dangers and the difficulties of estimating the potential contribution of future sources of energy, especially for the long-term future. The uncertainties surrounding such estimates are enormous, and we make no claim whatsoever to be able to make a more accurate assessment than anybody else. Most of this section is based on the contributions of many specialists in the recent burst of energy publications. It is as much our purpose to identify the uncertainties, problems and risks – in resource estimates, in technological development and in economic, environmental and political factors – as it is to assess the size of exploitable reserves and resources. Given the increases in energy prices and capital costs since many of these estimates were made, we can expect considerable revisions in the estimates (in both directions) over the next few years.

Coal Deposits of coal are classified according to their calorific value into anthracites, bituminous, sub-bituminous, lignites and peat, the last two having considerably lower calorific values than the first three. According to the World Energy Conference (1974), identified coal reserves (excluding peat) amount to 1.4×10^{12} tonnes, of which nearly 0.6×10^{12} tonnes were considered recoverable with then current technology and prices. Total coal resources available in the Earth's crust were estimated on the basis of geological evidence to be 10.8×10^{12} tonnes. Averitt (1969) estimated in 1967 that total coal resources were 15.3×10^{12} tonnes and Foley (1976) argues that, on the basis of past experience, about half this quantity could be considered as ultimately recoverable.

Although coal's role in energy supply has been steadily eroded by oil and gas during the twentieth century, production increased at an annual rate of

1.7 per cent to reach 2.5×10^9 tonnes in 1974. Given the considerable increase in oil prices since 1973, the size of coal reserves recoverable under the economic conditions prevailing in 1977 can be expected to be above the 1974 level of 600×10^9 tonnes, even allowing for the effects of inflation on capital investment programmes in the coal industry. Major chemical and oil companies are now amongst the keenest purchasers of coal companies and coal rights, particularly in the U.S.A., Australia, Canada and South Africa.

The mining, transportation, storage and use of coal still pose some difficult problems. Underground mining remains labour-intensive despite increased mechanisation, and imposes a high toll in human costs. Open-cast mining has led to large-scale environmental disruption in many countries, and neither type of mining has done much to enhance physical surroundings. Present methods of transportation are relatively cumbersome and expensive, especially over long distances, and coal is a more difficult and environmentally dirtier fuel to use than oil or natural gas.

As a consequence of the recently renewed economic attraction of coal, large funds are now being committed to research and development (R & D) programmes with the purpose of overcoming many of these problems. Advances in underground mining machinery should favour the continuation of the trend of the past twenty years towards better manpower productivity and working conditions and lower accident rates. Fluidised bed combustion of coal will, if successful, increase the technical and economic efficiency of coal use in electrical power stations and industrial boilers, as well as reduce environmental pollution from sulphur dioxide. The transportation of coal through slurry pipelines would reduce the difficulties of moving coal over long distances, as would its conversion into electricity or synthetic oil and gas at the pit-head or underground.

The liquefaction and gasification of coal would also increase the possibilities for substituting coal for oil and natural gas in many uses. The feasibility of liquefaction was demonstrated during the Second World War in a Germany cut off from major oil supplies, and is currently undertaken on a commercial basis in South Africa. Coal gas was used widely as town gas, but R & D programmes are now concentrating on producing methane-like gases similar to natural gas with a high calorific content and few impurities.

Oil Great uncertainty surrounds estimates of world oil reserves. In 1974 the World Energy Conference estimated proved reserves, recoverable under the economic and technological conditions prevailing at that time, as 92×10^9 tonnes.* Since then, British Petroleum (1976) has estimated proved reserves as 76×10^9 tonnes, in spite of the considerable increase in the price of

---

*Depending on whether one uses the conversion factors of the United Kingdom Government, of British Petroleum or of the United Nations, one tonne of oil is equivalent to 1.7, to 1.5 or to 1.3 tonnes of coal. We shall use the conversion factor 1 tonne oil equivalent (tce) = 1.5 tonnes coal equivalent (tce).

oil in the intervening period. In 1974, the O.E.C.D. (1974a) estimated total recoverable reserves (both proved and probable) as 200-250 × 10⁹ tonnes.

Even greater uncertainties exist about ultimately recoverable oil resources. Weeks (1962) and Ryman (1967) estimated them to be 273×10^9 and 285×10^9 tonnes, whilst the U.S. Geological Survey (Albers, 1973) estimated them to be between 184×10^9 and 1840×10^9 tonnes. Over long periods of time there have been substantial revisions in estimates of ultimately recoverable oil resources. Kahn, Brown and Martel (1976) have pointed out that between the years 1885 and 1949 there were many predictions that U.S. oil resources would soon be exhausted. Between 1948 and 1971 Weeks has increased his estimate of ultimately recoverable world oil resources by a factor of 3.75. However, since 1959, most estimates have stuck stubbornly around 270×10^9 tonnes, with the exceptions of a few dissenters and the obvious agnosticism of the U.S. Geological Survey, whose wide range of estimates must be based on the assumption of our continuing and considerable ignorance.

The sources of such ignorance are many. First, the World Energy Conference (1974) points out that many countries have not made comprehensive surveys of reserves and resources, and that reserves for China and the U.S.S.R. are perhaps underestimated, given that large areas of these countries are as yet unexplored. Second, considerable oil resources are thought to exist under the sea on the world's continental shelves, and perhaps even in deeper water. These are the new frontiers of oil exploration, so that reliable and comprehensive information is limited and rapidly reassessed. Third, the size of ultimately recoverable oil reserves depends heavily on trends in the rate at which oil is recovered from reservoirs – the current rate of recovery varying between 30 and 40 per cent. Enhanced recovery techniques and higher energy prices might eventually enable this rate to be increased to as much as 60 to 70 per cent. Every improvement of one per cent in recovery would add the equivalent of more than one year's production at current rates (Commoner, 1976). However, oil companies operating in the North Sea argue that investment in the more advanced recovery techniques is not attractive financially, when compared with the investment opportunities available elsewhere.

Fourth, most of the knowledge about oil reserves and about geologically promising regions for oil resources is in the hands of commercially oriented oil firms, or are state secrets, especially in the communist countries (Cheng, 1976; Elliot, 1974). Commercial considerations discourage the search for supplies beyond a time horizon of fifteen years or so; and, in some countries, stock exchange rules discourage optimistic or speculative estimates about future reserves. It is therefore not entirely surprising that the estimates made by experts close to the oil industry (such as Weeks, 1962, Hubbert, 1968, and Warman, 1973) conform to the same prudent conservatism, whilst those made by outsiders (like Odell, 1974, and Albers, 1973) reach different conclusions.

Growth in the trade and use of oil has brought environmental hazards associated with spills from oil tankers and with air pollution (especially sulphur dioxide). The new exploration frontiers also have their problems and hazards, such as oil leaks and losses from undersea drilling activities, the ecological effects of oil pipelines (particularly their thermal effects in Arctic and Antarctic regions), and the more general increase in the costs and risks of oil exploration, when compared to conditions prevailing in the Middle East in the 1960s.

Given these conditions and the proven advantages of oil as a fuel, there are likely to be two significant consequences. First, considerable technical and financial resources will continue to be devoted to overcoming new problems of exploration and production. Second, regions with plentiful supplies of oil will be subjected to political conflict and pressure. In this context, the Middle East will probably be joined by hotly disputed offshore territories, such as Spitzbergen (Norway and the U.S.S.R.), the Aegean Sea (Greece and Turkey) and the Falkland Islands (Argentina and U.K.).

Natural Gas Large amounts of natural gas are known to exist in most oil-producing areas of the world. Until recently, most natural gas apparently had little commercial value. In 1974, five Middle Eastern members of OPEC (Abu Dhabi, Iran, Iraq, Kuwait and Saudi Arabia) burnt off (flared) about two-thirds of their total gas production. Although the figures are not directly comparable, the U.S. Bureau of Mines has estimated that 13 per cent of world natural gas production was flared in 1973 (*Petroleum Economist*, July 1976). The absence of large populations and local industry, the near self-sufficiency until recently of the major gas-consuming countries, the lack of an infrastructure and an established world market for gas, and the stronger interest in oil, have all contributed to this situation. A number of the major 'flarers' are now giving much more serious consideration to petrochemical uses of natural gas, as well as to its export.

Given the relatively recent emergence of natural gas as a major world fuel, estimates of available reserves tend to be both very approximate and rapidly changing. Estimates in the *Petroleum Economist* (July 1976) of proved reserves, recoverable under prevailing economic and technological conditions, increased from the equivalent of 50×10^9 tonnes of coal at the beginning of 1970 to about 90×10^9 tonnes at the beginning of 1975 (assuming that 750 cubic metres of natural gas are equivalent to one tonne of coal (tce)). In 1974, the World Energy Conference estimated proved recoverable reserves as 70×10^9 tce. Given that these proved reserves have been estimated conservatively, that they do not include probable or possible reserves exploitable under prevailing economic and technological conditons, and that the potential for new gas discoveries is high, we can expect that the estimates of proved gas reserves will continue to increase in future. In the meantime, estimates of ultimately recoverable world resources of natural gas cannot be based on much systematic information. In 1972, Linden estimated them as 370×10^9 tce, and in 1973 the U.S. Geological Survey estimated them as between 150×10^9 and 1500×10^9 tce.

Compared to oil reserves, natural gas reserves appear to be relatively less concentrated in a few countries: the U.S.S.R. has 35 per cent, Iran 16 per cent and the U.S.A. 10 per cent. As a fuel natural gas has high calorific value, and is clean and efficient to burn. The main problems relate to its transportation and distribution. Technical advances in large diameter pipelines and in bulk refrigerated tankers carrying liquefied natural gas have eased these problems to a certain extent. Although there are large gas grids in the U.S.A. and Europe the establishment of an extensive system of pipelines for distribution would be expensive, and therefore unlikely to happen unless natural gas supplies and eventual substitutes are both plentiful and assured.

Oil shale Oil shale is a commonly found rock containing a solid organic material called kerogen. On heating to 300–400 degrees centigrade, the kerogen breaks down into gaseous and liquid hydrocarbons, which – after a preliminary upgrading process – can be fed into a conventional oil refinery. According to the World Energy Conference (1974), identified oil resources from shale oil amount to 100×10^9 tonnes in rocks containing 0.1 to 0.4 litres per kilogram, and to 360×10^9 tonnes in rocks containing 0.04 to 0.1 litres per kilogram. Speculative resources amount to about 2300×10^9 tonnes with the former, higher oil densities, and Hubbert (1968) has estimated the total 'oil in position' in shale to be $275,000 \times 10^9$ tonnes. Foley (1976) argues that the energy used in extracting oil from low oil density shale is more than the energy actually produced. Since 90 per cent of shale oil is in such low-grade deposits, and since only a part of the remaining deposits can be mined and then recovered, Foley estimates ultimately recoverable resources of oil from shale to be about 800×10^9 tonnes.

The large-scale extraction of oil from shale remains uneconomic under 1976 conditions, although the Occidental Oil Company in the U.S.A. has claimed – though not substantiated – success in the underground (*in situ*) preparation of oil shales. The energy costs are substantial and the environmental impact of mining and extracting shale oil are considerable, requiring substantial commitments of manpower, equipment and water, and creating a volume of waste in spent shale greater than the amount originally mined, and containing toxic materials.

Tar sands Tar sands consist of sands or sandstones impregnated with heavy oils. The largest known deposit, in Athabasca (Alberta, Canada), is estimated to contain 100×10^9 tonnes. According to the World Energy Conference (1974), Cashion has estimated a world total of about 150×10^9 tonnes of oil in tar sands in major deposits. A company called Great Canadian Oil Sands has been producing oil from tar sands in Alberta since 1967. At one stage there were plans to increase production almost tenfold by 1985, but these have been revised considerably downwards because of financial and technical difficulties.

The economic and environmental problems of tar sands are very similar to those of shale oil. Both involve the extraction of relatively small amounts of oil from large amounts of other materials. To produce large amounts of oil inevitably requires the mining and movement of much larger amounts of materials and an extraction process that uses considerable amounts of energy and leaves large amounts of waste. As a consequence, the capital and environmental costs of production are high.

Nuclear fission The possibilities of energy from nuclear fission grew directly out of the discoveries of twentieth-century physics. A naturally occurring radioactive isotope, Uranium-235 (U-235), occasionally splits into two approximately equal portions emitting considerable amounts of energy, as well as two or three neutrons, which can in turn be made to split further U-235 atoms. U-235 occurs in nature in U-238 in densities on an average of about 0.7 per cent. Natural uranium or enriched uranium, where the proportion of U-235 is increased, are the fuels for so-called thermal fission reactors, the main characteristics of which are determined by three factors: the degree of enrichment of the uranium fuel, the moderator, which regulates the neutron speed and energy release, and the coolant, which transfers heat from the nuclear reactors to turbine steam.

When U-238 absorbs a neutron, it decays radioactively and becomes plutonium-239, a radioactive substance, not found in nature but with the same property as U-235 of splitting and releasing energy when bombarded ' y neutrons. This reaction is the basis of the fast breeder reactor, in which a mixture of uranium and plutonium oxide fuel is the core around which a layer or blanket of U-238 absorbs neutrons and is converted to plutonium-239. Fast breeder reactors are claimed to be about sixty times more efficient in fuel use than thermal reactors. The core of the fast breeder reactor is necessarily compact, with high power density and without a moderator, so that a material with a high capacity for absorbing and transferring heat is required as coolant. So far, the favourite candidate as coolant has been liquid sodium, which reacts fiercely on contact with water.

Thorium supplies consist mainly of thorium-232, and like U-238 this isotope is not fissile but fertile, and can capture a neutron to form thorium-233, which decays to form uranium-233 – a fissile isotope. Thorium – like U-238 – can therefore be the basis of breeder reactors. As has been pointed out in the Sixth Report of the G.B. Royal Commission on Environmental Pollution (the Flowers Commission), it can already be used together with enriched uranium in two existing types of thermal reactor – the CANDU reactor and the High Temperature Reactor (HTR). As a result, the amount of uranium required in the thorium cycle could be about one-fifth that needed for reactors burning uranium alone. CANDU and HTR reactors can be designed to have a breeding ratio near unity or even slightly above. Fast reactors can be designed to work on the thorium / U-233 cycle and HTRs as the U-238/plutonium cycle, increasing the range of potential alternatives in nuclear power development.

Thus the fuels for nuclear fission are uranium and thorium. Assessing the reserves and the resources of these fuels is bedevilled by many difficulties. Uranium is the basis not only of nuclear reactors, but also of nuclear bombs. Rates and patterns of uranium exploration and mining have therefore been strongly influenced by military and political factors, and estimates of reserves are not available for the communist countries. Furthermore, after considerable increases in oil prices in 1973, the immediate response was to rush out ambitious plans for the expansion of nuclear energy. This induced a rapid increase in estimates of the apparent demand for uranium around 1985, so that prices of uranium sometimes increased sixfold. This essentially conjunctural problem of matching supply with a rapid and unforeseen increase in apparent demand has sometimes been mistaken for signs of eventual exhaustion of naturally occurring uranium reserves and resources.

However, as Hansen (1976) has pointed out, 'Only a generality about the past can be expressed – when a market existed, a supply existed'. Outside the communist countries reasonably assured uranium resources (those known to exist and recoverable with currently proven technology) at less than $10 a pound increased by 75 per cent between 1965 and 1973. By 1975, reasonably assured resources at less than £15 (1975 prices) a pound had reached more than a million tonnes. A similar trend exists in 'estimated additional resources' – that is, resources believed to occur in unexplored extensions of known deposits or in undiscovered deposits in known uranium districts.

Estimates of higher-cost resources available at between $15 and $30 a pound are based on much less data. Hansen estimates 'reasonably assured' and 'estimated additional' resources in this price range both to be about 700,000 tonnes. This means that reasonably assured and estimated additional resources at up to $30 (1975 prices) a pound amount to about 3.5×10^6 tonnes. This estimate seems somewhat less optimistic than the World Energy Conference, which concluded in 1974 (probably on the basis of 1973 prices) that reasonably assured and estimated additional uranium resources at up to $18 a pound amounted to just over 4×10^6 tonnes. The main discrepancy between the two estimates concerns the more speculative higher-cost reserves.

Finally, Hansen notes that only about 15 per cent of the Earth's land surface has been explored for uranium, and that a further 25 per cent is probably at the same time geologically interesting, politically and environmentally available, and logistically accessible.

The energy implications of these reserves can be calculated through the conversion factors used by both the World Energy Conference (1974) and

Hansen (1976):* 3.5×10^6 tonnes of uranium can be expected to provide between 26 and 30×10^6 megawatt-years of electrical energy through thermal reactors, and between 1600 and 1800×10^6 megawatt-years through uranium/plutonium breeder reactors. In terms of primary energy requirements, this would be equivalent to between about 80 and 100×10^9 tonnes for breeder reactors.

Information on thorium reserves and resources is less comprehensive and more widely scattered than that on uranium. Thorium is at present produced mainly as a by-product of the rare earths, and is used in aircraft alloys, lamp mantles and as a catalyst. According to the World Energy Conference (1974), 'reasonably assured' and 'additional' resources at prices up to $12 a pound could be as much as 2.7 million tonnes. This could provide about 1300×10^6 megawatt-years of electricity through breeder reactors, which is equivalent in primary energy requirements to about 4000×10^9 tonnes of coal. There is little doubt that thorium reserves would become much bigger than indicated above should the prospects of a thorium-fuelled nuclear reactor improve in the future. So far, no commercial thorium-based reactors have been built and it is unclear whether the technical difficulties with the thorium fuel cycle are as severe as those of the uranium/plutonium fuel cycle.

There is a powerful school of thought amongst advocates of nuclear energy that the present generation of water-cooled and gas-cooled thermal reactors will inevitably give way in the next thirty years to a plutonium-based breeder reactor, probably using liquid sodium as a coolant. Such a hypothesis is based *inter alia* on two key assumptions. The first is that resources of naturally available nuclear fuel will soon be scarce: as we have seen above, this is far from clear given the relatively small amount of exploration so far and the existence of considerable reserves of thorium. The second assumption is that, given its greater efficiency in the use of fuel, the plutonium breeder reactor is inevitably more economic. This is also debatable, given the relatively small part of total nuclear generating costs attributable to nuclear fuels (around 6 per cent) and the very high capital costs of the sodium-cooled fast breeder reactor. On the basis of data made available in West Germany, Otto Keck (1977) has estimated that the 300-megawatt breeder reactor being built there has capital costs eight times those of existing thermal light-water reactors. Admittedly, this relates to a single prototype, but given the particular safety problems posed by fast breeding nuclear cores and by sodium, there is room for doubt about whether 'economies of scale' or 'learning curves' will ever enable these cost disadvantages to be overcome (Bupp and Derian, 1975).

*According to these conversion factors, each tonne of uranium is capable of providing about 25 megawatts (MW) of thermal energy for a year in thermal reactors. Assuming that electrical power stations are 30 per cent efficient, this means that one tonne of uranium provides about 7.5 MW of electrical energy (MWe) for a year. Assuming further that electrical power stations have an average of an 80 per cent load factor and that a tonne of coal is equivalent to 7400 kilowatt-hours, then one tonne of uranium is equivalent to about 24000 tonnes of coal.

There have also been construction delays and technical and economic difficulties with existing thermal reactors, some of which are inevitable in any large-scale, technologically sophisticated programme, but some of which reflect political opposition to nuclear programmes, either at the national level as in Sweden, or at the local level as in France and West Germany (Surrey and Huggett, 1976). In addition, more stringent safety requirements have resulted in delays and increased costs (Krymm, 1975).

The economic uncertainties about the rate of introduction of nuclear power in the future remain considerable, and are increasingly bound up with the politics of nuclear technology. The latter will also influence control and trade in uranium and thorium resources. Even more important, given their close links with nuclear weapons, national and international policies towards plutonium, uranium enrichment and the reprocessing of nuclear fuels will remain highly 'politicised'. The unresolved problems of transport and storage of radioactive fuels and wastes, and their implications for both safety and civil liberties, are not simply the concern of just a few 'radicals' and 'eco-freaks'. Generally acceptable solutions are unlikely in the foreseeable future.

Nuclear fusion   The source of energy in nuclear fusion is the same as in nuclear fission, namely, the transformation of mass into energy. Fission takes place through the splitting of heavy elements, and is the basis of the atomic bomb. Fusion takes place through the coalescence of light elements, and is the basis of the hydrogen bomb. In particular, a combination of two isotopes of hydrogen — deuterium and tritium – together with the common metal lithium – can be transformed into hydrogen and helium, with the release of enormous amounts of energy. According to the World Energy Conference (1974), the available resources of deuterium, tritium and lithium are such that the potential energy from nuclear fusion can be considered as infinite.

The problem lies elsewhere, namely, in demonstrating the technical feasibility and economic viability of controlled nuclear fusion. The reaction takes place at temperatures of the order of 50–100 million degrees centigrade, when substances are no longer gases but 'plasma' (or atoms stripped of their electrons), and when no material container could hold such a plasma. The problems of keeping such a plasma stable at the correct temperature and getting energy out of it are far from being solved, in spite of the expenditure of considerable resources over the past twenty years. Other possibilities are also being explored, including the bombardment of small pellets of deuterium and tritium by a powerful laser beam or by beams of charged particles. Foley has concluded, '. . . fusion power is an attractive but distant possibility. For those countries that can afford the research it is probably a worthwhile speculative investment. But even if the work is success-ful . . . fusion power will make very little difference to patterns of world energy consumption over the next fifty years' (Foley, 1976, p. 197).

Geothermal energy   Geothermal energy derives from the internal heat of the earth's core. Favourable regions for the exploitation of natural geothermal energy are those where the earth's crust is thin or fissured, particularly volcanic regions. Small-scale commercial exploitation dates back to Italy in 1904, followed by Iceland in 1928 and New Zealand in 1958 (Garnish, 1976). By 1974 about 1200 MWe were generated from geothermal sources, mostly in Italy, New Zealand and the U.S.A. In Iceland, the main emphasis is on the use of hot water for space heating; the 60 per cent of the population that currently rely on geothermal district heating schemes will reach 90 per cent in the near future. Another such scheme operates on a smaller scale in Budapest. In New Zealand, the wet steam field at Wairekei has been supplying 192 MWe since 1958, and a further 110 MW of steam heat is used in a pulp and paper mill. Special conditions (of temperature and pressure) are required for geothermal based electricity production, but lower-grade heat sources have many direct applications.

Some sixty countries are known to be active in geothermal R & D, and all the main producers of electricity from geothermal sources have plans for expansion in the next few years. There are also plans for the expansion of use in district heating, in greenhouses and in pulp and paper mills. Sites on the Pacific 'ring of fire' – New Zealand, New Guinea, Japan, the U.S.S.R. and the Americas – are thought to be very promising for further development. Steam fields have been established along the African rift valley, and also in the Azores, Italy, the Balkans, the Middle East, Indonesia, India, China and some of the Caribbean islands.

According to the World Energy Conference, naturally occurring geothermal resources may amount to the thermal equivalent of 1500×10^9 tonnes of coal to a depth of 10 kilometres, and 300×10^9 tonnes to a depth of 3 kilometres. About 4 per cent of this total can raise steam of sufficient quality to produce electricity. Because of advances in oil technology, drilling at depths of 4–6 kms has become widespread and depths of over 9 kms have been achieved in the U.S.S.R. However, drilling costs rise steeply with depth, and the costs of distributing low-grade heat remain high. It is therefore likely that – electricity apart – the exploitation of geothermal sources will depend for some time to come on the geographical proximity of industrial and domestic users.

In the longer term, technology for using so-called dry-rock sources of geothermal energy would, if developed, increase the potential for geothermal energy enormously. The World Energy Conference (1974) estimated total heat in all rocks to a depth of 10 kms as thermally equivalent to about 50×10^{15} tonnes of coal, of which about one-quarter is situated under land.

Direct solar energy   According to the World Energy Conference (1974), the solar energy reaching the earth's surface each year is thermally equivalent to about 130×10^{12} tonnes of coal, four orders of magnitude greater than the world's commercial energy consumption each year. According to Foley (1976), about one-third of this solar energy is used in the hydrological cycle; one-third of one per cent in wind, waves and ocean currents, and the remaining two-thirds is absorbed and reflected. The amount required for maintaining life through biosynthesis is at present very small compared to these other magnitudes.

Since 1973 interest in solar energy has grown enormously, and, given its abundance, the objectives of R & D programmes are simply defined in terms of the costs of collection and use. Economically viable systems have so far been achieved on any scale only in greenhouses, the production of salt and distilled water, and the provision of domestic hot water in certain countries. Because of the low density of solar energy, high-grade uses will be difficult to achieve. The solar energy falling on twenty million square kilometres of the world's deserts may be about four hundred times total world energy production, but the technological and economic problems of collection and transmission are formidable. The same is true of some of the 'space-age' proposals such as the use of very expensive solar cells (though the collapse in transistor chip production costs *may* be repeated).

In the immediate future, greater possibilities for improvement exist in the relatively simple technologies for domestic water and space heating, cooking, and industrial process heat for small-scale industry in the poor countries. Between 30 and 50 per cent of energy consumption is in the form of low-grade heat in the rich countries, and an even higher proportion in poor countries. Mass production could eventually reduce equipment costs considerably. In the meantime, the key technological problems remain those of energy storage, and the efficient use of this low-density but high-grade energy source.

Hydro-electric power Although water power was traditionally used for mechanical applications, hydro-power installations are now primarily for electricity generation (HEP). Efficiencies in energy conversion of 90 per cent can be achieved, compared with a maximum of about 35 per cent in fossil-fuelled central power stations. The theoretical amount of energy obtained from an HEP system is determined by the volume flow of water and the vertical distance through which it falls. But only a fraction of the theoretical amount can be effectively converted into electricity. Seasonal variations in water flow mean that at some periods in the year sufficient conversion capacity may not exist. The building of dams leads to evaporation of water and to the slowing down of water flows because of silting. In some remote places it is physically difficult to build dams and to install turbines.

According to the World Energy Conference (1974), potential world HEP capacity amounts to about 2.3×10^6 MW, calculated on the basis of annual average flows through exploitable regions. Assuming an 80 per cent load factor in electrical power stations and a 30 per cent efficiency in energy conversion in fossil-fuel stations, this is the equivalent to a primary annual energy use of about 7×10^9 tonnes of coal.

At present, about 14 per cent of the world's HEP potential is being exploited. Immediate expansion of capacity is not without problems, especially for the world's poor countries. Capital costs are high and the product is electricity, the expanded use of which depends in large part on industrialisation and the ability to purchase durable consumer goods. Rivers and water have alternative – and not always complementary – uses for fishing, navigation and irrigation, and HEP schemes can cause widespread ecological damage.

Wind power Wind was, until a hundred years ago, the main motive force for ships and a major source of energy for industry and agriculture. The usable amount of energy available with existing technology has been conservatively estimated at between 1 and 20 million MW. Assuming that this were converted into electricity, it would be equivalent to an annual energy production of between about 3 and 60×10^9 tonnes of coal.

The feasibility of electricity generation from wind was proved by experiments on both sides of the Atlantic in the 1940s and 1950s, but these were abandoned given the abundance of cheap oil. Since then advances in the related field of rotor design for helicopters have led to robust and reliable engineering configurations that can be adapted for windmills without extensive development work. Because of the low energy density of wind, there are severe design constraints, effectively limiting electrical output to between 500 and 1000 kW at each installation. Enormous numbers would be required to contribute significantly to the capacity of large electricity systems, but the World Energy Conference (1974) argues that installations would be no more unsightly than an electric power grid, that the variability in power availability would be very little different from hydro-electric power, and that up to 10 per cent of total electricity supply through windmills could easily be accommodated in the U.S.A. and other industrialised countries. However, as with other unconventional energy sources, it is not necessary to assess its contribution by comparison with, for example, base-load nuclear stations connected by a grid. The contribution of numerous small units can be of great significance in certain remote localities, where the cost of grid extensions is high, or in the poor countries. Neither is it the case, in a well-planned system, that 'availability' from a mix of unconventional sources need be lower than from centralised power stations, especially if the problem of energy storage is resolved.

Wave power Wave power can be considered the hydraulic derivative of wind. No assessment of total or exploitable world resources of wave power appear to be available, although a recent report has estimated that 900 miles of wave generators off the north-east coast of Scotland would produce sufficient energy to meet about half the U.K.'s electricity requirements – namely, 30,000 MW (G.B. Central Policy Review Staff, 1974). However, many problems remain concerning stability of structures in a hostile environment, anchorage, danger to shipping and form of energy transmission (electricity or hydrogen).

Wood, dung and waste   Wood, dung and natural waste materials are renewable sources of solid, carbonaceous fuel. According to the World Energy Conference (1974), only 4 per cent of total world energy in 1967 was derived from them, whilst nearly half the world's population was dependent upon them. Desai (1977) has estimated that about 70 per cent of the energy consumed in Kenya and in India in 1970 was from these sources, as compared to less than 1 per cent in the industrially advanced countries. Makhijani and Poole (1975) have estimated that when wood, dung and waste are included, annual energy consumption per head in the world's underdeveloped countries increases from 0.2–0.7 tce to 0.9–1.8 tce. The more efficient production and utilisation of energy from these sources must inevitably be a major concern for the world's poor countries in the next twenty to forty years.

It has also been suggested they should become more important in the total world energy balance in future. Foley (1976) has argued that little reliance could be placed in this context on the possibilities of human waste. He calculates that if all the U.K.'s human waste were collected and treated, total energy production through 'biogas' plant would not be more than 0.37×10^6 tce in a country with a population of 55 million. If we assume a future world with a population of between 6 and 12 billion, then the total amount of energy produceable through human waste would be between about 0.04 and 0.08×10^9 tce in a world that, as we shall see later in this chapter, could have energy requirements a thousand times greater.

However, Desai's calculations suggest a more promising future for other carbonaceous sources. On the basis of his figures for India in 1970, 130×10^6 tce of energy came from firewood, vegetable waste and manure (including animal manure and fertilizer uses). Given the same future world population estimates as above, this could mean between 10^9 and 2×10^9 tce of world energy production from these sources, using Indian technology, 1970 vintage.

The development of 'fuel crops' offers the possibility of a novel energy source, albeit a small-scale one until much more research has been undertaken. Fast-growing plants, such as the water hyacinth, provide at least two crops a year in suitable conditions, compared with perhaps two crops a century for mature trees. Many other plants are under investigation (for example, seaweed, grasses, root crops), as well as agricultural wastes (such as straw) and algae, together with the relative merits of direct use of the dry matter for food, heating, paper-making, fertilizers, or for methane production (biogas) and fermentation and distillation into liquid fuels. It is too early as yet to ascertain the potential contribution from fuel crops, or to provide definitive assessments of net energy efficiencies and land, water and labour requirements, but it would be hasty to dismiss this area of research as inconsequential to world energy supplies over the next seventy-five years.

Tidal power   The source of tidal power is not the radiation of the sun, but the gravitational forces of the moon. The World Energy Conference (1974) estimates about 2 per cent of the world's tidal energy as being potentially usable, amounting to 64,000 MW. Foley (1976) and Hubbert (1968) conclude that, on the basis of achieved conversion efficienies of about 25 per cent, about 16,000 MW of electrical energy could be generated, equivalent in primary energy terms to about 50×10^6 tonnes of coal each year.

The Rance tidal power station in northern France has a maximum output capacity of 240 MW. Other schemes on the Severn Estuary in the U.K., the Dutch Delta plan and Passamaquoddy Bay (U.S./Canada) are currently receiving considerable attention. The greater exploitation of tidal power faces many problems. Given the fluctuation in tides, they are inherently inefficient. Availability depends on the lunar cycle, whereas demand tends to move on a solar cycle. Suitable sites are difficult to find. In particular, the building of barrages across wide estuaries could involve large, if often unforeseeable, costs and problems of a technological, ecological and environmental nature. Some of these problems could be overcome by the construction of an inner dam as a pumped storage facility.

Energy conversion   Some of the potentially important energy conversion processes have already been touched upon above: the gasification and liquefiaction of coal and the use of waste, dung, firewood and 'fuel crops'. During the twentieth century, the most significant energy conversion system has been the generation and distribution of electricity. Until the early 1970s world electrical energy production had been doubling roughly once every ten years. By 1971, about a quarter of total electricity output was generated by hydro-electric power, and three-quarters by fossil fuels. In terms of primary energy inputs, electricity accounted for just over a quarter of total world commercial energy.

The advantages of electricity – especially compared to coal – are ease of transportation and use and the possibilities of greater economies of scale in the burning of fuel. The spread of electricity use has been closely associated with the growth of mechanisation and the process industries and of consumer durables in the home. The disadvantages are now becoming more apparent with the higher real costs of energy.

The first is the inefficiency of energy conversion and transmission processes. At the beginning of the century the generation efficiency was about

10 per cent, and this has risen to about 35 per cent in a best practice plant today. Improvements in conversion have come about through higher turbine temperatures and pressures and through economies of scale; the possibilities of further improvement in existing technologies are now limited. Improvements in transmission have come about through using ever-higher voltages; here the possibilities for further improvements are technically greater than in generation but require large capital expenditures. Another major possibility may be much wider use of district heating, where low-grade waste heat from electrical power stations is recycled for use in space and water heating, or where heating is provided centrally from geothermal steam wells and boilerhouses.

The second problem of electricity use relates to the difficulty of storage. This is particularly important given the inability both of nuclear reactors supplying electrical energy to adjust their supply to fluctuating demand, and of solar, wind and even hydro-electric sources to maintain a steady and predictable level of supply. Considerable attention is therefore being given to various possibilities for the large- and small-scale storage of electricity – and of other forms of energy: for example, pumped or underground water, flywheels, compressed air, heat, electro-chemical (batteries), electro-magnetic, electrolytic (e.g. hydrogen). However, as yet, none of these methods has been shown to be technically and economically feasible on a large scale.

Another related problem receiving increased attention is the effective use of low-grade heat, which, as Lovins (1977) states, accounts for at least 30–50 per cent of energy used in the industrially advanced countries, and where a number of routes offer considerable potential for the future: district heating, waste heat recuperation, solar energy and geothermal energy. One promising line is the further development of the heat pump, which reverses the principle of the refrigerator and extracts heat from a low-temperature source and upgrades it to a higher temperature. For an electric heat pump, overall efficiency would be nearly 70 per cent compared to the 50–60 per cent of a direct fired central heating system, and heat pumps offer considerable flexibility in combination with other heating systems.

Conclusions on Energy Resources

Tables 5.4. and 5.5 summarise this discussion on resources. They inevitably include some degree of arbitrariness in the estimates of reserves and resources; in the conversion into tonnes coal equivalent sometimes on a thermal basis and sometimes on a primary equivalence basis; and in selecting the problems and the uncertainties to report. Three unambiguous conclusions can be drawn from them.

The first is that the physical availability of energy on the earth will not be a problem over at least the next one hundred years. Ultimately recoverable

TABLE 5.4   *Summary of reserves, resources and uncertainties for depletable energy resources*

Fuel	Proven & possible reserves (10^9 tce)	Ultimately recoverable resources (10^9 tce)	Uncertainties and problems
Coal	1000	5600–7700	Environmental costs of open cast mining; cost and ease of transport and use.
Oil	300–375	276–2760	Size of recoverable resources.
Natural gas	200	150–1500	Size of recoverable resources; transport and storage.
Shale oil	negligible	1200	Environmental and economic costs.
Tar sand	negligible	225	Environmental and economic costs.
SUB-TOTAL: (Fossil-hydrocarbons)	1500–1575	7451–13,385	
Uranium thermal reactor	80–100	?	Size of uranium reserves, radioactive wastes.
Uranium breeder reactor	0	At least 5000	Plutonium, proliferation, economics.
Thorium breeder reactor	0	At least 4000	Problems with the fuel cycle.
Thermonuclear fusion	0	Virtually unlimited	Proving technical feasibility.
Geothermal: Wet rock	12–60	300–1500	Using low-grade heat.
Dry rock	0	50,000,000	Proving technical feasibility.
TOTAL (excl. fusion and geothermal dry rock	1600–1700	At least 17,000–24,000	

Note: Equivalence in tonnes of coal calculated on a thermal basis for hydrocarbons and geothermal; on a primary fuel equivalence basis for nuclear energy.

fossil resources would last 200–300 years at annual rates of world energy consumption ten times those existing today. Similar annual rates could be satisfied a thousand times over by the theoretical potential of renewable energy resources. As with other natural resources, the problem is one of ensuring that there are technologies that make the use of these resources technically feasible as well as economically and environmentally acceptable.

TABLE 5.5   *Summary of potential problems and uncertainties for renewable energy resources*

Energy source	Proven potential (10^9 tce/year)	Exploitable potential (10^9 tce/year)	Theoretical potential (10^9 tce/year	Uncertainties and problems
Direct solar	?	?	80,000	Technologies of storage and use; large-scale applications.
Hydro-electric power	7	?	?	Capital costs, alternative uses of water in less-developed countries.
Wind power	?	3–60	400	Storage.
Firewood, dung, waste, fuel crops	1–2	?	40	Collection for use; net energy gain.
Tidal power	0.05	?	10	Environmental effects; capital costs; limited potential; storage.
TOTAL	At least 8	At least 11–69	124,000	

Note: Equivalence in tonnes of coal calculated on a thermal basis for solar energy and for firewood, dung and waste; on a primary fuel equivalence basis for hydro-electric, wind and tidal power.

The second conclusion regards the importance of coal in satisfying the world's future energy requirements. It accounts for well over half of proven and possible fossil fuel reserves. Even with the advent of breeder reactors, it could still account for nearly a third of ultimately recoverable energy resources.

The third conclusion is that, given both the practical difficulties of exploitation and the limited size of the theoretical potential, it is unlikely that tidal power or firewood, dung and wastes will ever play a major role in satisfying the world's energy needs.

Beyond these conclusions there remain many uncertainties, problems and risks. Assessing risks and uncertainties, and ranking the importance of problems, inevitably involves strong doses of both technical and value judgements. Ours will quickly become apparent in the identification of the factors that we think deserve particular attention in the production and efficient use of energy.

There are major uncertainties about the size of ultimately recoverable resources of oil and natural gas. Although these resources may turn out to be considerable, they also may not. A strong case can therefore be made for conserving oil and natural gas increasingly for premium uses. Unlike Kahn, we are not optimistic about the large-scale economic exploitation of shale oil and tar sands. The nature of the extraction process is such that environmental costs will be high and, in the absence of radical and unforeseeable break-throughs, so will economic costs. Future energy policies should not depend heavily on shale oil and tar sands.

We are not optimistic that nuclear energy will necessarily solve the world's energy problems. Like Foley (1976) we believe that the possibilities of thermonuclear fusion should be pursued as a potentially profitable long-term bet, but that we should not count on it being successful. Like Sir Brian Flowers and his colleagues of the U.K.Royal Commission on Environmental Pollution (1976), we are concerned about the large-scale introduction of the plutonium-fuelled, sodium-cooled fast breeder reactor, and its implications for safety, nuclear proliferation and civil liberties. We also have severe doubts about its supposed economic attractions. Even compared with other systems of generating nuclear electricity, the technology is very demanding and the technical and political consequences of nuclear accidents are unpredictable. It is a relatively inflexible and technically inefficient energy source, given that in most cases it can only be used to generate electricity at present. For all these reasons we favour a cautious and diversified policy towards the introduction of nuclear energy, with its gradual introduction after the careful testing of a variety of configurations including the High Temperature Reactor. We also think that greater attention should be paid to the thorium-fuelled reactors.

Given all these problems, we see no reason to ignore the large potential for the development of solar, wind and geothermal power. As Tables 5.4 and 5.5 show, the scope for growth could be enormous, and it is doubtful whether the technical or economic problems are any more difficult to solve than those of the sodium-cooled fast breeder reactor or of thermonuclear fusion.

5. ENERGY CONSERVATION

The considerable increase in energy prices since 1973 has led to greater concern about the conservation of energy. Governments have launched energy-saving programmes, set up committees of enquiry, published numerous reports and urged users to 'save it'. The rate of growth of energy consumption has slowed down, but the extent to which this has resulted from economic recession or from energy conservation is still a matter for analysis and debate.

Over the time horizons that we are considering here, there will obviously be considerable scope for improvements in the efficiency of energy conversion and use, just as there have been in the past. In the nineteenth century there were many improvements in, for example, the specific fuel consumption of the steam engine. Since then there have been many well-documented examples of increased fuel efficiency per unit of output in, for example, aluminium and iron and steel production, the generation of electricity, air and rail transport, and domestic space heating. In some cases these savings have been attributable to technical changes (for example, higher boiler temperatures and pressures), in others to changes in fuel mix (for example, from coal to oil and natural gas in domestic heating). But not all technical changes have increased the efficiency of energy use. The combination of price and convenience offered by the private motor car in the O.E.C.D. countries has led to a drastic shift from public and rail transport to private and road transport (Leach, 1972) and to the greater use of energy.

In this section we shall examine some of the possibilities for improving the efficiencies of energy conversion and use in the next twenty-five years and in the next seventy-five years. Our conclusions are summarised in Table 5.6. (p. 143). Needless to say, precise forecasts over such time horizons will probably turn out to be badly wrong, because of unforeseen changes in patterns of final energy demand and in techniques for energy conversion and use. Nonetheless, such long-term horizons are necessary for a comprehensive renovation of the housing, industrial and transport infrastructure, the nature of which will have a strong influence on the efficiency of energy use.

Domestic use   In the Western industrially advanced countries between a fifth and a quarter of all energy is directly consumed in the domestic (or housing) sector, where typically between 60 and 70 per cent is used for space heating and cooling and for water heating, and the remainder for cooking lighting, refrigeration and other appliances (Freeman, 1974; Chapman, 1976). It is, of course, a matter of judgement which of these categories of energy consumption are for essential, useful or frivolous purposes. We conclude that the main items of consumption are necessary for survival, while the remainder are essential for domestic comfort and liberation from domestic chores. We doubt that the main item of consumption – namely, heating – is influenced significantly by a desire to consume conspicuously, although it has been pointed out to us that energy is used to heat swimming pools in California. However, patterns of residential energy consumption will be influenced considerably by climate.

There is plenty of evidence that the technical efficiency of energy use in the home could be increased considerably, even in the short term. Much of today's housing stock is old, or was built when real energy prices were falling and energy conservation was not a major objective of building design. Much the same is true of energy-intensive domestic appliances. Relatively simple improvements in insulation could lead to considerable savings. According to both the G.B. Department of Energy (1976) and the Ford Foundation Study (Freeman, 1974), savings in useful energy (i.e. the energy needed to perform a given task) could be between 10 and 20 per cent by the year 2000. Beyond that time the effects of building new housing to higher standards of insulation and conservation would begin to make themselves felt. The G.B. Department of Energy estimates that total savings in useful energy between now and then could be 35 per cent, whilst Lovins puts them as high as 80 per cent (1977).

Services In the Western industrially advanced countries, services (private and public) account for between 10 and 15 per cent of useful energy consumption, once again mainly for heating of office buildings. Savings of between 10 and 20 per cent have been estimated as feasible for the year 2000 by a Ford Foundation study (Freeman, 1974) and the G.B. Department of Energy (1976). Beyond that time they could, according to the G.B. Department of Energy (1976) and to Lovins (1977) amount to between 35 and 50 per cent by comparison with today.

Industry Industry is the biggest consumer of energy in the Western industrially advanced countries, accounting for between 35 and 45 per cent of the total. A small number of sectors, mainly concerned with the processing of materials, typically account for about two-thirds of this total: iron and steel, chemicals, aluminium, building materials and paper. In most other industries energy accounts for a small proportion of total costs, a significant component being space heating. Most of today's stock of industrial capital was installed when real energy prices were falling. It is therefore all the more remarkable that increases in the efficiency of use have been achieved – for example, up to 20 per cent in the U.K. between 1960 and 1975 (Chesshire and Buckley, 1976). This has happened because of the continuous search for economies in energy consumption in the heavily-consuming process industries, the generally higher levels of technical efficiency embodied in the renewed capital stock (e.g. oxygen steel making and the dry cement process), replacement of many coal-burning appliances by those using oil and natural gas, and changes in the product mix and raw material base.

Given the heterogeneity of patterns of energy use and the rapid pace of technical change in industry, it is very difficult to foresee and to assess the potential for energy saving in future. No doubt similar economies in space heating can be achieved in industry as in the domestic and commercial sectors. But it is unlikely that oil and gas can be substituted for coal indefinitely. Improvements in methods of burning coal will become critical to the potential for industrial energy savings in future.

There are widely differing views about the feasibility of large-scale savings in energy in the process industries referred to above. A Dutch study (Over and Sjoerdsma, 1974) concluded that in process industries accounting for 42 per cent of industrial energy consumption in the Netherlands savings of only 8 per cent could be expected in energy process efficiencies by the year 2000. In a Ford Foundation study (Myers, 1974), however, it was estimated that savings in useful energy in these sectors in the year 2000 could be between 40 and 50 per cent. Perhaps these very different assessments reflect the relatively higher price – and consequently higher technical efficiency in use – of energy in Western Europe than in the U.S.A. It is our judgement that, compared with today's patterns of industrial energy consumption in Western Europe, savings in useful energy could be between 15 and 25 per cent until the year 2000, and between 30 and 50 per cent until the year 2050.

Transport Transport accounts for about a quarter of all energy consumed in the U.S.A. and about 15 per cent in Western Europe (Leach, 1973; Freeman, 1974). In both regions, road transport now accounts for the major part of total transport – the car for about 15 per cent of all energy in the U.S.A. and for about 10 per cent in Western Europe. Thus, whilst technical change will lead to improvements in diesel engines for heavy vehicles, loco-motives and ships, and in turbines for aircraft and ships, by far the most important area for potential energy saving is road transport. In 1970 the world's road vehicles consumed about 500 million tonnes of oil – about one-sixth of total production. Foley (1976) has estimated that if American cars were built to the standards of energy consumption already practised else-where in the world the savings of oil would amount to about 80 million tonnes a year.

Beyond this obvious and important saving, increases in fuel efficiency compared to present patterns of road transport will come from two direc-tions. First, those related to the road vehicle itself will involve reduced drag, improved and smaller engines, improved transmission, a special class of urban vehicle and the adoption of diesel engines. According to Wildhorn (1975), they could lead to fuel savings of 20–40 per cent in the U.S.A. It is our assumption that no technical obstacle will stop these savings being achieved by the year 2000.

Second, beyond 2000, there are the possibilities for redesigning cities, towns and transport systems so as to reduce drastically the demand for road transport. It would be particularly important to reduce the demand for private cars in urban areas, given that they use a high proportion of all trans-port's energy. Alternatives like buses, trains and trams are readily available.

In order to assess the longer-term possibilities of energy saving let us assume that, through urban design and public transport policy, we eliminate private road vehicles for passenger transport completely. According to Leach (1973), the efficiency in energy use of public passenger transport is three to ten times greater. Compared to present patterns of energy consumption, the total saving of energy would therefore be between two-thirds and 90 per cent of energy for private road passenger transport. According to Chapman (1976), the energy consumed in providing private road passenger transport accounts for about 16 per cent of the U.K. total (this includes the energy needed for making and maintaining cars). This means that total savings could amount to between 10 and 14 per cent of total energy consumption. If we also assume improvements in efficiencies in useful energy in commercial road transportation of 20-40 per cent, further savings amounting to between 1 and 3 per cent of total energy consumption could be expected.

Energy conversion Energy can be lost during its use, or during its conversion and transmission from source to point of use. In terms of the conservation of energy, fossil fuels are, in general, relatively efficient in transmission and inefficient in use; much of the above discussion has been about reducing such inefficiencies in use, particularly in space heating, industrial processes and the internal combustion engine. Electricity, on the other hand, is, in general, efficient at the point of use, but the conversion of heat into electricity is a thermodynamically inefficient process. In the U.K. for example, the average efficiency is 30 per cent and the best about 35 per cent. With present-day conversion technology, no further significant increases can be expected, although with present-day materials, the maximum theoretical efficiency of conversion from heat to work is about 60 per cent. The utilisation of waste heat from power stations would enable this efficiency to be reached, perhaps assisted by heat pumps. Since electricity accounts typically for about 30 per cent of primary energy inputs in Western Europe, we could – on the basis of the diffusion of existing best practice in electrical generation technology by the year 2000 – expect savings equivalent to 10 per cent of all primary energy consumption. Assuming overall efficiencies of 60 per cent in electricity generation through combined heat and power by 2050, energy savings by comparison to those of today would be about 18 per cent of primary consumption. Further savings could be expected by using waste heat from industrial processes, and from a better matching of low-grade heat needs through, say, a greater use of solar energy. Unfortunately we do not have the data that would enable us to assess how important these further possibilities for saving could be.

Conservation Proposals: Conclusions

Before attempting to summarise the implications of the above discussion for future energy savings, it is first worth stressing its limitations. To begin with, we have not examined systematically the effects of changes in product mix on the efficiency of energy use in the years 2000 to 2050. This is because we do not know what changes will take place. However, we think that we have discussed the main areas where changes would influence energy conservation significantly in future. We cannot conceive of a modernised world without considerable amounts of energy being used to transform materials, although such a world may restrict much more severely than today the use of the private passenger car with very considerable implications for energy conservation.

We have not said anything about the effects of energy pricing. Clearly, the higher the price of energy, the greater the incentive for conservation, but how high would it have to be over the next twenty-five to seventy-five years in order to achieve the savings set out in Table 5.6? Unfortunately we do not know, and we do not think that anyone does. In addition, energy conservation in space heating, in transportation and in the use of waste heat depends in the long run as much – if not more – on public policy decisions of a long-term nature about housing, urban development and public transport, than it does on individuals comparing alternative costs and benefits.

The very different experiences of the U.S.A. and of Western Europe in the development of public transport, in the fuel efficiency of the passenger car, in the use of energy in the process industries and in the domestic and service sectors, suggest that changes in the levels of energy prices of a magnitude equal to their variation across the Atlantic over the past seventy years can make a significant impact on energy conservation. Changes of such a magnitude have taken place since 1973, although relative costs have changed less dramatically than is often assumed. We still do not know whether they will be sufficient to bring about the level of energy saving that we have described above. With petrol for cars still at about 60 cents a gallon, we are inclined to doubt it for the U.S.A.

Table 5.6 summarises the possibilities for energy savings in both conversion and use that could be envisaged until the year 2000 and the year 2050. With perhaps the exception of the high estimates for the domestic and commercial sectors in the year 2050, the savings are considerable by comparison with the patterns of consumption and use technology prevailing in Western Europe in the early 1970s. By comparison with those prevailing in the U.S.A. they would probably be considerably greater. Schipper and Lichtenberg (1976) have estimated that the U.S.A. would use about one-third less energy if it were as technically efficient in energy conversion and use as Sweden.

By comparison with prevailing Western European technology, the scope for savings appears to be considerable: from a fifth to more than a third by the year 2000, and from nearly half to three-quarters by the year 2050. Unfortunately there are no comprehensive historical data on trends in energy conservation with which these estimates can be compared. However, they can be compared with estimates made by two people with very different positions on the future of energy, Herman Kahn and Amory Lovins of Friends of the Earth.

Kahn's (1976) estimates amount to an annual rate of improvement in energy use per unit of output of 1.4 per cent until the year 2025, and of 1.1 per cent from now until 2076. Our estimates have greater variance and a higher average: from 0.9–1.7 per cent until the year 2000, and 0.8–1.8 per cent between now and the year 2050. Lovins and Price (1975) argue that, as a result of a vigorous programme of energy conservation, the U.S.A. should be able to reduce primary energy consumption per head over the period 2010–40 to a third or a quarter of today's level: in other words, to a range of 3–4 tonnes

TABLE 5.6 *Possibilities for energy saving in conversion and use in the industrially advanced countries until 2000 & 2050*

Sector	% of total energy use	Main uses of energy	Possible % savings in energy use until 2000	Possible overall % savings in energy use until 2000	Possible % savings in energy use until 2050	Possible overall % savings in energy use until 2050
Domestic	20–25	Space heating (60%)	10–20	2–5	35–80	7–20
Services	10–15	Space heating (50%)	10–20	1–3	35–50	4–10
Industry	35–45	Process industries (60%)	15–25	5–11	30–50	11–23
Transport	15–25	Road transport (80%)	20–40 on road	3–10	67–90 (on road passenger) 20–40 (on other road)	10–14 1–3
Total percentage savings in energy use				11–29		33–70
Percentage savings in energy conversion			10 (of 2000 energy demand)	7–9	18 (of 2050 energy demand)	5–12
TOTAL PERCENTAGE POTENTIAL SAVINGS IN ENERGY CONSERVATION AND USE				20–36		45–75

143

TABLE 5.7   Profiles of future energy demand: a comparison of alternatives

	The year 2000			The year 2050		
Profile character	Annual consumption (10⁹ tce)	% in 1974 poor countries	Cumulative consumption 1974–2000 (10⁹ tce)	Annual consumption (10⁹ tce)	% in 1974 poor countries	Cumulative consumption 1974–2050 (10⁹ tce)
High growth, unequal						
United Nations (1971)	36	17	485	700	20	11500
Saturation variant	12–21	20–40	260–350	26–70	65–75	1000–2000
Low growth, unequal						
Zero energy growth	8	17	208	8	17	608
Low growth, more equal						
Zero energy growth	8	74–79	208	8	77–85	608
Zero per head energy growth	10–13	74–79	230–270	12–22	77–85	800–1100
High growth, more equal						
Energy to burn	45–70	40	585–1000	171–326	77–85	7000–13000
U.S.A., 1970	25–40	40	390–540	74–142	77–85	3000–6000
Sweden, 1970	18–25	40	330–390	37–71	77–85	1500–3000
Low conservation	15–22	40	290–370	20–39	77–85	1200–1800
High conservation	11–15	40	250–290	10–19	77–85	700–1200

Note: For the high-growth/unequal profile, cumulative energy consumptions were calculated as the areas under an exponential curve. In all other profiles, the curves are logistic. The areas under them were calculated both by assuming a straight line growth of energy consumption between 1975 and 2050, and by measuring the area beneath a smooth curve on semi-logarithmic paper. The latter method was also used to calculate annual energy consumption between 1974 and 2000 for the zero per head energy growth and for the high growth, more equal profiles.

coal equivalent each year. Our estimates, based on a relatively high level of Western European energy consumption of 6 tonnes coal equivalent in the early 1970s, would amount to between 3.8 and 4.8 tce in the year 2000 and to between 1.5 and 3.3 tce in the year 2050. The lower estimate for 2050 is, therefore, considerably lower than that of Lovins.

However, Lovins goes on to say that 'even in the case of four-fold shrinkage, the resulting society could be instantly recognisable to a visitor from the 1960s and need in no sense be a pastoralist's Utopia . . .'. Neither is the society that we are envisaging, but the lower estimate assumes the abolition of the private passenger car, which is a considerable change by comparison with the 1960s. If we relax this assumption and assume instead a 20–40 per cent improvement in energy use in the private passenger car between now and 2050, then the maximum energy saving in the year 2050 would be 67 per cent compared to today, implying a consumption level equivalent to 2 tce per head per year, and an annual rate of improvement of 1.5 per cent. This is still above the level and the rate of improvement suggested by both Lovins and Kahn.

For all these reasons, we shall consider two possibilities for conservation in the profiles that we shall now go on to discuss. First, 'low conservation', with an annual rate of improvement in conservation of 0.8 per cent until the year 2050. Second, 'high conservation', with an annual rate of improvement of 1.8 per cent, aiming beyond the simple elimination of obvious waste from the existing system towards major changes in physical planning, public transport and pricing compared to Western Europe in the mid-1970s.

Finally, we must mention one major gap in this discussion of conservation, namely, the possibilities for improvement in the utilisation of non-commercial energy in the agricultural regions of the poor countries (already mentioned in chapter 4). We suspect that the possibilities are enormous, but we do not have the space to discuss them in this paper, the main focus of which is the possibility of world-wide modernisation.

6. Profiles of Energy Demand

Before elaborating profiles for the future based on economic growth and international equality, we must define them in terms that are meaningful and operational in the debate about energy futures. Our view is that the high-growth/unequal profile can be equated to a continuation of the situation existing between, say, 1960 and the oil crisis of 1973. The low-growth/unequal profile can be equated either to a world in economic crisis, where there is no growth in energy demand because there is no economic growth, or to a world that is at the same time elitist, politically conservative and very concerned about ecological balance. The low-growth/more-equal profile might reflect the concern of certain groups about the ecological and social effects of continuing growth in energy production and use. The high-growth/more-equal profile reflects the traditional goal of most political and economic philosophies, namely, material plenty for all of mankind. The implications of these profiles for future energy demand are set out in Table 5.7.

High Growth with Unequal Distribution: A Return to 'Normality'

The large discoveries of oil and natural gas after the Second World War increased available world energy reserves, led to a lowering of real energy prices, reduced national energy self-sufficiency in some of the major industrialised countries and enabled industrial and urban development to become more footloose. It provided a stimulus to new industries and to the growth of mass vehicle ownership and use, reinforcing the decline of indigenous higher-cost coal industries and of much of the public transport system.

By the late 1960s some warning signals began to appear. Demand for energy increased at a faster rate than GNP in the O.E.C.D. countries and exceeded forecast levels. The coal industry was beset with many difficulties and the growth of nuclear capacity fell short of earlier expectations. An inevitable upwards pressure on prices followed the emergence of a seller's market. One of the key factors leading to this situation, if not the most important, was the increase in the absolute level of U.S. oil imports from 25 million tonnes in 1950 to 173 million in 1974 – from 14 per cent U.S. consumption in 1954 to 40 per cent in late 1974 – and a sharp and sudden rise in its dependence on OPEC sources. In 1976 the U.S.A. imported 265 million tonnes of oil, 46 per cent of total consumption.

Since the huge increase in world oil prices by the OPEC cartel, some people have argued for a return to the good old days of low-priced oil. Sometimes the argument is dressed up in the clothes of neoclassical economics: monopolies are bad and the costs of producing oil in the Middle East are low. Sometimes it is straight power politics: the OPEC cartel is a declaration of economic warfare imposing a huge drain on the Western industrialised countries' balance of payments, increasing inflationary pressures, imposing huge economic transformations and provoking a huge indebtedness in the world's poorer countries. Both types of argument are particularly prevalent in the U.S.A. An almost pure version of the latter appeared recently in *Business Week* (20 December 1976) entitled 'How OPEC'S High Prices Strangle World Growth'. However, it is the case that higher oil prices in the U.S.A. would not only tend to restrain further demand growth, but would improve the economic viability of higher domestic oil production and of alternative energy sources.

But what would happen to the production and consumption of energy if we did return to the 'normality' of low energy prices existing before 1973? It is instructive to begin by looking at forecasts about energy made before then.

An interesting example is provided by the United Nations in 1971, which fore-cast that world energy consumption in the year 2000 would be 36.5×10^9 tce, of which 54 per cent would be in the developed market economies, 36 per cent in the centrally planned economies and 10 per cent in today's poor countries (excluding China and North Korea, which were included under centrally planned economies). Oil would provide 55 per cent of all energy, gas 30 per cent, coal 12 per cent and hydro-electric and nuclear 3 per cent.

Starting from 1974, and assuming a steady exponential increase until the year 2000, cumulative oil consumption would under such circumstances be equivalent to about 250×10^9 tce, and cumulative energy consumption just under 500×10^9 tce.* Assuming a continuation of such a trend until the year 2050, world annual energy consumption would reach just under 700×10^9 tce each year, cumulative energy consumption about $11,500 \times 10^9$ tce, and the poor countries would still be consuming about 10 per cent of the total.

It is all too easy to ridicule such projections. But the assumptions behind them are not very different from those made elsewhere at that time. The United Nations forecast assumed that per head energy consumption in the developed market economies would reach nearly 21 tce each year by the year 2000. This is more than the 16 tce assumed by Landsberg *et al.* in the early 1960s in their projections of U.S. energy consumption in the year 2000, but considerably less than those made by the Ford Foundation (Freeman, 1974), when after a further decade of falling energy prices and increased energy con-sumption, an 'Historical Growth Scenario' assumed a level of annual energy consumption in the U.S.A. of just under 28 tce in the year 2000. It is impor-tant to remember that throughout most of the post-war period until 1973 real energy prices were falling. 'Normality' was a situation where the incentives to use energy efficiently in the technical sense were diminishing and energy was rapidly becoming almost a 'free good'. If such conditions were to re-emerge, such projections might be plausible.

But there is another possible definition of pre-1973 'normality', where energy prices are not falling but simply stable at a lower level than those pre-vailing in early 1977. Under such circumstances, there will be more incentive to economise – or, perhaps more important, less incentive to waste – energy than in the 1960s and one could argue that per head energy consumption would not increase beyond that existing in the U.S.A. today. As we have seen, modernisation of the industrial and domestic capital stock results in a more efficient use of energy compared to previous vintages; and the composition of economic growth in future is likely to be less energy-intensive than in the past. The possibilities for further rapid diffusion in the use of household consumer durables, of home and factory heating and of private automobiles are

*Under conditions of exponential growth for N years from a level of annual energy consumption E_1 to a level of annual energy consumption E_2, cumulative energy consumption is

$$\frac{N}{\log \frac{E_2}{E_1}} \times (E_2 - E_1)$$

industries will probably not expand at the same rate in the industrialised countries as in the past. On the other hand, low energy prices will discourage strong efforts at energy conservation.

What implications would these assumptions have for future energy consumption? One could assume, at one extreme, that all the industrialised world (North America, Europe, U.S.S.R. and Japan) gradually moves up to present U.S. levels of energy consumption (12 tce per head) by the year 2000; or at the other extreme, that North America remains at its present level, whilst Europe, the U.S.S.R. and Japan stabilise at present levels in the E.E.C. and Comecon (about 5 tce per head). Under such circumstances, annual energy consumption in the industrially advanced countries would be between 8 and 16×10^9 tce in the year 2000.

By the year 2000, the poor countries would have reached GNP levels where, in the early 1970s, the level of per head energy consumption was about 1 tce. If one assumes further that growth in GNP and energy consumption would be maintained independent of demographic trends, then energy consumption in the poor countries in the year 2000 would be between just under 4 $\times 10^9$ tce and just over 5×10^9 tce. Thus total world energy consumption in the year 2000 would be between 12 and 21×10^9 tce, compared to 36×10^9 tce in the U.N. forecast described above. If one assumes a steady exponential trend in energy demand from present levels then cumulative world energy consumption between 1974 and 2000 would be between about 260 and 350×10^9 tce.

It is much more difficult to speculate about the consequence of the continuation of such trends until the year 2050. If per head energy consumption continued to remain stable in the industrialised countries, their consumption in 2050 would be between 9 and 17×10^9 tce. If the GNP per head of today's poor countries grew at $2\frac{3}{4}$ per cent per annum, it would reach a level in 2050 where energy consumption per head could be anything between 3.5 and 5.5 tce per annum. Since, as we have already said, the likelihood of further conservation at pre-1973 prices would be small, the level of energy consumption in the year 2050 of today's poor countries would be between 17 and 53×10^9 tce, depending on population levels and per head energy consumption. Thus world annual energy consumption in 2050 could be anything between 26 and 70×10^9 tce and, assuming a steady exponential trend between 1974 and 2050, cumulative energy consumption between these two dates would be between about 1000 and 2000×10^9 tce.

Low Growth with Unequal Distribution: Zero Energy Growth

From 1973 to 1975 the world lived in a state of zero energy growth. This happened as a result not of deliberate and desired choice, but of a brusque slow-down in economic activity. Even without a nuclear war zero energy growth could continue or recur unintentionally in the future if the world is unable to maintain, or to foster, economic growth. This could happen for any number of reasons in the future just as it has often happened in the past: continuing 'stagflation' in the advanced capitalist countries; stifling bureaucracy and economic rigidities in the centrally planned countries; political disorganisation, economic exploitation or a basic lack of investment resources in the poor countries. Zero energy growth resulting from zero economic growth and happening unintentionally has historically been frequent.

If, as a result of economic stagnation, energy production did not increase in future, cumulative world consumption between 1974 and 2000 would be about 200×10^9 tce, and about 600×10^9 tce by 2050. Over this period, the already significant differences in per head energy consumption between the industrialised and the poor countries of the world would increase still further. In 1974, average annual per head energy consumption was 6.3 tce in the developed market economies, 5.1 tce in Eastern Europe and the U.S.S.R., and 0.4 tce in the poor countries. By the year 2050, demographic trends could reduce per head consumption by up to 30 per cent in the industrialised countries, but by between 40 and 70 per cent in the world's poor countries to between 0.1 and 0.25 tce a year.

Low Growth with More Equal Distribution: Zero Energy Growth

However, there have been advocates of a conscious policy of zero energy growth coupled with a large-scale redistribution of resources. Some, like Illich (1974), have criticised the social and spiritual consequences of energy-intensive methods of living, working and travelling, and have predicted their ultimate breakdown. Others, like Dumont (1974), have moved from assumptions of approaching ecological and Malthusian limits in energy and other natural resources to advocate a materially simpler, more equal world. What would happen if, through the actions of some totalitarian regimes, for example, there were to be no more growth in world energy consumption beyond the level of 1974, but energy resources were redistributed world-wide on a more equal basis?

World-wide, per head energy consumption would be about 1.9 tce a year. This would be slightly above the 1972 consumption level of Spain, but well below those of Italy and Japan. This level would not last for long. Given the inevitable population increases over the next sixty years, energy consumption per head would be reduced to between 1.2 and 1.5 tce a year in the year 2000, and to between 1.3 and 0.7 tce a year by the time that world population levels off between 2030 and 2050. At the higher level, world energy consumption per head would then be slightly more than that of Mexico in 1971, and at the lower level somewhat above that of Brazil and Turkey in 1972. The annual rates of improvement in energy conservation necessary to make this level of consumption equivalent to 6 tce per head in 1974 would be between 2 and 2.9 per cent a year, which is higher than the 'high conservation' alternative that we defined as 1.8 per cent a year at the end of section 4.

If, on the other hand, world energy production were increased in line with population, in order to keep per head energy consumption constant, then world annual consumption would be between 10 and 13×10^9 tce in the year 2000, and between 12 and 22×10^9 tce in 2050, whilst cumulative consumption from 1974 would be between 230 and 270×10^9 tce until 2000, and between 800 and 1000×10^9 tce until 2050. The annual rate of improvement in energy conservation necessary to make 1.9 tce equivalent to 6 tce in 1974 would be 4.6 per cent by the year 2000, and 1.6 per cent by the year 2050. Achievement by the former date is, therefore, unlikely, but the latter appears possible if a 'high conservation' policy were followed.

High Growth with More Equal Distribution: Enough for All

Profiles of a high-growth/more-equal world depend essentially on three assumptions: the size of the world's population and the time that it takes to stabilise; the time it takes for today's poor countries to industrialise; and the rate of energy consumption necessary to sustain modernisation. As in all of these profiles, we assume, on the basis of the projections of Mesarovic and Pestel, that world population will reach between 5.2 and 6.7×10^9 in the year 2000, and will stabilise at between 6.3 and 11.2×10^9 by the year 2050. We shall also assume that today's poor countries will have fully industrialised by this latter date. This may be regarded as over-optimistic, but individual countries have experienced such economic transformation in the last seventy-five years.

The rate of energy consumption necessary to sustain development in the year 2050 is far more difficult to predict, so we have chosen a very wide range of five possible levels. First 'energy to burn', where the world's energy consumption per head moves towards the level forecast in the early 1970s for the U.S.A. in the year 2000, namely 28 tce a year; such a variant implicitly assumes that energy is more or less a 'free' good. Second 'U.S.A., 1970', where world energy consumption per head would reach 12 tce a year. Third, 'Sweden, 1970', where it would reach 6 tce a year. Fourth, 'low conservation', where on the basis of 'Sweden, 1970' levels of demand there would be an annual rate of energy conservation per unit of output of 0.8 per cent per year, probably stimulated by continuing pressures from OPEC and other energy suppliers to maintain and even increase somewhat the present level of real energy prices. Fifth, 'high conservation', where on the basis of 'Sweden, 1970' levels of demand there would be an annual rate of energy conservation of 1.8 per cent a year, probably stimulated by a vigorous public policy for energy conservation, and a level of energy prices much higher than those existing in 1977. We have not examined a profile with a completely equal distribution of income at either Swedish or U.S. income levels, since the implications for patterns of energy demand are negligible (see Freeman, 1974).

As one might expect, the level of future energy consumption varies enormously amongst these variants, as is shown in Table 5.7, which summarises the main characteristics of all the profiles examined. Between 'energy to burn' and 'high conservation', annual energy consumption in a fully industrialised world could vary over very wide ranges: between 11 and 70×10^9 tce in the year 2000, and between 10 and 326×10^9 in 2050; and cumulative consumption between 250 and 1000×10^9 tce for the period 1974 to 2000, and between 700 and $13,000 \times 10^9$ tce for the period 1974 to 2050.

7. COMPARISONS AND CHOICES

Comparisons

The first conclusion to be drawn from the comparison of the profiles in Table 5.7 is that, in terms of their implications for energy consumption, there is often as much variation within each profile as there is between them. In the high-growth/unequal profile, annual world consumption could vary by a factor of 3 by the year 2000, and 25 by the year 2050; the equivalent variations for the high-growth/more-equal profile are 6 and 30. Even in the zero growth profile there is an equivalent variation of 0.6 in 2000, and 3 in 2050.

There are also some similarities between profiles. The more equal profiles for zero per head energy growth and for high growth with high conservation are almost the same in their implications for demands on energy resources. And the saturation variant of the high-growth/unequal profile is in some ways very similar to the more equal profile of 'Sweden, 1970'. The reasons for these differences and similarities emerge from the wide range of assumptions that can legitimately be made about energy demand within each of these profiles. Whilst they do serve as useful ordering devices for considering a range of possible futures, profiles defined in terms of growth and less inequality offer no particular insights into patterns of energy demand.

Putting aside the two profiles that assume 'energy to burn' (United Nations, 1971) and the one assuming 'U.S.A., 1970' as the world pattern of energy towards which to move, the range of cumulative demands on energy resources in the year 2000 is relatively narrow: from 208×10^9 tce in the cases of zero energy growth to 390×10^9 tce at the higher end of the 'Sweden, 1970' profile. The considerable differences begin to emerge strongly only beyond the year 2000. However, given the long lead-times involved, the basis for these very different longer-term trends will to some extent be predetermined by technological activities and the investment decisions that are executed and planned in the next twenty-five years.

Implications for Resources

The 'energy to burn' and the 'U.S.A., 1970' profiles would probably put a heavy pressure on resources and technology, as a comparison of Tables 5.4 and 5.7 shows (pp. 135 and 144). Cumulative energy consumption since 1974 could reach between 390 and 1000 $\times$ 10^9 tce by the year 2000, and between 3000 and 13,000 $\times$ 10^9 tce by the year 2050. By this latter date the ultimately recoverable resources of fossil fuel resources (estimated at between about 7000 and 13,000 $\times$ 10^9 tce) and thermal fission resources (80-100 $\times$ 10^9 tce) could well be exhausted, unless there were a large-scale introduction of nuclear breeder reactors, or some other novel technology. There would be very little recoverable reserves of anything left for posterity.

Even by the year 2000, such high energy demand profiles could be running into problems of oil supply. As we can see from Table 5.4, proven and probable reserves could be equivalent to between about 300 and 375 $\times$ 10^9 tonnes of coal, and some experts have concluded that ultimately recoverable reserves may not be much more than this. In 1974, oil provided about 45 per cent of all energy resources and by 2000 it could be providing about 62 per cent if the trend in its importance in total energy supplies were allowed to continue. Cumulative demand for oil between 1974 and the year 2000 would then be between 210 and 540 $\times$ 10^9 tce in the 'energy to burn' and 'U.S.A., 1970' profiles. Even on the assumption that oil continued to supply just 45 per cent of all energy resources, cumulative demand would still be between about 180 and 450 $\times$ 10^9 tce. Assuming the same proportional contribution of oil in all other profiles, cumulative demand would be between about 90 and 180 $\times$ 10^9 tce, so that the danger of pressures on oil reserves and resources would be much less.

It is also clear that official estimates of installed nuclear energy capacity in the year 2000 will be realised only in a world with very high growth of energy demand. Up to 1974, about 70,000 MW of electrical generating capacity of nuclear origin had been installed in the capitalist world. As a result of the huge increase in oil prices, the nuclear energy agencies of the O.E.C.D. and the United Nations were jointly predicting in December 1975 the installation of between 2,000,000 and 2,500,000 MW of electrical generating capacity of nuclear origin by the year 2000 (Patterson, 1976); in other words, an annual rate of increase in capacity of 14-15 per cent during the last twenty-five years of this century.

The estimates of installed nuclear capacity for the year 2000 had already been revised downwards by the beginning of 1976 to between 1,500,000 and 1,800,000 MW, which still implies an annual growth rate of 13 per cent (Krymm and Woite, 1976). They are equivalent to about 5 $\times$ 10^9 tce of primary energy inputs. Assuming that, in the year 2000, the present non-communist world will still be producing about 70 per cent of the world's energy, and that nuclear energy could not be equivalent in primary energy inputs to more than a third of the total because of its sole application to the generation of electricity, then the minimum level of world energy demand in the year 2000 necessary to make the estimated nuclear capacity feasible would be just over 20×10^9 tce. This assumes that *all* electricity would be generated by nuclear reactors. If we make the further assumption that only a third to a half of all electricity in the non-communist world will be generated from nuclear energy in the year 2000,* the minimum level of world energy production would have to be between 40 and 60×10^9 tce, which is well into the 'energy to burn' type of profile. If, on the other hand, we assume that world energy consumption is between 15 and 25×10^9 tce, and nuclear energy generates between a third and a half of all electricity, then nuclear energy in the non-communist world in the year 2000 would be equivalent in primary energy to between about 1 and 3×10^9 tce, or between about 0.3 and 1.0×10^6 MW of electrical energy, namely, between a half and a sixth of present official projections. As in the past, official projections continue to be over-optimistic.

The final conclusion can be briefly stated. Population is not the main, direct determinant of future levels of energy demand. This could vary by a factor of only two by the year 2050. The main determinants are the extent of world economic development and the degree of its energy intensity.

Choices

Choices of desirable energy profiles for the future inevitably involve both technical and political judgements about what is important and what is not. The factors affecting our judgements are, first, the level and the international distribution of material quality of life that the profile offers and, second, the degree of pressure that the profile is likely to place on resources – be they natural, environmental, technological or economic.

On this basis, we can immediately reject the United Nations 1971 profile, on grounds of both the international distribution of material benefits and the pressure on all types of resources. We would add that, unless oil turned out to be much more plentiful by the year 2000 than even the optimists believe, such a profile could not be sustained, since oil prices would soon start increasing again. We also reject the 'saturation variant' of the high-growth/unequal profile. Although its distributional and resource disadvantages are far less severe than those of the United Nations 1971 profile, it still has considerable drawbacks and dangers. By the year 2050 there could still be wide inter-national differences in levels of income per head, and the further economic growth of today's poor countries could put considerable strains on resources if this growth is highly energy-intensive.

We also argue that although the low-growth/unequal profile would put no

---

*Given that nuclear electricity can be used only for base-load, at present, this seems a reasonable assumption.

pressure on resources, its material implications for the world's poor would be more unpleasant than the high-growth unequal scenarios, especially when population in today's poor countries increases over the next 30-50 years. We also reject a low-growth/more-equal profile, without energy conservation, even if it allows energy production to keep pace with population increases. Per head energy consumption in such a profile would be at a level of the poor countries around the Mediterranean where, as we know, a certain number of people do lead materially simple, yet stylistic and varied lives. But they live off the economic surplus created either by a semi-feudal peasantry, or by an industrialised and energy-intensive hinterland. And if for no other reason than climate, such an option is not open to the inhabitants of Moscow, Peking, Chicago, Hamburg, Glasgow or La Paz.

The profile of more equal, zero energy growth per head coupled with high conservation has greater attractions, since it offers the possibility of a sufficient material base for all the world's population. However, in so far as it is linked to a low or to a zero rate of world economic growth, it has two disadvantages. First, it is highly unlikely under such conditions that sufficient resources could be diverted to the very considerable investment and technological requirements of a high conservation world. Second, in the absence of energy growth or economic growth, the diversion of large-scale resources towards the poor will be politically more difficult.

The variants on the high-growth/more-equal profile, by definition, satisfy both our material and distributional requirements. However, the 'energy to burn' variant is clearly unacceptable because of its resource implications, and is very unlikely too unless unexpectedly large new reserves and resources of oil are discovered in the next twenty years. We are then left with a choice amongst four variants, where world energy consumption in 2050 could be anything between 10 and 100×10^9 tce, and where choices cannot be made quite so easily as for other profiles. However, we reject the 'U.S.A., 1970' variant because we think that towards the upper end of its range it could put too great a pressure on fossil resources. In addition, per head useful energy consumption in the U.S.A. is not significantly higher than in Sweden (Schipper and Lichtenberg, 1976); and Lovins (1977) argues that the costs of energy conservation in the U.S.A. are considerably lower than for opening up equivalent new sources of energy.

However, even if it is true that the 'U.S.A., 1970' variant is simply a more wasteful one than 'Sweden, 1970', what increase in requirements for useful energy can be expected beyond the present Swedish model? Brookes (1972) has argued, on the basis of data for the 1960s, that increases in GNP per head are associated with more or less equivalent increases in useful energy consumed per head. We are not convinced that this will be the case in the late 1970s, the 1980s and beyond, given the changing structure of demand with higher living standards. Consumer durable and space heating requirements will be more or less saturated, as will the demands for processed materials.

The demand for transport will be highly income elastic, but urban and sub-urban passenger car transport – where there has been tremendous growth since the Second World War – will continue to suffer increasing restrictions in the face of environmental and congestion costs and the renovation of public transport. The mining and processing of materials may also require increasing amounts of energy in future, in so far as there is movement towards lower-grade ores, but we doubt that this will have significant effects, and there is always the possibility of switching, at least to some extent, to less energy-intensive recycling of used materials.

For all these reasons our own preference is for the 'Sweden, 1970' and the 'low conservation' variants, or for some combination of the two, which would increase the amount of useful energy available beyond that of 'Sweden, 1970.' But stating preferences about the future is not enough. It is also necessary to talk about their feasibility, which is what we shall now do.

8. POLICY AND POLITICS

The feasibility of our preferred profiles of future energy development depends upon the factors that will determine the degree to which today's poor countries develop over the next seventy-five years. Here we shall concentrate on only those that are directly related to energy.

Future Energy Supplies

We have already discussed the constraints and opportunities on the ex-pansion of future energy supplies (pp. 134-7). In Table 5.8 we summarise a pattern of future energy supply that tries to take account of these constraints and opportunities, whilst at the same time meeting the energy requirements of our preferred profiles. No mention is made of thermonuclear fusion, dry-rock geothermal energy, shale oil or tar sands because, for the reasons set out in section 4, we do not think it is desirable to count on them. We have also left out wave and tidal power because we think that their overall global signifi-cance is limited. The main elements of our supply profile are as follows.

Coal: If the rate of growth of coal output from 1900 to 1975 were main-tained until 2050, annual production would reach about 10^{10} tonnes. If, as we suggest below, increases in the production of oil and natural gas were re-strained, the rate of growth in world coal production could return to that existing in the period 1900-29, before the large-scale introduction of oil and natural gas. In this case, annual production in 2050 could level out at 20×10^9 tonnes, and reserves could last for at least a further 200 years. In addition to considerable investment, such an expansion would depend on technical

TABLE 5.8   *Our preferred pattern of future energy supplies (Unit = 10⁹ tce)*

Fuel	Annual 1974	Annual 2000	Cumulative 1974–2000	Annual 2050	Cumulative 1974–2050	Further production possibilities after the year 2050
Coal	2.5	4–6	80–140	10–20	400–850	At least for another 200 yrs at 2050 rates.
Oil	3.6	4.5–6	100–125	5–10	325–500	Very large uncertainty. Could last for up to 500 yrs or could be virtually exhausted.
Natural gas	1.7	2.8–4.6	55–70	5–10	250–450	Very large uncertainty. Could last for up to 200 yrs or could be virtually exhausted.
Uranium: thermal reactors	0.2	1.0	13	5	110	
Uranium: breeder reactors	negl.	negl.	negl.	negl.	negl.	Considerable possibilities based on further discovery of uranium, on use of thorium, and on uranium-based breeder reactors. Minimum of 9000 × 10⁹ tce.
Thorium: breeder reactors	negl.	negl.	negl.	negl.	negl.	
Geothermal sources: wet rock	negl.	1.0	10	6	150	Between 25 and 225 years at 2050 rates.
Hydro-electric power	0.4	2	25	7	280	Indefinitely at 2050 rates
Solar energy	negl.	1	5	2–12	70–300	Indefinitely at much higher levels than in 2050.
Wind energy	negl.					
Natural waste & fuel crops	negl.	0.5	2	1–2	36–50	Indefinitely at 2050 rates.
TOTAL	8.4	16.8–22.1	290–390	41–72	1620–2690	Coal, nuclear, solar & wind resources remain considerable.

Note: Methods of calculating cumulative consumption are the same as in Table 5.7. The 1974 annual total is different from that in Table 5.2, since in this table nuclear and hydro-electric energy have been counted in terms of equivalent primary inputs.

156

change in methods of mining and transporting coal, in gasification and lique-faction, and on other improvements in combustion. Most important of all would be the potential manpower constraint, and the environmental conse-quences of carbon dioxide release to the atmosphere.*

Oil: Given the world's growing dependence on oil today and the consider-able uncertainty surrounding the size of ultimately recoverable oil resources, the rate of expansion of oil production should be reduced, so that it reaches between 4.5 and 6×10^9 tce by the year 2000 and accounts for a quarter of the world's energy production, compared to 3.6×10^9 tce and about 45 per cent of the total in 1974. Cumulative consumption between 1974 and 2000 would then be between 100 and 125×10^9 tce, well within all estimates of proven and probable reserves. Unless ultimately recoverable oil resources turn out to be at the high end of the estimates being made at present, oil production should then continue to expand slowly to reach between 5 and 10×10^9 tce in the year 2050 or between 12 and 14 per cent of total energy production. In such circum-stances, cumulative oil production between 1974 and 2050 would be between about 325 and 500×10^9 tce. Given what is said at present about the world's ultimately recoverable resources this could mean that these resources are more or less exhausted, or that they could last for up to a further 500 years!

Natural gas: Given that the present level of gas production is lower than that of oil, and that the recent spate of technical change offers more possi-bilities for transportation and use, the rate of expansion of gas production should be higher than that of oil, but not too much higher, given the same enormous uncertainties about the size of ultimately recoverable resources. Production should reach between 2.8 and 4.6×10^9 tce in the year 2000, so that cumulative production would be well within currently estimated proven reserves. By 2050, annual production could reach between 5 and 10×10^9 tce, when – as with oil – ultimately recoverable resources could be exhausted, or they could last for another couple of hundred years.

Nuclear energy: For a mixture of environmental, political and economic reasons we advocate an expansion of nuclear energy capacity over the next seventy-five years of just over 4 per cent a year, to reach the primary energy equivalent of 5×10^9 tce in 2050, and cumulative consumption since 1974 of about 110×10^9 tce. Production in the year 2000 would reach about 10^9 tce, which is at the low end of the estimate that we made in section 7. This slow rate of build-up would enable a thorough testing and evaluation of a variety of thermal and breeder reactor types including those based on thorium, without large-scale commitment to nuclear energy in general, or to any one type of breeder reactor. We think that this approach is more likely to provide

*However, the amount of carbon dioxide released by the year 2000 will be less than that envisaged by the authoritative S.C.E.P. Report (1970).

a sound basis for the further development of nuclear energy, since it would
reduce the dangers of public rejection, of nuclear proliferation, and of
premature commitment to a reactor type (the sodium-cooled fast breeder
reactor) that could turn out to be disastrous economically as well as environmentally.

Geothermal energy: We suggest a growth of wet-rock geothermal energy
sources of up to an annual production equivalent in primary terms to 6×10^9
tce in the year 2050. Cumulative production by then would be about $150 \times$
10^9 tce since 1974, which is more than estimates of proven and probable
reserves ($12-60 \times 10^9$ tce), but well within the range of estimates of ultimately
recoverable resources ($300-1500 \times 10^9$ tce). Depending on how big these
resources are, production at the levels of the year 2050 could continue for
between a further 25 to more than 200 years.

Hydro-electric power: We suggest that by the year 2050 all the identified, exploitable resources of hydro-electric power should be developed. This will
mean an annual production equivalent in primary energy terms to about $7 \times$
10^9 tce, and a cumulative production between 1974 and 2050 of about $280 \times$
10^9 tce.

Solar and wind power: Solar and wind power offer considerable
potentialities for supplying low-grade heat energy,* provided that technical
problems related to storage, conversion and heat pumps are solved in the
next twenty years. These sources could also become important during the
process of development of today's poor countries. And, given their virtually
inexhaustible potential, they could offer considerable possibilities for
expansion beyond the year 2050. In the initial stages at least the exploitation
of solar and wind power would be through the installation of a large number
of relatively small units. The process of diffusion may therefore be slow and
we would not expect, even under the most optimistic assumptions, a significant proportion of the world's energy to be generated from these sources by
the year 2000. However, by the year 2050, we envisage the possibility of
providing between 2 and 12×10^9 tce from these sources, or between 5 and 17
per cent of total energy. The possibilities of expansion beyond this date
would be considerable.

Natural waste and fuel crops: Although the ultimate potential for
producing energy from natural waste and fuel crops may be limited, these
sources may be particularly important in today's poor countries and may
eventually be feasible for exploitation on a systematic, commercial basis. We

---

*So does waste heat from industrial processes. However, to include waste heat from electricity
generating power stations here would be double counting, since we have already considered this
possibility in section 5 under savings in energy conservation.

therefore envisage the possibility of producing between 1 and 2×10^9 tce from them by the year 2050.

Overall characteristics: The fuel mix that we are suggesting for the future has the following characteristics. First, the overall potential production varies between 17 and 22×10^9 tce in the year 2000, and 41 and 72×10^9 in the year 2050; cumulative production between 1974 and these two dates would be between 290 and 390×10^9 tce, and between 1600 and 2700×10^9 tce, respectively. It could therefore satisfy both our 'high conservation' and our 'low conservation' profiles; and, depending on population growth and degree of conservation, it could probably satisfy our 'Sweden, 1970' scenario too.

Second, the fuel mix is more varied than that existing in 1974. Coal, oil and natural gas together account for between two-thirds and three-quarters of the total in the year 2000, and for about a half in the year 2050, compared to more than 90 per cent in 1974. Whilst coal will more or less retain the relative importance that it has today, dependence on any one type of fuel will be reduced.

Third, the mix offers some flexibility. If oil resources turn out to be at the low end of present estimates, there is the possibility of expanding coal, or solar and wind power. Geothermal and thermal nuclear sources may also offer possibilities, provided that the technical obstacles to the former are overcome, and that recoverable uranium resources turn out to be more than today's estimates.

Fourth, the mix offers possibilities for further change beyond the year 2050. There will still be plenty of exploitable coal in the ground, and considerable potentialities for the further expansion of nuclear energy, on the one hand, and solar and wind power, on the other.

Thus, our preferred profiles appear to be feasible in terms of physically supplying energy resources without large-scale disruption of the environment, and at costs that are economically acceptable. However, this conclusion assumes away politics, both international and national, as well as the problems of sustaining technical change. It is to these subjects that we shall now turn.

Regional Imbalances

International geopolitical stresses are one of the most significant possible hindrances to the achievement of the above pattern of energy supply, which implicitly assumes that energy resources will be traded freely across national boundaries. Between 1950 and 1973 this was indeed increasingly the case, with growing trade in oil and reduced national self-sufficiency, at least amongst the Western industrialised countries. However, since 1973, the dangers and difficulties of increased 'interdependence' in energy have become apparent, and the international pattern of energy supplies has become explictly and highly politicised, with inter-state bargaining increasingly taking precedence over conventional commercial transactions.

Attention has focused on the Middle East and its enormous reserves of oil, where in the space of thirty years its component countries have moved from the status of quasi-colonies of Western industrialised countries to that of participants in a well-organised and powerful cartel. At the same time, an energy-dependent country like France can no longer dominate its potential oil suppliers, either politically or militarily, and is attempting to reduce its dependence on them through an ambitious nuclear energy programme.

Thus, this mismatch between the location of the major fossil fuels and that of the major needs for energy can influence not only international politics but also the pattern of development of energy supplies. In Table 5.9 we try to identify where these major mismatches might be by comparing estimates for the major regions of the world of ultimately recoverable fossil fuel resources (coal, oil and natural gas, excluding shale oil and tar sands) with the cumulative energy consumption between 1974 and 2050 required for them to reach and sustain an annual level of energy consumption of the 'Sweden, 1970' profile.

Requirements would clearly be lower for the 'low conservation' and 'high conservation' profiles, but the differences would not alter substantially the conclusions that we shall draw from the figures in Table 5.9. Much more important are the limitations of the data on fossil fuel supplies. The location and reporting of such supplies is more thorough and systematic in the Western industrialised countries than elsewhere; the resources of many of the world's economically underdeveloped regions, and of China and the U.S.S.R. may be underestimated by considerable amounts. The data do not capture the considerable heterogeneity of various of the regions, in terms of both number of nations and level of their fossil fuel resources. Compare, for example, the coal and oil reserves of the generously-endowed U.K. and the poorly-endowed France.

What emerges from Table 5.9 is that, in the long-term perspective of its needs for modernisation, the Middle East is not the region best endowed with fossil energy resources. Depending on the size of ultimately recoverable oil and gas resources and on future population levels, Middle Eastern oil and gas resources could cover regional requirements by between a factor of about 1.3 to more than 20. The indefinite continuation of a policy of large-scale exports of oil and gas could, in certain circumstances, lead to problems of supply for regional needs as could the unabated political stress between Middle Eastern states.

It is the U.S.S.R. and Eastern Europe (mainly the U.S.S.R.) that are best endowed in relation to local needs, which are covered by a factor of between 30 and 50, followed by North America (mainly the U.S.A.), whose needs are covered by a factor of between about 15 and 26. China's needs are covered by

TABLE 5.9   Indigenous fuel supplies and energy needs, by region, 1974–2050 (10⁹ tce)

Region	Ultimately recoverable resources				Cumulative needs for 'Sweden, 1970' profile, 1974–2050.	Uranium	
	Coal	Oil	Natural gas	Total		Thermal	Breeder
North America	1596–2195	25–248	48–475	1669–2918	112	69	4152
Western Europe	157–216	11–114	7–75 (All Europe)	175–405[a]	84	11.7	702
Japan	5–7	0	0	5–7	34	negl.	6
E. Europe & U.S.S.R.	3287–4520	24–236	39–390 (U.S.S.R. only)	3762–5221[a]	112	?	?
Latin America	10–14	58–578	14–137	82–729	100–200	2.5	150
Middle East	17–24	78–779	14–139	92–918[b]	40–70	} 11.5	690
Rest of Africa		58–576	13–130	88–730[b]	70–125		
China	420–578	2–23	} 12–115	434–716[c]	200–300	?	?
Other South East Asia	36–50	17–172		65–337[c]	370–700	1.7	102

Notes: (a) includes the total for natural gas for all Europe.
(b) total for coal included in Africa other than Middle East, since most of it is situated there.
(c) includes combined total for natural gas for China and other South East Asia.

Sources: Regional totals for coal, oil, natural gas and uranium from World Energy Conference (1974) and Table 5.4 above.
Cumulative needs based on 6 tce per head in year 2050, and high and low population estimates of Mesavoric and Pestel (1974).

a factor of between about 1.4 and 3.6, on the basis of the limited data available, and those of Western Europe by between about 2 and 5, although the variation amongst countries in the region is considerable. West Germany and the U.K. are particularly well-endowed with coal and, for a shorter period, Norway and the U.K. with oil and natural gas.

For Africa outside the Middle East, future sources of indigenous supply are far more uncertain, depending very heavily on how much recoverable oil is eventually found and on access to the coal resources of South Africa and Zimbabwe, which account for more than 85 per cent of the total. Similarly the position of Latin America is highly uncertain, depending on how much oil is eventually found and also on the eventual exploitation of the huge shale oil deposits of Colombia, the recoverable portion of which has been estimated by the World Energy Conference as equivalent to about 120×10^9 tonnes of coal, and on the prospects for exploitation of heavy oil deposits of the Orinoco Tar Belt.

However, the region of the world where the gap between needs and resources is greatest is without doubt the region of Asia outside the U.S.S.R. and China. Japan can cover only between 15 and 20 per cent of its needs until 2050 from indigenous coal, and so far it apparently has no oil and gas. The rest of South East Asia can be expected to cover between about 10 and 90 per cent of its needs, depending on how much oil is found and how fast population grows. For these regions, the assumptions of regional autarky are much more questionable.

Thus, apart from possible intra-regional causes of tension (amongst which offshore rights could, as we have said, loom very large), what emerges from this analysis is the dominant position of the U.S.A. and the U.S.S.R. in supplies of fossil fuels, the possible vulnerability of Africa and Latin America, and the heavy degree of dependence of South East Asia. The behaviour of the two super-powers in future could have a considerable influence, both on the provision of energy for purposes of modernisation, and in the temptation for the dependent regions to launch themselves into large-scale programmes for the expansion of nuclear energy. We know that very often such programmes are undertaken for reasons other than a legitimate concern for the security of energy supply. However, just as the decision of the French government in 1976 to build a full-scale, sodium-cooled, fast breeder reactor was without doubt influenced by uncertainties surrounding supplies of oil from the Middle East and by the unwillingness of the U.S.A., Norway, the U.K. or anybody else to guarantee alternative sources, so similar decisions could be taken in many countries in future. If the U.S.A. and the U.S.S.R. are seriously concerned about the dangers of nuclear proliferation, they should avoid ambitious and unnecessary programmes of their own for the expansion of nuclear energy and concentrate instead on coal. They should also carry through policies enabling assured provisions of fossil fuels to countries that need them. The obstacles to achieving this latter objective are considerable; on the whole they relate to energy demand in the U.S.A. and to energy supply in the U.S.S.R.

As we have seen, the U.S.A. has a higher and more wasteful pattern of energy use than any other country in the world. However, by the year 2050, North America will not account for more than 5 per cent of the world's population. Thus, at a first glance, the future would not be much influenced if the U.S.A. alone were to maintain its high energy consumption levels whilst the rest of the world moved to those of Europe. However, the indirect effects of U.S. behaviour will be enormous. As the richest world power the rate and direction of the development of the U.S.A.'s energy technology will influence the energy technology that other countries adopt, either through trading relations or through providing an example that other countries wish to follow.

We cannot be very optimistic about the possibilities of a conscious U.S. policy to reduce energy consumption. Our preferred profiles are far more radical than the apparently most radical ones proposed in the Ford Foundation study. (Freeman *et al.* 1974). These were resisted strongly, as has been 'Project Independence', which was formulated after the 1973 crisis in order to reduce U.S. dependence on foreign energy sources. U.S. oil imports have continued to increase since then, a trend that has led to strong criticisms by the E.E.C. Commission and by a number of countries in the International Energy Agency, and to a specific request to reduce imports from the president of France.

We do not know whether the arrival of Alaskan oil and the projected increase in U.S. energy prices in the next couple of years will make an appreciable difference. Suffice it to say that, as with other natural resources, the U.S.A. has historically been well-endowed with energy and has had a high level of per head energy consumption for a long time (see Table 5.1, p. 114). Institutions and pressure groups sustain habits of consumption. In particular, U.S. citizens appear to want to keep their low-priced energy and large automobiles, whilst being more choosy and difficult about expanding indigenous energy production. As the unhappy experience so far of Project Independence suggests, any energy conservation policy will require strong political leadership, including a willingness to increase quite heavily the tax on energy use or to otherwise adjust prices closer to long-run marginal costs. This one measure, more than anything else, is likely to bring the lagging U.S.A. up to international best practice in the conservation of energy.

In the U.S.S.R. the problems are different. Although energy consumption has increased enormously over the past fifty years, it is still less than half the per head level of the U.S.A. The problems relate to the longer-term incentives for the U.S.S.R. to increase its energy supply for export. Despite very large oil and gas reserves, its dominant energy resource is coal, the large-scale movement of which will depend on technological improvements in transportation, in liquefaction and in gasification. As in other areas of technology the

U.S.S.R. may eventually have to import Western technology to exploit its fossil fuels. An agreement may eventually be struck with energy-poor Japan, which can offer hard currency and advanced technology in return (Russell, 1976). For these reasons, and as part of the general process of détente, similar deals may eventually be struck with certain energy-poor countries in Europe. But the energy-poor regions of South East Asia apparently have very little to offer in return, unless the U.S.S.R. is very anxious to woo them away from the political influence of China.

Producers' Interests

The pattern of future development of energy supplies that we are suggesting is very different from that of the past and very different from that proposed for the future by the proponents of nuclear energy. Some producer interests are bound to resist the pattern that we are suggesting. Some oil companies may not relish a slower expansion of oil production. But most of them are increasing natural gas production, and some – together with chemical companies – are already diversifying into coal. Given their technological, production and market base, both chemical and petroleum companies can be expected in future to make major contributions to coal-based technologies just as they have done in the past.

Potentially far more vigorous could be opposition in industrialised countries from electricity generating companies and two of their supply-side allies, the advocates of nuclear energy and the makers of electrical generating and transmission equipment. Our preferred futures will certainly require a considerable expansion of electricity production, but not at the rate or in the countries that they would prefer. Furthermore, the capital intensity, technical sophistication and large scale required for nuclear energy are unlikely to make it appropriate for most poor countries in the next thirty years; and we have argued that the long-term forecasts and expectations put forward for the rapid expansion of nuclear energy in the industrialised countries are both unrealistic and undesirable.

Strong opposition to both the low – and *a fortiori* the high – conservation futures that we have explored can be expected from the motor-car industry. Unfortunately, no powerful and organised producer interests exist as yet to advocate the energy conservation, the unconventional energy sources and the growth of public transport that we propose as part of our preferred energy profiles. In addition, improvements in space heating and public transportation will be closely tied to government for physical planning. The production and distribution of equipment to exploit solar and wind power will be much more decentralised and varied than that of power station equipment, and will depend heavily on the behaviour of building contractors and of local government.

Resistance to these unconventional energy sources could be weaker in today's poor countries, in which large-scale electricity generating companies and plant suppliers have relatively less influence. It would be silly to suggest to these countries that windmills, solar energy and 'biogas' will suffice for the large-scale manufacture of steel and the chemical fertilizers that they need. But it is equally silly to suggest that centrally generated electricity is the only way to perform energetically low-grade tasks in the domestic sector: a system that uses fast breeder reactors to meet these needs has rightly been described as 'thermodynamic overkill'. A steady upgrading of traditional, inexhaustible sources of energy could be a more efficient method – both economically and thermodynamically – of meeting these needs. A strong programme in the basic technologies of solar and wind power, heat pumps and energy storage would be of great benefit to both the advanced and the less-advanced countries.

However, political considerations are also relevant to any discussion of possible technological obstacles confronting the achievement of our preferred profiles. Coal industries in many countries are under state ownership and depend ultimately on government political decisions for the resources they will need for capacity expansion and technical change; and in countries where coal mines have remained in private hands, traditional management attitudes and the strong and sustained competition from oil and natural gas have left coal companies without the resources or the competence to promote expansion and technical change.

Furthermore, electricity generating companies are either nationalised or heavily regulated, and groups for the promotion of nuclear energy are heavily state-financed. Their advice weighs considerably in the deliberations of government and they naturally tend to advocate what is in their self-interest. For this reason alone one must be wary of technical judgements of these groups about unconventional energy sources. For example, it certainly is the case that the domestic use of wind and solar power runs up against the unsolved problem of storage. But the same is true of electricity, and it is far from certain that this technical problem is more difficult in magnitude and complexity than the problems surrounding the development and operation of thermonuclear fusion. And is it fair to compare the feasibility of technologies in which organised R & D efforts have been virtually negligible with the feasibility of a technology on which governments have already spent hundreds and sometimes thousands of millions of dollars on research and development activities? We do not think so.

Technology, Prices and Diminishing Returns

It would be wrong to subsume all problems of technical change under those of politics. *None* of the future energy profiles that we have advocated would be possible without improvements beyond the existing technologies of energy production, conversion and use. Certainly the emphasis would shift from energy production to energy use as one moves from a 'Sweden, 1970' profile to a 'high conservation' profile; in either case technical change is necessary.

It has been the thrust of arguments in certain circles in the past three to four years that the costs of technical change and of opening up new sources of energy supply are forever increasing, and that the return (or net energy output) on each new investment in terms of energy obtained is similarly decreasing. Unfortunately, we do not have access to systematic, comparable and accurate cost data in order to assess whether or not this is the case, although Lovins (1977) provides some plausible information. But if it is the case, and if the trend continues, the implications for world economic growth would be no different from the implications of Malthus' assumptions about diminishing returns in agriculture in the nineteenth century: it would eventually stop.

The problem therefore deserves to be taken seriously, and it must be admitted that what might be advance warning signs can be detected. The economic rent to energy producers has increased considerably, just as it would have done to landlords in a Malthusian world. The dominant economic power – the U.S.A. – has begun importing significant amounts of energy, just as the dominant economic power in the nineteenth century – the U.K. – began importing food in large amounts following the Malthusian concerns expressed by, amongst others, David Ricardo.

However, it can also be argued that the pattern of technical change in energy since the Second World War has been conditioned by three factors: the exceptionally low cost of Middle East oil, the neglect of the social costs of greater energy production and use, and the misallocation of resources to energy R & D by the governments of all the major industrially advanced countries. It will take many years before energy prices can be adjusted to reflect long-run marginal costs of replacing Middle Eastern sources.

During the 1950s and 1960s low-cost Middle Eastern oil, and the consequently falling real prices of energy, reduced the incentive to undertake the types of R & D activities and technical change that now reveal themselves to be essential for the future: the improvement of coal-based technology, the development of unconventional energy sources and greater technical efficiency in energy conversion and use. It can be argued, but not proved, that provided that energy prices remain at least at their present (1977) levels, technological activities in these three areas should begin to bear economic fruit in the next five to ten years. Admittedly the much higher energy prices now prevailing inevitably require big economic transformations, especially in the countries that are poor both economically and in indigenous energy resources. We have already argued that the resolution of this problem depends more on the U.S.A. and the U.S.S.R. than on the OPEC countries.

The neglected social costs of increased energy production and use have taken many forms, from pollution to the reduction of urban amenity through the increased use of the private automobile to the long-term political and ecological implications of the large-scale introduction of nuclear energy. The growth in public awareness of these costs has often been rapid and the resulting action often effective although sometimes unreasonable. This awareness is unlikely to diminish, and the internalisation of these costs has already had significant economic effects in nuclear energy, strip mining and the exploitation of shale oil and tar sands. They cannot be neglected in future.

Finally, governments have concentrated most of their energy R & D on the nuclear option since the Second World War, and, within the nuclear option, on the sodium-cooled fast breeder reactor. Growing environmental and social concern about nuclear energy has pushed up costs (Krymm, 1975); neglect of elementary economic considerations may make the sodium-cooled fast breeder reactor an even bigger white elephant than Concorde. It is perhaps an inherent danger in the operations of government to put too many eggs into one technological basket, on the basis of unrealistic or non-existent analyses of the cost, market and other factors likely to influence the technology's widespread acceptance (Eads and Nelson, 1971; Jewkes, 1969). It is to be hoped that the welcome trend in some countries towards more open and informed public debate and criticism about energy technology will ensure that many more energy options are explored in future, both inside and outside nuclear technology. This and the maintenance of energy prices are essential features of an insurance policy against diminshing returns in energy investment in future.

9. SUMMARY AND CONCLUSIONS

Our main conclusions are that, provided the right policies are followed, it will be possible to avoid both the Malthusian trap of restraining world economic growth because of insufficient energy supplies and what some have even called a 'Faustian bargain' of a rapid and large-scale introduction of nuclear energy. Our preferred future would involve a continuous effort to improve energy conservation, most of all in North America, but also elsewhere in the industrially advanced world; an expansion in the production of coal, coupled with technical improvements related to its mining, transportation and use; a slowdown in the rate of expansion of oil and natural gas production; a cautious and diversified exploration of alternative nuclear reactor designs; the expansion of hydro-electric power; and the expansion of the unconventional sources of geothermal energy and wind and solar power. An insurance policy against diminishing returns in energy investment will involve the maintenance of real energy prices at post-1973 levels, a growing contribution of the petrochemical industry towards improvements in coal-based technology and a much more flexible and diversified pattern of investment by governments in energy R & D than has hitherto been the case.

The achievement of these objectives will depend on the containment of the nuclear and electricity lobbies, and may be resisted by the automobile industry. It will also depend on compensating countries that are energy-poor – and particularly those in South East Asia – for the increased costs of energy. Given their very generous endowments with energy resources, both the U.S.A. and the U.S.S.R. have a particular responsibility to provide energy resources for export. Such a policy would also reduce – although not eliminate – the dangers of nuclear proliferation.

Simplistic policy prescriptions like 'a return to the market' or 'the adoption of socialist planning' do not help us much to understand the problems and possibilities of energy, whatever their wider significance might be. The workings of the market in the U.S.A. and West Germany have produced widely varying levels of per head energy use. Differences in resource endowments and in policies for energy pricing and for public investment have resulted in very different patterns of energy consumption between capitalist North America and capitalist Western Europe and Japan.

Similarly, the levels of energy consumption in socialist Eastern Europe and the U.S.S.R. are slightly higher than those in capitalist Western Europe, in spite of the less widespread use – for the moment – of the motor car in the U.S.S.R. There are probably several reasons for this: the greater emphasis on heavy industry; the greater use of coal, which is less efficient in use at present than oil and natural gas; in the U.S.S.R., the availability of vast indigenous energy resources and the consequent lack of a balance of payments constraint; and perhaps industrial inefficiency in energy use, related to emphasis on the maximisation of production and inadequate attention to the pricing of industrial inputs.

It is surprising that energy has received less attention than food, even amongst the neo-Malthusian futures writers. In the M.I.T. models, for example, energy did not even merit separate treatment. This may have had an effect on government views of the longer-term future. A recent U.K. publication by the Cabinet Office concluded that long-term energy supplies for the U.K. were not a problem, given the advent of the fast breeder reactor, but that food supplies could become a problem. Given the conclusions of this and the previous chapter, we cannot agree.

CHAPTER 6

Some Non-Fuel Mineral Resources

William Page*

This chapter is concerned with non-fuel minerals and materials, in particular with metals, about whose future availability most qualms have been expressed. The central question is whether long-term supplies can be sufficient to meet long-term demands. The range of issues involved is broad: mineral resources, exploration, extraction technology, the financial and other costs of mining, the end-uses of materials and the scope for greater efficiency of use, substitution, the role of recycling and trade, geo-politics and lifestyles.

In view of the complexity of each of these issues, let alone their interactions, we shall begin with a brief survey of some past trends and current features of the material sector. This will be followed by an examination of how other forecasters have seen the future of materials. Only then shall we turn to our own effort at forecasting, first by examining some of the building blocks for making statements about the future of materials and then by looking at the issues raised in each of the four profiles for demand and supply.

STARTING POINT FOR THE FUTURE: PAST AND PRESENT

Table 6.1 describes some of the principal properties and uses of major materials in industrialised societies. It is illustrative and not comprehensive. The statistics in this table generally refer to the U.K., although they provide an indication of the situation in other industrialised countries. The main uses of some materials are relatively specific: e.g. tin in cans and lead in transport

*For their assistance in preparing this chapter thanks are due to John Clark, Paul Gardiner and Sam Cole. I also want to thank the Nuffield Foundation who financed my field trip to South America.

TABLE 6.1   *Introduction to some materials: prices, properties, end-uses, 1975*

Material	U.K. price per tonne Nov. 1975* (£)	Key properties	Estimated main end-uses in U.K.†
Mild steel	100–150	Strong and tough	Transport 19%, construction 18%, mechanical engineering 16%, plus electrical goods, containers, etc.
Other ferrous metals: Chromium	2000	Makes steel stainless	Stainless and other steels account for most of their uses (especially manganese); other uses include, e.g., plating, batteries, magnets (depending upon metal)
Nickel	2500	Makes steel more workable	
Manganese	550	Chemically useful in steel making, improves the metal	
Aluminium	400	Light, strong, resists corrosion, conducts	Transport 27%, electrical 14%, packaging 10%, plus machinery, consumer goods, etc.
Copper	580 (has exceeded 1500)	Conducts, alloys with zinc, etc.	Electrical 48%, construction 17%, general engineering 17%, transport 10% (W. Europe)
Zinc	350–400	Easily forms tough castings, protects steel, alloys well	Brass 28%, galvanising 26%, die castings 20%, plus chemicals, batteries
Lead	170 (sométimes over 400)	Chemical, resists corrosion, soft but heavy	Batteries 25%, petrol additives 17%, cable covering 14%, plus sheet, pipe, solder, chemicals
Tin	3000 (has exceeded 6500)	Protects steel, low melting point, alloys	Tinplate (cans, etc.) 42%, alloys (bearings, pewter, etc.) 33%, solder 8%, plus tinning, chemicals, etc.
Platinum group metals	3m.	Catalytic properties	Chemical industry 36%, petroleum 19%, electrical 18%, plus ceramics, glass, etc. (U.S.A., 1973)
Silver	69,000	Photographic chemicals, conducts, looks good	Photography 26%, electrical 23%, sterling ware 21%, solders, etc. (U.S.A., 1973)
Mercury	2600	Liquid, conducts, forms amalgams	Caustic soda production 49%, electrical 25%, dentistry 5%, etc. (W. Europe, 1972)

TABLE 6.1   *(continued)*

Material	U.K. price per tonne Nov. 1975* (£)	Key properties	Estimated main end-uses in U.K.†
Portland cement	15	Cheap and strong, binds sand, aggregates	Construction
Phosphate rock	25	Chemical/life-supporting properties	Fertilizers, plus minor uses in detergent, industrial chemicals

*For some materials, the 1975 price was unusually low; in these cases, other prices reached since 1974 are indicated.
†Percentages given when 10% or over of total consumption.
Sources: Prices from *Metals Bulletin* (various issues) and *Industrial Minerals* (various issues); uses mainly from Metallgesellschaft (1974).

(batteries and petrol), so that demand for them is highly dependent upon these products. Steel, on the other hand, has a great diversity of uses.

The key properties of materials together with prices help to explain their types of use, such as conducting electricity, providing strength, or protecting steel, but it would be wrong to assume that any material with a particular property can be used whenever that property is required: it is always a combination of properties that is sought. A conductor, for instance, must do more than conduct; it must also have sufficient strength, minimal corrosion at connections, be compatible with whatever covering is used, be sufficiently flexible and, of course, be acceptable in terms of final cable cost.

Today's demand for materials is the result of a very rapid growth since 1900, and especially since 1950. Table 6.2 shows that world production (generally equivalent to consumption in the long run) has grown faster for some materials than for others, but few, if any, have shown declines since 1900. Steel is important because one hundred times more of it is used than of any non-ferrous metal and its production increased more than twenty-fold between 1900 and 1970; more than half of this growth occurred after 1955. Before 1900 only a few hundred tonnes of aluminium had ever been produced; the million-tonne mark was passed in 1941, and nearly seventeen million tonnes per year were being consumed around the world in the early 1970s. Copper production rose from 10,000 tonnes a year average for 1800 to 1810, to 750,000 a century later, to around seven or eight million today. Thus a continuation of present trends would lead to yet greater quantities of raw materials being produced in the future.

Although there are problems with the statistics, the consumption of these materials is certainly concentrated in the developed world. Per head consumption of many materials in the poor countries is around 5–15 per cent

TABLE 6.2   *Growth in world production of some materials, 1900–70 (thousand tonnes)*

	1900	1925	Growth since 1900 (% p.a.)	1950	Growth since 1925 (% p.a.)	1970	Growth since 1950 (% p.a.)
Steel	28,000	80,000	4.1	169,000	3.0	590,000	6.5
Aluminium (primary)	negl.	180	–	1510	8.9	10,300	10.1
Copper (smelter)	500	1400	4.2	2520	2.4	6310	4.7
Lead (refined)	870	1510	2.1	1850	0.7	4000	4.0
Zinc (smelter)	470	1140	3.6	2060	2.4	5230	4.7
Tin (smelter)	90	149	2.1	187	0.9	220	0.9
Nickel	7.6	37*	6.6	148	5.7	607	7.3

*Mine production.
Sources: Steel from Sutulov (1972); others from Metallgesellschaft (1975).

TABLE 6.3   *Per head apparent consumption of some materials in different regions in 1972*

	O.E.C.D.-rich*	Rest of the world	Africa	Asia	Central and South America
	Weight (kg.)				
Steel	566	82	27	55	77
Aluminium	13	1.0	0.3	0.3	0.8
Copper	8.8	0.7	0.2	0.2	0.8
Zinc	5.8	0.6	0.2	0.2	0.5
Lead	3.8	0.5	0.01	0.01	0.5
Nickel	0.64	0.05	0.01	?	0.01
Tin	0.26	0.02	0.01	0.02	0.03
	Comparative index				
Steel	100	14	5	10	14
Aluminium	100	8	2	2	6
Copper	100	3	2	2	9
Zinc	100	10	4	3	9
Lead	100	13	0.2	0.3	14
Nickel	100	8	2	?	2
Tin	100	7	3	7	10

Note: 'O.E.C.D.-rich' includes all members of O.E.C.D. except Greece, Spain and Turkey.
Sources: Metal statistics from World Bureau of Metal Statistics, *World Metal Statistics*; population statistics from U.N. *Statistical Yearbook*.

of that found in the richer O.E.C.D. countries; Table 6.3 provides some comparative data for regions of the world.

Two aspects of the supply side merit highlighting. First, contrary to a widely held belief, mining activity is concentrated in the industrialised world rather than in poor countries. Table 6.4 shows the countries that account for

TABLE 6.4   *The geographic concentration of mineral production in 1972*

Mineral	No. of countries accounting for 50% world production	Country, and percentage share of global production
Molybdenum	1	U.S.A. 64
Cobalt	1	Zaire, 50
Manganese	2	U.S.S.R. 44, South Africa 14
Phosphate rock	2	U.S.A. 42, U.S.S.R. 22
Iron ore	2	U.S.S.R. 40, U.S.A. 11
Nickel	2	Canada 36, U.S.S.R. 20
Asbestos	2	Canada 34, U.S.S.R. 26
Vanadium	2	South Africa 31, U.S.A. 31
Chromium	2	U.S.S.R. 28, South Africa 24
Potash	3	U.S.S.R. 26, Canada 17, W. Germany 12
Tin	3	Malaysia 31, Bolivia 13, U.S.S.R. 11
Bauxite	3	Australia 21, Jamaica 20, Surinam 10
Zinc	4	Canada 23, U.S.S.R. 12, Australia 9, U.S.A. 8
Copper	4	U.S.A. 22, U.S.S.R. 15, Chile 11, Zambia 11
Petroleum	4	U.S.A. 19, U.S.S.R. 17, Saudi Arabia 11, Iran 10
Tungsten	4	U.S.S.R. 19, China 18, U.S.A. 8, Thailand 7
Silver	4	Canada 17, Mexico 13, U.S.A. 13, Peru 13
Lead	4	U.S.A. 16, U.S.S.R. 13, Australia 12, Canada 11
Cement	6	}(many countries with small percentage shares)
Salt	15	

Sources: Mainly Metallgesellschaft (1975) and U.N. *Statistical Yearbook* (1974).

TABLE 6.5   *Rich and poor regions' shares of mine and smelter production and consumption, 1974*

	% mined in		% smelted/refined in		% consumed in	
	poor	rich	poor	rich	poor	rich
	countries		countries		countries	
Aluminium	51	49	7	93	8	92
Copper	44	56	34	66	10	90
Zinc	28	72	13	87	13	87
Lead	29	71	17	83	15	85
Tin	86	14	75	25	13	87

Note: 'Rich countries' includes Eastern Europe.
Sources: World Bureau of Metal Statistics (1975); Metallgesellschaft (1975); U.N. *Statistical Yearbook* (1975).

half the world production of a number of minerals. The U.S.A., U.S.S.R. and the old 'white' British Commonwealth countries account for 35 of the 49 entries on this list; poor countries predominate only in the mining of cobalt, tin and bauxite of the commodities listed.

Where poor countries do play a greater role is in trade, given that most of the U.S. and Soviet production is for internal consumption. Table 6.5

TABLE 6.6   *The shift towards poor countries, 1899–1974*

	rich*		poor	
Percentage mine production from countries that are now:				
	1899	1974	1899	1974
Iron ore	99	63	1	37
Copper	90	56	10	44
Lead	90	71	10	29
Zinc	**	72	**	28
Tin	13	13	87	87
Mercury	91	67	9	33

*Western and Eastern Europe (including U.S.S.R.), U.S.A., Canada, Japan, Australia, New Zealand.
**While statistics were not locatable for zinc in 1899, it can be noted that only one of the seven main mining regions is in a poor country (Algeria).
Sources: 1899: *Encylopaedia Britannica* (1902); 1974: Metall-gesellschaft and U.N. *Statistical Yearbook*.

summarises the proportion of world mining and smelting/refining activity that took place in poor countries in 1974. It shows that their share in mining is considerably higher than in processing; for instance, 51 per cent versus 7 per cent for aluminium, 44 per cent versus 34 per cent for copper. This situation differs from that at the turn of the century, when the role of poor countries was considerably less (except for tin). Thus there has been a sizeable shift towards investing in mines in these countries (see Table 6.6).

Over the last decade or so the politics and economics of mining appear to have become much more fluid. While few of the changes are new to the scene – nationalisation, tax and royalty increases, talk of new price-setting and marketing arrangements and so on, all have historical precedents – they are becoming less easy to ignore when looking at the world mining situation. This means that forecasters can make even fewer safe assumptions about the continuation of existing patterns of production.

RAW MATERIALS IN THE FUTURES DEBATE

As Table 2.2 in chapter 2 has shown (pp. 14–15), forecasters are as concerned with raw materials as they are with food and the environment, and the spectrum of opinion is similarly varied. Forrester and Meadows argued that demand for materials will outstrip supply within a century, following the depletion of all deposits that could be exploited at even a very high but still tolerable cost. In contrast, Kahn, the Soviet authors and many experts from the minerals industry itself assume that no insuperable difficulties will arise from long-term mineral shortages. For Kahn, 'alarm is genuinely misplaced', and for Modrzhinskaya, the threat of great shortages is 'illusory'.

Most futurologists consider the demand for materials to be more or less insensitive to deliberate policy changes, being mainly determined by the general level of economic activity. Some see a larger role for recycling, substitution or more physically efficient use of materials and argue that the link between demand and economic activity is not necessarily linear. Kahn and his colleagues, for instance, suggest that the material inputs to a post-industrial society would rise more slowly than incomes, since the major growth would be in the service sector, which is less materials-intensive than manufacturing industry. Specialists in the minerals sector itself (such as those with the U.S. Bureau of Mines or Resources for the Future) pay considerable attention to demand factors, but less commonly discuss the subject at such an aggregate level as the 'futures' writers and generally consider shorter time horizons.

The supply side is as a rule regarded as meriting most attention. For the authors of *The Limits to Growth*, only 250 years' supply of non-renewable resources at 1970 rates of consumption – or 'optimistically' five times this amount – are available world-wide; but as the rate of consumption increases exponentially, non-renewable resources run out over the next century and their unit cost will rise by a factor of 20 near to the point of total depletion. Precise estimates of reserves do not, say the authors, affect their overall conclusions. If depletion of a finite resource is taking place at an exponential rate, then even assuming a larger quantity of reserves would put off exhaustion by a relatively insignificant period. At the other extreme Kahn and his colleagues suggest that, 'even with a factor of 60 [increase in the world's annual requirement for raw materials] we would reject out of hand the notion that we could *run out* of any really critical material resource, one that would prevent the growth we envisage from actually occurring' (Kahn, Brown and Martel, 1976, p. 87). They expect prices to decline in the long run.

In their model the Bariloche group simply assume a 'non-limitation of natural resources in the foreseeable future'; the total amount of material is 'intrinsically unknowable'. In their view the evidence indicates that 'minerals have been extracted at continuously decreasing social costs' (Herrera, 1976, p. 29). Although they caution that 'in the unrestrained pursuit of economic growth, faith in the inexhaustibility of essential natural resources [energy and food included] cannot be taken for granted', in their model they assume that prices will be more or less steady. Mesarovic and Pestel appear in their model to make similar assumptions, even though they say in their text that consumption must be reduced in preparation for the 'age of scarcity' (Mesarovic and Pestel, 1974, p. 147). After analysing supply prospects for specific materials and dismissing the prospect of long-term exhaustion, Leontief and his colleagues (1976) predict increases in the costs of extraction by the turn of the century by a factor of two or three. This is comparable with the increase predicted in *The Limits to Growth* model for the year 2000.

One of the major constraints on raw materials production pointed to by several neo-Malthusian authors, including Spengler and Heilbroner, is energy supplies. The Ehrlichs, like Heilbroner, see the problems of energy and waste as 'gigantic'. Kahn argues that, although certain areas of the world may be designated 'junk piles' while strip mining or other degrading activities are proceeding, this need only be temporary, and subsequently the region would be restored 'if practical' (Kahn, Brown and Martel, 1976, p. 158).

The authors of *The Limits to Growth* say that their pessimistic conclusions are further exacerbated when geographic factors and international relations are taken into account. Although many other authors disagree with their conclusions about physical and technological limits, on this second issue there is more consensus, but views about the manner in which such difficulties should be dealt with differ considerably.

For two reasons it is not surprising to find these widely differing views of the prospects for material supplies. First, different authors examine these problems with different perspectives and expectations. For instance, authors who come from a mining background may be predisposed towards expecting major problems to be solved, because they have been solved in the past (see, for example, Prain, 1975).

The second reason, which politeness often forbids to mention, is that a fair degree of ignorance about mining and material-using industries is to be found amongst some of the futures writers, while many of those who are immersed in the industry itself can lose sight of broader horizons. Given the magnitude of the task when looking at the future of the world, these shortcomings are understandable, but this does not change the situation. To single out examples would be unkind, but credit should be given to Heilbroner who later changed his original and simplistic gloomy views about materials. As a recent O.E.C.D. paper remarks, 'the amount of literature on [this] subject [is] mainly due to verbal inflation and an abundance of repetition which concealed a serious lack of new ideas and original study' (O.E.C.D., 1977, p. 3).

In much of the forecasting literature there is a major contradiction in assumptions. On the one hand, everyone is agreed that prediction is impossible; on the other hand, the authors are attempting to demonstrate that the world will or will not face serious material shortages. An alternative approach is employed in this chapter: *to identify the main conditions* under which various long-term futures may be viable and, if and when possible, to indicate what action (if any) might enhance the likelihood of those conditions being met.

ISSUES IN FORECASTING MINERAL SUPPLY AND DEMAND

Economic Activity and Materials Consumption

In terms of materials futures, the important differences between the four profiles examined in this book are the rates of economic growth assumed for rich and poor countries. High or low rates in rich countries distinguish between two pairs of profiles, while high or low rates in poor countries distinguish between another two pairs. We shall examine the implications of high and low economic growth rates in rich or poor countries for the demand and supply of materials, first seeking a relationship between levels of economic activity and materials demand.

The standard measure for levels of economic activity is gross national product, and the standard measures for material demand are weight and value. There are two ways of comparing these: to compare per head GNP with material consumption per unit of GNP (e.g. tonnes of steel per million dollars of GNP), or per unit of population (e.g. tonnes of steel per head). Figures 6.1 and 6.2 show comparisons for some industrialised countries in 1973, and Table 6.7 shows changes between 1960 and 1972 in the former.

These figures show that there is a relationship between economic activity and materials demand, but the correlation is not perfect. The point can be made by comparing per head metal consumptions in Austria and Japan, countries whose GNP per head were within $100 of each other in 1973. Austrian per head consumption of aluminium was about 70% of Japan's, and that of steel and copper, about half. In contrast, the Austrian lead consumption was greater than Japan's.

Table 6.7 compares the 1960–72 growth rates in GNP and materials consumption in seven countries. The quantity of materials used per unit of GNP is henceforth called the 'materials intensity' of the GNP; the table shows that some materials intensities have been increasing, some declining. Aluminium consumption has grown faster than GNP in five countries (i.e. increasing intensity), whereas tin has lagged in all seven countries. In the U.K. and France, GNP has grown faster than consumption of any of the five materials (showing that these materials intensities have declined), whereas Japanese and Italian intensities of steel, aluminium and nickel have all increased.

There are two main reasons for this variation between countries. The first has to do with the nature of the statistics. 'Consumption' statistics do not exclude those materials that have been incorporated into manufactured goods subsequently exported (nor do they include such imports). There are very few solid facts to guide assessment of the effects of this factor upon what strictly should be called the 'apparent' consumption of materials. Crude calculations, based on trade statistics for manufactured goods and guesses as to their individual materials content, suggest that there are cases where

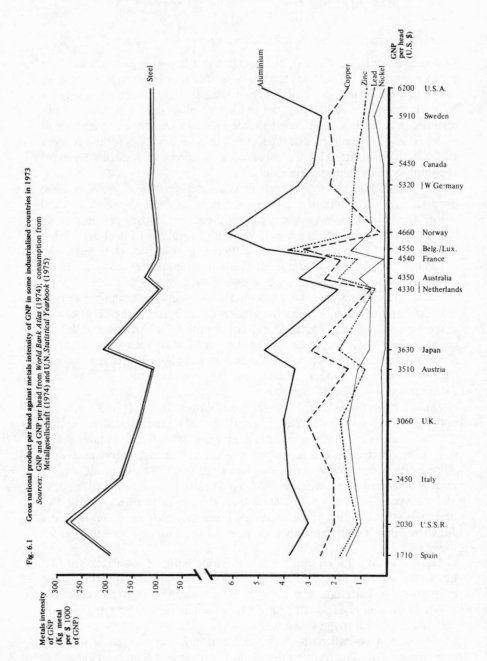

Fig. 6.1   Gross national product per head against metals intensity of GNP in some industrialised countries in 1973

Sources: GNP and GNP per head from *World Bank Atlas* (1974); consumption from Metallgesellschaft (1974) and U.N. *Statistical Yearbook* (1975)

178

Fig. 6.2   Gross national product per head against metal consumption per head in some industrialised countries in 1973

Sources: GNP and population from *World Bank Atlas* (1974); consumption from Metallgesellschaft (1974) and U.N. *Statistical Yearbook* (1975)

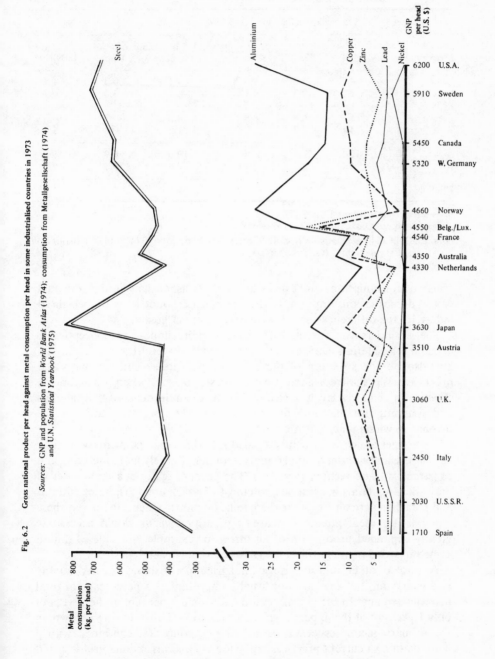

179

TABLE 6.7   *Growth rates in GNP compared with growth rates in apparent consumption of some materials, 1960–1972*

| | | Average annual growth rate in: | | | | |
| | | | apparent consumption of: | | | |
Country	GNP	Steel	Aluminium	Copper	Tin	Nickel
U.S.A.	4.1	3.6	8.9	**4.4**	0.3	**4.7**
U.K.	2.5	0.2	1.0	−0.3	−3.3	0.7
France	5.7	4.5	5.4	4.2	−0.3	4.0
West Germany	4.6	2.7	7.5	2.2	0.8	**5.4**
Japan	10.6	**11.1**	19	10.0	6.9	**16**
Italy	5.1	**6.9**	9.8	3.6	3.3	**9.9**
U.S.S.R.	6.8	?	7.1	4.4	3.5	4.4*

*Eastern Europe, including U.S.S.R.
Note: Numbers in bold type indicate growth rates higher than that of the GNP.
Sources: GNP and steel statistics from U.N. *Statistical Yearbook* (1974); other statistics from Metallgesellschaft (various years).

apparent consumption can be as little as half, or as much as double, the final or real domestic consumption. In the case of small countries with specialised industries the differences could obviously be much greater.

The second reason for the differences is more important conceptually: demand for materials depends not only on levels of overall economic activity, but also on the structure of the economy with its specific products and processes. We shall consider some of these, focusing attention upon the effects of high or low levels of economic activity on the demand for materials and assuming, for the moment, that there will be no great changes in the manner in which materials are used.

Economies are conventionally divided into three sectors: primary (mainly agriculture and mining or quarrying), secondary (largely manufacturing and construction) and tertiary (services). The primary sector is a major user of only a few materials or minerals, foremost of which are phosphates, nitrates and potash in agriculture. Were there to be no improvements in the way these minerals are used, greatly increased agricultural yields would necessitate greatly expanded production of all three; for example, one rule of thumb sometimes used is that fertilizer use grows 2.7 times faster than yields.

A range of other materials is used in agriculture, fishing, forestry, mining and quarrying, but they are not usually important as a percentage of total material demand. In Britain, agriculture is around 3 per cent of the GNP, but only 1 per cent of the apparent steel consumption. However, high growth in the primary sector, especially in developing countries, combined with a continuation of current practices in the use of minerals and materials, would still lead to increased demands upon the industries that supply them.

TABLE 6.8   *Materials consumption in capital goods, transport and construction, U.K., 1968 (in money terms)*

As percentage of total value used of:

	All materials included	Iron castings, etc.	Other iron, steel	Aluminium and its alloys	Other non-ferrous metals
Capital goods	32	22	32	26	40
Transport	20	32	21	27	8
Construction	9	12	11	0*	6
TOTAL	61	66	64	53	54

*As aluminium is used in construction, this figure is misleading despite its appearance in the U.K. input—output tables. Metallgesellschaft (1975) gives 7.5%

Definitions: 'Capital goods' consists of agricultural machinery, machine tools, pumps, etc., industrial engines, textile machinery, construction and mechanical handling equipment, other machinery, other non-electric machinery, industrial plant and steelwork, other mechanical engineering, instrument engineering, electrical machinery, insulated wire and cable, electronics and telecommunications, and engineers' small tools.
   'Transport' consists of shipbuilding and marine engineering, wheeled tractors, motor vehicles, aerospace equipment and other vehicles.
   'Construction' is only construction.

Source: Central Statistical Office, *Input—Output Tables for the U.K., 1968*, H.M.S.O., 1973. (The totals, from which the above percentages were derived, were obtained by subtracting the intra-sectoral quantities (the diagonals) from Total Intermediate Output in Tables B and C.)

There are three major users of materials in the secondary sector: capital goods, transport equipment and construction. Table 6.8 shows their respective shares of the U.K. consumption of some materials in 1968, by value. Capital goods accounted for 32 per cent of the total consumption of the materials included, transport equipment for 20 per cent, and construction for 9 per cent, a total of 61 per cent. While other users are sometimes of greater importance for specific materials (e.g. around 40 per cent of the tin used in the U.K. is for cans), these are of lesser importance in overall terms (packaging accounting for under 2 per cent of the metal used in the U.K.). The inclusion of non-metals makes a significant difference only in construction, where out of a total materials bill of around £1065 million in the U.K. in 1968 non-metals such as aggregates, cement, bricks, timber, glass and plastics accounted for £850 million.

The tertiary sector does not make such great use of materials. Taking the U.K. in 1968 again, 'distributive trades' took £8 of metal and cement inputs for each £1000 of gross output, and 'communications' £22; in contrast the production of motor vehicles used £182.

A common model of economic growth is that, as poor countries develop, it is their secondary sector that grows fastest; in contrast, in the industrialised countries it is the tertiary sector that is expected to grow fastest as incomes rise. Thus, for the poor countries, high rates of economic growth would be associated with greatly increased demands for materials, probably growing at a rate greater than that of the GNP (given the materials intensity of the secondary sector). On the other hand, demand for materials in the industrialised countries would be expected to grow more slowly than GNP at some point. Let us briefly look at what this model could mean for the world demand for materials, taking just one case.

Table 6.3, which compared consumption of materials in different regions of the world, implied that the per head consumption of materials in the poor countries would have to grow by at least ten times if it were to reach the present levels of O.E.C.D. countries. About two-thirds of the world population currently live in developing countries. Bringing per head consumption up to the O.E.C.D. levels would require roughly a tripling of world materials production, if there were to be no increase in population size. If the population of the poor countries were to double in size while the industrialised world population remained constant, then world-wide consumption would increase by a factor of six.

However, this of course assumes that there will be no great changes in the manner in which materials are used and takes no account of international trade patterns. By ignoring the possibility of improvements in the efficiency with which materials are used, the estimates for future demand given above are likely to be near the top of the range of possible future demands. Introducing this element of improved efficiency can only produce lower estimates.

Technical improvements leading to a reduced materials input for a given output have been of great importance historically. In the U.S.A. between 1947 and the early 1970s the steel intensity of capital goods dropped by 20 per cent, as did the metallic intensity of transport equipment; the steel intensity of the construction industry fell by 12 per cent, while its copper intensity was more than halved; the steel intensity of electric and service equipment was also halved.

Such data do not necessarily imply reduced overall materials intensity, because they can hide substitutions that have taken place, with corresponding increases in the intensities of use of other materials. For instance, aluminium and plastics intensities have increased in many of the American economic sectors over the above period. Furthermore, reductions may have occurred not only because materials are being used more efficiently when making specific products, but also because a different range and mix of products are being produced now. These influences are best illuminated by considering individual products.

Tin cans are made from steel plate with a protective coating of tin, and there have been variations over time and between countries in the thickness of that coating. In 1941, the U.S. tinplate industry used an average of 15.4 kg of tin for each tonne of tinplate. By 1950, the traditional hot dip coating technique was being replaced by electrolytic coating, and the average was down to 8.7 kg. Continued technical improvement and the replacement of old coating plant gave a 1975 average of 5.0 kg in the U.S.A. The Italian and British averages for the same year were 6.8 kg and 5.8 kg, respectively (figures from Metallgesellschaft, various years). An even more conspicuous illustration is the pocket calculator: ten years ago calculating machines were large and heavy mechanical beasts; small pocket calculators are not just smaller and lighter, but also offer many more mathematical functions.

The average car or lorry battery of 1960 used a similar quantity of materials as did its mid-1940s counterpart but its useful life was 50 per cent longer. Thus 25 million replacements were required in 1960, 13 million fewer than would otherwise have been the case. The lead–acid batteries now produce around 10 watt-hours per pound weight; silver–zinc batteries can produce four times that (albeit at five times the final battery price per watt-hour, with penalties in volume). Another instance of an increased product lifetime is the monochrome television receiver; the average age of those scrapped in the U.K. in 1957 was 5.1 years, as against 10.6 years in 1971 (R. J. Smith, n.d.). The weight of glass containers has declined by about 30 per cent over the last twenty years as a result of surface treatments, which allow more of glass's potential strength to be realised; further reductions have come about by using yet thinner walls combined with strengthened shoulders and bases.

Redesign is often, if not always, required to reduce the quantity of material used. A specific combined clutch and fan has been redesigned to use 20 per cent less material, while also providing better service. The commutator of a Hoover electric motor used £3.50 worth of materials per hundred before redesign, and 50p worth after. A one horse-power electric motor now uses half the weight of materials of its 1930s' equivalent.

This listing could go on virtually indefinitely, but we should also consider how future reductions might be achieved. There is much less literature available on this, but some points can be highlighted.

First, there is evidence of straightforward wastage of materials in industry. One survey of stores' issues compared with final shipments in a company showed that 33 per cent of the metal sheet and strip issued was not utilised and likewise 48 per cent of the metal bars, 12 per cent of the diecastings, 18 per cent of plastic mouldings and 73 per cent of the paint and enamel (Harwell, 1974). Information at sectoral or national levels is scarce, but such examples show there is clearly scope for some improvement.

Second, the main objective of those who design products is not to minimise the weight or value of the materials used but to minimise the final cost of the required product. Weight for weight, steel is cheaper than zinc, but diecasters use zinc because it permits cheaper manufacturing costs. A tonne of galvanised steel products can cost less than a tonne of copper, but copper's final installed costs are less for domestic plumbing or central heating systems, partly because it is a much easier material to work with. This suggests that scarcity and price increases could have a very considerable effect on substitution and reduction in materials intensity.

When considering possibilities for the long-term future, the questions are of a different order of magnitude from those normally posed by commercial or associated researchers. We are concerned with the possibilities of achieving great reductions in the materials used in the long term. A doubling of per head GNP in rich countries, or a quadrupling in the wealthier poor countries, would not increase total demand for materials if it were associated with a drop in the average materials intensity of GNP to half, or quarter, its present levels.

The closest approximations to the kind of study we are seeking can be represented by those published by the U.S. National Materials Advisory Board. In their study on silver, for instance, they report industrial views that up to 15 or 25 per cent (two views) of the silver then used for electrical contacts could be eliminated by redesign 'without serious consequences to the quality of the devices. However, this would be accomplished only with a very large expenditure of engineering effort. A 50% curtailment would have a severe impact on the industry, requiring extensive redesign, de-rating and probably the curtailment of the output of new devices' (1968, p. 9). Their conclusion on silver in photography is even less firm: on the one hand, this use is, 'as far as is known, without anything approaching a satisfactory substitute'; on the other hand, an 'authority' is quoted as saying that, 'in the course of time', they expect their present lines of research to provide substitutes suitable for some applications. (There is no discussion of how to avoid substitutes but still use less silver – except for recycling more.)

While such conclusions may be the best that can be drawn from current research, they hardly provide a sound basis for pronouncements about future possibilities. That they often suggest favourable omens is true, but they rarely substantiate the future feasibility of major changes, or indicate the range of savings that may be possible by given future dates.

Major changes were stimulated in the past by high prices, fluctuating prices or threats of real shortages. In pre-war Germany and in many other countries during the Second World War legislation changed the demand for materials; certain civilian uses of certain materials were banned. However, this was often at the cost of quality and greater expense in such items as cans, electrical cable or machine-tool steels. The balance between some substitutes is fine at present, strongly indicating that the cost differences are not large. Aluminium, copper and plastic components in car radiators, copper and aluminium in conductors, tinplate and tin-free steels in cans, are three instances. In a generally optimistic article entitled 'The Age of Substitutability', Goeller and Weinberg (1976) quote some materials that 'may have' substitution problems (e.g. manganese in steel making, tungsten in tool making) and conclude by saying that, 'more study is needed on these and to identify other such critical situations' (p. 689). However, their general conclusion that most materials have a wide range of substitutes in most applications is an extremely important one.

Recycling is a final means by which the demands for virgin material could be reduced. Recycling is already used on a large scale; it accounts for around 40 per cent of world copper and lead production, and probably much more of the total steel production. In the U.K., scrap accounts for around 55 per cent of crude steel production, 20–25 per cent of copper consumption, slightly over 20 per cent of aluminium and zinc production, over half the lead, and 10–15 per cent of the tin.

The scope for increasing these secondary supplies appears somewhat limited, despite recently fashionable views to the contrary. When finished with, most products are already collected and recycled – industrial equipment, wire and cable, ships and aircraft, rolling stock and so on. Many of the exceptions, such as beer cans or cooking foil, generally involve smaller quantities of materials, but have caught public attention because they are conspicuous in domestic rubbish, little of which is recycled; this waste is currently a subject of much study and several countries have built pilot plants to test the feasibility of recycling more of the materials it contains.

There are significant exceptions to these fairly high levels of recycling. Between one-third and one-half of the tin used in the world goes into cans, which are rarely reclaimed. The zinc coating used to protect steel (galvanising) is generally lost when the steel is recycled. But these problems are also currently receiving much attention in many countries, and solutions are already being implemented. Future developments that may occur in recycling include means of reducing the costs of collecting and reprocessing materials, and of improving the recovery rate of certain non-metallic materials, paper and plastic products in particular. We may conclude that, while there is some room for improvement, recycling rates cannot be greatly improved. This does not mean, of course, that even a small improvement in recovery and recycling rates is not worth striving for, though big changes in recycling technology or in costs of recycling are unlikely to have a large influence on supply.

Some authors would contest this conclusion. Chapman (1973) has claimed that around three-quarters of the old copper scrap and half of the aluminium scrap arising in the U.K. currently goes unused. However, his conclusion depends on assumptions concerning how long products made in the past will last, where there is little empirical data available; in the one case where a survey has since been conducted (old aluminium scrap in the U.K.), the results do not support his conclusions. Most experts in the scrap trade appear unconvinced by him because they cannot see how it is that such large quantities of old metal could be disappearing from their view.

There is a way in which some materials are currently lost to the environment without being counted as a source of post-consumption scrap: corrosion. The rusting of iron and steel is especially significant, given the quantities of steel produced and an estimate that one-fifth of this is lost through rust every year (Zinc Development Association, 1975). This could be greatly reduced by a more widespread use of protective techniques, especially coatings, which could result in significant increases to the amount of steel available for recycling.

Thus it seems certain that in many cases there are, or will be, means of reducing the quantities of virgin and recycled materials required to produce a given product or to fulfil a given function, although there is little data available from which to estimate the scope for aggregate long-term savings. We conclude that relatively little used material is left out of recycling activities. Under these circumstances can we reliably estimate the extent to which demand for virgin materials could be reduced in the long term while maintaining (or even improving) the material standards of living found in the richer countries now? Insufficient data and problems of measurement rule this out. What can be done is to consider some alternative possibilities that the above analysis suggests to be plausible. For instance, we may consider whether it is realistic for per head consumption to be reduced by, say, 25 per cent or 50 per cent. Given that total per head consumption has generally been growing in all countries, this would represent a break with past trends, and would probably require considerable R & D and other technical efforts. However, the attractions of greatly reducing the consumption of virgin materials will partly depend upon the relative attractiveness of the alternative: mining more.

Before leaving consumption issues, attention should be drawn to the trend towards increased use of materials more complex in terms of their chemical composition. While we tend to talk of 'aluminium', 'zinc' and so on, these metals are often, perhaps usually, alloyed with other metals and elements, and much metallurgical and materials research is the study of how new additives improve the characteristics of materials. Consequently, the various metals and other materials are slowly becoming more intermeshed and this, in turn, means that a supply problem in any one of them could have a greater impact on more finished materials than before. Against this potential danger must be noted the tendency to increase the number of materials capable of providing given properties, and the increased number of 'materials scientists' aware of this danger. Some authorities consider the education of designers to be of central importance (NATO, 1976).

Mining More

The main reason for using less virgin materials could be because of problems in obtaining supplies from mining as reflected in high costs. Mining activity depends on three conditions: the required minerals must exist in the earth's crust (or, if appropriate, in the oceans or atmosphere), there must be a satisfactory means of extracting them and there must be sufficient capital actually as well as potentially available for investment in this sector.

(i) *Absolute physical limits* There can be no reasonable doubt that the earth's crust contains more of the chief elements used in the production of materials than could be used for millenia to come. At present consumption rates the top kilometre of the land surface contains over ten thousand million years' worth of aluminium, a hundred million years of iron, and over ten million years of – amongst others – lead, zinc, chromium and mercury. This calculation is based on average crustal abundance, the volume of the top kilometre, and current consumption statistics. Sea water and the ocean floors, especially manganese nodules, also contain equally gigantic quantities of various elements (see, for instance, Mero, 1968). The problem is not that of insufficient absolute quantities existing on the planet.

(ii) *Means of extracting materials* The second condition is that there be a satisfactory means of extracting a material. This includes both technological and cost factors. In principle, any chemical element can be extracted from any rock that contains it. In fact platinum is already extracted on a commercial basis from rocks containing it in concentrations lower than the average crustal concentration of aluminium, iron, calcium (for, e.g., cement), manganese, chromium, zinc, nickel, copper, cobalt, lead, uranium, tin or tungsten, to name just the better-known elements.

This proposition is of little practical consolation to an industry whose production must be measured in thousands or millions of tonnes each year. The real question is not can it be done, but at what cost can it be done? After all, platinum costs around \$5 million per tonne. This question of costs and their future trends is one of the main issues that differentiates the neo-Malthusian pessimists from the optimists. We shall briefly illustrate the type of argument that is in use.

Most long-term price data suggest that real prices of materials have not risen. Indeed, this is often the case even using current money prices; when these have not risen, real prices certainly have not. The average 1920 list price for 99 per cent pure aluminium in the U.S.A. was 33¢/lb; in 1950 it was 20¢/lb, and 25¢/lb in 1973. Corresponding prices for copper were 25¢/lb average for 1915–18, 15¢ in the 1920s, 12¢ during the last war, and 30¢ in 1960. Barnett and Morse (1963), in one of the most quoted of all these studies, analysed real prices between 1880 and 1960, concluding that both the capital and the labour inputs had declined since 1890 for each unit of output. Nordhaus (1974) has compared the prices of four metals (aluminium, copper, iron, zinc) since 1900 with an average cost of labour in the U.S.A.; the only evidence of a rising real price on this basis was copper between 1960 and 1970.

Such studies are often quoted by the 'optimists' (Kahn, Brown and Martel,

1976; Herrera *et al.*, 1976; Page, 1973), and these conclusions may be right. However, the optimists do not give much weight to some of the defects of such studies. Since the First World War materials prices have often been subject to government control; during booms and recessions the aluminium list price has often been partly ignored; when the same material has a dual pricing system, such as a producers' price and a 'free market' price, it is by no means obvious which to use. The more fundamental question is whether tendencies that have operated in the past (say from 1950 to 1970) will also continue into the future: for this question such studies are not conclusive.

Mining history reveals many instances of discontinuity. When high-grade copper ores started to become scarce at around the turn of this century, there was a shift to the exploitation of low-grade ores, with a very different approach to their mining (introducing the bulk processing of rock and in effect moving the industry more into the earth-moving business). The American iron ore industry switched partly to taconites after the last war, having depleted much of the conventional ore; other examples include changes in the ores of nickel and beryllium.

The important principle underlying these changes is that the designation of the rocks that can be described as constituting an ore can change rapidly. An ore is a mineralised zone from which materials can be extracted commercially, given the likely prices obtainable for that production and the technology at hand. Thus a change in prices or in extraction technology can convert a commercially uninteresting deposit into an ore; the recent increases in the price of gold led to many gold deposits being promoted to ores, while the changed technology in copper or taconite mining had similar effects on other deposits.

The rate at which new ores must be found in the future by further exploration or by redefining what constitutes an ore will in part reflect the cumulative demand for the material in question. Let us take copper as an example.

We take a relatively extreme case because, if the problems that it presents can be solved, then there is less need to worry about less extreme cases. For this hypothetical future we assume that the world average per head consumption of primary copper reaches three times the present O.E.C.D. average (that is, slightly more than Sweden's or Belgium's apparent consumption was in the early 1970s), and grows up to this level at a rate double the highest seen in any major region over the last twenty years (see Table 6.9). Similar results would emerge from taking a lower growth rate to a higher final level. Cumulative world demand by 2000 would then be 500–600 million tonnes of copper, with around three billion tonnes by 2030. The former figure is about double the known reserves of 1970 (300 million tonnes), and the latter figure is ten times greater. Known world reserves would have to grow by an average of 2.2 per cent per annum from now to 2000, and by 5.5 per cent annually for the thirty years thereafter, if they were

TABLE 6.9 *Average annual growth rates in apparent per head consumption by region, 1952/3–1972/3*

	O.E.C.D.	E. Europe	Latin America	Africa	Asia
Steel	4.2	4.1*	4.9	3.0	13.0
Aluminium	6.9	8.5	13.2	18.0	12.2
Copper	2.8	5.2	3.5	3.5	8.6
Lead	1.6	4.9	2.9	1.4	8.5
Zinc	3.2	4.6	5.7	6.4	10.0
Nickel	5.7	2.1	12.4	?	38
Tin	0	1.3	−2.1	0	2.6

Unweighted average = 7.9% p.a.

*U.S.S.R. 1962/3–1972/3
Sources: U.N. *Statistical Yearbook* (various years) and Metallgesellschaft (various years).

to be adequate to meet this demand. (The relatively low figure up to 2000 reflects the starting point of presently known reserves and the lower total consumption levels.)

These percentage rates are in line with past achievements. Known reserves in the country that has mined the most copper, the U.S.A., grew at an average rate of 7.9 per cent between 1950 and 1971, while total world reserves grew at around 3.0 per cent per annum. (During parts of this period prices were increasing.)

Average ore grades declined during this period; in the U.S.A., the 1950–6 average was 0.8 per cent (copper metal per tonne of ore mined), as against 0.59 per cent in 1970, and 3 per cent in 1880. There has also been a trend away from underground copper mining to open-pit mining. Despite the exploration activity of companies and government agencies, there is little knowledge about the location and grade of copper deposits around the world or more than a few hundred metres below the surface. Thus it is not possible to reason from forecasts of cumulative production to specification of the ore grades that would have to be exploited if a tenfold increase in reserves were to be achieved. What can be said with some certainty is that the present form of open-pit mining of current grades (say 0.4 per cent copper or more) must slow down at some future point, as the immense deposits required for such operations become even more scarce; at present, around 60 per cent of world copper production is from such mines. With high growth in the demand for copper, this would probably be around 2000.

There are at least three ways of continuing copper mining under such conditions, all of which merit attention: the use of even larger amounts of near-surface, but even lower grade deposits; the use of the smaller deposits of the higher grade found near the surface (at present, low-grade ores must be worked on a large scale if they are to be economic); or moving back underground, where deposits may prove to be high- or low-grade but, with present practices, are expensive to exploit.

A halving of ore grades means doubling the quantity of rock moved for each tonne of metal and thus somewhat higher costs. A move to underground mining implies with current technology a tendency towards less easy mining (the problem of access shafts, access to the optimum working area, ventilation, compact equipment for confined spaces, etc.) and so, once again, higher costs. Smaller deposits imply less output over which to spread overhead and infrastructure costs.

As in the past, both incremental and radical innovations in both equipment and mining practices may counteract these cost-raising tendencies. Former radical innovations include such processes as surveying with instruments mounted in aircraft, blasting with ammonium nitrite/fuel oil explosives, using one piece of equipment to perform various loading, hauling and dumping operations underground, using floatation methods to concentrate mined ore and, for some metals, the replacement of the traditional blast furnace by other smelting techniques. Future possibilities that are still in the early stages of development include the use of earth resource satellites for exploration and leaching for extraction. In this latter technology chemicals are passed through the rock, become impregnated with the desired minerals and are then collected and treated. At present this method is being tried only experimentally and mainly on uranium mines – apart from its more widespread use in treating mine wastes (*Mining Magazine*, February 1976, p. 152). It is too early to put much faith in an economic evaluation of the technique; it can only be put forward as an illustration of what could be successfully developed.

The same observation applies to the mining of manganese nodules on the ocean floors. These nodules are rich in other minerals as well as manganese – copper, cobalt and nickel, for instance. They present novel problems both in raising them from several thousand feet down and in their processing, since mining metallurgists have little experience of handling this mixture of minerals. The prospects appear favourable and they are the subject of much commercial interest, but despite this, it would still be premature to assert that they *will* provide a potential source of these materials. There are, for example, the possible environmental and ecological consequences, which are little understood at present, but which must be thoroughly considered.

With some minerals the actual mining and beneficiation of the ore is the major component of the final cost; mining and concentrating copper ores accounts for around 70 per cent of the final cost of the metal, smelting and refining for 30 per cent. For steel the corresponding percentage is lower and for aluminium the intermediate product (alumina) may be under 20 per cent of the final ingot price. Thus the relative importance of the mining stage versus smelting varies with implications for which of them will require most attention in the future if total costs are to be kept down.

The availability and costs of energy are often seen as a major constraint upon future supplies of materials. The energy required to produce a tonne of metal in the U.S.A. in 1973 (mining through to ingot) ranged at least from 408 million Btu's for titanium through 244 million for aluminium and 112m for copper to 65m for zinc or 24m for steel slabs (Hayes, 1976). The two main concerns are that increased energy inputs will be required to handle inferior ores, and that unit energy costs will increase. The former will be reflected in the energy requirements of mining and the initial stages of concentrating; as long as the same raw material is used by the smelters in the future, their energy inputs should not change significantly, except for energy needed in pollution control. Under 15 per cent of the energy cost of producing aluminium is attributable to obtaining the concentrate (i.e. alumina), so that increased energy inputs in mining will not have a great impact upon total costs. Chapman (1974) estimates that extracting aluminium from bauxite uses only around 9 per cent less energy than from lower-grade clays, although Goeller and Weinberg (1976) estimate this figure as 20 per cent. For copper, where mining and concentrating account for around 57 per cent of the energy used (Hayes, 1976), it is estimated that a shift from a 1 per cent ore to a 0.3 per cent ore doubles the total energy requirements (Goeller and Weinberg, 1976).

Future energy requirements per tonne of metal will depend upon the quality of the ores and the technology available. For instance, the above-mentioned 0.3 per cent copper ore is only slightly inferior to the 0.4–0.5 per cent mined in some places now; future grades may be considerably lower, say under 0.1 per cent or 0.05 per cent, with much greater energy requirements. In this case, alternative technologies may be introduced, reducing if not halting the rise in energy demand; Battelle Columbus (1975) estimate that current leaching practices on waste copper ores (tailings) require around three-quarters of the energy used in more conventional techniques, suggesting an important role for leaching if energy costs are high.

It should be noted that the energy required to produce some materials is considerably greater than the energy theoretically required to break down the chemical compounds containing them. Some difference is to be expected, given the inevitability of some physical inefficiency and for activities related to extraction, such as grinding, transport, pollution control and so on. However, around 0.7–2 million Btu's are theoretically required to electrolyse copper oxide or sulphide (the main minerals in the ores) to one tonne of copper metal; the actual requirements of U.S. industry in 1973 were about 48 million Btu's per tonne, i.e. twenty-five to sixty times greater. For lead the differences are around twenty to forty times, and for zinc, twelve to sixteen. This suggests that there is still considerable room for improvement. In comparison, the actual U.S. energy input per tonne of aluminium from mine to ingot was only eight times greater than the theoretical need in electrolysis, and the figure for iron ore through to crude steel slab only 3.5 times greater.

This indicates that fairly high degrees of energy efficiency already exist in these two industries, where relatively high energy inputs for at least aluminium have stimulated improvements in energy use.

Water is another major input to parts of the industry, especially those engaged in concentrating ores prior to smelting: many of their processes, such as floatation, involve the use of water. In the future this will be an increasingly important problem given that much mining (and thus concentrating) is undertaken in relatively dry areas (see, e.g. Lloyd, 1974).

Several other aspects of mining and smelting will also require continuing attention. The quantities of mine waste are immense; a 1 per cent ore produces 99 tonnes of such tailings per tonne of metal, and that only if one assumes 100 per cent recovery of contained metal and that the tailings are dried to their former degree. The volume of tailings also increases as a result of processing. The question of how to handle tailings will become more important, yet there is currently very little research being undertaken into novel approaches. Leaching, if proved viable on other grounds, could reduce the problem by eliminating the production of tailings. Pollution from smelters and refineries is another important consideration and effective control has increased costs: in the U.S.A., for instance, pollution control has cost the steel industry around $3.5 billion, has increased the cost of copper production by around 5–8 per cent, and has caused seven zinc smelters to close (*Business Week*, 30 June 1973, p. 59). The consequence has been the shift of smelting and refining from industrialised countries; this will be discussed later.

(iii) *Investment* The third condition for mining and smelting activity to expand is that capital must be available. The absolute availability of capital in the world may be a serious constraint but, in this section, we examine only the problem of attracting investment into the mining and smelting sector.

The capital costs of this industry are high. In 1975 there were thirty-nine projects outside Eastern Europe and the U.S.S.R. involving $400 million or more; eighteen of these were over $600 million, and two were over $2000 million (*Mining Magazine*, September 1975, pp. 201–21). About 70 per cent of world metal production comes from only 170 mines and 90 per cent of Western production from only about 1000 mines (Govett, 1975). Consequently companies are inevitably obliged to seek reassurance about continuity of operations. There are two major deterrents to investment in mining and smelting at present: unresolved conflict over ownership and control, and low prices.

The former have been manifest in nationalisations and great tax or royalty increases, especially during the last five or ten years. Foreign copper mining interests have been nationalised in Chile, Zambia, Zaire and Peru, bauxite companies in Guyana, iron ore in Venezuela. The taxes payable by foreign bauxite companies in some Caribbean countries have increased, eightfold in

Jamaica for example. Some similar developments have occurred in Canada, with potash and asbestos nationalisations, and taxes increased greatly in some Australian and Canadian provinces.

Part of the expertise that the large multinational mining companies and houses have is that of arranging large financial packages, sometimes of $600 million or more. The risk of changing conditions for investment, such as nationalisation or great increases in taxation, may deter them from arranging investment, which could be serious for countries that do not yet possess the necessary skills. The multinationals offer expertise in technology and mine management, which are currently scarce in most poor countries engaged in mining. This reduces the credit ratings of such governments or their state-owned companies when seeking to raise funds directly for exploration, mining or smelting.

An alternative method of financing is to re-invest profits from mining activities. Historically, around 70 per cent of the investment in mining in the U.S.A. has come from this source (*Mining Journal*, 14 February 1973, p. 113). As world prices for materials have become a politically sensitive issue there are major repercussions for the pattern of new investment. The capital costs of mining have increased greatly since 1970 (see, for example, British–North American Committee, 1976), partly because of increased costs for capital goods themselves and in some countries because of the need for additional plant to control pollution. Operating costs have also risen, with energy prices and interest rates being significant factors. Since 1974 these increases in costs have been combined with lower prices for many materials, and the result has been a reduction in the profits available for re-investment.

Prices tend to be set by institutions geographically located in industrialised countries: producer prices by the major mining companies, 'free market' prices by such institutions as the London Metal Exchange. Many mineral-exporting poor countries feel that they are somewhat excluded from price-setting decisions; suspicion and tension result when they also feel prices to be too low. This has been reflected in the creation of associations of poor world mineral exporters of copper, bauxite and iron ore, and similar tentative steps have been taken for silver, mercury and manganese. It is also evident at meetings on prices and related issues at the U.N., UNCTAD and elsewhere; and affects the nationalisations and tax changes already mentioned.

Proposed agreements for solving present and future conflicts over investment, control and prices abound (Institute of Development Studies, 1976). They include the use of buffer stocks to moderate price fluctuations, controlled by joint producer–consumer organisations as in the International Tin Council – a long-established and much-cited organisation which, in early 1977, was in danger of collapsing through disagreements over target price levels; maintaining high prices but assisting importers who would otherwise be damaged by them; the widespread use of standard forms of guidelines or agreement for investment; the provision of legal expertise through the U.N.

to host governments negotiating with foreign companies; greater access to (say) the International Centre for the Settlement of Investment Disputes. All of these proposals and equally the desire to continue the present investment arrangements reflect the widespread conflicts of national interests.

The more militant approaches of the copper, iron ore and bauxite exporters seem to have abated since 1975 or early 1976; the calls to follow the example of OPEC in October 1973 are now rare, as the feasibility of repeating that action in most other minerals appears increasingly remote, except possibly in bauxite where there have been great changes (Bergsten, 1976). What is less certain is the extent to which such plans may be revived if and when the next boom comes and producer power in the market increases (for example, Barker and Page, 1974; Bergsten, 1973; Ray, 1975).

Social effects of mining investment One last condition must also be met, although its controversial nature induced us to put it last: there must be countries with mining potential prepared to engage in mining. Examples of countries with that potential but still deciding to ban mining are few and far between; the only examples known to us are a local Inca ban on Spanish gold mining (see Hemming, 1972, p. 337) and a Roman ban on mining in Italy for a time.

Why should there be any change in this policy? Because the benefits to be derived from mining for export may not compensate for the costs; this may not be true at the financial level, although some mining sectors have run at a financial loss for some years, such as the Bolivian state tin mines, but may be true in the context of the national development objectives of some countries engaged in non-fuel mineral exports.

The essence of the argument can be illustrated with South American examples. Most developing countries desire foreign exchange earnings to pay for imports of capital goods, fuel, services, weapons and so on; but while large mining sectors are good at earning foreign exchange, they are also good at spending it. Fifty-nine per cent of Chile's foreign earnings between 1952 and 1970 came from the copper and other exports of her five largest mines but, between 1957 and 1969, these five spent 50 per cent of the foreign exchange they generated. In 1971, 72, 73 Peru's non-fuel mineral exports were valued at $401m, $480m and $634m; the average annual foreign exchange expenditure of two state-owned companies planned for the period 1975–9 was about $500m. Thus, when assessing the foreign exchange contribution of mining in these countries, it is necessary to consider net and not gross earnings. (For the many sources drawn on in this section, see Page, 1976.)

Some parts of the South American mining industry offer jobs with exceptionally poor working conditions. According to one far from revolutionary source, 'Working and living conditions in most mining camps in the Andes have been a disgrace ever since the days of the Spaniards' (*Mining Annual Review*, 1975, p. 341). Improved conditions are found in modern mines, but these jobs tend to be very capital-intensive; for instance, a concentrator costing $10 million or more directly employs only twenty-five people (i.e. $400,000 per job). Neither are the total numbers of jobs created in modern mines plentiful; Chile's state-owned copper mines, which account for most of her production, employ 30,000 people from a total population of 12 million, and Guyana's mines employ around 6 per cent of the national workforce, despite her being the world's fourth largest producer of bauxite. Thus mining does not play a major role in direct employment in these countries, despite the size of their mining sectors, but does require considerable capital inputs.

Other drawbacks to placing great emphasis on mining in national development include the creation of elites whose interests may conflict with those of the government or 'the nation'; while miners were instrumental in giving Bolivia her first socialist government in 1952, they also contributed to the downfall of Allende's government in Chile in 1973. Those working in modern mines tend to be highly paid, receiving sometimes two or three times the wages paid in other sectors; their example and interests may upset attempts at introducing national wage policies (as in Chile, Peru and Bolivia), and their spending patterns can divert economic resources away from directions preferred by the government and towards imports of luxury goods and the provision of other goods and services that have little immediate prospects of meeting the needs of the mass of the population.

Local political and social structures have sometimes been upset in the past by mining activity, the best two illustrations being Bougainville in Papua New Guinea and Ocean Island in the Pacific. The copper mine in Bougainville nearly caused the political break-up of the country, as the mining area sought independence; it may do so yet. The phosphate mining on Ocean Island led the British Phosphate Commissioners to encourage the locals to move to another island over a thousand miles away, with consequences that seem to have pleased none of them.

Adequate assessment of the impact of mining upon development would require an examination of the available alternatives, but we should stress that the fundamental characteristics of mining in these countries have received little critical examination in the past. For present purposes we should note the possibility of great changes occurring in policies towards new investment in mining in these countries in the future, in addition to the changes of the last decade or so.

Use Less or Mine More?

There is nothing new about these two basic alternatives and they are of course interdependent: high mining and refining costs are reflected in high prices, and so encourage users to reduce their demand. (Tin, the most expensive of the major tonnage materials, has had one of the slowest growth rates recorded; aluminium and steel – both cheap – have grown rapidly in their respective periods.)

Costs and prices must play a role regardless of the general political, economic and social framework that may exist in the future. While we cannot expect to forecast exact prices and costs of mining or of material-using processes and products, we can point to some considerations that must affect the framework for future possibilities.

The materials industry is concerned with security of supply and safeguards for investment. There is a desire for assurance that supplies will not be disrupted and investments in mineral extraction will not suddenly be nationalised or become entangled in civil or military disturbances. This has a bearing upon supplies from, or investment in, poor countries and – to differing extents – in Canada, Australia and South Africa. If there were to be a long period of international disharmony, there would thus be pressure in both rich and poor countries to become more self-sufficient by domestic mining or by using less virgin material. For the industrialised countries, whose wealth gives them greater medium-term flexibility than most poor countries have, there are several reasons why using less may be preferred over domestic mining.

Limiting consumption is likely to lead to lower environmental and energy costs than mining more at home. The environmental costs of improved efficiency of use of materials appear to be negligible, if not non-existent; recycling does involve some environmental costs, be they the aesthetics of collection centres and reprocessing plants or the pollution created by reprocessing – none of which is a significant problem. Most of the environmentally costly stages in the total life cycle of a material have been passed once it reaches ingot (or comparable) form for the first time; the mine tailings, the pollutants in the original ore, such as sulphur or arsenic, the holes in the ground, are all mainly problems of primary extraction and not of recycling.

In the long term there is the possibility of primary extraction techniques that have fewer environmental impacts than present techniques, and these could change the balance. However, for the medium term it is hard to envisage the development of techniques that are environmentally superior to best practices in recycling.

The energy requirements of recycling are also less than for primary extraction. Chapman (1975) estimates that recycling copper, zinc or lead needs only 12–13 per cent of the energy used in primary production, and aluminium 3 per cent. On the other hand, using materials more efficiently may require a marginally greater energy input; using less steel for a given product may mean using steel of greater metallurgical sophistication (and so more heat treatment, cold working, alloying stages, etc.) and more machining or other fabricating stages.

While high long-term prices for materials would encourage users to reduce their demands, the monthly or yearly fluctuations in those prices are also relevant. Fluctuations are reputed to deter consumers and are not generally welcomed by producers. Copper and tin prices have been especially prone to fluctuations – world copper prices in mid-1976 were roughly one-third of the mid-1974 level, for instance. This creates budgeting and managerial problems for both suppliers and users, and provides an incentive to reduce uncertainties by substituting less volatile materials or reducing total materials requirements.

There are other factors that, depending upon the material, country or company, may be of greater or lesser importance. Balance of payments, employment, the influence of mining companies, the economic lifespan of existing material-producing or material-using plant, and so on, are all real or potential concerns and, depending upon the circumstances, could work in favour of either option. Some examples will arise when discussing the four profiles of future patterns of economic growth.

Contracting demand has one further appeal: if successful, it reduces uncertainties about the future. In a sense, reducing demand is a one-off activity, whereas mining is a continuous activity. A rich country that, say, halves its virgin materials requirements will have less to worry about regarding the long-term availability of those materials.

THE FOUR PROFILES

High Growth, More Equal Distribution

In this profile high long-term growth in the poor countries could result in their achieving levels of economic and material well-being comparable to those in the rich countries, whose own growth rates have been less rapid.

What would be the consequences of the world average consumption per head of materials climbing up to the present O.E.C.D. average? We gave a rough answer to this question earlier (page 182); we now consider it in more detail in relation to specific materials. The present average consumption of non-O.E.C.D. countries is about one-tenth of O.E.C.D. levels (Table 6.3). We assume a growth rate in per head consumption of about 5 per cent a year, which is a convenient figure reflecting past growth rates (shown in Table 6.9) and giving weight to steel.

On this basis it would take about fifty years (to 2025) for the average per head consumption levels outside the industrialised countries to reach their present level. If we take present world-wide annual consumption to be one unit, the world cumulative consumption of materials between 1975 and 2025 would be between 130 and 170 units. The range arises from taking alternative population forecasts, as shown in Table 6.10. Total cumulative consumption

TABLE 6.10   *Cumulative consumption of raw materials in all regions,*
1975–2050 (total world consumption in 1975 = 1)

If per head consumption grows to:	Cumulative consumption from 1975 to:	If population size is:		
		Low	Medium	High
50% of present O.E.C.D. average	2000	39	41	43
	2025	93	100	120
	2050	150	170	210
100% of present O.E.C.D. average	2000	43	45	47
	2025	130	140	170
	2050	230	270	350
200% of present O.E.C.D. average	2000	62	64	66
	2025	180	190	210
	2050	380	440	570

Assumptions: (1) the per head consumption of materials in poor regions averages 10%
of that in O.E.C.D. (see Table 6.3);
(2) a growth rate of 5% p.a. in per head consumption dropping to
0% once the limit is reached; the two exceptions are for the industrialised regions: in the '50%' row, their per head consumption is
assumed to fall by 1% p.a. until it is halved, and in the '100%' row,
it does not change;
(3) the population projections come from Mesarovic and Pestel (1974).

by 2025 could be greater than this since the assumption of no further increases in the average per head consumption in O.E.C.D. countries may be
conservative, especially for a high growth profile; for many individual
materials, several countries already have double or even triple the average
consumption. Secondly, an annual growth rate of 5 per cent in poor
countries' per head demand may also be a conservative estimate. Asian consumption of steel (excluding Japan's) grew by 13 per cent per annum between
the early 1950s and 1970s and Latin America, where there are plans for a
great expansion in steel output, achieved 4.9 per cent over the same period.
Thirdly, demand in poor countries could grow to levels beyond the present
O.E.C.D. average; Table 6.10 shows that, if all regions had average per head
consumption growing to double that previously assumed, then world
cumulative demand by 2025 will be 180–210 units. By 2050, cumulative
demand would be around 230–350 units using the first, more conservative,
assumption and 380–570 units using the second assumption. Table 6.11
shows that most of these totals can be ascribed to growth in demand in the
poor world.

Few materials have known and measured reserves as large as this. Of the
eight metals shown in Table 6.12, only chromium has reserves exceeding 300
units (i.e. years at current consumption rates), with iron and nickel also
exceeding 130 years. A high growth, more equal world must either find
more reserves, or limit its demands below these levels. Tables 6.10 and 6.11

TABLE 6.11   *Cumulative consumption of raw materials in developing countries, 1975–2050 (total world consumption in 1975 = 1)*

If per head consumption grows to:	Cumulative consumption from 1975 to:	If population size is:		
		Low	Medium	High
50% of present O.E.C.D. average	2000	17	18	20
	2025	55	64	79
	2050	96	120	160
100% of present O.E.C.D. average	2000	17	18	20
	2025	76	90	110
	2050	160	190	260
200% of present O.E.C.D. average	2000	17	18	20
	2025	80	95	120
	2050	240	300	410

Assumptions: (1) the per head consumption of materials in poor regions averages 10% of that in O.E.C.D. (see Table 6.3);

(2) a growth rate of 5% p.a. in per head consumption dropping to 0% once the limit is reached; the two exceptions are for the industrialised regions: in the '50%' row, their per head consumption is assumed to fall by 1% p.a. until it is halved, and in the '100%' row, it does not change;

(3) the population projections come from Mesarovic and Pestel (1974).

TABLE 6.12   *Known world reserves in 1970 and growth rates 1950–70*

	Known reserves, at present usage rate (years)	Growth since 1950* (% p.a.)
Aluminium (bauxite)	100	6.6
Chromium	420	11.0
Copper	36	6.7
Iron	240	14.0
Lead	26	6.4
Manganese	97	2.0
Tin	17	2.9
Zinc	23	5.1

*Calculation includes cumulative mine production between 1950 and 1970

Sources: Include Paley (1952), Metallgesellschaft (1972), U.N. *Statistical Yearbook* (various years) and U.S. Bureau of Mines publications.

indicate the effects of providing O.E.C.D. materials standards of living while using half her present per head consumption; cumulative demand by 2050 is reduced to about 60 per cent of the former level.

Because of her total population size, the greatest demands would arise in Asia. By 2000, Asian annual demand for raw materials (excluding that of Japan) would be roughly three-quarters of the present world total; in fifty years' time, it would be three times greater, and the cumulative demand, seventy times. If we assume that the required reserves were found and that the capital costs of mining and smelting were comparable to those in the U.S.A. in 1975, we have a total capital cost of $650 billion for providing capacity to produce five major materials (aluminium, copper, lead, zinc and iron ore pellets). This is equivalent to two years of total Asian GNP at its present levels (still excluding Japan); given high rates of economic growth this is not a tremendous amount. However, we have assumed that none of the plant built during this period will need replacing (which is implausible), and that 1975 U.S. costs are applicable, which is controversial; they may well be higher, but could be lower. Despite this, it still seems reasonable to assume that the capital costs of meeting such demands would not be crippling, given high rates of economic growth. Even if capital expenditure were to be ten times greater, it would still contribute only 4 per cent of Asia's GNP if that were growing at 7.5 per cent a year (or 6 per cent if GNP grew at 4 per cent per annum).

While the conclusion for Africa would be similar, except for smaller total quantities, the superior starting points of Latin America and the industrialised countries place them in a better position regarding likely capital costs – still assuming that reserves are not a problem.

Because of the differences between materials it is necessary to consider reserves material by material. Take aluminium, which is more abundant in the crust than any other metal and twice as abundant as iron. Because it has had an exceptionally high growth rate in the past, we take the case of world average per head consumption growing by 10 per cent a year to double the present O.E.C.D. level (rather than 5 per cent annually to only that level). Under these conditions known world reserves would not suffice much beyond 1990 or 1995. A continuation of past growth rates in known deposits (12 per cent p.a. during the 1950s and 1960s) would be adequate, and the prospects appear favourable. Large deposits are being found in several countries (e.g. Australia and Brazil), and the estimates of known reserves do not take into account immense deposits that are known to exist but still await measurement. Technology for using clays of inferior quality to the traditional bauxite is under active development, looks commercially attractive in the medium term, and would expand usable deposits of aluminium almost indefinitely. Thus more than adequate reserves of aluminium are not far from being secured.

The reserve situation for copper is not so clear, as a need for continuous improvements in technology (or increases in prices) is likely. The general nature of the technological problems was discussed earlier. Most metals are closer to copper's position than aluminium's; lead, zinc and tin are not too different. At least the major single metal – iron – is nearer to aluminium's relatively secure position. Thus, for metals like copper the more attractive long-term proposition may be to find means of using less. Goeller and Weinberg (1976) argue that since raw materials consumption is so dominated by the relatively abundant iron and aluminium, even if the prices of those metal that are more sensitive to ore grade increase by a factor of five to ten, the unit price of 'avalloy' would only increase by a factor of two.

It was argued earlier that there is insufficient data on which to base estimates of the long-term possibilities for reducing demand for materials, let alone what the financial costs would be. Despite this, we can still make some points about the merits of reduced demand in a high growth and more equal profile; Tables 6.10 and 6.11 assumed final per head levels of half the present O.E.C.D. average.

First, it stretches credulity to argue that the poor countries could achieve O.E.C.D. materials standards of living without increasing their materials requirements. Whatever the minimum material needs may be for capital and consumer goods, transport, construction and so on, they are surely greater than 5–10 per cent (see Table 6.3) of current O.E.C.D. consumption. For instance, about nine tonnes of steel exist in buildings, machinery, vehicles, etc. in the U.S.A. per head of population; to build up to even 25 per cent of this at a rate of 20 or 30 kg a year (higher than the present rate in many countries) would take nearly a century. This growth rate must be incompatible with a more equal high growth profile.

Secondly, we note that even a sizeable reduction in the use of materials would still require some new mining to be undertaken. Take a material such as copper, where 40 per cent of world supplies currently comes from recycled material. Assume that this quantity could be increased by half (which is very optimistic, given earlier arguments); then mining could only be eliminated if there were a 40 per cent reduction in the demand for copper. Such a target might be achieved for copper in the industrialised countries over the long term, but to do so without resorting to substitutes is likely to prove difficult. (Many past reductions have come from using substitutes, especially aluminium.) To use substitutes would increase demands for other materials, thus making it even less likely that recycling could satisfy demand.

Reduced demand does offer the advantage of pushing back the timing of many of the problems faced by the suppliers of virgin materials. The developments required to continue copper mining could be postponed by a few decades if primary demand were to be reduced sufficiently. As before, the same applies to lead, zinc, tin and other such materials. Other impacts, on energy resources, water supplies, places of natural beauty, etc., would also be kept at lower levels by reduced mining activity.

A high demand for primary materials would suggest that material prices have remained relatively low. This would be compatible with high rates of economic growth in countries that have to import most of their supplies (especially in developing countries), since high import prices can hinder growth, as witnessed by the effects of the oil price increase on poorer countries. This, in turn, would suggest that the technological and economic problems of mining will not have proved serious, and that attempts to maintain high prices by political action will have failed. Indeed, the threats of such action may be a stimulus to research and development into technological escapes from political holds; much of the present research into alternatives to bauxite for aluminium production is spurred on by the desire for greater independence from bauxite-producing countries. High levels of consumption would also suggest that environmental concerns had been handled, by employing technologies with few environmental impacts, by reduced worldwide concern about environmental problems, or by a greater shift of mining and smelting activities to those countries or areas that are prepared to accept the environmental costs in exchange for the benefits they receive.

The alternative of relatively little virgin materials being used suggests that the costs or prices of virgin materials are high as a result of technological and/or political problems. The former cause would not worry most parties, given that in this profile it will not have seriously hindered economic growth, but high prices for virgin materials through political action could have been caused by relatively aggressive moves by at least some mineral-exporting countries. Those industrialised countries previously more dependent upon imports could have some retaliatory powers in the form of demand-reducing technologies, which they would only release to other countries in return for price concessions from the mineral exporters. This would not be relevant if the high prices resulted from political actions mutually agreed by rich and poor countries, but it is doubtful whether high prices could be thus sustained in the long run without governments having much greater control over the production and use of materials (i.e. the market) than they have now.

High Growth, Unequal Profile

If the industrialised countries consume more materials in this profile than in the preceding one, then total world demand could be greater than in the high growth but more equal profile. Consequently, the physical, technological and related problems of mining could be that much greater. But whether this particular development is assumed or not, political factors could aggravate the situation in specific regions.

In the past, an increasing proportion of the materials used by industrialised countries has originated in poor countries (see Table 6.6, p. 174). This has given the industrialised countries greater geographic freedom of movement, thus allowing them to exploit lower-cost deposits, but in recent years has led the poor countries to seek new conditions for such investment or trade (as discussed earlier). It is possible that such negotiations might be dropped, but a much more likely prospect is that they will continue. In that case, it is hard to see the mineral-exporting countries being willing to support rapid growth in the industrialised world (through low prices and guaranteed supplies) while they themselves remain relatively poor (even if richer than now).

Consequently, we would anticipate that in this profile the industrialised countries would have to revert to self-sufficiency through domestic mining and/or using less. More mining would add to the energy, environmental and other problems mentioned above, and the power given to the major industrialised mining areas could destroy any impression of a harmonious and unified industrialised world. In particular, the U.S.A., U.S.S.R., Canada and Australia could have great bargaining power, especially over Japan, Western Europe and other import-dependent countries. It is not implausible that the mining countries could each have internal conflicts between their mining regions and national governments (Western Australia and the Federal Government have already engaged in squabbles over who should control and benefit from mining undertaken in that state). The poor countries that do not mine materials could be trapped between high material prices on the one hand and lack of access to demand-reducing technologies on the other, both of which could contribute to low rates of growth.

This argument suggests that great reliance would have to be placed upon reduced demands in most of the industrialised countries. As an overall assessment of the profile, we note that its successful achievement appears highly dependent upon this one course proving feasible. A future that is highly dependent upon the achievement of one uncertain development, the other options having virtually disappeared, seems unattractive.

Low Growth, More Equal Profile

Perhaps surprisingly, this profile could prove more troublesome from the materials perspective than the high growth profiles. This is because sufficient economic resources may not be available to solve the problems faced. Very high costs for mining or for reducing demand could aggravate shortages; in *The Limits to Growth* it was assumed that mining costs increase so much that the world economy collapses. This situation might not be amenable to control by policy; when the physical and technological problems are immense and the economic resources severely limited, the options are few. The balance between the material and other sectors would clearly have been drawn wrongly if the consequence were unintended long-term shortages of materials.

Certain policies could have the result (probably unintended by some parties) of enforcing low growth upon rich countries and the transfer of resources to poorer countries. For instance, a succession of effective cartels of poor country mineral exporters could slow down growth in the rich countries, while the resources thus transferred to the exporters could benefit them and perhaps their non-mining peers. The three assumptions – achieving cartel action, it leading to resource transfers, and the transferred resources then being used for the common good of poor countries – are all tendentious, suggesting that this profile might be more easily achieved with active cooperation from the rich countries.

If we do assume such cooperation (without prejudging its likelihood), several possibilities emerge. One is that the rich countries encourage high material prices, while somehow controlling the consequences of creating some even wealthier industrialised countries and companies, who would otherwise benefit greatly; and that, simultaneously, the poorer material-importing countries are somehow compensated. The practical danger of such an arrangement is that it will encourage overproduction, with the accumulation of unwanted stocks that have to be kept off the market (if prices are not to fall again). A great degree of mutual trust between countries would be called for: the mineral exporters would have to be convinced that the stocks were not going to be sold, while the financial supporters of the scheme would have to be convinced that the money was well spent.

Transferring 'value-adding' processes to poor country mineral exporters is another way of transferring resources, and is already under way. Many, perhaps most, of those countries that still export ore concentrates have plans to process them to the next level of intermediate product or final ingot. Some also have plans for expanded exports of semi-fabricated or fabricated goods, but are often at a disadvantage when competing in industrialised country markets, given tariff and other trade barriers and relatively high shipping costs for such goods. These disadvantages would need lifting, and the qualms of groups within the industrialised countries over the export of jobs would need allaying. Moving to more value-added products still requires mining, and we can note the earlier discussion on the possible incompatibility of mining with economic development in poor countries.

On the other hand, we might return to our three 'tendentious' assumptions. Some analysts would argue that all three possibilities are rendered unlikely only by the existence of capitalist political systems, and if the governments of these countries were replaced by socialist regimes with no class ties to international business, all three assumptions would be rendered much more feasible. It remains doubtful, however, whether the economic circumstances of revolution in poor countries would permit rapid growth in materials consumption without a protracted period of capital accumulation.

Low Growth, Unequal Profile

The demand for materials would be low in this profile, especially in most poor countries, and so the technological problems to be faced will be less than perhaps even in the high-growth/material-saving profile. Some aspects of this profile are similar to the preceding one. The reasons for low growth could include the severity of the technical problems faced in mining more or using less, cartel actions that created long-term economic recessions without benefits to any major party, or ineffective attempts to transfer value-adding activities to poorer countries.

In several respects, this profile might contain all that one would hope the other three profiles could avoid; it represents the dustbin of their unresolved problems. We have already said enough about reserves, energy, environment, investment conflicts, pricing conflicts, increased efficiency of use, recycling and so on to eliminate the need for repetition here.

SUMMARY AND CONCLUSIONS

In this chapter we have attempted to bring a long-term perspective to bear on the problems of the materials sector. One obstacle that arose frequently was that the kind of data required are not generally available. The industry is primarily concerned with specific mining areas and the short or medium term; the futures debate is concerned with the long-term global situation; material users are concerned with the total costs of specific products more than with halving their materials inputs across a wide range of products.

This severely limited the potential for making quantitative assessments of the future costs, monetary and otherwise, of many of the qualitative choices that are available. What could be done was to identify the kinds of condition under which a tonne of material would be cheap or expensive in the future, and the conditions under which that tonne could be forgone without impairing the standard of living. In some instances we also obtained a feel for the feasibility of meeting those conditions.

Absolute physical limits, in terms of the crust's contents, are not a problem. In some cases, such as aluminium and iron, it was also argued that their physical distribution in the crust was not itself a barrier, but that obstacles might arise from the availability of energy, capital, water or other inputs. For some other metals, such as copper, lead, zinc, or tin, it was argued that major technological changes may well be required if high outputs are to be maintained while prices are kept down. Economic and political difficulties in investment and trade are important and the benefits derived from mining by poor countries are themselves by no means unambiguous.

Capital goods, transport and construction are the three largest users of most materials, the exceptions being such instances as agriculture's dominant use of fertilizer minerals. The quantities of materials required to produce specified goods has often declined over time, although changes in the mix of goods produced in an economy make some types of comparison difficult, as do substitution and changes in the overall characteristics or service performance of individual goods. The prospects for reducing demand for virgin materials by increased economy of use of materials appear greater than by more recycling.

These uncertainties regarding mining and conservation make it difficult to be categorical about the feasibility of the high growth profiles. The high growth, more equal profile is the most attractive, but does entail risks of running into materials constraints. To an extent, this trade-off is a matter of social and political values, but must be compared with the risks that are associated with the low growth, more equal profile, and with the less attractive aspects of the less equal, high growth and (especially) low growth profiles.

One conclusion is irresistible: the allocation of resources to R & D in material-saving technologies and recycling technologies must be a very high priority for the attainment of high growth scenarios. This and the similar conclusions in relation to agriculture and energy lead us in the next chapter to a more detailed consideration of the problems of technical change.

CHAPTER 7

Policies for Technical Change

Christopher Freeman, Charles Cooper and Keith Pavitt

Our ability to predict the rate, the nature and the consequences of broad patterns of technical change has unfortunately not improved very much since Malthus and Marx were writing. The dominant modes of Western economic analysis in the twentieth century – neoclassicism and Keynesianism – have in general treated the rate and direction of technical changes as exogenous to the economic system. Technology has received far less attention from academics and policy-makers than the other 'heavy' variables in long-term development. Even among marxists, who have generally treated technical change more seriously, there are relatively few who have devoted much attention to it. Bernal among scientists and Mandel among economists are rather exceptional. Improvements in our understanding have come from theoretical rogue elephants in economics like Joseph Schumpeter and John K. Galbraith, and from empirical work by assorted economic historians, industrial economists, scientists and sociologists. Only in the past twenty years have research and development (R & D) activities and the process of technical innovation and diffusion become more widely recognised as significant factors in international economic activity, and incorporated into theories of productivity growth, industrial behaviour and international trade.

Schumpeter said that the management of technical change would become a routine, predictable activity and Galbraith sometimes asserts that this is now the case. But empirical study shows otherwise. In spite of the proponents of 'technological forecasting', 'technology assessment' and 'project programme planning', neither industry nor government has shown much accuracy in predicting the time and money required to develop a new piece of technology or the extent of its acceptance by users once developed, let alone the longer-term and secondary effects of a social, psychological or ecological nature. Market and user acceptance uncertainties are, in general, much greater than purely technological uncertainties (Freeman, 1974). In relation to the broader impacts of technology on public and international affairs there have also often been wrong predictions. Thus in the early 1960s it was observed that a 'technological gap' existed between the U.S.A. and Western Europe and some people, such as Servan-Schreiber (1968), predicted that it would grow and result in the technological and economic depletion of Western Europe. Now there are some Americans who are afraid that a technology gap may develop in favour of Japan and Western Europe (Gilpin, 1975).

Nonetheless, some significant and far-sighted work on the links between technological and economic and social trends has been undertaken. In the 1930s both C. Furnas (1936) and the National Resources Committee (1937) of the Department of the Interior (under the strong influence of the sociologists W. F. Ogburn and S. C. Gilfillan) looked at future technological trends. The work of the Committee remains remarkable even today for its scope and foresight. It identified many of the important technological trends and their economic relevance in each of nine sectors: agriculture, the mineral industries, transportation, communication, power, chemicals, electrical goods, metallurgy, construction. It also identified some of the social problems that future technical change would cause and over which we are still brooding today: the introduction of the mechanical cotton picker in the southern United States and its effects on migration from rural areas; the time wasted travelling between city centres and airports; and the social impact of television.

But both Furnas and the Committee underestimated, or did not identify, some important technologies that emerged in the following ten years: atomic energy, computers, radar, antibiotics and the jet engine. They did not foresee the social discontinuity of the Second World War, nor the huge impact that it would have on the development of these technologies. By 1945 some of the scientists working on the development of the atomic bomb were predicting with uncanny accuracy the consequences of its use: the institution of a permanent, science-based international arms race (Jungk, 1958). This major problem for the world's future will be discussed in chapter 10.

The influence of technical change on the nature and conduct of foreign policy has been explicitly recognised ever since, and it is not confined to the military field. In the late 1950s the U.S. Senate Committee on Foreign Relations commissioned a study by the Stanford Research Institute on the impact of non-military scientific developments on the foreign-policy problems facing the U.S.A. This study also identified many of the technology-related problems of international affairs that are still with us today: radio-active waste from nuclear reactors; the exploitation of undersea resources; U.S. dependence on foreign sources of raw materials; the availability of fossil fuels; U.S. attitudes to the emergence of strong foreign competition in manu-factured products; and a range of problems related to the plight of the world's poor countries – the population explosion, the availability of food, the inappropriateness of advanced-country technologies to the needs of the poor, the lack of scientific and technical effort directed specifically to meeting these needs, and the harmful effects of synthetic substitutes on poor countries' exports.

But with the benefit of hindsight it can be seen that the study did not identify all the emerging problems and possibilities. It underestimated the rate of technical advance in, and the political impact of, application satellites: communications, navigation, weather forecasting, resource detection. At the same time it overestimated the impact that would be made by the machine-translation of language, by the use of teaching machines in the world's poor countries and by the role of the social sciences in contributing to the development of the world's poor countries. Finally, it underestimated the problems that the U.S.A. would face in exporting – or not exporting – technologies with both civilian and military uses: for example, rocket launchers, enriched nuclear fuels, nuclear reactors and reprocessing plants, large computers and advanced electronic components.

These and many other examples serve to remind us that there is no way in which we could predict the emergence and acceptance of all future technologies, even for a relatively short period ahead. This is obvious not simply from a hindsight review of earlier forecasts, impressive though this always is in its revelation of bias and blindness, but also on straightforward logical grounds. Much scientific research is concerned with the exploration of the unknown. By definition we cannot know the outcome of such explorations and still less can we know its future impact on technology. Consequently any review of possible and probable future technologies is inevitably deficient in at least two senses. First, it is bound to omit some completely new developments that can in no possible way be foreseen within our present limitations. Secondly, it is bound to err in its assessment of the feasibility, cost and social acceptability of some technologies that are on the horizon or in the early stages of application. Thus, although we may certainly applaud futurologists such as Kahn and Wiener (1967) or Kosolapov (1976) for attempting to list and assess the technologies that are likely to be important in the next fifty to one hundred years, both we and they know that these lists are sure to be incomplete and inaccurate.

However, general and more qualitative forecasts about technology can be made on the basis of the present world pattern of allocation of resources to R & D activities. The present huge commitments to military R & D and to nuclear energy R & D are more likely to produce weapons and fast breeder reactors than small-scale agricultural techniques for tropical regions or cheap and reliable energy from wind and solar sources. Our analysis has considerable implications for the according of R & D priorities, to which we shall return in the conclusions of this chapter.

TECHNICAL CHANGE IN MANUFACTURING INDUSTRY

In one sense our task is much easier than the listing and assessment of a large number of specific technologies. The question we have to answer is: can we assume that the overall rate of technical change (whatever the combination of specific new and old technologies) will be sufficient to sustain an improvement in living standards of the world's population, at least as great as that which has occurred over the past fifty years, and more equitably distributed? Or to put the question another way around: how strong is the evidence *either* that the rate of technical change in general is likely to decelerate to zero, *or* that specific blocks may be encountered that will cause sudden discontinuities? We may readily recognise that, even in attempting to answer these questions — though they are easier in principle than the comprehensive prediction of all new trends in technology — we can answer only in terms of degrees of probability and credibility. There is no question of proof, only of plausibility and of consistency with the evidence.

First of all, then, from what we know about the process of technical change, is it likely to decelerate and come to a halt during the next half century? Here we have a relatively firm starting point. As the Bariloche group and many economists have pointed out, even with the extreme — and barely credible — assumption of no major new discoveries in science, technical change could continue at a high rate for a fairly long time. This derives first from the simple fact that 'best practice' techniques are so far only in use in a very small proportion of the world's productive enterprises and that the productivity 'gap' between 'best' and 'worst' practice is large.

Salter (1961), in one of the best-known and most authoritative economic studies of technical change, has demonstrated the extent of this gap *within* industrialised countries in manufacturing firms, and indeed it can be illustrated from any census of production. He attributes the existence of the gap in the main to differences in technology embodied in successive vintages of new capital investment. He shows that the best firms often have a productivity level two or three times as high as the worst.

Empirical studies of the diffusion processes of new technology within industrialised countries generally indicate a period of ten to fifty years from first adoption to saturation. Moreover, they also indicate a steady process of productivity improvement for many years after the embodied investment, resulting from 'learning by doing' in using the new technology. Salter places the main emphasis on the installation of new plant as the vehicle of technical change, but empirical studies such as Hollander's (1965) study of the rayon industry have amply confirmed the additional importance in many industrial processes of 'incremental innovation' associated with experience of using new plant and machinery.

There is no precise means of quantifying the possible productivity growth within industrialised countries with existing technology; but it is certainly technically possible to treble or quadruple existing levels, if we allow for what is in the R & D pipeline as well as for the diffusion of existing best practice in enterprises. This takes no account of inter-country differences in production techniques and productivity levels. The gaps within any of the industrial countries are large, but between countries they are enormous. Thus, possibilities for a prolonged catching up process in the world's poor countries are substantial. With no major new developments in science or even in technology, it is *technically* possible to raise productivity levels in industry and agriculture in the world's poor countries by at least an order of magnitude, and probably more than twenty times. This is not to say that the poor countries should simply adopt the present-day rich country techniques of production. On the contrary, they should modify and adapt these technologies to suit their own requirements and factor endowments and develop some quite new technology of their own. We shall return later to this important and complex issue.

Thus, even on the extreme assumption of no new developments in science, it is evident that technical change could continue at a fairly high rate for at least thirty years and that within this period, given appropriate institutional and social changes, the poor countries could make substantial progress in catching up with the rich countries. For illustrative purposes a notional rate of technical change of 2 per cent in the industrialised countries might be associated with a GNP growth of about 3 per cent, and a notional rate of technical change in the poor countries of 3 per cent might be associated with a higher GNP rate of growth of 5–7 per cent. This difference is probable because of the greater possibilities of 'extensive development' in the poor countries from the unused reserves of labour and the increase in capital stock.* Indeed on purely *technical* grounds their growth could continue for another generation beyond this, as it would be in the industrial countries that the constraint of no major new developments in science would first make itself felt.

If there were no such developments, it is conceivable that early in the next century technical change in the rich countries would decelerate and ultimately come to a halt as more and more enterprises reached the limits of

*Technical change is of course not the only source of improvements in productivity and growth of GNP. Economists normally use the term to cover not only improvements in the physical techniques of production and distribution, but also improvements in managerial methods and other skills. In much econometric work, it is defined as a 'residual factor', which includes all growth not attributable to an increase of capital or labour. After a long period of experiment with unsatisfactory statistical data, this stream of econometric work on the 'aggregate production function' appears at least temporarily to have run into the sand. Most economists now appear to have abandoned the attempt to estimate statistically the 'contribution' of capital, labour and technical change to aggregate growth of the economy. Most of the earlier measures are now discredited and the emphasis is on the complementarities in the process, rather than on artificial disaggregation (i.e. the recognition that new technologies are largely embodied in new equipment and/or new skills of the labour force). However, we should note that many of the world models we have discussed do use aggregate production functions.

existing technology with modern plant and the inevitably continuing variation in the capacity of management, labour and social institutions. If we relax this highly artificial assumption and allow for some major new developments in science and science-related technology, then a continuing high rate of technical change and productivity growth seems plausible well into the twenty-first century.

The view that science is reaching its limits rests on an interpretation of the scientific enterprise analogous to the exploration of the land surface of the globe. The big discoveries have all been made and all that remains is filling in the details on the maps, with a few corners in equatorial forests and Antarctica still unexplored. On this view there are now rapidly diminishing returns to scientific research. The opposite extreme view is that the scientific enterprise is facing limitless horizons and infinite surprises. Kahn and his associates suggest that future innovations 'may even seem to contradict the laws of physics' (Kahn and Wiener, 1967, p. 69).

Clearly there are fundamental questions of philosophy involved here as well as more pragmatic issues, and we do not propose to embark upon a discussion of them. We note only that, on the one hand, previous assumptions that final truths and ultimate limits had been reached did not prove justified, yet on the other, the evidence of diminishing returns in the cost sense seems to be fairly strong in some areas, for example particle physics. From this we draw the pragmatic conclusion that some discoveries will continue to be made, that old theories will be modified and new ones continue to be generated, but at a higher cost in real resources committed to scientific endeavour.

In so far as technology is closely related to advances in fundamental science, its progress could also be expected to slow down and to become more costly. Many historians and economists have argued, however, that much technological progress occurs independently of basic science or of organised research and development, so that any deceleration might not be directly related to the progress of fundamental research and applied research.

Consequently we agree with the Bariloche group that basic human needs in food, shelter, education and health could be met by the early decades of the twenty-first century for the whole of the world's population, even with no more than existing science and technology. If we postulate some continuing advances in technology over the next fifty years, as seems plausible, then a scenario of further productivity growth for another half-century is feasible in the technical sense, even if there is some deceleration in the rate of technical change.

These conclusions leave no room for complacency. The area of uncertainty is considerable, even though mainstream proponents of most schools of economic theory would find them acceptable. Moreover, they are subject to three important qualifications. First, they assume the continuing effectiveness of social mechanisms for stimulating, generating, disseminating and applying new technology. Secondly, they are based on generalisations at a high level of abstraction about a multitude of discrete and varied change processes. Even though we cannot predict the future developments in each and every one of these technologies, there may be *specific* blocks in sectors of the economy, which might falsify our expectations in all other sectors; for example, there may be difficulties in the continuity of supply of energy or materials. Thirdly, our conclusions have not been related to the problem of bias in technical change: bias in the general sense of an orientation towards the problems of the rich countries, and bias in the related and narrower sense in which economists use the expression – towaıds labour-saving technologies.

It could be that the continuity of technical change would permit the realisation of our high-growth/unequal world profile, but not a high-growth/more-equal world profile. Let us now see how far these qualifications may lead to modifying our conclusions and then examine their implications for policies for science and technology.

SOCIAL MECHANISMS FOR THE GENERATION AND APPLICATION OF NEW TECHNOLOGY

We have already noted that none of the main schools of economic thought (and the same is largely true of sociology and political science) has devoted much attention to the detailed analysis of the sources and consequences of technical change. Policy-making in the field of science and technology has proceeded on a pragmatic ad hoc basis with little general theory to guide it. This has been changing slowly with the growing recognition that simply to spend more money on scientific research or technological development has often been both wasteful and ineffective. As long as research and development were only on a very small scale, and the flow of innovations seemed to be relatively cheap and easy, albeit unpredictable, not too many questions were asked. But as a result of the massive increase in research and development during and after the Second World War, and its increasing professionalisation, science and technology are now matters of growing social concern. Expenditures on research and development may often now be a substantial fraction of the total budget of a government department or an industrial firm and, in the aggregate, they are typically of the order of two per cent of total GNP in industrial countries.

Policy-makers in government and industry have inevitably become increasingly concerned with these activities from what may be loosely described as a 'managerial efficiency' angle. At the same time other social concerns have also increased. Nuclear weapons and nuclear energy, to take the obvious examples, have made everyone aware of the complex social and ecological problems associated with the introduction of new technologies; the current controversy about genetic manipulation is another example. These and innumerable other instances have led to an increasing demand for the public assessment and regulation of technical change, especially in the fields of transport, energy, drugs and chemicals.

This growth of public interest in the origins, effectiveness and consequences of innovations and inventions has helped to stimulate academic and policy-related research into all these problems. It is beyond the scope of this chapter to survey the results of this work.* Here we are concerned only with the relevance of the findings to the problem of continuity of technical change and their consistency with the established schools of thought in the social sciences.

In Part III we shall be discussing the ways in which alternative theories and 'worldviews' within social sciences lead to different visions of the future. But there is greater agreement than might be expected between marxist, Keynesian and neoclassical approaches, at least on policies designed to sustain a high rate of technical change. Broadly speaking, all schools of thought accept both the desirability and inevitability of a major public (governmental) investment in the resources devoted to stimulating and sustaining scientific research and technical change. This agreement is most obvious with respect to fundamental research and education. But there is also general acceptance of the need for substantial public investment in a number of other fields of research, such as agricultural research, medical research and environmental research. Agreement extends also to related dissemination, training and information services designed to ensure effective diffusion and application of new technology. It is not necessary here to go into the precise theoretical economic justification for the use of public investment rather than reliance on the market mechanisms to ensure adequate endowment of these activities. Suffice it to say that neither classical, neoclassical nor Keynesian economics has ever found any major difficulty in accepting this stance.

Differences become sharper in relation to the social consequences of technical change and it is at the enterprise level that disagreement is obvious and fundamental. Neoclassical and, to a lesser extent, Keynesian economists tend to stress the great importance of decentralised, entrepreneurial, profit-motivated decision-making to ensure continuity and effectiveness of technical change in industry and many services. They stress also that planned socialist industry is likely to be bureaucratic, slow and lacking in that degree of imaginative initiative which is the essence of technical innovation. Marxist economists, on the other hand, generally accept that capitalist industry has been very effective in generating and sustaining a high rate of technical

---

*A convenient and fairly comprehensive survey is available in the volume edited by Ina Spiegel-Rosing and Derek de Solla Price (1977).

change, but hold that socialist industry can also do this and with fewer adverse social and environmental consequences. In particular, they argue that socialist societies need not and do not experience the cycle of booms and slumps and the associated unemployment and slow-down of economic growth.

However, with very few exceptions neither the marxist critics of capitalist society nor the critics of socialist society have argued that there are social reasons (as opposed to technological reasons) for expecting a complete cessation of technical change in either system. Even those who, like Sutton (1968), argue that most technical change in socialist societies is based on imported capitalist technology, do not expect this transfer to stop, even if the embargoes he advocates were actually enforced by governments and enterprises. Similarly, the expectations of some socialist economists that the social contradictions of capitalism will lead to its ultimate collapse are usually tempered by realism about its technical achievements over the last quarter-century.

Nevertheless it would be absurd to paper over a genuine and deep difference between the Marxists and other schools. Marxists do believe that capitalist social relations are in many ways a major constraint on the further growth of the productive forces and on useful applications of science and technology. The critics of Marxism often maintain that market economies are inherently more flexible, adaptable and innovative than any state-planned system could ever be. Thus, in terms of each view there would be some serious constraints to technical change in the other system.

It is not possible to bridge this gulf by an appeal to the empirical evidence of the experience of various social systems. There has undoubtedly been a high rate of technical change in the socialist countries and, associated with this, a massive expansion of technical education and investment in research and development and in many other scientific and technical services. However, it is still open to the critics of socialist societies to point to the high rate of import of foreign technology into the socialist countries and the continuing world leadership of the capitalist countries in many branches of technology. Advocates of 'convergence' hypotheses can argue that each system is gradually coming to resemble the other. There has been substantial decentralisation of research and development activities to enterprise and university level in the socialist countries and a growing use of contract techniques, whilst public investment and involvement has increased in the capitalist countries. Moreover, essentially similar technologies are now being developed and applied on a world-wide scale, which provides a strong continuing basis for convergence.

It is not possible to resolve this partly ideological dispute here. For our immediate purpose, what matters is that an assumption of continuity of technical change over thirty to sixty years in industrial countries is not inconsistent with various social theories, or with the empirical evidence about various social systems, or with various alternative assumptions about their spread during that time.

But even if our assumption of continuing technical change is tenable in terms of an accepted level of commitment of public and private resources, are there other problems associated with the social mechanisms for technical change that might lead to deceleration in either or both systems? There are at least two major problems that require serious and intensive study: the possibility of diminishing returns to research and development, and the inadequacy of contemporary methods of technology assessment and project evaluation.

In a number of industries some evidence has been produced that shows that the real costs of generating a new product or a new process have been rising fairly sharply, both in capitalist and in socialist economies. This is true, for example, of new drugs, new insecticides, new aircraft and new types of nuclear reactor. This cost escalation is due to a variety of factors including sheer technical complexity and scale, environmental legislation, and other social concerns. In some cases the costs of experimental development are now so high as to constitute a serious barrier to entry for many firms and countries; even super-powers find some of them expensive. On an optimistic view these rising costs might be circumvented by breakthroughs in science and technology providing new and cheaper alternative solutions. The example of transistor technology in relation to the older valve technology is often cited in this connection. But in view of the growing concern with safety, environmental and other social aspects of technical change, escalating costs of investment in research and development and other technical services might become more general.

In support of this more pessimistic view, it is possible to point not only to the rising costs of generating and using new technologies in a whole number of industries, but also to the possibility of diminishing private returns to the research and development system as such. It is possible that the spurt in the rate of technical change that occurred during and after the Second World War was due in large measure to the 'social invention' of the professional research and development laboratory and its extensive adoption, particularly in industry. The rapid expansion of the professional research and development system between 1940 and 1970 is evidence of the immediate competitive advantage, that capitalist firms derived from it. But this competitive advantage, as with the corresponding expenditures on advertising, is eroded when most firms have learned to play this game. The same is partly true of the technological arms race and other forms of inter-governmental rivalry and competition.

It has, of course, always been recognised in all schools of analysis that professional research and development is only one of many sources of technical change, and some of the others may prove more prolific. It is also possible that other social innovations may prove even more effective than the research and development laboratory has been. Nevertheless it would be reasonable to draw two conclusions from this discussion. First, the question of diminishing returns to investment in research and development and other sources of innovation deserves far more serious attention and investigation than it has so far received. Secondly, the possibility of long-run diminishing returns to research and development is serious enough to justify very careful attention to global priorities and 'insurance' strategies in endowment of science and technology.

The inadequacy of contemporary methods of technology assessment and project evaluation is obvious, not only from the continuing enormous cost and time over-runs that occur in both capitalist and socialist economies, but also and more seriously in the possibility that irreversible damage to the environment and/or to human society might be caused by the introduction or widespread adoption of some new technologies. We have argued in chapter 5 that fast breeder reactor technology is such a case, although the risks may be reduced by further research and development. Most governments in both capitalist and socialist societies have not accepted so far that the risks are serious enough to warrant a moratorium on the commercial application of this technology, but the proponents do accept that there are some very serious risks. It must be a matter of judgement, probability and trade-off in assessing whether these risks are acceptable. But it is in any case clear that methods of assessment and debate are grossly inadequate compared with the magnitude of the risks involved. This together with the increasing cost and complexity of much advanced technology provides some justification for the view of Meadows (1972) and Schumacher (1973) that technology has tended to outstrip the capacity of social systems to understand and control it and provides powerful justification for very careful consideration of priorities in research and innovation.

Greater openness and stronger public accountability could make R & D systems more efficient in their use of resources in relation to society's needs. Independent centres of countervailing scientific and technical power are needed, both inside and outside government, in order to monitor and assess what the big battalions in government and industrial laboratories are doing and in order to give independent scientific and technical advice to individuals and groups who need it.

CRITICAL INPUTS

As we have seen, there is almost universal agreement among those involved in the futures debate that the three most important sectors are those discussed earlier in this part of the book: food, energy and materials. A severe discontinuity in the supply of any of these would undoubtedly cause acute problems throughout the system. We do not think it probable that purely *technical* problems will prevent a steady expansion of supply of food and materials over the next fifty years. Here we are in agreement with Kahn's analysis, and in particular we accept the view that there are *many* different ways in which greatly increased future world requirements might be met. The evidence from the past on the speed and effectiveness of the technical response to specific shortages of materials is very impressive. The range of technologies and the possibilities of substitution are so great that it is difficult to envisage any local or specific block or discontinuity that would be fatal for the system as a whole. So, too, is the evidence on the scope for long-term productivity improvements in agriculture through a variety of demonstrably feasible techniques.

This does not mean, of course, that there is no need to devote further resources to the promotion of continuous improvement in agricultural and materials technologies. This is indeed essential if we wish to maintain improvements in productivity well into the twenty-first century and if we wish to resolve the innumerable specific local problems of adaptation and substitution. It is also essential as an insurance policy. Even if we are fairly confident about the range and capacity of existing technologies, chapters 4 and 6 have shown that the uncertainty that exists is still great enough to make it prudent to continue investment in their extension and enhancement. For example, the possibility of serious discontinuities arising from climatic change or from social disasters such as war can by no means be excluded. Consequently it makes eminently good sense to have insurance policies not only in the form of global stockpiles of foodstuffs and commodities, but also in the form of available means of coping with new supply situations that may suddenly confront various countries in food and materials production.

Some obvious priorities in agricultural R & D are the development of techniques that can be extensively applied to food production in poor countries, that are not capital-intensive and that are less energy-intensive than those now in use in Europe and North America. Among the promising possibilities are the direct fixation of nitrogen, the use of biological techniques of pest control, the breeding of new strains of livestock particularly suited to tropical conditions, new cheap and robust small tools and equipment and ocean farming techniques.

In the supply of materials one of the most urgent needs is the development of less energy-intensive and less capital-intensive methods of mining, extraction and processing, for a wide variety of minerals. Chapter 6 has shown that the capital costs of mining and mineral processing are likely to be a serious problem unless further capital-saving technologies are developed. At the same time there is enormous scope for large numbers of projects concerned with economy in use of materials, scrap recovery and recycling techniques. The whole question of obsolescence and product life will also require increasing attention from industry, government and social scientists.

Unlike food and materials, the physical availability of energy supplies *could* be a serious constraint on the achievement of the objective of sustained high rates of technical change and productivity growth. Increased energy supplies will inevitably be necessary for increased industrial production, as well as for higher food output, use of lower-grade ores, higher rates of materials recycling and reduced levels of pollution. At the same time, supplies of fossil fuels are finite and non-renewable. Nuclear energy is technically and economically feasible, but carries with it some major potential hazards such as radioactive wastes and the proliferation of materials and technologies capable of being used to make nuclear bombs. Supplies of solar and wind energy may not be available for centralised, large-scale uses; and controlled thermonuclear fusion has yet to be proved technically feasible. Thus it is conceivable that energy supplies could be a serious constraint on the growth of the global system unless there are successful R & D programmes in the supply and conservation of energy.

Energy R & D and related activities to stimulate technical change therefore deserve very high priority. In chapter 5 we have identified the following areas as particularly important within the energy sector: conservation, particularly space heating, transport and the use of waste heat from power stations; the mechanisation of underground coal-mining, and coal gasification and liquefaction; the storage and transport of natural gas; geological surveys of oil reserves and resources; the widespread use of solar and wind power as low-grade energy sources; fuel crops; and, within nuclear energy, more resources for the storage and disposal of radioactive wastes and for thorough testing of alternative reactor configurations, including breeding alternatives – based on uranium and thorium – to the sodium-cooled fast breeder reactor.

TECHNICAL CHANGE IN POOR COUNTRIES

We turn now to the most difficult of the three major qualifications on the continuity of global technical change.* The international division of labour has practically excluded poor countries from the creation of new industrial technologies. The bald facts about international distribution of research and development skills, engineering capability and other skills – like machine-making – that are parts of the process of innovation, are reasonably well known. As a rough measure, the developing countries accounted for about two per cent of world expenditures on research and development some ten years ago. Today, the percentage might be a little higher – though not much.

---

*As this issue has been too little discussed in the futures debate, or indeed anywhere else, we make no apology for a relatively long exposition of a fairly complex argument, cast mainly in terms of economics. For a much fuller treatment of this whole range of problems see Cooper (1971 and 1978 forthcoming).

And even though there may have been a small increase in their scientific and technical resources, it is open to question whether this has made any significant contribution to their social welfare. In agriculture, as we have seen in chapter 4, only a small proportion of world research is concerned specifically with the problems of the poor countries, in spite of the critical importance of this sector in terms of employment, growth and welfare.

The notion that this international division of labour results in a pattern of comparative advantages from which poor countries can gain – by trade in technology – has been put in question increasingly over the past decade. The comparative advantage idea initially found expression in the concept that there are great benefits in being a technological late-comer. Today this concept is regarded with the deepest scepticism by the political leadership and the intelligentsia in most of the poor countries. It is also questioned by many in industrialised countries. More and more it is counterpoised with the concept of 'technological dependence', which, it is argued, is a specific aspect of the more general state of 'dependence' poor countries have to overcome in order to develop at all.

The theories of technological dependence borrow a great deal from earlier theories of imperialism. It is perhaps not surprising, therefore, that they have never enjoyed much prestige amongst Western political leaders. In more concrete terms Western countries, pre-eminently the U.S.A., have generally reacted against the dependence arguments and, in particular, they have tended to brush aside the arguments that international transfers of technology by large, multinational enterprises can take place on terms that are distinctly disadvantageous to poor countries. The battlelines in the UNCTAD debates on international transfers of technology are generally very clearly defined. The various UNCTAD resolutions calling for international intervention in the interests of poor countries have remained just resolutions; there is very little willingness in the advanced economies to contemplate any constraint on the action of large Western enterprises in the poor countries. Equally, very little has been done to assist them in building up their own technical resources.

In part, this division of views about the international distribution of benefits from new industrial technologies is easily explicable. The 'technology dependence' theories, which provide the intellectual prop for the political positions taken by poor countries, generally have a somewhat absolutist ring to them. The arguments seem often to proceed along the lines that dependence is self-evidently evil and that anyone who fails to accept the fact is in bad faith. The normative conclusions that emerge are not of a kind to recommend themselves to the Western countries, or to large Western enterprises. Furthermore, far too often the call for action to control the power of the multinational enterprises in poor countries seems to come primarily from the already rich nationalistic business classes of those countries. The action that is proposed (e.g. to control pricing behaviour, encourage re-investment, etc.) seems more appropriate to increasing the material welfare of those classes than to 'development' in any wider sense.

However, for all the reluctance on the part of Western governments to accept the negative implications of 'technological dependency', there are certain features of the present division of labour in technology that are profoundly disquieting and that need to be faced more squarely. We need not dress up these problems in a theory of 'dependence' at all. In fact, it aids recognition and might improve the chances of a more liberal and comprehending response from the industrialised countries, if we refrain from doing so. The analysis is reasonably consistent with Keynesian and marxist economic theory and not wholly inconsistent with some interpretations of neoclassical theory, although not generally accepted there.

The first problem is that the ready supply of technology and technical skills from more advanced economies tends to act as a *substitute* for building up local capabilities in less-advanced countries and this, we argue, can rebound to their disadvantage. For example, even locally owned enterprises in poor countries, undertaking investments in new lines of production, generally prefer to use foreign product and process technology, foreign designers and foreign construction engineers, even though local counterparts and substitutes might be available. The problem often lies in the comparative inexperience of, for example, local engineering designers. This means that it is very risky to use them. Foreign designers may be more costly, but the risks of delay in construction or malfunctioning of plant are much less. Equally, tried and commercially proven process technologies, even if they have to be purchased at the cost of a degree of control by multinational enterprise, are much less risky than untried local processes.* Foreign plant contractors evidently have wider experience and are more likely to be efficient than local ones.

These, however, are typically situations in which there are important 'external economies'. Put more simply: if the local engineering designers had been used, there might well have been economic gains from a social point of view. Partly these would take the form of foreign exchange savings. More importantly, they would take the form of 'learning by doing' in the local engineering design enterprise. This process of 'learning', if sustained, might eventually produce a local engineering group capable of competing with foreign groups. However, these social gains of foreign exchange and technical skill matter little to local investors. From their individual standpoints, they are asked merely to stand the risks and possibly pay the costs of the present inexperience of the local engineer. The experience gained by the local engineer might well be at the cost of mistakes, and the local investing

---

*There are a number of cases in India where industrial processes developed by the national Council for Scientific and Industrial Research (CSIR) have been rejected by private business in favour of importing similar but proven foreign techniques.

company – in the absence of government intervention – is rationally unwilling to meet these costs, since from its individual standpoint they will not be covered by future gains. Generally speaking, these private incentives to use foreign technical skills and technology operate over a wide range of activities. They lead to a substitution for local skill development to a greater extent than is desirable from a development point of view.

In other words, there is a rational economic argument, based on the incapacity of market forces to encourage sufficient development and use of local technical skills, underpinning many of the ideas of 'technological dependence'. It is an argument that is greatly strengthened when we go beyond the implicit assumption of a more or less competitive market situation and consider the imperfections that characterise 'technology markets' in the real world. Briefly, these deficiencies in the market mechanism are strongly reinforced by the way in which 'technology' is actually transferred internationally. The substitution for local skills is all the greater, because foreign owners of technology often use their bargaining power to ensure the use of experienced foreign engineers, designers, contractors and the like rather than local ones. Once again, this is simply an outcome of privately rational decisions. Foreign supplier firms, no less than local recipients, are put off by the risks and potential costs of using local technical capabilities. In addition, the opportunity costs to the foreign supplier of using its own engineering staffs may be very low. If the foreign supplier has plant production facilities, even if only for some sub-processes in the production line, the incentives to use its own facilities and its customary engineering sub-contractor will be all the greater. And finally, problems of maintaining secrecy about 'proprietary' processes can also reinforce the reluctance to involve local laboratories, design consultants and contractors. Broadly speaking, the superior bargaining position of technology suppliers – based often on a technological quasi-monopoly, but also on such things as brand-names and trade-marks – seems to be used frequently in favour of using foreign sources of technology.

It is this type of substitution effect, pushed to greater levels than is socially desirable in poor countries, that underlies the argument that local science and technology in these countries are 'marginalised'. This horrible term is meant to convey the idea that market forces and imperfections in technology transactions undermine the links that should exist between local R & D laboratories and production. As a consequence, it is argued, local R & D objectives, as they emerge in an ad hoc way, have little to do with local requirements. To the extent that there is a local scientific research community, it naturally enough develops broad scientific objectives oriented often towards basic science. This is because the alternative of a socially relevant programme is simply not open.

If these arguments are accepted, they lead to the conclusion that there are self-reinforcing tendencies in the international division of labour in science and technology towards increasing or at least maintaining concentration of these skills in the industrialised countries. To summarise the problem: the only way local researchers or engineers can acquire the experience that might make them 'competitive' in the future, is to be employed actively in the development of production processes now. But market forces and the organisation of technology transfers more or less prevent this and, at the same time, ensure that foreign technical people are used, who thereby acquire experience of the local environment from which local agents are excluded. Underlying the 'technological dependence' theory there is a Myrdalian 'circle of cumulative causation' of this kind (Myrdal, 1957).

So much for the long-run problem (at least for the moment; we shall return to it later). However, in most poor countries it is the short-run consequences of this situation that inevitably claim most attention. There are two main issues: the costs associated with overall reliance on foreign technology and the inappropriateness of foreign technology. Of these, the 'costs' question gets by far the most attention.

The question of what 'technology' *per se* costs in poor countries is difficult to answer. It is, however, easier to see how technology suppliers are able to use the advantages of superior technical skills and the proprietary technology so as to enhance their bargaining power in transactions with enterprises or governments in poor countries. The outcomes of this superior bargaining power (in some comparatively uncontrolled situations) show up in the terms and clauses that appear in contractual transactions for technology, e.g. in licence contracts, and in some of the practices of the multinational suppliers of technology. Vaitsos' (1974) work in Colombia and the other Andean Pact countries has provided a powerful empirical analysis of costs, and has shown how monopolistic control of technology can underlie the imposition of restrictive clauses on sales and exports of technology recipients. He also shows how technology suppliers can achieve a captive market for intermediate goods by selling 'technology' on the understanding that purchasers commit themselves to using materials, inputs or capital equipment from the technology supplier or some designated sub-contractor. Vaitsos' research showed that very substantial over-pricing of intermediate inputs can result with consequent losses of foreign exchange, government revenue and domestic income. These studies led to a widespread political concern in the Latin American countries in particular, a concern that found some expression in Article 24 of the Cartagena agreement of the Andean Pact. Subsequently, the preoccupation with the social costs of foreign technology sparked off the UNCTAD programme and a succession of attempts in UNCTAD to initiate an international debate on the issue. It has also led a number of countries to introduce systems of administrative control to deal with the terms on which technology is transferred.

By and large, Western governments have followed two lines of response in answer to all this. One has been that the problems encountered by the poor countries are largely the outcome of their own policies, e.g. policies of import-substituting industrialisation, or alternatively of their own inaction. This rather unsympathetic response may have been tempered in recent years by the recognition that 'transfer-pricing' practices by multinational enterprises can have negative effects in industrialised countries too (for instance, the recent Monopolies Commission enquiries in the United Kingdom – e.g. Chlordiazepoxide, 1974). A second line of response from the rich countries has been that the international supply of technology is a matter for the private sector, where they as governments have very little say and hardly any control. This response is greatly weakened by the fact that many of the practices in technology transactions that poor countries find objectionable are subject to various forms of anti-trust control within the domestic economies of the advanced countries. There is, of course, a very considerable intervention by government in most industrialised economies in situations of potential monopoly.

The question of how to control the costs of international technology transfers has exercised governments of a wide variety of ideological persuasions in poor countries. It is evidently an issue on which governments of very different political colour can ally. Fundamentally, it is about international distribution of income and while the matter is kept at the level of international distribution there can be considerable agreement between governments whose policies on internal distribution differ widely. The debate on technology transfer has produced the interesting contradiction of 'radical' responses to multinational enterprise from governments whose internal policies are anything but radical. These 'radical' responses essentially reflect the interests of local business classes in obtaining a larger share of income from the introduction of new technologies.

The second question of concern in poor countries is about the 'inappropriateness' of Western technology. The arguments underlying the concept of inappropriateness are widely familiar and have already been mentioned in Part I. The most common one is that Western technology is inappropriate in a capital-starved, labour-abundant economy, because it is relatively lavour saving, i.e. capital-intensive in the sense that it requires a lot of investments per worker. In political terms this line of argument has received support in Western aid agencies in recent years, largely because of profound concern about the humanitarian and political implication of mass unemployment and 'unproductive' employment in poor countries. The perceived threat to social and political stability has strongly reinforced what used to be mainly an argument about economic efficiency and the full employment of factors of production. However, the concept of inappropriateness is also more widely interpreted. For example, it includes the idea that Western technology and technical knowledge is ill-adapted to the proper exploitation of natural resources in poor economies. It also includes the idea that modern Western industry is generating social organisations and patterns of consumption in these economies that are alien and disruptive, and that foreclose options for alternative lines of social development.

These questions are probably less seriously considered in real political terms in many poor countries than the 'costs of foreign technology' question. This is mainly because the problem of 'inappropriateness' is so closely related to internal social and political issues. 'Inappropriate' technologies are often introduced because they are needed to produce the Western-style consumption goods that the comparatively high income elite wish to consume. Controlling their introduction – by indirect taxes on output, for example, or by direct loans on certain consumption goods – has proved politically difficult in some countries and has never been seriously considered at all in others. A switch to more 'appropriate' technologies may also raise political problems; for example it may require a shift of investment resources from large modern sector producers to small firms in rural areas.

However, there are no doubt situations where the social possibilities for using alternative technologies beneficially exist, and in these situations the central question is how those technologies will be created. There are two main lines of approach to this problem; they are not strictly speaking mutually exclusive but they can, for the sake of argument, be put forward as polar cases. The first response is to rely on Western technological capability to generate new technological systems that are more appropriate. It is a response that is regarded with deep suspicion in many of the poor countries, largely because it implies multinational enterprise will become the main vehicle for the supply of the new technologies. Indeed, there are some signs that multinational corporations are moving in this direction already – partly by creating new products and processes for poor countries and partly by transferring the comparatively labour-intensive stages of production to those of them that have set up export-oriented industrialisation policies. There are two main reasons for the suspicious response to this situation. The first is that it essentially implies a continuation of substitution for local skill development – the 'circle of cumulative causation' continues to operate, but in a different form. The second is that, whatever short-run benefits may result, in employment generation for example, there are also likely to be costs because of new forms of technological monopoly.

The second response to the need for 'appropriate' technology is that poor countries should build up their own technical capabilities to create it. This proposal is far-reaching in some of the conditions it seems to imply. One condition would be much greater control over technology imports and a conscious effort to use and develop local technical capability. A second condition might well be that these countries will have to develop more substantial machine fabricating capabilities than they have at present; since machine-making and design play a critical role in innovation in 'mechanical industries'. Those who advocate this response support their arguments by pointing out that many poor countries could quite readily develop a comparative advantage in machine-making activities, especially those related to 'more appropriate' types of capital goods. However, this notion of a much more widespread local innovative capability has not received much attention in Western policy, and conceivably would not get much political support.

At this point we may turn to the question of how Western governments might respond to this international situation in the future. The first point we want to make has no doubt an air of special pleading. Nevertheless, we are convinced it is worth stating. It is simply that the issue of the international development of technology should be treated with much greater seriousness and awareness than in the past. Any real commitment to improving economic development and social welfare in poor countries implies a direct pre-occupation with the operation of international markets for technology and a serious examination of the issues that we raise in this chapter, however they may be resolved. This has not been recognised in action by Western governments except in limited ways. In our view it is important to generate public debate on these issues within the industrialised countries themselves, and that is one of the purposes of this book.

More directly, however, there is a need for reconsideration and realignment of polcies. International discussions and negotiations on transfer of technology have been pretty sterile up till now. They have been dogged by pro and anti positions on the issue of 'technological dependence'. Unfortunately, that issue has often been expressed in terms that have obscured the fact that the way international technology markets work creates real problems for the development of and demand for relevant technical skills in poor countries, and is one of the reasons for a 'brain-drain' of qualified scientists and engineers from poor to rich countries. A clear recognition of these problems and their causes by several governments might be the first step out of the impasse that has been reached in UNCTAD.

This should be accompanied by the recognition that the 'substitution' problems in poor countries cannot be solved by technical assistance programmes to educate skilled scientists and engineers. Whatever value such components of the aid programme might have, their effects are frequently undermined by the fact that technology is supplied in international markets on terms that in effect exclude engineers and scientists in these countries from participation in the productive sectors (except in non-scientific and non-engineering occupations), or at least restrict their role and potential contribution. It is true, no doubt, that changing this situation ultimately depends on action by these governments themselves. Some governments are already attempting various direct controls. However, we believe that this process could be directly aided by industrial country governments, and that it will not be difficult to find ways of doing so.

This raises a more general point. In most industrial countries there is frequently a contradiction between policies on 'aid' and policies on trade and investment. The case of skill development we have just discussed is the outcome of such a contradiction. The aid programme trains technical people, whose role in local industry – or at least in technology development and adaptation – is circumscribed by the way in which companies 'sell' technology or transfer it to the recipient country. Equally, programmes of capital aid are offset in certain respects (e.g. in balance of payments terms) by the income flows that technology suppliers are able to appropriate by virtue of mono-polistic positions based on technology itself or some other factor (e.g. market power or brand-names). In many industrialised countries, the agencies of government that deal with foreign trade and investment are not only substantially out of touch with 'aid' agencies, but actually implementing policies that in their broad impact are contrary to the development aims of 'aid' policy. In our view one of the major political challenges of the coming twenty years is to search for the resolution of these contradictions. This would involve much more than just departmental coordination in government.

A possible approach to this issue would be for the U.S.A. and other industrial countries to take the initiative in an extension of anti-trust law to international operations, especially in poor countries. Such an initiative would be a logical extension of the commitment to development and a very crucial component of an aid programme. It would of course entail a very considerable realignment of aid, trade and foreign investment policies, and some would regard such a change as improbable on the basis of past experience of 'aid' policies.

Finally, there is the question of the development of technical capability within poor economies, specifically in the interests of new types of technological development. In our view this raises some fundamental questions for world priorities in research and development, as well as in 'aid' policies. In the first place, we support the argument that the main hope for new lines of appropriate technical change lies in building innovative capability *within* poor countries. We share many of the doubts, described earlier, about the use of multinational enterprises in this field. In our view, therefore, if the governments of industrial countries are committed to long-run development in poor countries, they should considerably increase their contribution through the aid programme to local technological development.

This probably implies a realignment of aid policies in terms of country priorities, which will, of course, raise major political issues. The point is, however, that the best hopes for generating alternative types of technology are in countries where employment and greater equality in welfare are major objectives, and where the political and social organisation is to some degree amenable to such objectives. These are not necessarily the types of country that receive most aid at present.

The objective of encouraging local technology also implies that aid policy should encompass a shift towards much less reliance on foreign technology and foreign investment in overall development strategy and much greater control by poor countries of such technology transactions as may take place with foreign enterprises. Under these conditions the aim of aid policies in this area would then be to reduce as far as possible the comparative costs of using local rather than foreign technology. This implies a policy oriented towards training of suitable types of technical personnel, and of contributing towards local research and development and other innovational institutions. It also implies a major shift towards the development of machinery production in poor countries themselves.

Summary and Conclusions

From the earlier chapters and from the above discussion we conclude that no insoluble problems, which might frustrate the achievement of high growth profiles, should be posed by technical change in manufacturing industry or in the production and distribution of food. Continuing technical change will be desirable and necessary, and there appear to be no insuperable scientific or technological obstacles to its achievement. However, given that the future is uncertain and that these sectors are critical to world economic development, it will be desirable to take out what could be described as global insurance policies, which include continuous large-scale support for basic research and for scientific and engineering education related to them, as well as the development of a wide range of alternative technological solutions.

The main problem in relation to technical change in agriculture and manufacturing is a global reorientation towards the solution of the problems of the poor countries. This will in our view involve a massive increase of scientific and technical resources in those countries themselves.

The provision of sufficient energy and materials for future world development poses many new and challenging technical problems, so that R & D in these fields both deserve high priority. Such R & D should be much more diversified, both inside and outside the nuclear energy sector, than is the case at present. Because of its central importance for all other sectors of the economy and because of the difficulties associated with nuclear power described in chapter 5, we would give this sector the highest priority of all. The materials problems, although serious, are inherently more tractable and the variety of possible solutions far wider.

We have argued throughout this chapter and the earlier ones that the future rate and direction of technical change cannot be divorced from the wider economic and political setting within which it takes place. The cost and feasibility of technical change in, for example, materials, transport and energy, will be heavily influenced by social, safety and environmental legislation; more generally, the pace and direction of technical change will be strongly influenced by the system of rewards and incentives influencing both

R & D teams and industrial firms. The way in which these rewards and incentives encourage or discourage the development of technologies and skills for poor countries will depend, amongst other things, on the anti-trust behaviour of the governments of industrialised countries and the policies for importation of foreign technologies in poor countries.

Government policies will also be critical to the rate and direction of technical change in energy. The behaviour of the governments of the U.S.A. and the U.S.S.R. will have a major influence on future world availability of fossil fuels. In all industrialised countries energy technology will be critically influenced by general policies towards energy prices, public investment, public regulation, the international transfer of energy technology and the allocation of R & D resources amongst competing claims.

In other words, technical change and the allocation of resources to R & D cannot be divorced from wider questions of the future of the world's political economy. These questions are the substance of the final part of this book. Here too we discuss the still more fundamental question of the 'quality of life'. Man does not live by bread alone, and even though we may be able to provide enough bread, this leaves these more important questions still unanswered.

PART III

Prospects for Social Change

CHAPTER 8

Worldviews and Scenarios

*Ian Miles**

In this chapter we shall present three 'worldviews', which offer contrasting perspectives on world development. We shall use them as guides to the controversies about the historical evolution of the present world economy and its possible and desirable courses of development, and to work out our own scenarios of alternative world futures.

The 'worldviews' may be regarded as three different political standpoints: conservative, reformist and radical. Each standpoint will be defined here by a mixture of analytical and prescriptive statements about how the world operates and what should be done to influence its operation. Before setting out these worldviews it will be useful to consider briefly the way in which the differing theoretical analyses have themselves evolved. This will mean covering some ground that may already be very familiar to some readers, but it is a necessary basis for the subsequent discussion of development theory, growth and international equity.

CLASSICAL ECONOMICS, MARXISM AND KEYNES

Adam Smith's *An Inquiry into the Nature and Causes of the Wealth of Nations*, published in 1776, is generally regarded as marking the beginning of classical political economics. Though it is often now seen as a source of conservative philosophy, in its time it was a radical influence. Smith's arguments supported the vigorous new class of industrial capitalists in

*The ideas which shape this chapter arose from an extensive re-evaluation of our forecasting approach, largely stimulated in the first place by Charles Cooper, Gordon MacKerron, Joe Townsend and Andrew Sayer. Charles Cooper submitted earlier versions of the chapter to extensive and valuable criticism, and Keith Pavitt made many valuable editorial suggestions. Sam Cole and Jay Gershuny helped develop the scenarios and John Irvine made very useful detailed criticisms.

Britain and undermined the position of the landed classes. As the book's title suggests, at the heart of his analysis is a concern with the causes of economic growth and national incomes per head; he did not tackle directly the question of 'world development', although he paid considerable attention to the colonial system.

Adam Smith propounded a labour theory of value, later given a revolutionary interpretation by Marx. Smith argued that the true value of a commodity was determined by the quantity of labour-time typically needed to produce such a commodity. Market prices might fluctuate around this level according to supply and demand. In the long term, resources would be shifted to gain the highest available returns, and assuming the existence of competition the unaided market would allocate investments to their most efficient and profitable users, ultimately drawing market prices back to the true values of the commodities in question. Economic growth is largely based upon increases in the productivity of labour, particularly those yielded by the division of labour, and upon the employment of large proportions of the labour force in 'productive labour' (producing physical goods), which depends on the accumulation of capital, i.e. the investment of profits in productive enterprise by the capitalist class.

Smith recognised that the pursuit of self-interest might not necessarily be to the general good. In his system the 'invisible hand', which enables the self-interested behaviour of individuals to be at the same time in the community's interest, required the existence of appropriate legal systems and institutions. However, within such a framework, free competition and free trade were desirable. Restrictions on imports and exports should be removed, and protection of agriculture should be abandoned, since it could not pay a nation to produce itself what might be bought more cheaply elsewhere (although even here Smith notes that protection may be needed to allow infant industries to develop). Whilst he argued for free trade to enable capitalists to specialise and take advantage of the world market, his discussion of an international division of labour was not fully worked out.

The years following the publication of *The Wealth of Nations* saw major economic changes in Britain. The bad harvests during the Napoleonic wars and the subsequent hardship and stagnation gave widespread credence to Malthus' ideas of over-population. By the time David Ricardo's *Principles of Political Economy* was published in 1817, industrialisation and urbanisation had proceeded apace and interest in trade and economic growth amongst economists and politicians was intense.

Ricardo extended Smith's analysis, using the principle of comparative advantage to demonstrate the benefits of the international division of labour and trade. He sought to prove more rigorously than Smith that under conditions of free trade everybody would benefit. He did not completely clarify, however, whether one country might gain more than another from free trade. Ricardian ideas were used to justify a wide range of trade and colonial policies in the early nineteenth century. They provided a theory well-adapted to win support from the manufacturing capitalists who saw free trade policies as a way of expanding their markets and cheapening their imported raw materials. They were particularly acceptable at a time when Britain was becoming an industrial workshop for a world that would supply her with agricultural produce. Ricardo himself took the prospect of Malthusian limits very seriously. He believed that a law of diminishing returns would lead to rising costs in agriculture as progressively less-productive marginal land was brought into cultivation. This was at the heart of his attack on landlords and on the protection of British agriculture, which prevented the purchase of wheat from agriculturally resource-rich countries, inflated food prices and labour costs, and thereby tended to reduce profits and capital accumulation.

As the most industrialised European country and the dominant economic power, Britain provided a unique environment for economists. It is not surprising that despite common interests in problems of trade and economic growth, political economy in other countries took different directions, and acceptance of the ideas of Smith and Ricardo on free trade and related issues was by no means unanimous. In the 1840s in Germany, for example, Friedrich List was arguing in his economic texts that free trade between nations would be predominantly in the interest of the most developed countries. With a focus on neither individuals nor classes as economic actors, but on nations, he argued that the less-industrialised states should set up tariffs to protect manufacturers from competition from more advanced countries. List saw the prospects for economic growth in his country as intimately connected with the pattern of world trade and the international division of labour. Ironically, his arguments have now been taken up by leading Cambridge economists to justify protectionist policies for the ailing British economy. It is thus the turn of German economists to remind Britain of the virtues of free trade,

Marx's economic theories owed a great deal to British classical economics, as he was the first to acknowledge. Whilst he despised Malthus, he always wrote admiringly of Ricardo. However, he believed that the further development of economics as a science beyond the Ricardian system could be undertaken only by those who were prepared to question the fundamental institutions of the system, rather than simply accept them.

In his theory, capitalists exploit the proletariat by appropriating the surplus value produced by labour. They are able to do this because the workers have nothing to sell but their labour power and so are obliged to work for wages. In a few hours they may create the value of their own means of subsistence, and in the remaining hours of the working day they produce a surplus for the capitalists. A future communist society must be based upon the proletariat's seizure of ownership and control of the means of production. Marx argued that modern industry was creating the conditions for such a change, especially through increased concentration of ownership and centralisation. Economic growth and the advance of technology under capitalism meant that scarcity was no longer a consequence of under-production of the essentials of life. The acute crises of capitalism, manifest in business cycles, were in fact crises of temporary 'over-production' resulting from investment decisions governed by competitive market forces. Further-more, the increase of capital-intensity meant that it became continually harder to maintain the rate of profit on industrial investment, thus providing a powerful impetus to technical change and other means of increasing productivity. This tendency for the rate of profit to fall was one factor that Marx saw as deepening the crisis of capitalism. Another was the sharp conflict of interest between workers and owners and the experience of organisation and collective action that industry gave the working class. Marx's theory was based squarely on the notions of class and class conflict, rather than on the notion of economic society as an aggregation of individuals. The class-conscious proletariat would be the agent of social revolution.

Marx often seems to suggest that capitalist development would spread out from the industrial countries to encompass the world, with all countries following a similar path and workers' revolutions taking place in the most advanced ones. But he also discussed the processes whereby colonies might be impoverished, their growth retarded and distorted by the imperial powers, and even considered the possibility of revolutions taking place first in the poorer, peripheral countries, such as Russia. The relative prominence of these two aspects of imperialism and world development is an issue of contention among present-day Marxist and radical economists.

Marxists regard imperialism as a stage in the development of world capitalism (Lenin, 1917) and not simply as a consequence of nationalism or some other anomaly distorting the operation of the capitalist economy. The expansion of capitalism reflected not only a search for raw materials and new markets, but also an effort to counter the tendency of the profit rate to fall. Profit rates could be maintained through cheaper materials, the expansion of the market and the available labour force. Lenin saw imperialism as tending to move the world more rapidly towards the point where a transformation to socialism could be made. However, like most other developments of capitalism, imperialism could not be welcomed. Not only did it involve violent repression of colonial peoples, but it could also enable the industrial states to 'buy off' some more highly paid sections of their working classes. In Lenin's view this was the economic basis for 'reformist' ideologies in the European socialist movement.

Marxist economic analysis made more headway among the working-class movements on the European continent than in Britain; it influenced the perspectives of mass political parties and, eventually, the Russian revolutionary movement. Marx's concepts, however, were never well received by the majority of influential economists. By the time that the later volumes of *Capital* were published, classical political economy itself had given way to theories of marginal utility and the neoclassical schools of economics.

By the middle of the nineteenth century, free trade policies had been established in Britain, the owners of manufacturing industry had a secure position in the power structure, and the problems of industrial capitalism were more obviously those of combating the labour movement and securing more stable and efficient administration than of contesting the hold of the old aristocracy on the English economy. Classical political economy had played a major role in this contest and the landed classes had been forced to accommodate to the new order. The grand issues of economic growth and the distribution of its benefits were now of less concern than questions about price changes and the economics of public utilities such as gasworks. The labour theory of value seemed unwieldy for predicting market prices and their fluctuations, and positively subversive in the distinctions drawn between productive and unproductive labour and in the way in which it was used to define exploitation.

In the last half of the nineteenth century, and particularly after 1890, new approaches to economics were developed by such theorists as Jevons, Marshall and Walras. In their view of capitalism, both the labourer and the entrepreneur were alike productive, and every factor of production was rewarded because of its utility. In neoclassical economics the purchasing decisions of individuals reflect their assessments of satisfactions to be gained from different goods (their relative 'utilities'). Individuals make rational use of their resources to maximise utility. Investment decisions and production follow the expression of demand in the market as indicated by price-signals. Orthodox economic wisdom was increasingly dominated by the neoclassical approach and it was used in the twentieth century by Fabian socialists, advocates of pure *laissez-faire* and corporatists alike. However, for many years neoclassical economists did not develop the notions of international division of labour and world development much beyond the perspectives of Smith and Ricardo. Imperialism was largely viewed as an aberration in the world market, stemming not from economic but from political factors. With the liberalisation of international trade it was still maintained that the workings of the market would ensure that nations produced at an optimum level according to the principle of comparative advantage.

In chapter 3 we saw how marxist analysis was applied by Russian revolutionaries faced with the task of achieving social and economic transformation in an under-developed country. Even before the Bolsheviks came to power and confronted the problems of 'socialism in one country', Lenin had described development under capitalism as extremely 'uneven': regions were affected in very different ways, with some colonies and non-industrial nations maintaining a mixture of advanced capitalist enclaves in a hinterland of semi-feudal and other pre-capitalist economic formations.

After the 1920s analysis and discussion of these issues in the Soviet Union was stifled by the dogmatic theories and ruthless repression of Stalinism. The rich countries faced new concerns: they moved into the Great Depression and many observers felt that the Marxist predictions of the collapse of capitalism were about to be fulfilled. In the U.S.A. Roosevelt's government initiated the New Deal, a major move from *laissez-faire* to government intervention in domestic economic affairs. In Germany the Nazis employed even more drastic means to combat depression, including military spending, heavy public investment and internal repression of trade unions. In Britain the work of Keynes provided a new formulation of economic theory that justified governmental economic activities such as the New Deal was attempting and which non-Marxist social reformers had been seeking in many industrial countries.

Keynes's account of the problems regarding growth in the 1930s is sometimes described as an 'under-consumptionist' approach. He argued that stability could be restored by fiscal policies that would keep effective demand up to levels which would sustain full employment. Against orthodoxy he argued that unemployment need not stimulate automatic market adjustments, that it might instead trigger a spiral of decreasingly effective demand and investment. If the 'invisible hand' would not move to restore full employment and growth, the state could do so by public spending and by influencing private spending and investments through changes in taxation and interest rates.

Keynesianism provided the intellectual framework for the strategies which industrial states were forced to follow during the Second World War (even if they had resisted them in the Depression) and for the policies of full employment that they adopted afterwards. It was used by European social democrats as part of the rationale for the mixed economy. Contrary to the expectation of sceptical observers, the new role of the state was apparently one of the factors that enabled Western countries to reduce the impact of trade cycles and achieve high and relatively uninterrupted economic growth for two decades. It seemed as if the new economics was able to guarantee stable growth; but there were doubts about the continuing inflation, which by the early 1970s was to become a pressing problem.

DEVELOPMENT ECONOMICS

The Keynesian tradition, which was focused on the problems of the industrial countries, had little to offer the Third World, however. Large numbers of former colonies became independent after the Second World War, and the East and West vied for influence over them. Development studies mushroomed and attracted many leading economists in all parts of the world, who attempted to grapple with the problems of formulating 'optimal' growth strategies and of assessing the effects of policies actually followed in poor countries. 'Development economics' increasingly established its own theoretical approaches.

Many poor countries sought to develop rapidly through industrialisation in order to increase incomes at a rate faster than that of population growth. An important strategy was the attempt to reduce balance of payment problems and to offset declining terms of trade by domestic production of industrial goods that would otherwise be imported. In the 1950s ECLA (the U.N. Economic Commission of Latin America) and its leading economist Prebisch developed a 'Latin American' development economics that justified such policies. The ECLA economists viewed the world as divided between a rich industrial centre and a poor, primary-producing periphery whose development could be stimulated if local entrepreneurs could be protected from competition from overseas producers in the domestic market. Import-substitution might increase prices of industrial goods, but it could provide employment, save on foreign exchange and encourage the acquisition of technical skills. At the same time it would call for large investments to establish industries; foreign financing seemed to be an appropriate strategy.

More orthodox Western economists warned that import-substitution ignored the principle of comparative advantage and could damage the economies of the poor countries. These warnings seemed to be borne out by the stagnation of much of Latin America in the 1960s despite some industrialisation. However, neoclassical trade theory was itself changing. The Heckscher–Ohlin theory of the 1950s, which stressed the role of the relative factor endowments of different countries in establishing trade patterns, met with increasingly severe criticism. Under the impact of experience, research and changing policies, a more dynamic notion of comparative advantage was developed. Technological change, training and the discovery of new resources were accepted as major influences on the balance of comparative advantages, and intangible capital investment in education and research was recognised as a major factor endowment. The influential study by Little, Scitowsky and Scott (1970) analysed the failures of import-substitution and then advocated that many poor countries would benefit from producing manufactured goods for export as well as increasing their primary exports. Such export-promotion could lead to the acquisition of important skills and would not commit these countries to remaining primary producers indefinitely.

Some writers originally closely aligned with the ECLA position, such as Furtado, became dissatisfied with both its achievements and its theoretical focus on industrialisation and terms of trade. Latin American economists took to analysing the ways in whish social structures of poor countries led the local industrialists to develop ties with foreign capital. They argued that the problems of import-substitution stemmed not from the policy itself, but from such factors as the structure of land tenure, the unequal distribution of wealth associated with domestic production of luxury goods rather than mass consumption items, and the collaboration of local manufacturers with both the landowning aristocracy and foreign multinational corporations, taking advantage of protection for the maintenance of their own power and privilege.

Similar analyses of under-development, stressing institutional obstacles to growth and pointing to state intervention as a means of overcoming the inability of a market economy to surmount them, have been made by a wide range of economists and have been labelled the 'structuralist' approach. One version of structuralism is 'dependency' theory, which relates the problems of poor countries to the historical formation of their economies as primary resource suppliers; this is used to argue for the creation of strong national capitalist groups in order to overcome the power still exerted by the rich industrial countries.

Some contemporary Marxists have put forward perspectives similar to those of dependency theorists, agreeing that the poor countries have been 'under-developed' because of their links with the world economic system. To such theorists development is unlikely to be achieved by attempts to secure greater national autonomy by supporting local capitalists. The ruling classes' close links with overseas interests can be broken by nothing short of revolution. Other marxists do not use terms such as 'dependency' but talk of neocolonialism as a major force retarding development (and benefiting the capitalist classes of rich countries). Yet others argue that economic development may take place under the stimulus of foreign investment.

Thus, like other social sciences, development theory today comes in many varieties. Neoclassical economists promote the ideal of the free market, although they disagree about such issues as the protection of infant industries and the effects of multinational corporations. Keynesian and structuralist economics are used to justify state intervention to stimulate and stabilise capitalist development. A neo-Ricardian school of trade theorists has emerged as a non-Marxist 'radical' challenge to the orthodoxies. Marxist approaches usually stress imperialism as a continuing major factor in world development, but there are many disputes within this tradition.

In this necessarily simplified account of development theory we have attempted to show how the theories generated at a given time both reflect contemporary problems and draw upon previous theories. Some of them are mutually incompatible, but other concepts are more widely shared. Different kinds of analysis will often be directly employed to advance political interests. Thus, at the UNCTAD and other conferences the proposals made by various groups drew upon these different traditions of development theory. Admittedly interests and alliances are complex, as are the terms of the debate between proponents of different theoretical traditions. There need be no one-to-one correspondence between such broad political classifications as conservative, reformist and radical orientations and such theoretical perspectives as neoclassical, Keynesian and marxist analyses. Nevertheless, at least some matching of theory and interests in international development appears to exist today, as in the nineteenth century. Dominant industrial powers such as the U.S.A. and West Germany tend to favour *laissez-faire* approaches in international trade reform (although seeking some kinds of regulation, such as guarantees about the security of foreign investments). Other industrial countries, e.g. some members of the E.E.C., want the world economy to be planned to such a degree as to safeguard their industries against price fluctuations, while the poorer countries seek a structural change in the world economy.

Rather like the political debate about world development, the forecasting literature has drawn upon the ideas of development theorists. We have argued that the use by forecasters of specialist work on such issues as trade and industrialisation was unsystematic and superficial. We may now add that there is little acknowledgement of lack of consensus in this specialist literature. To present a single theoretical perspective as the latest and best wisdom is the approach of most forecasters, including some who have a background of solid achievement in economics.

The existence of divergent social-philosophies/development-theories postulating significantly different means of achieving international equality and growth must also be taken into account. Analysis of the crucial questions posed by the Malthusian problem has only taken us a little way in this direction. As part of an alternative approach for assessing and advancing the world futures debate, the concept of 'worldviews' may prove useful.

WORLDVIEWS

Different traditions of economic analysis, such as neoclassical, Keynesian and Marxist, are by no means monolithic. We can often characterise particular writings or theorists as belonging to one or other tradition, but we would be mistaken either to construe any one perspective as unchanging or to expect all its representative thinkers to produce identical analyses and conclusions. Some continuities do, however, exist within each tradition. The way in which different approaches focus on different primary units – individuals, nations or classes – is one such continuity. The use of different theoretical approaches – e.g. the focus on the efficient allocation of resources and the principle of comparative advantage as opposed to a concern with different modes of economic organisation – is another. Nevertheless, within each group of theories we observe significant changes in attitude over time as well as major controversies between theorists at any one time. The Neoclassical economists debate the monetarist thesis, the legitimate extent of state authority and whether the monopolistic features of multinational corporations offset their positive contributions to world development; Marxists disagree about the reality of the falling rate of profit, the feudal or capitalist nature of poor countries and the composition of the working class; and structuralists and Keynesians cover much of the widely varying terrain between these two theoretical poles.

This diversity of analysis means that we cannot possibly acknowledge all shades of opinion. For our present purposes it can help to group different approaches into a limited number of schools of thought, because we need to venture beyond economic description. Furthermore we cannot possibly assume that common *theoretical* approaches yield common political perspectives and prescriptions for action. While neoclassical economists are often caricatured as uniformly conservative, some economists have tried to derive arguments for major shifts in the distribution of wealth from neo-classical principles; structuralists may or may not urge changes in the power balance of national groups as a concomitant of nationalistic reforms; the terms 'left-' and 'right-Keynesian' are common enough to need no comment; and marxian analysis has been used not only in revolutionary and reformist proposals but also, on occasion, for extremely reactionary purposes. Representatives of the three worldviews tend, nevertheless, to draw or develop their analyses from the theoretical apparatus of different traditions of social or economic thought. However, although the 'political' labels – conservative, reformist, radical – given to them can be used to summarise policy prescriptions, they do not adequately reflect theoretical assumptions underlying the prescriptions.

We are by no means the first to classify different political positions or social theories in order to organise a bewildering number and range of different writings. For example, both Barratt-Brown (1974) and Gilpin (1975 a, b) analyse international economic relationships in terms of three perspectives. Gilpin goes so far as to provide descriptions of the alternative futures that each perspective implies, providing one image of the future for each viewpoint.*

---

*In *The Next 200 Years* Kahn et al. (1976) contrast four different perspectives on the future. However, these simply represent different assumptions about the Malthusian problem, ranging from extreme technological pessimism to extreme optimism. Grouping analysts in this way masks important differences in their political and economic persuasions.

Several authors have contrasted different theoretical approaches in specific areas of social research in a way similar to our use of 'worldview'.

Among recent American and British writings in this vein the following authors provide bibliographies that are useful in following up particular research traditions – development theory: Barratt-Brown (1974), Chilcote and Edelstein (1974), Foster-Carder (1976); sociology: Chambliss (1973), Lazarsfeld (1973); social problems and welfare: George and Wilding (1976), Horton (1966), Shostak (1974); political development and regional issues: Hechter (1975), Katzenstein (1976).

Theoretical analysis by conservatives tends to draw on such sources as the neoclassical school of economics, structural-functionalism in sociology and functionalist approaches in the study of international relations. These approaches share many conceptual underpinnings: the essential features of society are seen as consensus, order and the forces that maintain the integrated functioning of its different components; the ideal social order is often portrayed as an equilibrium, maintained by liberal economic policies and fairly conservative political strategies. Society is viewed as a system composed of elements that contribute to its overall functioning. Social change occurs through evolution and diffusion: new ideas, technologies and institutions are assimilated into the social order if they can perform society's functions more efficiently than their predecessors. Diffusion tends to progress from more advanced to less advanced sectors, regions or social groups, and attempts to accelerate or control it are often disruptive. Efforts towards directing the course of social and economic development are likely to upset the balance of functions in unpredictable ways. Intervention in the spontaneous interaction of ideas, institutions and goods in an established 'normative system' of social values and structures, whether arising from self-interest or well-meaning but short-sighted interference, in many cases may actually reduce the overall level of welfare by preventing properly adaptive evolution. Such assumptions have led many observers to describe proponents of the conservative worldview as spokesmen for private intersts, fearful of state intervention in their affairs.

In outlining worldviews we bring together analyses from a variety of authors who share roughly the same position: no one writer or work, then, is likely to be fully representative of any worldview and, similarly, writers whom we would associate with a particular worldview might well object to some points in our account of that position. Nevertheless, it may be useful to mention authors whose work has, we believe, made a substantial contribution to each worldview. In the case of the '*conservative*' worldview, we might cite Adam Smith, Durkheim and Pareto as historical sources, Karl Popper as social philosopher, P. T. Bauer, Harry Johnson and Milton Friedman as economists, and R. A. Dahl, Mancur Olson and Talcott Parsons as political scientists and sociologists.

We label a second perspective the '*reformist*' worldview. It differs markedly from the conservative perspective in that the theories largely employed here stress the problems rather than the advantages of a *laissez-faire* approach to socio-economic systems. Thus, Keynesian economics proposes that free markets can create unemployment and under-use resources. Government intervention to regulate the economy is needed to avoid stagnation and consequent political instability. In modern sociology and political science, writers on 'post-industrial society' have often taken a similar stance on the need for social engineering directed towards the solution of social and environmental problems. This worldview can also be characterised by a greater emphasis on conflict. The ideal social order in this view is a mixed economy in which a regulating agency, often the state, plays the role of arbiter in social conflicts and carries out liberal politics. While social change in the past has largely been a matter of advances in technology and knowledge, which have been used to advantage by particular groups or nations, it is now possible, these writers argue, to use existing mechanisms for directing change in a more deliberate and equitable way. They maintain that they are seeking to safeguard pluralist decision-making while ameliorating the social costs of unregulated social systems. Many observers have described these views as special pleading for bureaucrats and technocrats who wish to gain or legitimate personal power and prestige without risking major social change or challenges to powerful vested interests.

Perhaps the most obvious historical precedent for the contemporary development of this worldview is J. M. Keynes; Heilbroner is an economist whose work is largely in this tradition, while Daniel Bell is a sociologist whose futurological books *The End of Ideology* and *The Coming of the Post-Industrial Society* seem to fit the worldview (albeit at the more conservative end of the reformist spectrum). Indeed, reformist conceptions have been employed by many forecasters, development economists and others concerned with contemporary social trends. Other prominent figures we might name here are J. K. Galbraith, Gunnar Myrdal and Furtado as economists and Ralf Dahrendorf as political theorist, but it seems rather unfair to single out individuals from a tradition of analysis that in many ways consists of sophisticated statements of much of the 'collective wisdom' of recent decades and of attempts to fuse together the two other worldviews.

We call our third perspective the *'radical'* worldview: the dominant theoretical tendencies here are Marxism and neo-Marxism in their various forms, but we might also cite anarchist and libertarian political viewpoints. The social analysis used in this worldview is founded on the notion of a dialectical interplay between ideology (the 'consensus' of the conservative worldview) and social relations (especially class conflict). Peoples' consciousness is conditioned by their social life, but since the social system has contradictory features there is the possibility of revolutionary consciousness developing and playing a role in transformation. Major structural changes in society follow seizures of power by different classes. These changes themselves establish preconditions for further change. Rather than social change being due to an evolutionary process of 'natural selection' among ideas, institutions and technologies, the interests of the ruling classes are seen as moulding the dominant features of society. Whilst based on human interests these features appear as natural arrangements or technical necessities with autonomous power of their own. Radicals look to a new social transformation in which power will be seized by the working class (in classical Marxism) and/or the peasantry (as in Maoism). Only then can the evolution of society be placed under democratic social control so that it may follow the interests of people rather than the search for profit; only then can the economic system be free of periodic crises and continual imbalance. Inequalities of economic power limit freedom, and democracy cannot be fully realised in societies where some individuals have access to massive resources that can propagate their views and restrict the choices of others. Critics of these arguments often assert that they are put forward by would-be rulers and dictators, discontented with their lack of power in a free society.

Obviously the historical sources of this radical worldview may be traced back to Marx and other socialist writers and activists. Contemporary radical analysts include economists such as Ernest Mandel, Samir Amin and André G. Frank, political theorists such as Ralph Miliband, and social philosophers such as Herbert Marcuse and Perry Anderson. Some radicals resent being compartmentalised into disciplines in this way, and contend that it is necessary to analyse society as a totality; that while some division of labour may be necessary, the fragmentation of academic disciplines encourages mystification and reformism.

These political labels convey the sense of theoretical analysis infused with prescription. However, there are several dangers about using them. One is simply that they already carry so many associations that important distinctions may be overlooked. By 'conservative', for example, we refer to a particular blend of analytical and prescriptive orientation, which we shall seek to outline in sufficient detail to avoid confusion with a particular political party. Likewise it would be wrong to treat the three worldviews as if they were different points on a single 'left–right' dimension of political orientation. Whilst in some respects this is a reasonable approximation, there are in other cases surprising convergences and divergences between their theoretical analyses. Related to the above points is the matter of differences in 'foreign' and 'domestic' analysis. It is by no means uncommon, for example, to find an advocate of revolutionary change in the world economy simultaneously supporting reactionary policies at home, or vice versa. Our accounts of three worldviews, then, impose a degree of order on political and theoretical controversies which, although it is useful for our analysis of alternative futures, ignores a great deal of their characteristic diversity.

There is one particular purpose, however, for which we do find it convenient to represent the three worldviews as if they are simply upon a single dimension. Figure 8.1 is a graphic presentation of how the forecasting authors might be placed in terms of both their political views and their positions in the Malthusian debate as technological optimists or pessimists. Positions on this diagram were assigned to authors on the basis of their writings as summarised in chapter 2 (Table 2.2). Figure 8.1 deals with *international* political analysis and does not depict their positions on domestic matters. It will be apparent that authors have only been assigned approximate positions given the ambiguity and sometimes inconsistency of much of their work in terms of the three worldviews. Classifying authors in this way is

Figure 8.1   Forecasters' positions summarized in graphical form

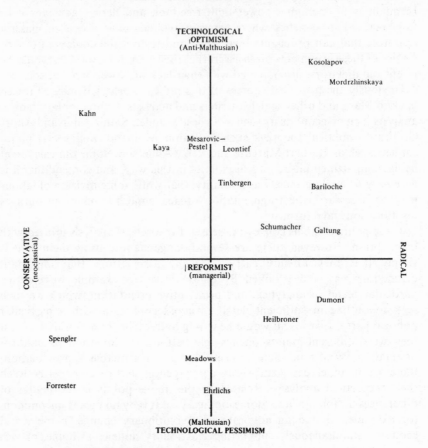

Note: This figure presents a speculative 'mapping' of forecasting authors in terms of their views on Malthusian issues and matters of international political economics. Authors have been assigned to different positions here by Sam Cole and Ian Miles, largely on the basis of the prescriptive statements drawn from their works and summarised in the tables of chapter 2.

nevertheless of value in understanding their differing pronouncements. Compare, for example, Figures 3.6 and 8.1: there are highly suggestive similarities. The major difference between them seems to be that both reformist and radical authors believe that their proposals would bring about fairly equitable futures. The profiles of their forecasts in terms of international equality thus tend to converge even where their political prescriptions diverge. Whilst a discussion of Malthusian attitudes clearly plays a role in forecasters' assessments of future world economic growth, the international distribution of incomes in the future is related to a different set of political attitudes.

Judgements of what is, and what is not, plausible will often differ between proponents of different worldviews. Even variables that appear nominally to have a direct physical meaning are ultimately defined according to a political or philosophical viewpoint. Which resources are 'known' or 'proven' in the year 2000 will largely be a result of the global political changes between now and then. Attitudes towards the relationship between nature and society affect estimates of human ability both to extract resources from the ground and to overcome 'surprises' such as those resulting from climatic change. Similarly, conflict is for some writers inevitable rather than surprising, a creative necessity rather than anathema; redistribution will not take place without social reforms, and social reforms will not take place without conflict. The comparison of worldviews is therefore crucial to the study of alternative futures.

PERSPECTIVES ON WORLD DEVELOPMENT

Associated with the three worldviews are very different accounts of past history. There are, of course, areas of agreement on the larger historical trends that have shaped the world, e.g. on the economic 'take-off' of a number of Western European nations between the fourteenth and sixteenth centuries, which has transformed them into wealthy, industrialised, urbanised countries. But beyond such general descriptions we find different analyses.

Of most relevance to our present purpose is the controversy over the relationship between the historic political and economic expansion of European nations and events elsewhere in the world. Some writers argue that the poor countries of today have always been 'under-developed' because of essentially internal political problems or cultural barriers. If their position has worsened, it has been through warfare and population growth resulting from the application of modern medicine and insecticides. We identify an emphasis on such forces in accounting for inequality in the world economy as a view propounded by many conservatives. Reformists would agree to some extent, but would argue that the slow growth rates of the poor world can be partly accounted for by the long history of colonial domination to which it has been subjected and by covert mercantilist discrimination against its produce by the rich countries. Radicals often describe 'under-development' as a condition that has been imposed upon the poorer countries, whose skills and entrepreneurship were crushed by the power of rich-country capitalists and whose political structures and productive resources are to this day distorted by neocolonialism. (Again, some reformists would agree with much of this analysis.)

The worldviews also differ about the processes of Western growth. In conservative accounts, the emergence of new social values (the 'Protestant ethic') or mercantile and then industrial capitalism was the spur to growth and technological change in the previously stagnant and feudal economies of Europe. There is an emphasis on how competitive capitalism liberated the worker from serfdom, gave rise to new freedoms of social mobility, and encouraged the efficient use of resources. Reformist accounts also often stress the new ethics of hard work, thrift and accumulation, but place more emphasis on the conflict between social groups and nations and suggest that mercantilist tactics, rather than unfettered trade, helped establish the predominant industrial economies. The power of these economies was partly founded on the exploitation of the poor world, but industrialisation was also associated with a good deal of impoverishment and disruption for the European labour force. Some radical accounts go beyond this to argue that the superior power of the West was derived not from any cultural superiority – such as the values or 'spirit' of capitalism – but in the first place from access to the wealth of the Americas. Capitalism was established through conflict and struggle between rising and declining classes and the exploitation of the working class, on which it remains based; its industrialisation required the extraction of wealth from colonies, thereby giving an international dimension to exploitation.

In addition to these different interpretations of economic history, distinct analyses of the underlying tendencies of the world economic system may be associated with the three worldviews. One conservative ideal is for economic rationality to prevail: as more economic actors come to accept the common norms of the competitive market economy, the system should be freed of the 'exogenous factors' that disrupt its smooth functioning, its 'moving equilibrium'. In practice many conservatives are pessimistic on this point; they sometimes end up supporting authoritarian regimes in poor countries as the only chance of reasserting rationality in world development. Reformists consider the picture of 'economic rationality' too rosy. Power, politics and other 'exogenous factors' are an inevitable part of an economic system World and national economic structures will require regulation and continuing adjustment in order to reduce instabilities and inequalities. Radicals view even this as not enough. The capitalist system is inherently prone to crisis and is founded on exploitation and inequity. Nothing short of its abolition will suffice.

The three worldviews also reflect distinctive analyses of the ways in which different types of future – high or low economic growth, much or little international disparity – might be attained. Since any future evolves inevitably from tendencies existing in the world today, we must consider further what the three worldviews say about them. All three agree in recognising major changes that have occurred in the world economy in recent decades, but they disagree about their causes and their implications for the future.

In assessing both the rapid economic growth of industrial nations in the

1950s and 1960s and prospects for the future, conservatives direct attention towards the interdependent nature of the world economy. National economies have been increasingly tied together by trade and foreign investment. Governments should be more aware of the costs of policies of economic nationalism; administrators in nations of all types should recognise the common self-interest in liberal economic policies. Trade liberalisation since the Second World War did indeed permit the multilateral expansion of trade and an achievement of high rates of economic growth. However, these achievements were threatened in the recession of the 1970s as governments sometimes tried to cope with domestic problems of unemployment, stagnation and inflation by protectionist means. Causes of inflation diagnosed by conservatives include wage rises produced by trade union pressures in the rich countries, governments printing money to cover their increasing expenditure, thus effectively devaluing money, and the economic nationalism of OPEC and others in increasing energy and resource prices.

To many conservatives, multinational corporations have become the most dynamic economic actors on the world scene, unlike relatively short-sighted national governments. Although some conservatives regard these corporations as dangerously oligopolistic and liable to distort the market, others see them as increasing world-wide economic efficiency by shifting operations to countries where national resources and labour are cheap. In the search for stability, they are oriented to long-term investment planning and marketing strategies, which make them internationalistic in outlook. Large corporations may be emerging as rational economic powers capable of responding to changes in international politics, and nation-states should be encouraged to relax their nationalistic grip on the international economy.

In the conservative worldview a rational world economic system should tend towards establishing an international division of labour in which countries specialise in producing those commodities most appropriate to their factor endowments. Few conservatives would now argue that poor countries should restrict themselves to primary production. The present specialisation of many poorer countries in exporting primary produce reflects their comparative advantage, but comparative advantages are now seen to be dynamic and to some extent malleable. The abundance of cheap labour in such countries may in the future lead to the transfer of much manufacturing industry to them. In this desirable eventuality, multinational corporations can act as agents of development, transferring capital, technology and modern attitudes, aspirations and practice. This process of diffusion has been inhibited by local cultural barriers and the vagaries of world politics, but that it is practicable has been demonstrated by the rapid growth of some Third World economies such as Brazil, South Korea and Taiwan.

For conservatives a desirable pattern (and to some a likely pattern) of growth for poor countries is the diffusion of modern technological and economic practices and attitudes from the industrial nations to the metro-politan parts of the poor world, and thence to their more backward agricultural sectors. In many respects this resembles the viewpoint of Soviet writers – with the crucial difference that they see such trends occurring in socialist development rather than under the impetus of the profit motive. Workers would transer from the agricultural to the industrial sectors as agricultural production was modernised. This smooth transition has in many cases, however, been disrupted by the malign political interferences that have been portrayed in detail by neoclassical economists. Many ex-colonies have tried to emulate the rich countries by import-substitution, which means in most cases producing a range of goods unsuited to their comparative advantages; they have protected unprofitable industries and so have ended up by distorting investment patterns and paying above world prices for goods of below standard quality. Labour has been over-priced, leading to explosive levels of migration to the cities and to foreign investment in capital-intensive operations (which fail to provide substantial employment). These policies, and related practices such as over-valuing of exchange rates and subsidisa-tion of interest rates, have effectively discriminated against agricultural production, in which many of the poor countries should have specialised, given the comparative advantages of geography and climate. Furthermore, rapid population growth, encouraged by the spread of Western insecticides and medical practices, requires strict controls if it is not to hinder growth of incomes per head.

Reformists offer different perspectives on these problems. They often argue that nations either do or could, and certainly should, exercise substantial influence over multinational corporations. National interests and power politics are underestimated by both conservatives and radicals. The 'liberalisation' of trade has really served to disguise mercantilist practices by the advanced countries. The long period of relatively uninterrupted post-war growth was due not to a liberalised world economy, but to countries either consciously following Keynesian principles of economic management or doing so unwittingly with heavy military expenditures. The interdependence of the world economy was made possible and desirable to the richer countries – and especially to the U.S.A. – largely because of their continuous economic growth, their dominance over the rest of the world and their relative command over technological and material resources. To be sure, there are changes in the relative power of different countries. Other industrial nations have risen to challenge U.S. leadership, and poorer countries have aggressively sought a redistribution of world wealth. Under these strains mercantilist practices have become more visible, with trading groups like the E.E.C. and the U.S.A. disagreeing on policy. Multinational corporations have had to adapt increasingly to government economic policies, which reflect domestic political goals more than a growing consensus on the virtues of a liberal world economy. These corporations may thus become less power-ful as international competition for resources and markets intensifies.

Nevertheless reformists do attribute the lack of development of many poor countries partly to cultural and institutional factors, and to resistance by powerful groups to any change that would threaten their authority and privilege. The failures of import-substitution strategies are seen not simply as penalties for flouting the principle of comparative advantage, but as reflecting the importation of tastes and technologies from the rich countries by the affluent groups in poor countries. Also important, however, has been the balance of power within the world economic system. Historically the colonies were led to specialise in particular forms of produce, which rendered them particularly susceptible to trade fluctuations, and they have suffered as terms of trade have changed in the post-war era. Genuine liberalisation of world trade has been against the domestic political interests of the richer countries; industrial development along the Western path has been made even more difficult through discrimination by the industrialised powers against goods manufactured in poorer countries.

Reformists often analyse the world recession of the 1970s in terms of economic conflicts resulting from shifts in the balance of geopolitical power. The U.S.A. encountered balance of payments problems and was threatened by intense competition from the Western European and Japanese economies she helped to rebuild in the 1940s and 1950s. Some resource-rich developing countries were able for the first time to act in unison against a divided group of consuming nations to push up their prices (in the process displaying their potential power over multinational corporations). This may encourage the larger industrial countries and regional groupings of economies (such as the E.E.C.) to compete with each other for zones of influence. In order to establish world economic growth with a more equitable distribution of incomes, many reformists have argued for international agreements that go beyond preventing imperfections in competition or making exchange rates flexible. They argue for adjustments of the terms of trade so as to distribute the profits of trade more equitably and for agencies to monitor and direct the investments of multinational corporations and assist the transfer of foreign-owned assets to local investors. For example, investment could be directed towards projects to aid poor countries to diversify their economies and to stimulate the use of 'appropriate technologies', so as to provide more employment for local labour and greater consumption of indigenous products.

Radicals generally agree that the multinational corporations have become increasingly powerful relative to national governments and see the interests of the former as conflicting not only with those of national governments and elites, but also with those of humanity at large. Smaller countries have often been pushed into economic policies unfavourable to their long-term interests and to their populations, taken as a whole, by the power of international big business to grant or withhold investment. Multinational corporations represent the culmination of the long-run tendency for the size of businesses to increase, centralising capital and power as well as concentrating production in large units. Some radicals, however (e.g. Emmanuel, 1976), argue that multinational corporations can in fact stimulate development of productive forces in poor countries, and are not necessarily more oppressive than local business interests in capitalist development would be.

World economic growth was possible until the 1970s through the high levels of private investment, and the operation of international agencies such as the I.M.F. and World Bank, and state expenditures. These succeeded in delaying the emergence of world recession, but at the cost of high levels of inflation. State subsidies, expenditure and intervention, including prices and incomes control, are not themselves the sources of crisis but simply responses to difficulties encountered in a market economy. The present reductions in state expenditure not only represent an attack on working-class living standards, but also make it likely that by removing the 'cushioning' of the economy future recessions will be even more severe than that of the early 1970s. Economic problems are likely to be expressed as financial crises in the first instance (with speculative attacks on national currencies being prominent), but they essentially remain crises of the system as labour and recessions tend to permit and encourage the further concentration of production and capital in the largest firms of the leading nations. Competition between firms intensifies. This produces pressures for greater exploitation nationally and internationally, which provides the circumstances for the emergence of revolutionary consciousness and conflict. The crises, imbalances and cutting of state expenditure in advanced capitalist countries may undermine the 'welfare consensus' on which the acquiescence of workers in their own exploitation has been founded.

Radicals cannot accept that multinational corporations would be ready to submit to international schemes involving their further taxation, and doubt whether capitalism can generate any degree of equity. They see the under-development of the Third World as part of uneven world development, characteristic of capitalist expansion, and, in some respects, reinforced during the neocolonial post-war decades. The ruling classes in industrial countries continues to extract wealth from labour in the ex-colonies, but now rely upon the assistance of the local bourgeoisie rather than direct force to safeguard investment and profits. Capitalist economic growth in poorer countries, sustained in only a few cases, has tended to be unbalanced and to impoverish large sections of the population. Such countries have either industrialised under state direction behind protective barriers, created massive internal pockets of poverty by exploiting internal colonies (e.g. Pakistan's treatment of what is now Bangladesh) or else temporarily benefited from the fact that as colonies their economies were aligned to the efficient production of specific foodstuffs or minerals for export.

Even if the world economy were transformed into a 'welfare capitalism' with substantial efforts to reduce regional disparities, radicals argue that it would remain a crisis-prone system where attempts at planning could at best represent the need of an exploitative and powerful class to regulate the real producers of the world wealth. As it is, many radicals maintain that the dynamics of the capitalist system tend to establish a hierarchical world structure, with power and wealth concentrated in the capitals of the leading industrial nations. Poor countries may stagnate or achieve enclaves of growth in a sea of deepening poverty. Their government policies are shaped by the local ruling class, which is usually aligned with the international big businesses on which they depend for luxury goods, capital and some degree of power and security. Populations expand as the peasantry seeks to ensure security for its old age. But there has also been a growth of revolutionary anti-imperialist conciousness among the 'wretched of the earth' (though this has been sometimes intertwined with anti-foreign chauvinism). This has led to several revolutionary wars and the establishment of a number of socialist-oriented regimes in the poor world. These countries may try to sidestep capitalism by extricating themselves in varying degrees from the world market. Few small countries, however, can be expected to achieve autarky, even though socialist development must require some separation from the global capitalist economy.

SCENARIOS FOR THE FUTURE

Thus, the three worldviews draw upon very differing accounts of the trends in world growth and inequality and make very different prescriptions for the future. In the conservative view growth can best be assured by freeing the market system from constraint; in the reformist view a substantial degree of government control is necessary; and in the radical view a total transformation away from capitalism is required. Our next task is to relate these perspectives to the features of the world's future that concern us – growth and equality. Our three worldviews represent different analyses of the tendencies inherent in the world system that might guide its development in different ways. For each of the four profiles of the future we can therefore specify three variants, thus constructing twelve alternative scenarios in all.

Three High Growth, Inegaliterian Scenarios (H.I.)

These alternative socio-political scenarios rest on a more or less optimistic assessment of the physical availability of food, energy and raw materials. In some cases very great changes in the technological structure of society, especially in the efficiency of use of basic materials, are probable. In this they follow many of the conclusions about technological possibilities in chapters 4–7.

A future with high rates of growth in the world economy and with larger gaps between the rich and poor nations is one that might be derived from projecting post-war trends in world development. The differences between the three worldviews relate particularly to the role of the state vis-à-vis private interests and to patterns of world trade.

For conservatives an extremely uneven pattern of world development might suggest that there is some barrier between the poor and the rich countries (although the principle of comparative advantage itself gives little clue about the distribution of gains between trading partners). The rich would be achieving high levels of economic activity, while the poor would be insulated from or impervious to modern economic practices. This could result from a future with extensive trade and mobility only among the industrial nations, whose political strategies are presumably fairly united.

From a reformist perspective a period of disturbance and threats in economic affairs might stimulate competition amongst industrial countries to form stable trading alliances with poor countries. An H.I. scenario could thus consist of the development of regional blocs, in which the super-powers established distinct zones of economic influence around the world, their competition involving a disproportionate accumulation of wealth in the richer countries.

Radicals would probably assign a greater role to multinational corporations and their influence on nations or the development of trading blocs. The large corporations could continue to exploit the world's workers and concentrate wealth and power within the richer nations, if supported by political settlements which weaken world revolutionary movements and socialist countries, and by continuing technological change and government policies that offset and minimise capitalist crises. We summarise the three alternatives for the profile in Figure 8.2 (These flow diagrams' of the future omit feedbacks and reciprocal interactions in order to simplify the presentation.)

Conservative high growth, inegalitarian scenario   In the conservative world-view economic rationality – unfettered trade, division of labour and pursuit of profit – is the sovereign route to a rich world. Futures in which the industrial countries become richer while the developing 'South' remains impoverished would involve processes that distribute rationality unevenly between rich and poor countries. This would be the future against which Kahn and Spengler appear to be warning the poorer nations.

A lack of rational attitudes and policies means that there is a failure of modernisation processes in poor countries, though some exceptions, such as South Korea and Taiwan, would join forces with the industrial countries. Traditional patterns of life, ethnic allegiances and the mentality of sub-sistence farming prove resistant to change. Governments act on the basis of nepotism, intrigue and national prestige. They continually obstruct the free development of wealth-generating industrial and commercial institutions. The poorer countries might display irresponsibility in their economic and

Figure 8.2.   High Growth, Inegalitarian Scenarios

'CONSERVATIVE' H.I. SCENARIO

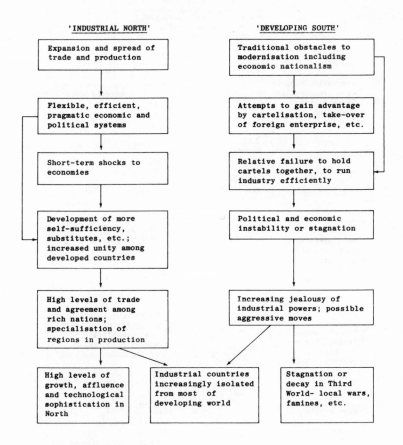

'INDUSTRIAL NORTH'

Expansion and spread of
trade and production

Flexible, efficient,
pragmatic economic and
political systems

Short-term shocks to
economies

Development of more
self-sufficiency,
substitutes, etc.;
increased unity among
developed countries

High levels of trade
and agreement among
rich nations;
specialisation of
regions in production

High levels of
growth, affluence
and technological
sophistication in
North

'DEVELOPING SOUTH'

Traditional obstacles to
modernisation including
economic nationalism

Attempts to gain advantage
by cartelisation, take-over
of foreign enterprise, etc.

Relative failure to hold
cartels together, to run
industry efficiently

Political and economic
instability or stagnation

Increasing jealousy of
industrial powers; possible
aggressive moves

Industrial countries
increasingly isolated
from most of
developing world

Stagnation or
decay in Third
World- local wars,
famines, etc.

'REFORMIST' H.I. SCENARIO

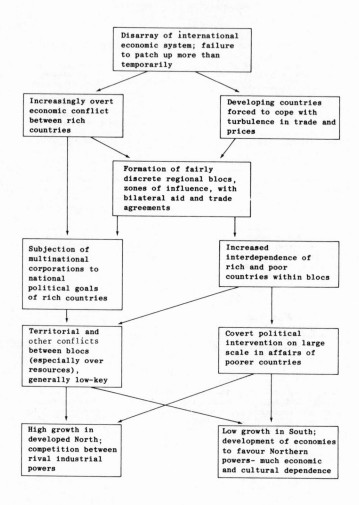

'RADICAL' H.I. SCENARIO

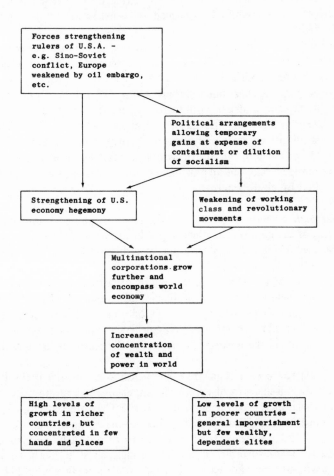

political relations with the rest of the world. There might be attempts to black-mail the 'Northern' powers, to set up resource cartels, to nationalise local branches of multinational business, and to subject trade agreements to the whims of territorial disputes.

These problems could lead the more industrial countries to turn inward, preferring more reliable trading partnerships. The economic nationalism and political instability of poor countries would in many cases mitigate against successful cartelisation. The poorer countries would be unable to impose any long-term arrangements upon the rich ones, who would probably reduce their reliance on products and markets of the poor world. The North would become more self-sufficient: the role of scarce or imperilled materials in industrial economies would be reduced by substitution, conservation and recycling strategies.

Increasingly the industrial countries would come to recognise their common interests. Tensions between the developed East and West might decrease and their political and economic systems converge. They might cooperate in maintaining independence from the turbulent and unreliable South. Jealousy and distrust would grow with the economic and social gap between North and South. The stable and increasingly wealthy North might even be sealed off economically and militarily from all but a few poor countries. Other parts of the South would be beset by local wars or famines, or would manage to eke out an existence of impoverished stagnation, such as that described by Heilbroner.

Reformist high growth, inegalitarian scenario   Judging by the projections that several of the global modellers (e.g. Mesarovic and Pestel, 1974) make, this is the scenario which they envisage would result from a continuation of present trends.

The reformist H.I. scenario develops out of current instabilities in world trade, which herald the end of an unusual and temporary phase of economic co-operation and the return to a world of mercantilist rivalry. Industrial countries would here renew the struggle over obtaining and protecting sources of supply in the wake of challenges to the economic leadership of the U.S.A.

A plausible route to a high growth, inegaliterian profile is the intensification of a disguised form of economic imperialism. The super-powers and groups of developed nations such as the E.E.C. would attempt to set up spheres of influence, institutionalising close connections with groups of more or less dependent poor countries. The strains of old-fashioned imperialism are probably insupportable in modern times, so it is likely that covert political manipulation and selectively repressive local elites would be used to maintain the influence of the industrial powers in the poor world.

The industrial nations would thus be able to secure markets and, becoming service-oriented 'post-industrial' societies themselves, would export the more boring, dangerous or polluting aspects of production to the poor countries. The latter would remain as the sites of much primary production and many would probably experience some economic growth, but this would be development largely in the interests of the rich. The rich countries might work out some of their rivalry in the arena of the poor world, possibly being involved in local and civil wars there. They would probably make a show of their 'paternal' concern for their dependent partners by 'aid' in the form of food hand-outs, labour camps for migrant workers, big urban development projects and the like, while blaming any signs of discontent on subversion by their rivals.

Radical high growth, inegalitarian scenario   High growth in the capitalist world is threatened by the long-term tendency of the rate of profit to fall. While many radicals in North America and Europe expect industrial societies to be shaken by crises of increasing severity, instabilities need not necessarily prevent further high inegalitarian growth, which according to many Third World radicals is the outcome of present tendencies. There is some dispute among radicals as to whether this tendency will inevitably appear. The whole post-war boom period refuted contemporary expectations of immediate large-scale capitalist crisis, although there are no signs that the propensity of capitalism to have periodic and potentially revolutionary crises has waned. In an H.I. scenario such crises would have been contained at the cost of the world's workers and especially of those in the poorer countries. Galtung (1977) suggests that there might be a similar future if poor nations do not recognise their common interest.

The room for manoeuvre of multinational corporations would be expanded by policies that, while going under the name of détente, effectively reduce the socialist countries' commitment to revolutionary movements in the poor world and elsewhere in exchange for Western technology and capital. This might follow failures in Soviet agricultural policies, Sino-Soviet conflicts, dissent in the East European bloc and similar problems that find no mention in the Russian futurology of Modrzhinskaya (1973) and Kosolapov (1976). Many radicals in capitalist countries, however, have developed critical analyses of state socialist countries that make such prospects appear quite plausible. This scenario postulates political stabilisation of the world favourable to the industrial giants of the richest countries. U.S. economic hegemony would probably be restored.

The U.S.A., Western Europe and Japan would be at the apex of a hierarchical system of world exploitation, whose base would consist of poor countries and the peripheral regions of the richer ones. Capitalist development would polarise wealth and power in the world, and within countries. High levels of military expenditure would prevail, not so much to secure the balance of military power as to repress insurgency in the poorer regions and to stabilise capitalist economies. Social conflict and environmental degradation might be prevented from reaching critical levels, but at ever greater cost to personal liberties.

Three Low Growth, Inegalitarian Scenarios (L.I.)

The following low growth scenarios are more likely to involve 'Malthusian' shortages, i.e. circumstances in which there are failures to apply technology to releasing the potential of the physical world. However, low growth may be attributed to institutional or political factors rather than to physical limits or purely technological problems.

A future in which world growth rates are low and international inequalities similar to the present, might at first glance appear to mean a respectably wealthy world; at growth rates of one per cent per annum, gross world product would more than double in eighty years. But with population growth exceeding this figure in many parts of the world, an L.I. profile could actually mean a world of declining living standards. In the accounts developed from the three worldviews the L.I. scenarios look superficially similar: for example, they all include world inflation, economic nationalism and failures of technology. But the processes singled out as likely causes of such a future are very different.

Conservatives, for example, would see the fundamental causes as outside the economic system, which would be distorted by political or other pressures. The fault would lie in over-management, and in distortions of economic rationality. Reformists would probably point to institutional bottlenecks or inefficient management as responsible for the world's stagnant inequality. A lack of trust and co-operation between nations might prevent a desirable restructuring of the world economy. Radical thinkers, in contrast, see tendencies towards crisis and recession as inherent in capitalist economic relations rather than arising from exogenous sources or institutional mismatches.

Conservative low growth, inegalitarian scenario   In this scenario the economies of both the industrial North and the poor South would be stagnant. The problems of the former could stem from debilitating cultural attitudes (environmentalism, erosion of the Protestant work ethic by a counter-culture), trade-union monopolistic power ('Luddite' attitudes to innovation and rationalisation), ethnic conflicts aggravated by pressure groups, bureaucratisation, over-management, etc. These problems are identified by pessimistic conservatives as constituting a breakdown of political consensus into a mass of competing interest groups, to which weak governments can only respond by inflationary and short-sighted attempts to please all parties – at least at first. Later it is just the strongest parties who are important and the fate of democracy depends on who gains the upper hand. This resembles the future predicted by Forrester (1971) as an outcome of

Figure 8.3.   Low Growth, Inegalitarian Scenarios

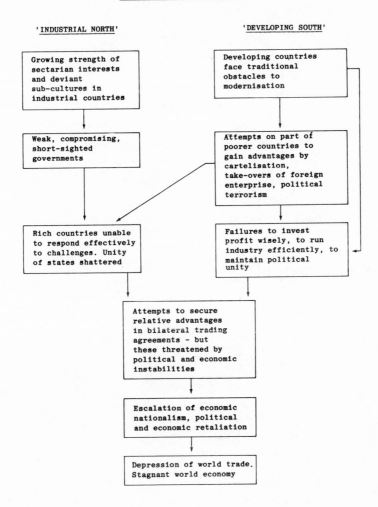

'CONSERVATIVE' L.I. SCENARIO

'INDUSTRIAL NORTH'   'DEVELOPING SOUTH'

Growing strength of
sectarian interests
and deviant
sub-cultures in
industrial countries

Developing countries
face traditional
obstacles to
modernisation

Weak, compromising,
short-sighted
governments

Attempts on part of
poorer countries to
gain advantages by
cartelisation,
take-overs of foreign
enterprise, political
terrorism

Rich countries unable
to respond effectively
to challenges. Unity
of states shattered

Failures to invest
profit wisely, to run
industry efficiently, to
maintain political
unity

Attempts to secure
relative advantages
in bilateral trading
agreements - but
these threatened by
political and economic
instabilities

Escalation of economic
nationalism, political
and economic retaliation

Depression of world trade.
Stagnant world economy

'REFORMIST' L.I. SCENARIO

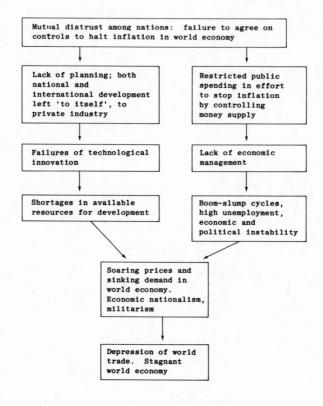

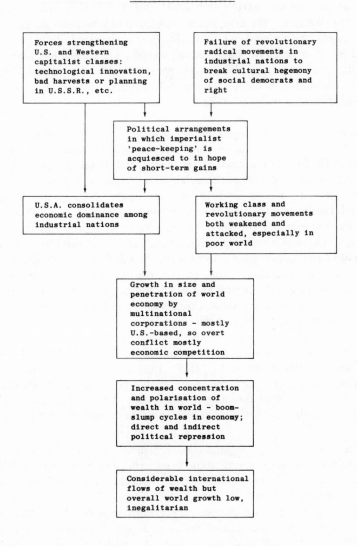

'RADICAL' L.I. SCENARIO

Forces strengthening U.S. and Western capitalist classes: technological innovation, bad harvests or planning in U.S.S.R., etc.

Failure of revolutionary radical movements in industrial nations to break cultural hegemony of social democrats and right

Political arrangements in which imperialist 'peace-keeping' is acquiesced to in hope of short-term gains

U.S.A. consolidates economic dominance among industrial nations

Working class and revolutionary movements both weakened and attacked, especially in poor world

Growth in size and penetration of world economy by multinational corporations - mostly U.S.-based, so overt conflict mostly economic competition

Increased concentration and polarisation of wealth in world - boom-slump cycles in economy; direct and indirect political repression

Considerable international flows of wealth but overall world growth low, inegalitarian present trends; which directly stems from Malthusian shortages, although these might be aggravated by humanitarian aid and trade policies. It is also a future indicated by Kahn if too much attention is paid to 'environmentalists' and similar groups.

Although this retreat from the gains of Western culture is ultimately the responsibility of those who fail to guard their heritage, this scenario could be triggered off or reinforced by actions of the poorer countries. Perhaps they might attempt to form cartels or institute trade boycotts or encourage acts of terrorism. Whatever the case, these tactics would prove counterproductive; prices might rise but trade would be drastically depressed. Petty nationalism would be the rule of the day; nations would treat each other with mutual hostility and suspicion. Private enterprise would be shackled. The best intellects would turn away from worldly affairs, or become entangled in political, religious or racial feuds.

Reformist low growth, inegalitarian scenario   The reformist view is likely to be a world of management and technological failures, corresponding closely to the futures indicated by Heilbroner (1974) and the Ehrlichs (1970). Attempts by governments of the richer countries to curb inflation by cutting public spending would lead to chronic unemployment and depressed demand, inadequate training of scientists and technologists, and insufficient investment in research to cope with the environmental problems and resource shortages due to insufficient planning. Profit and investment levels would fall in the industrial countries, and there would be a decline in world trade. If well-endowed with resources, the poorer countries might manage some growth in semi-isolation from the capital and technological skills of the North; but this might be precarious and limited, threatened by jealous neighbours, conflicts over resources and population problems.

There might be attempts to form regional blocs, but these would fare badly because of mutual suspicion and inflexibility. The deep depression would stimulate political unrest leading to a variety of authoritarian governments. Some of these might indeed restore growth temporarily in their countries, but often this would be at the price of militarism. There would be a slow disintegration of the infrastructure of social welfare in most Western countries.

Radical low growth, inegalitarian scenario   In this scenario, which corresponds in some respects to the fears expressed by Dumont (1974), the capitalist economy has not achieved much success in overcoming its tendency towards periodic crises. Perhaps here we would find world economic problems aggravated by intense competition between different capitalist powers such as the U.S.A., the E.E.C. and Japan. The risk of major military conflict in such a future would be high. If conflict between multinational corporations from different national bases were reduced, which in itself seems to point to an interdependence between the richer capitalist powers founded on U.S. hegemony in international trade, such risks might be reduced.

The scenario would involve the continued under-development and exploitation of large regions of the world through international business, whose representatives would throw up smokescreens of free-trade rhetoric and point to isolated enclaves of Westernisation in the poor world as signs of their achievements. The impoverishment of larger areas would be blamed by these apologists on local cultural or personal failings. While some socialist revolutions might be possible in the poorer countries and there would probably be many attempts at guerrilla war and mobilisation of the peasantry, it is likely that the industrial nations would try to keep a firm grip on their markets and resource bases, if necessary with military action. Competition between different capitalist countries might, however, provide some bargaining opportunities for the poorer countries, which might thus achieve some gains relative to the H.I. scenario, although rich countries would have less 'largesse' to distribute.

Power and wealth would increasingly accrue to a few centres in the North, while production would slowly shift to the South and to peripheral areas. Development would be uneven and unstable, with intermittent periods of slump and stagnation, limited conflicts against insurgents, and much waste in the system. The Eastern European powers would be somewhat neutralised by economic concessions made in order to obtain American technology, grain and even investment; radicals would disagree about the growth prospects of socialist industrial states (and China) in a world of low economic growth. The disaffected and insecure working classes of the industrial countries would be kept in their place by pervasive indoctrination through powerful mass media, by fragmentation along conflicting regional, ethnic and occupational lines, and perhaps by wide-ranging state repression publicly justified by reference to acts of subversion and terrorism.

Three Low Growth, More Equal Scenarios (L.E.)

This profile of world development entails that the richer countries generally grow only slowly, if at all, and the poorer countries by and large show more rapid economic growth. If rapid growth is largely confined to countries at the lower stages of development and gradually slows as income levels approach and/or surpass those of the industrial nations, then we have a situation of low overall world growth. This is a profile favoured by several radical authors and world forecasters. However, they have different reasons for preferring low growth and also envisage different final levels of consumption as ideal.

For conservatives this future could come about in the industrial countries through the operation of extra-economic factors the effect of which would be to transfer income and opportunity to the poorer regions of the world. While several such factors might be named – wars or debilitating political conflict

Figure 8.4   Low growth, more equal scenarios

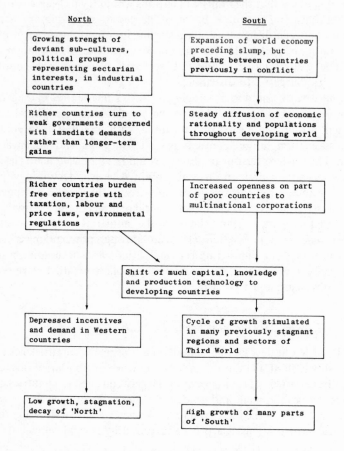

'CONSERVATIVE' L.E. SCENARIO

North   South

Growing strength of   Expansion of world economy
deviant sub-cultures,   preceding slump, but
political groups   dealing between countries
representing sectarian   previously in conflict
interests, in industrial
countries

Richer countries turn to   Steady diffusion of economic
weak governments concerned   rationality and populations
with immediate demands   throughout developing world
rather than longer-term
gains

Richer countries burden   Increased openness on part
free enterprise with   of poor countries to
taxation, labour and   multinational corporations
price laws, environmental
regulations

                Shift of much capital, knowledge
                and production technology to
                developing countries

Depressed incentives   Cycle of growth stimulated
and demand in Western   in many previously stagnant
countries   regions and sectors of
                               Third World

Low growth, stagnation,   High growth of many parts
decay of 'North'   of 'South'

'REFORMIST' L.E. SCENARIO

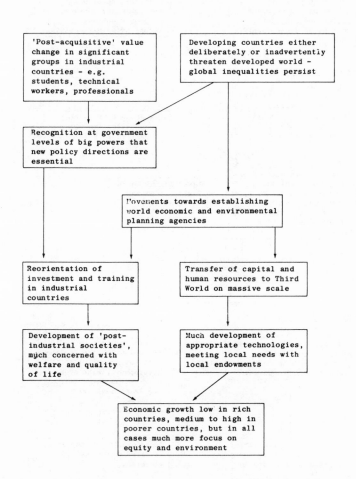

'RADICAL' L.E. SCENARIO

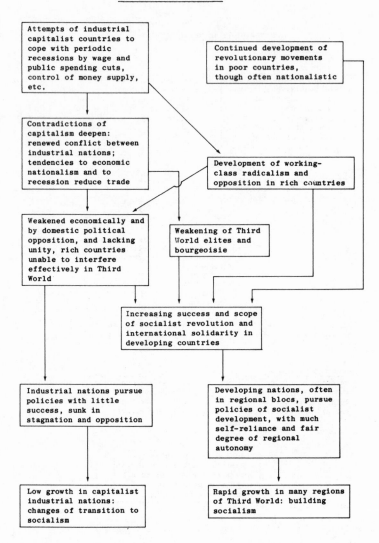

between European countries, major mistakes in technological development, or even climatic change – the most likely diagnosis would be in terms of the cultural factors that we have already encountered in the conservative L.I. scenario. Reformists would envisage such a profile arising, not by chance or mistake, but as the result of a deliberate policy of redistributing world wealth. International planning for development, environmental management and improved quality of life could take the direction of an L.E. scenario rather than an H.E. one, according to some reformist thinkers. Conservatives might argue that a change in the terms of trade against industrial countries would bring about an L.E. profile, although they might see its origins as lying more in conflict and conspiracy than in planned agreements. Radicals would be likely to see in this scenario a world on the verge of revolution and in transition to an H.E. pattern of growth. The industrial capitalist nations face economic collapse and have successfully been challenged for control of the poor world by local socialist initiatives, which secure more balanced paths of development.

Conservative low growth, more equal scenario   The problems inhibiting economic growth in the industrial nations would have to be severe to prevent the emergence of adequate leadership over an extended period. One of these factors could be cultural decadence, with family breakdown, permissive education and mass media dominated by 'progressives' contributing to inadequate socialisation. The incentives and rewards of work could thus be undermined by grievances and egalitarian legislation; anti-technology attitudes might grow, especially if there were some disasters in high technologies; financial and intellectual resources could be squandered on welfare and environmental projects rather than on the generation of more wealth.* Industrial economies might lack sufficient strength of will and solidarity to resist a massive change in the terms of trade in favour of poor countries.

Attempts by governments in the North to control the activity of big corporations by imposing restrictive regulations about the environment, and about hiring, firing and equal opportunities for workers, or by imposing taxation policies, might lead to a transfer of capital and expertise to the poor nations. Both market and centrally planned poor countries might seize the opportunity of allowing increased access to multinational corporations. This would encourage rapid growth in these economies, especially where resources are rich and strong governments deal forcefully with problems of cultural lag and transformation. While large areas and groups in the South

---

*Kahn suggests two similar scenarios in *The Year 2000* and *The Next 200 Years* (p. 259 and p. 280) with his criticism of growth-endangering environmentalism. That poor nations might overtake industrial nations is otherwise hardly commented upon in the literature we have reviewed, although we do remind ourselves of Spengler's concern in the 1930s that the demographic growth of poor nations would also result in their increased economic and strategic power.

would still cling to traditional ways, there would be a strong demand for labour, and modern ideas would diffuse rapidly. By the middle of the twenty-first century, what now constitutes the poor world would have become a whole range of different 'worlds', containing all extremes of cultural and economic development.

Reformist low growth, more equal scenario   The image of a world of steady transition to a stable and equitable society has a lengthy pedigree, with Plato, Thomas Aquinas, J. S. Mill and Keynes forming part of it, although they clearly had immensely different notions of the level at which economic growth might become zero. According to some reformists, the richer countries might reorient their policies under the impact of a spreading humanitarian environmentalist ethic spearheaded by professionals, elements of the counter-culture, alternative technology and ecology movements and the like. They would turn their economies away from continual increases in consumption levels to a more leisurely concern with quality of life. There would be a new emphasis on production that conserves resources and, where possible, can help create technologies suitable for poor countries.

Many reformists would argue that, however desirable such a transformation might be, it would be unrealistic to imagine it coming about without much stress, and it would perhaps call for draconian measures. Further, it might be doubted that industrial societies could thus change their production without relying upon poor countries to carry out their 'dirty work', as in the reformist H.E. scenario. Nevertheless, the poor world might play an active role in a rather different transformation of the richer countries: perhaps cartelisation and other strategies, or perhaps unintended events such as ecological or health catastrophes, might turn the big powers towards more co-operation. Sizeable transfers of capital and equipment to poor countries together with a slow-down of growth in the richer ones might be agreed upon. In the world futures debate, Schumacher (1973), Bariloche (Herrera *et al.*, 1974), Dumont (1974) and Galtung (1977) and, with less conviction, the Meadows (1972), the Ehrlichs (1970) and Heilbroner (1974) all postulate futures resembling this scenario. However, Galtung and Heilbroner in particular foresee many difficulties here. Heilbroner suggests that only authoritarian regimes would be able to carry out the required transformation (which he sees as desirable on the basis of assumed Malthusian limits).

In this scenario world trade would be fairly high, as would flows of knowledge and labour. Poor countries would aim for greater diversification of their economies. In a more ecologically conscious and planned world there would be much more emphasis on intermediate and appropriate technologies. Planning would be such as to encourage local enterprise along these lines, with small-scale businesses pursuing locally appropriate projects, and larger investments being carried out by the state with the backing of international aid.

Radical low growth, more equal scenario   Whilst it is rather difficult to develop plausible conservative and reformist low growth, egalitarian scenarios, many radical thinkers would probably find an L.E. profile fairly realistic in broad outline. The developed capitalist states would be embroiled in crisis: economically they would face low rates of profit, as well as inflation and unemployment, with political conflict about the distribution of wealth and the inadequacy of social services, problems over state intervention in private enterprises, and the like. There would be less capacity for them to intervene in the affairs of the poor world: traditional and bourgeois regimes in the South could be increasingly overtaken by socialist revolution, further weakening capitalism in the industrial states.

While political change in poor countries would undoubtedly progress in a halting way with many setbacks, socialist regimes would gradually be consolidated and begin to pursue and extend policies of regional self-reliance and socialist aid. Human and material resources would then be employed to achieve more balanced and less unequal growth. Unable to exploit the resources and cheap labour of these countries, the industrial nations might become increasingly withdrawn and preoccupied with their own problems. Eventually the masses of the North, too, might turn to radical programmes; some of them might join the new world-wide socialist alliance. The formation of strong regional alliances would be the most effective guarantee against capitalists trying to solve their problems by force. While this scenario has no exact correspondence in the futurology literature, there are some echoes of the works of Bariloche and Galtung, and perhaps of a non-Malthusian revision of Dumont's forecast.

Three High Growth, More Equal Scenarios (H.E.)

One common characteristic of the three worldviews is the projection of a fairly high level of world trade in the H.E. profile. For conservative theorists world development would best be accomplished by freeing trade from constraints. If national governments would agree to dismantle their trade barriers, to stop discrimination and protection, then private enterprise would provide the transmission belt for ideas, skills, capital and goods to move to where they would be most efficiently employed. Reformist writers, however, would argue that whilst it is necessary to remove those restrictions on trade that represent discrimination by the powerful against the producers in poorer countries, world development requires much restructuring of the existing world economy and cannot be entirely left to the market. Trade relationships would be expanded on a planned basis and linked with aid programmes; this would require the firm commitment of industrial countries to supranational economic agencies. Radicals would argue that such planning on a world scale would be subverted (if, indeed, it were allowed in the first place) by commercial interests, unless it received the support of powerful socialist forces. World planning here is seen as contingent upon world revolution. (See Figure 8.5.)

Conservative high growth, more equal scenario In essence this scenario makes the diffusion of economic rationality the guiding social principle. Conservatives draw from neoclassical economics the argument that a competitive market economy results in the maximisation of output. In the H.E. scenario this principle has been accepted by the world powers in their agreements about trade and other relations.

In this future, governments would increasingly recognise that liberal economic policies benefit their own interests more than short-sighted attempts to support declining home industries against foreign competition, to set fixed rates of exchange for reasons of national prestige, and the like. A positive role in development for multinational corporations would be recognised, as would the need to participate in the international economic community. This is very close to the view put forward by Kahn in *The Next 200 Years*. He accepts that there will still be considerable inequality in the world for a long time to come – but less than in any other future he can imagine. Counter-tendencies would not, of course, disappear overnight. In the poor world social change may be inhibited by persistent cultural traditions or by traditional elites such as landowners, while resistance to enterprise may emerge anywhere from trade unions, bureaucracies and other entrenched interests. Perhaps the bad example of a country meeting with disaster by trying to 'go it alone' or develop into a paternalistic welfare state would actually aid the diffusion of good practice. The countries of Eastern Europe would possibly constitute such bad examples, but they might also reform their economies away from central planning, perhaps after widespread domestic unrest about living standards.

The liberalisation of world trade might be accomplished through the agency of supranational organisations in which both national leaders and the managers of large companies participate. These agencies would help governments steer themselves through the processes of dismantling trade barriers and reforming the international monetary system, perhaps over a period of several decades. The growth rate of poor countries would be increased by the contributions of multinational enterprises and by the increased markets for their produce, once the industrialised nations relaxed their protectionism. Aid would be made multilateral and used to promote local initiatives, programmes of population control and research directed at overcoming other problems of poor countries, such as low agricultural productivity.

Reformist high growth, more equal scenario Reformists are less confident than many conservatives about the benign role of multinational corporations in developing countries and see substantial economic cooperation between countries as involved in an H.E. scenario. This would

Figure 8.5   High growth, more equal scenarios

"CONSERVATIVE' H.E. SCENARIO

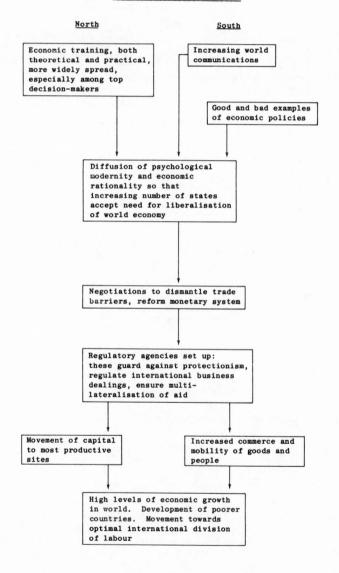

'REFORMIST' H.E. SCENARIO

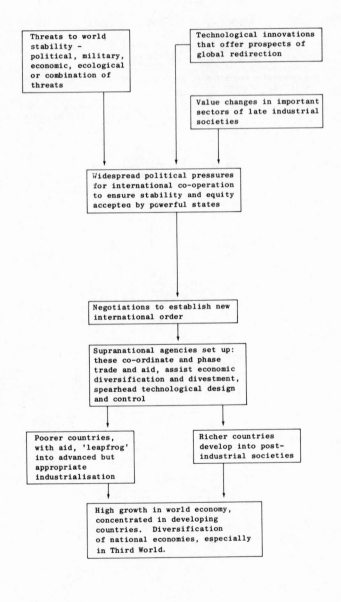

Threats to world stability - political, military, economic, ecological or combination of threats

Technological innovations that offer prospects of global redirection

Value changes in important sectors of late industrial societies

Widespread political pressures for international co-operation to ensure stability and equity accepted by powerful states

Negotiations to establish new international order

Supranational agencies set up: these co-ordinate and phase trade and aid, assist economic diversification and divestment, spearhead technological design and control

Poorer countries, with aid, 'leapfrog' into advanced but appropriate industrialisation

Richer countries develop into post-industrial societies

High growth in world economy, concentrated in developing countries. Diversification of national economies, especially in Third World.

'RADICAL' H.E. SCENARIO

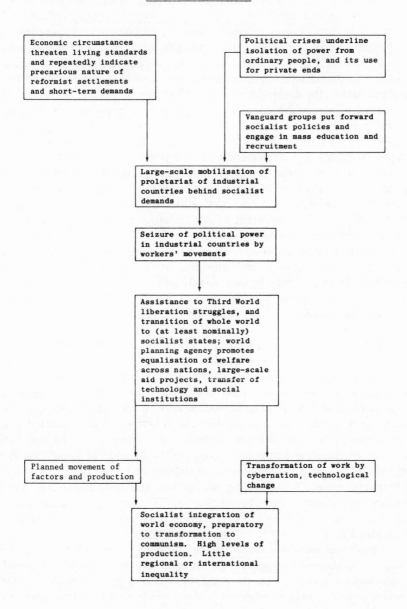

Economic circumstances threaten living standards and repeatedly indicate precarious nature of reformist settlements and short-term demands

Political crises underline isolation of power from ordinary people, and its use for private ends

Vanguard groups put forward socialist policies and engage in mass education and recruitment

Large-scale mobilisation of proletariat of industrial countries behind socialist demands

Seizure of political power in industrial countries by workers' movements

Assistance to Third World liberation struggles, and transition of whole world to (at least nominally) socialist states; world planning agency promotes equalisation of welfare across nations, large-scale aid projects, transfer of technology and social institutions

Planned movement of factors and production

Transformation of work by cybernation, technological change

Socialist integration of world economy, preparatory to transformation to communism. High levels of production. Little regional or international inequality need more to trigger it than the simple diffusion of ideas about world unity. Reformists here resemble some of the world forecasters; in many respects this H.E. scenario is similar to the forecasts of Tinbergen (1976) and Leontief (1976), who would, however, place less emphasis on high rates of overall global growth. Dumont and several of the more 'radical' futurologists also share this aim – and indeed Kahn does not rule out the possibility either.

The international agreements involved in this profile could include setting up a multilateral clearing agency to regulate investment and plan the terms and expansion of trade and aid; commodity currency reserve bodies, which could grant special trading rights for developing countries; and regional financial organisations to encourage the divestment of foreign-owned assets and counteract the development of local imbalances. Over time the activities of these bodies would become increasingly well co-ordinated, although they would probably be far from resembling anything like a world government. Indeed it is likely that the emphasis would be on regional bodies, but there might be attempts to implement plans for world development.

The shape of world development would probably involve the transformation of many of the richer countries into 'post-industrial' societies, with developing countries avoiding the worst aspects of Western industrial growth. Expertise is important in this scenario: in the richer countries for social engineering to develop a high quality of life; in the whole world economy to prepare and monitor world and regional plans; to help generate appropriate technologies and products for poor countries. Social and economic planning would be increasingly well co-ordinated across countries. The rapid growth of the world's population would slow down as the poor of the world experienced greater economic security.

Radical high growth, more equal scenario To radical thinkers, the precondition for world development in an H.E. scenario is fundamental political change in the capitalist countries. Many would argue that sweeping changes would also be needed in socialist countries. Such changes would involve the mobilisation of large sections of the working class and progressive social groups. Mass struggle would need to be co-ordinated through class-conscious parties and Marxist organisations. There would be open class conflict as the state attempted to oppose the upsurge of popular activity, expressed in factory occupations, large-scale strikes and the setting up of alternative means of managing production and public services. Among radical forecasters, Modrzhinskaya (1973) proposes a high growth, egalitarian future, although her description skirts many issues of the scenario developed here.

The establishment of socialism in the industrial countries would give a vital impetus to liberation movements in the Southern hemisphere. The period of turbulence involved in transforming the world might well be called 'world revolution'. After the wresting of power away from the ruling classes of the world it would be possible to set up world planning agencies, which could direct development according to human needs rather than those of competing businesses.

Reliance on capitalist production would be eliminated as far as possible. Large firms would be automatically nationalised, and small-scale production in agriculture and elsewhere speedily brought under public control. Land reform (and collectivisation) would be important elements in the development strategy of the non-industrialised countries. Consumption would be restrained while production capabilities were built up, which in many cases would mean reducing consumption, particularly among wealthier groups. Much aid would be forthcoming from the now-socialist industrial nations, who would be concerned to eliminate inequalities between nations. Technologies would be transferred on a massive scale, enabling the poor countries to leap into industrialisation, perhaps resembling the development of the central Asian republics of the U.S.S.R. Economic growth would be rapid, but its nature would be transformed, as production took place for social need rather than for profit, and the role of money diminished as more and more needs were satisfied free of charge.

Conclusions: Worldviews and Scenarios

Questions of social change and economic power are central to the human future. Our concern with economic growth and international equality has led us to set out some of the different answers given to these questions in terms of three 'worldviews'.

This is not to deny any significance to the physical attributes of the world: they are often of the greatest importance, and not only in determining the location of conflicts about scarce resources. There may well be shortages of certain materials, fuels and foodstuffs, or difficulties in promoting the technologies needed for world development; but these problems do not mean that our planet is physically exhausted and do not automatically imply suffering and hardship.

Like the world futures literature, these twelve scenarios throw up a bewildering variety of prospects for the future. Among them are some that remain well in the background of the futures debate. The scenarios also point to significant factors in the world today that need to be taken into account in futures studies.

The profiles and scenarios presented here should provide guidance in assessing the long-term implications for economic growth and international equality of developing trends and counter-trends in the real world. Whilst it is unlikely that the course of future history will closely follow any one of the narrow courses we have depicted, the scenarios should provide a framework for monitoring on-going trends, events and innovations and for assessing the robustness of policies towards alternative patterns of change.

We have not assigned probability ratings to the different scenarios or made claims about which are the most likely or feasible; indeed we would argue that such an approach is wrong both in principle and in practice. Different world-views each constitute different criteria of plausibility when we consider descriptions of the workings of the world. The likelihood and internal consistency of any scenario will therefore often be assessed differently by proponents of different viewpoints.

CHAPTER 9

Images of the Future

*Ian Miles, Sam Cole and Jay Gershuny**

INTRODUCTION

What would it feel like to be living in the future world emerging from one of
the twelve scenarios which have just been outlined? The evaluation of living
conditions and lifestyles is an enormously complex issue, where empirical
evidence is often tenuous, disjointed or simply not available; it is also charged
with political significance.

The scenarios provide a basis upon which to build more detailed images
of the future. Although we cannot consider the desirability, or otherwise,
of different profiles without considering the 'quality of life' of the futures
involved, this is not to say that we shall supply an index of desirability for
comparing them. The search for a single measure of social welfare is at best a
political rather than an 'objective scientific' task, and is at worst futile (Encel,
Marstrand and Page, 1975). However, what can reasonably be attempted is
the elaboration of the twelve images of the future. Here too, the proponents
of the three worldviews differ considerably in their assessment of what it is
that makes for a good life and a good society, in their interpretation of human
nature and about the significance to be attached to such values as equality,
liberty and concern for the environment. Among the futurologists, views on
these issues are also diverse; compare, for example, Kahn, Ehrlich, Dumont
and the Soviet authors.

Using as a basis our interpretation of the worldviews, ideas from other forecasters and some relevant social science literature we have chosen a set of
variables that jointly influence the quality of life. We do not claim that this set
is comprehensive. Indeed, it is unlikely that a comprehensive analysis of
future alternatives for the quality of life is feasible; much of the knowledge

---

*Like chapter 8, this chapter is based on a great deal of collective work. The discussion of health
draws upon work carried out by John Powles. John Irvine and Keith Pavitt provided useful
criticisms and suggestions.

needed for it has not, at least not yet, been created. The following elaboration of a range of quality of life issues for each of the twelve scenarios inevitably contains, therefore, a large element of speculation.

CONTRASTING IMAGES OF THE FUTURE

Tables 9.1 to 9.17 cover the following areas in turn: (1) geopolitical issues, (2) political development and change, (3) social stratification, status and power, (4) distribution and equality of material living standards and wealth, (5) social values and perceptions, (6) action, order and conflict, (7) social services and welfare, (8) food and nutrition, (9) health, (10) work, (11) leisure, (12) education, (13) shelter, (14) transport, (15) energy issues, (16) materials and resources issues, and (17) environment. The twelve different futures are contrasted by taking the four profiles as the columns and the three worldviews as the rows of each table. A great deal of abbreviation and 'telegraphing' of content is involved. In many cases we shall be talking about 'ideal types' in a given future rather than describing the range and types of variation that would be present: in particular the gross distinction made between rich and poor countries do not allow for the inevitable heterogeneity of any group of countries.

Text continues on page 316

TABLE 9.1: GEOPOLITICAL ISSUES   Key: P = poor countries
                                                          R = rich countries

High Growth, More Equal

(1) International agreements gradually
dismantle trade barriers, multilateralise
aid, reform monetary systems, etc. As
national boundaries diminish in
importance, there are shifts towards
optimal international division of labour,
with much trade and mobility of capital
and people. Culture and tastes become
increasingly global. Multinational
corporations transmit enterprise and
skills around world.

(2) Combination of domestic political pressure
in R, global political or economic threats,
and opportunities offered by new technology result in international agreements
to stabilise resource prices and
co-ordinate expanded trade and aid
interchanges. An economically diversified
world emerges, reflecting local diversity
as well as specialisation.

(3) Period of struggle and turmoil, culminating
in metropolitan and world revolution likely
to follow on major economic crises of
capitalism, but only with adequate
preparation of socialist movements; might
be sparked off by 'political' events such
as new colonial confrontations undertaken
during recession. Socialist states formed
in R move toward internationalism,
eventually set up world planning agency,
pooling resources and knowledge and
transferring skills and technologies.

High Growth Inegalitarian

(4) R isolate themselves from P in reaction
to P's economic and political caprice.
R turn to each other for resources and
technology, with a convergence of
political systems and much trade and
mobility. While some P become more
integrated with R, others are locked
in expansionist and chauvinist struggles,
civil wars, etc.

(5) 'Ultra-imperialism'; because of trade and
resource conflicts the world effectively
partitioned into regional zones of
influence; competitive but mainly
tolerant, not overtly hostile except
around borders. While blocs differ, most
likely pattern for R is shift in primary
production, environmental problems and
political repression of P and peripheral
areas.

(6) Failure of liberation struggle in P. R's
strength put behind groups in P oriented
to R's imperialism, who act as agents of
the world capitalist system. Socialist
countries' contribution reduced by
technology failures, internal conflicts
or dependence on capitalist R.
Multinational corporations consolidate
influence in the world: globe becomes arena
of their competition, with U.S.A. firms
probably overwhelmingly dominant.

Conservative | *Reformist* | *Radical* (row labels)

Low Growth, Inegalitarian	Low Growth, More Equal

(7) Protracted trade wars across world, perhaps sparked by attempts to form cartels or selfish action to secure resource supplies; possibly continuing world inflation tied to commodity price increases. Tide of economic nationalism grows until few nations retain any significant commitment to free trade. Squabbles over territory, attempts at subversion of neighbours, small-scale wars.

(10) R pursue misguided policies: welfare state and extreme environmentalism cripple industry, restrictive trade practices deter multinational enterprise and restrict expansion, leading to stagnation or decline With some exceptions (doctrinaire and under-endowed nations), P are much better in attracting investment, rapidly expand industry, trade and influence, forming trade and customs unions, and more stable political organisations.

(8) Monetary instability, inflation, shortage of vital resources, failure of technology, and other strains lead to triumph of 'malevolent mercantilism'. Economic and propaganda warfare is continuing state of affairs; R may pursue military conflicts in P in attempts to establish or retain zones of influence and access to resources.

(11) Political and cultural changes in R, signs of global ecological pressures, and threats from P mean that an 'environmental ethic' is slowly put into practice. Perhaps some form of international 'income tax' used to achieve balanced growth in P, while R's economies reoriented away from resource-consuming goods towards 'conserver' and service economies.

(9) Some R disadvantaged in jockeying for power in the world economy, perhaps by being denied access to vital resources (e.g. energy). Possibly U.S.A. dominance, more likely increased rivalry among industrial capitalist powers leading to economic instability on grand scale, but failure to offset declining rate of profit and escape periodic recessions. Pockets of growth and increasing centralisation of global power and wealth in the North, but general stagnation and decline. Industrial production shifts to P and R's periphery; class conflict intense, especially in these regions.

(12) Wars of national liberation in many P: R's interference discouraged by socialist countries and by conflicts of interest among R. Revolutionary movements and governments in P provide each other with mutual support, operate as regional blocs in pursuit of common development goals. Political alignments in R in state of flux: moves towards socialism in Western countries, break-up of NATO-type alliances under impact of economic conflicts.

Text continues on page 316

TABLE 9.2:   POLITICAL DEVELOPMENT AND CHANGE

	High Growth, More Equal	High Growth, Inegalitarian
Conservative	(1) Global trend towards establishment of liberal-pluralist states. In many P the emphasis of regimes puritanistic, with religious overtones. In R much more tolerance of differing lifestyles. State regulates unions and other particularistic interest groups, ensures welfare of infirm and aged, prevents discrimination against individuals or products arising from race, national origin, etc.	(4) R: liberal-pluralist states, possibly linked in loose federation. Important policies decided consensually among Northern countries. P: varieties of totalitarian regime in many countries; some communistic, some nationalistic; many small millenarian, separatist movements. Some P would be exceptions, with probable links to R and effective exploitation of local resources.
Reformist	(2) R: political power balance affected by pressures from youth, professionals, technical workers, etc. Much delegation of responsibility to local authorities. State attends to national and global growth; redistribution of wealth. P: progressive forces and sectors of society challenge traditional elites, development proceeds with more attention to local accumulation and less cost to poorer sections of society.	(5) R: governments very concerned with economic efficiency and maintaining stability, but social welfare needs also the focus of social engineering. P: variety of dependent political regimes. Some aspire to paternal liberalism, some with wherewithal to develop along social democratic lines, some simply repressive.
Radical	(3) R: workers' states, with national goals determined by delegates from workers' and community councils. Strong central governing bodies under public control and scrutiny but with much regional autonomy. P: socialist states, possibly with some remnants of state capitalism which are being phased out; development towards communism under way.	(6) R: highly repressive, manipulative regimes, possibly masquerading as democratic with two-party system but no real choice. High degree of surveillance of public. P: often puppet military regimes, corruption rife, strong links between state and organised crime, terrorism against dissenters.

Low Growth, Inegalitarian

(7) R: many states in various stages of
decline. Failed 'welfare states' now
heavily overbureaucratised, discouraging
enterprise and trade. Possibly some
military regimes, probably much regional
separatism.
P: as in (4), but lacking enclaves of
development.

(8) R: degenerate pluralist states, now non-
meritocratic and largely governed by
ruling elites (in name of socialism,
nationalism, or whatever).
P: some strictly dependent as in (5);
others pursuing autarkic policies with
little success and under continual
military threats.

(9) R: much as in (6), but with some states
less successful and possibly propped up
by U.S.A. or other contending powers where
in their interests. Socialist countries
probably recovering from economic setbacks.
P: much as in (6), but less non-military
assistance from R and likelihood of
guerilla and peasant warfare recurring in
many areas, with some major successes
possible.

Low Growth, More Equal

(10) R: domestic policies may resemble (7),
but possibly less conflict between R.
P: stresses for rapid social change need
containment, hence the most stable
governments in the short-term would be
military regimes aligned with business
interests, giving way to more
pluralistic states as development proceeds.
In some cases, a Japanese model.

(11) R: depending on timing and scale of world
political change, and on local initiatives,
different R may resemble (5) or (8), with
resource-conserving. P issues prominent in
government policy. Services often collectivised, some decentralisation of public
policy-making in less hard-hit countries.
P: many countries are networks of village
or commune republics, integrated by states
based on a middle-class backbone, regulating regional trade and technological
development.

(12) R: socialist countries fairly affluent;
others ranging from right-wing
totalitarianism to early stages of
socialism.
P: variety of states and much conflict;
the most successful are socialist or left-
inclined state capitalist, acting together
in preservation of mutual interests.

Text continues on page 316

TABLE 9.3: SOCIAL STRATIFICATION, STATUS AND POWER

	High Growth, More Equal	High Growth, Inegalitarian
Conservative	(1) R: wage rates similar in different countries; entrepreneurs and business leaders highly respected. Power diffused among many heterogeneous social groups. Occupational stratification marked, but only one of many bases for social differentiation. P: as above except more income inequality, traders and small businessmen highly regarded, pluralism still somewhat rudimentary although traditional elites waning.	(4) R: as (1); also scientists and defence workers highly rewarded and respected; status symbols (such as a country house, private transport, and other indicators of high consumption) important. P: traditional criteria of status, such as local and tribal power, religious authority, etc., mediated through control of state administrative system by dominant tribes, families, etc.
Reformist	(2) Almost everywhere technical experts, associated diplomats and statesmen highly regarded. Otherwise, high status in P to local organisers and businessmen, in R to state officials. Professional and social-service work are favoured careers. In R salience of occupational status reduced, since status needs replaced by more pride in craft work, concern with community.	(5) R: premium on well-paid technologists; status determined by job prestige and income. Elite in industrial society consisting of only a few powerful groups, but their influence moderated by separation of different branches of economy and polity. P: power mostly held by elites associated with interests, probably drawn from traditional ruling groups.
Radical	(3) R and P: labour much praised, but mental work still higher status; power may be linked to service to the Party. Continuous attempts to reduce inequalities between regions and labour, but slow erosion of established cultural attitudes.	(6) Real power wielded by small capitalist class controlling giant firms; in R this obscured by high status of and publicity given to managers, state officials and media personalities. Token recruitment of minorities to visible posts in organisations. In P, power vested in top bureaucrats, foreigners and security forces.

Low Growth, Inegalitarian	Low Growth, More Equal
(7) R: formal power largely concentrated in military and state institutions – although actual wielders of power despised by population at large. Corruption likely, and possible development of 'underworld'. P: probably resembles (4).	(10) R: as (7) in many ways. P: high respect given to local traders, researchers and foreign businessmen and entrepreneurs. Development of occupational prestige hierarchy typical of industrial societies.
(8) In R probably confusion of different status systems, with many groups in society owing allegiance to different hierarchical structures, including corporate, political, quasi-criminal and possibly religious groupings, with their own sub-cultures.	(11) R: depending on ease of adjustment to low growth, may resemble (2) or (8) with overt respect and covert resentment of government officials. P: local middle classes in ascendancy. Innovators, 'star performers' and educators in appropriate technologies achieve much popular prestige.
(9) Both R and P follow pattern established in (6), but probably considerable (if publicly muted) dissent from norms imposed by ruling classes.	(12) R will differ: socialist states follow pattern of (3), others of (9). P: continuing class conflict likely, while much local planning done by soviets and communes; central party officials have much national power, military figures much status where counter-revolution resisted. Teachers, doctors etc. much respected.

Text continues on page 316

TABLE 9.4: DISTRIBUTION AND EQUALITY OF MATERIAL LIVING STANDARDS AND WEALTH

	High Growth, More Equal	High Growth, Inegalitarian
Conservative	(1) While some P still relatively poor and national levels of wealth differ quite substantially, globally an unprecedented affluence. Large wage differentials in all countries; pockets of poverty in some.	(4) R: as (1), no discrimination on grounds of birth, but lack of effort or ability correlated with low rewards. Possibly antagonism to P. P: conditions much general squalor, gross inequalities; government officials living like feudal lords.
Reformist	(2) R have established and P are moving towards basically meritocratic society with moderate income differentials, and probably graded increases in wealth through the career. Minimum wages and free or subsidised provision of many basic needs would be ways of protecting the poor.	(5) R: essentially meritocratic, with wages notably higher in large corporate sector than in more traditional market sector P: still many poor people, wide urban-rural and regional gaps; traditional forms of favouritism, nepotism, etc. in appointments and remuneration.
Radical	(3) Equalisation of living standards proceeding across countries and occupations. Attempts to remove manual/non-manual and town/country distinctions. Abolition of money on agenda as goods are produced on basis of social need.	(6) Huge inequalities in R and P, although most obvious in P. Large police forces and other means needed to protect wealth; some return to systematic slavery in form of labour camps for unemployed and criminals.

Low Growth, Inegalitarian

(7) R: pressures for egalitarian society have undermined traditional reward systems; some levelling of incomes, but in general living standards are lowered in consequence; probably much crime and corruption.

P: are much as in (4).

(8) R: situation varies considerably from country to country; most common type might consist of low-level, highly taxed egalitarianism, with some wealthy elite groups.

P: much as in (5), but standards more depressed and local and national elites far less favoured.

(9) R: as in (6), wide differentials in wealth, income, opportunity. Periodic crises engendering unemployment and insecurity for large proportions of population.

P: islands of wealth in general poverty, but increasing impoverishment the norm. Some exceptions found in countries and areas striving for self-reliance, where conditions often fairly primitive, though improving.

Low Growth, More Equal

(10) R: much as in (7).

P: income differentials between regions and economic sectors fairly high, but slowly diminishing. Pattern of rewards across occupations corresponds to that developed in past industrial societies.

(11) R: some as in (2), but less affluent, probably with more regional and occupational variation in wages, but more social provision of services. Others as (8).

P: much regional variation; probably some social stratification at very local levels, thus quite large variations in living standards. Some redistribution at state and international levels.

(12) R: socialist countries achieve high degree of internal equality; others range between extremes like those in (9).

P: many countries have achieved land reform and other steps to equalisation (notably equality of the sexes).

Text continues on page 316

TABLE 9.5: SOCIAL VALUES AND PERCEPTIONS

	High Growth, More Equal	High Growth, Inegalitarian
Conservative	(1) World moving towards a society of leisure, with discontents stemming more from interpersonal conflicts than social injustice. Some 'alienation' in R expressed in cultism, sensation-seeking and the like; in P some protest about change expressed as trade unionism, revival of traditional dress and customs, etc.	(4) R: might expect general consensus on just distribution of social rewards and close approximation of this to reality. P: traditionalism in decay but not replaced by values of achievement or universalism. Much discontent, expressed as separatist and millennial consciousness, resentment of R and those associated with them, and intrapunitive aggression.
Reformist	(2) Sense of identity established by exaggerating cultural styles, lifestyles, etc., but also ethos of restraint dominant. Attitudes liberal (or liberalising) towards sexual behaviour and non-harmful deviance; collective responsibility for emotional 'casualties' by provision of counselling services, social workers, etc. Widespread belief in legitimacy and responsiveness of 'technocratic' government. More so in R than P, but P are tending in this direction.	(5) R: along lines of (2), but greater degree of local chauvinism, antagonism to other blocs and to P. Possibly some 'future shock' and anomie. P: conditions variable across time and place: some areas and ethnic groups continually resent inequalities, others experience low self-esteem and stifled by dependency.
Radical	(3) Process of building socialist consciousness under way; early fervour may face challenges from pockets of discontent, from confrontation of ideals with 'practical' short-term conflicts. Widespread sense of personal potency and community power in determining collective interests and action.	(6) While much local variation, in both R and P consciousness fragmented across various lines: individuals feel frustration and resentment, often appearing as racism, censoriousness, nostalgia, rather than class consciousness. Attempts to arouse working class may take despairing, 'romantic' forms, by small groups who have lost contact with and faith in the oppressed. Much apathy, resignation, sectionalism. If U.S.A. has hegemony "Americanisation' of world culture.

Low Growth, Inegalitarian

(7) R: fragmented societies with diverse but impoverished and reactionary sub-cultures. Grievances and crime abound; little sense of community wider than own family or street. Scapegoating, perhaps fanatic or terrorist movements. The wealthy retreat to secure or isolated estates. P: as in (4).

(8) Rather like the more unpleasant aspects of (5). In R and P some social groups scapegoated (probably minority ethnic or religious groups). Lifestyles frenetic, especially for young, with large revolutions of manners and generation gaps. Much resentment of authority, rejection of cultural heritage (except when fashionable).

(9) In many respects resembles (6). Culturally the process of Americanisation less notable. More potential for development of class consciousness and revolutionary movements; though these might well be localised, their struggles and symbols could be taken up elsewhere by small extremist groups engaging in minor cultural experiments.

Low Growth, More Equal

(10) R: as in (7).
P: much patriotism, pride in local culture and support for new achievements in industry, construction and communications. Respect for thrift, work, clean living; widespread belief that rewards generally appropriate. Some pockets of discontent and reaction likely, e.g. among newly urbanised and those rapidly moved from one economic sector to another.

(11) R: either as (8) or more accepting attitude to low growth, with society becoming 'communal'. In latter case general sense of satisfaction and equity, possibly some frustrated 'achievers' with increased interest in aesthetic issues, self-fulfilment, craft and workmanship rather than status and recognition.
P: Gandhiesque work ethic, but status distinctions probably remaining and legitimated by religious/village loyalties, and by association of local leaders with overseas experts and agencies.

(12) R: as in (9), except widespread resentment; possible rise of radical groups inspired by revolutionary ideologies of liberation struggles and by own experience.
P: anti-consumerist society, emphasising moral incentives; resurgence of traditional culture, technology, etc., but linked to socialist goals. Sometimes debate and mass participation, sometimes over-enthusiastic rooting out of deviant thought where change accomplished rapidly at cost of roots in masses.

Text continues on page 316

TABLE 9.6: ACTION, ORDER AND CONFLICT

High Growth, More Equal	High Growth, Inegalitarian
Conservative (1) Many voluntary organisations, much interest in leisure and hobbies. Fashions important. P's culture mirrors that of R but slightly less developed. Little crime, due to general affluence and efficient security.	(4) R: mostly as in (1). Deviant sub-cultures exist but integrative systems (religion, education for leisure) limit their influence and appeal. R see P as chaotic blend of militancy, reaction, and bare eking out of survival. P: some much like R's perception, some adapt to accept inferiority.
Reformist (2) Emergence of diverse lifestyles, much energy expended in 'pursuit of identity' and in finding variety. Experiments with different lifestyles and ways of regulating communal organisations. R: participative society, much involvement in local community management, in aesthetic and environmental design, much use of advanced communications systems. P: as in (1).	(5) While most lives will be spent routinely, anomie probably widespread, with juvenile delinquency, marital instability and industrial conflict. In P, nationalist movements may emerge, often to be repressed by R and local troops.
Radical (3) In R and P mass participation in political activity; networks of organisations establishing and linking local, regional and world production, development goals and social affairs. Much concern with self-education, both through experience of different communities and through more conventional means of instruction.	(6) R: most people sublimated in conformity, acquisitiveness, spectacle sports, and swings in morality from callous licentiousness to puritanism. Political opposition fragmented, voluntaristic, in many cases reduced to terrorism. P: peasant rebellions probably meet crude suppression. Crime on massive scale might be one relief from bleak improverishment of body and mind; another might be the carefully controlled importation of R's communications technology for mass 'entertainment' and ideological training.

Low Growth, Inegalitarian   Low Growth, More Equal

(7) R: repression of frequent upsurges of   (10) R often resemble (7); perhaps greater
    protest. These upsurges stimulated by and   sense of international rivalry. In P
    contributing to anomie. The breakdown of   firmness by authorities and industry
    rule of law becomes increasingly unjust   defuses trade unions, squatters and
    and inefficient. Widespread grievance   other sources of conflict, by breaking
    and hostility against welfare services,   their strength or incorporating them
    state officials, police forces.   into non-confrontational institutions.
    P: as in (4).   Development of educational and leisure
                                                    associations; mass political parties
                                                    feasible as main stresses of rapid
                                                    change recede.

(8) R: organised crime and intimidation on   (11) R: some perhaps as in (2); those
    a large scale would make the allegiance   maladapted to low growth as (8), possibly
    and loyalties of large portions of the   with more authoritarian regimes.
    population problematic. Violence routine   P: renaissance of oral culture, hard-
    in some urban areas.   working and prospering village
    P: as R in wealthier areas, elsewhere   societies.
    the apathetic, poorly-fed peasantry
    support militarised traditional rulers.

(9) R: strong but inward-looking counter-   (12) Conditions in different R might range
    cultures, separatism and sectionalism   from socialist mass action to breakdown
    on the part of organised labour (e.g.   of bourgeois state as in (9). P can have
    no support for the unemployed, for   had inadequate resistance from old
    foreign workers' struggles). Otherwise,   elites to prevent revolutionary change.
    R and P as in (6).   Mass movements producing such change
                                                    characterised by highly motivated
                                                    collective action, although probably
                                                    sometimes lacking democratic organisation.
                                                    Deliberate effort to advance cause of
                                                    regional development.

Text continues on page 316

TABLE 9.7: SOCIAL SERVICES AND WELFARE

	High Growth, More Equal	High Growth, Inegalitarian
Conservative	(1) R: facilities highly developed, largely under private initiative and incentives of profit as much as of charity; state aid restricted largely to aged and infirm. P: lacking advanced technology of service delivery used in R, but able to employ chemotherapy, contraception, etc. Fairly well-developed welfare services, especially in industrialised areas.	(4) R: much as in (1). P: health and welfare services rudimentary or based on traditional systems of relief and begging. Possibly some charitable provision of medical equipment and food from R, but this likely to be used by elites.
Reformist	(2) R: health and welfare services fairly egalitarian and collectivised, with focus on prevention, associated with educational campaigns, environmental protection, minimum wage legislation, etc. P: much development of paramedical services, state protection of workers' health, collective provisions for aged.	(5) R: similar to (2), but more focus on cost-efficiency and less concern with 'rights'. P: poorly developed and often token services, except for tourist areas and industrial labour force. 'Reservations' for the surplus population described as charitable institutions.
Radical	(3) Essentially similar forms being developed in R and P, with many basic goods and services free. Stringent health standards at work, preventive medicine, provision for care of elderly and continuing education.	(6) R: extensive, over-extended and shoddy services for ordinary people, unless technological innovations make services sector profitable and relatively cheap in labour. Specialised services might be developed, benefiting mostly higher income brackets. P: minimal services except for wealthy and essential parts of the labour force.

<u>Low Growth, Inegalitarian</u>

(7) R: welfare services over-extended, over-
subscribed and inefficient. They support,
however, large unproductive masses, even
if not very healthily.
P: as in (4).

(8) R: all services deteriorating, inefficient
and largely operating in favour of small
elites.
P: government action probably hopeless in
face of population size and environmental
degradation.

(9) R: similar to, but shoddier and nearer
collapse than (6). Social services used
as tool of repression; to shift people
around, break up subversive groups,
prevent industrial action, etc.
P: conditions also similar to (6).

<u>Low Growth, More Equal</u>

(10) R: similar to (7).
P: rudimentary but efficient services,
some provided privately (e.g. company
health insurance, aid with housing).
Some state coercion necessary to check
population growth, threats to health
and order, squatter settlements, and
other possible social problems.

(11) R: possibly a cheaper version of (2),
with much concern with community medicine,
distributive justice, underlying the
social services. Otherwise as (8).
P: as above, but less reliance on
highly trained technical staff, more
on mass campaigning.

(12) R: except in socialist countries and
those moving leftwards, conditions of
(9) are probable. In the exceptions,
fairly efficient services would be
developed.
P: in revolutionary regimes local and
low-technology services established;
reliance probably on paramedicals,
education drives, community care of
aged, etc.

Text continues on page 316

TABLE 9.8: FOOD AND NUTRITION

High Growth, More Equal

Conservative

(1) R: high and varied consumption with
imported styles of cooking, many
convenience foods.
P: robust, adequate diet with fish and
meat. Because of trade patterns a
tendency to global homogeneity, with
differences in eating following social-
status rather than national or regional
divisions. Possibly some areas and social
groups still malnourished; much over-
eating in affluent areas.

Reformist

(2) R: plenty of food, but emphasis not on
high consumption or convenience as much as
on variety and good cooking.
P: tendency to follow R styles - some
developments of novel farming methods in
arid regions, of local meat animals and
modifications of local crops. Revival of
traditional diets, but cross-fertilisation
of cookery across different cultures.

Radical

(3) Attention paid to production and
distribution of food to meet regional
standards, with orientation towards
upwards convergence of standards.
Probably reinforcement of many national
and regional dietary styles, but these
also affected by development of farming
technologies in previously unproductive
regions.

High Growth, Inegalitarian

(4) R: high demand for food but supplies short;
with rising price, food a major item of
household expenditure. Natural farming
insufficient; manufactured foods become
staple of poorer R groups; if ample energy,
then simulated meats, otherwise diet
modification. Eventually 'technological
fixes' give cheaper food again.
P: some populations approach 'Malthusian'
limits: famine, food riots, food wars
might follow bad harvests. In many regions
malnutrition prevalent, indeed normal.

(5) R: high levels of consumption, food styles
imported from 'colonies'; thus little
reliance on industrial manufacture of
foodstuffs, though this might attract some
R either for security reasons or because
of technological advances. Many P engaged
in 'estate' production of food for R. In
P local supplies probably adequate if
basic. Economically unproductive P
outside R 'spheres of interest' might rely
on subsistence farming and face severe
food shortages.

(6) Much food produced in P for R consumption;
North American grain might remain major
contribution to world supplies. Some parts
of P might face repeated hardship and famine,
while in R regional and class inequalities
might lead to shortages in crises such as
recession or war.

Low Growth, Inegalitarian

(7) R: good and varied food expensive and scarce for all except very rich. Sporadic rationing with little fresh fish or meat available. Staple diet might be basic manufactured protein and allotment vegetables.
P: might resemble (4).

(8) World wide, food consumption levels probably restricted, with widespread malnutrition. But some P may have marginally better food supplies owing to reduction of bias in production to R interests.
R: food supplies restricted and probably rationed on occasion; food quality poor, and diet supplemented by gardening, small-scale produce, etc.

(9) In many ways similar to (6), except that R are drained by military expenditure, hence food rationing and shortages likely to be more prevalent.
P: might be marginally better off.

Low Growth, More Equal

(10) R: conditions probably basically similar to (7), though whether better off because of trade with productive P, or worse off because prosperous P buy up more produce, is unclear. Many P booming; diet likely a combination of heavily advertised branded goods or provided by 'company town' or canteen organisation. Very intensive, possibly non-conventional farming methods.

(11) R: tend to simpler, restricted diets, possibly food cultism; imported diets might be authentic rather than heavily 'Westernised'. Stress on undemanding innovative techniques such as fish farming.
P: increasing agricultural productivity based on appropriate modification of traditional technology might lead to constantly improving standards of nutrition and more varied diets.

(12) R: depressed and unstable as in (4) except where R have moved to socialism or some other strategy adopted in which nutritional planning is important. More emphasis on P technologies and cuisine.
P: food production functional, diets fairly simple, but with emphasis on distribution of basic food requirements.

Text continues on page 316

TABLE 9.9: HEALTH

	High Growth, More Equal	High Growth, Inegalitarian
Conservative	(1) R: possible heavy emphasis on curative medicine, with fast technical advance in prosthesis and cure of disease. Preventive medicine (in addition to basic sanitation, etc.) might be minimal, but exhortations to exercise common in 'leisure society', with economical exercise technologies - isometrics, home exercise machines - prevalent. P: routine welfare benefits, sanitation, contraception introduced. Probably advanced curative technologies for the rich. Massive health campaigns to eradicate particular diseases likely.	(4) R: might resemble (1), though need to concentrate more production in R might lead to higher mortality rate (as might reliance on industrial foodstuffs). P: traditional medical practice and remnants of twentieth-century health services fighting a grim battle against epidemics and malnutrition. Possible that R provide medical assistance as self-insurance against disease; thus attempts to eradicate some diseases by inoculation.
Reformist	(2) Both preventive and curative approaches to health and medicine likely. High standards set to secure protection from harmful effects of foods and drugs; an international F.D.A. might be set up. But concern for individual liberty might limit effectiveness of such developments. P: gradual development to R standards via paramedical-based systems.	(5) R: might resemble (4), but with probably more regional diversity in health systems and regulations. P: often fairly primitive and reliant on expertise, drugs and instruments produced in R.
Radical	(3) Emphasis on preventive medicine and technological (bionic) treatment of accident injuries, etc. High levels of protection from harmful substances might be imposed, e.g. severe restrictions on smoking; also possibly compulsory medication for some physical illnesses. Welfare of community probably dominating individual liberty.	(6) R: probably strongly oriented towards curing diseases of civilisation, particularly among managers and professionals. Token regulation of industrial conditions and pharmaceutical industry, but high prevalence of iatrogenic and work-related disease. P: minimal health services, except where drugs sale profitable; possible exploitation of poor for health of rich (e.g. transplant organs, blood plasma, testing new products).

Low Growth, Inegalitarian

Low Growth, More Equal

(7) Quality of health services in both R and
P decline, and health levels with them.
Breakdowns in sewerage and water supplies
possible, leading to large emergence of
contagious diseases and hasty
responses to limit spread. In P
malnutrition associated with heavy
tolls.

(10) R: likely to resemble (7).
P: movement in the direction of (1),
but probably large regional, urban-
rural and class differences in access
to medical care.

(8) Expensive health services, only rich can
be adequately cared for. Just possible
that some diseases of civilisation
reduced by declining pollution levels
and dietary changes, and that better
nutrition in some P associated with
health improvements; but generally
health standards probably deteriorating
alarmingly in R and P.

(11) Some R and P might greatly rely on
preventive approaches, with emphasis
on community medicine, health education
and paramedical services. In some ways
would resemble (2), but less large-scale
state medical intervention; possibly
higher health standards due to improved
environmental controls. Other R might
be similar to (8), and P to (5).

(9) Probably similar to (6), but lower
health levels overall as standards are
reduced to cope with low profits and
high inflation in R and P.

(12) R: a range of circumstances; some R
resembling (7), others realising plans
for adequate food production, and so
achieving healthy, if uninspiring, diets.
Circumstances also varying across P,
tending towards those in (3).

Text continues on page 316

TABLE 9.10: WORK

	High Growth, More Equal	High Growth, Inegalitarian
Conservative	(1) R: automation on grand scale; many forms of manual labour archaic, employment even being seen as privilege for highly educated. P: work likely to be more labour-intensive, particularly in primary sectors. Much work taking the form of information-processing or service employment, unless these too were the focus of technological innovation.	(4) R: many jobs automated, but need for primary and secondary production to be located in R might place limits on this. In most P work would follow mixture of traditional patterns and approximate to factory work in early stages of European industrialisation.
Reformist	(2) R: most wearing and boring tasks probably automated, but emphasis most likely on job enrichment. Attempts to integrate work and leisure, making the former more creative with group technology, industrial democracy, flexitime, etc. P: technologies less sophisticated and work typically in factories resembling agglomeration of craft workshops. Industry fairly labour-intensive.	(5) R: many of more unpleasant or polluting jobs probably exported to P, migrant labour employed for tedious service sector jobs such as roadsweeping and catering. Work-force resident in P divided between industrial sector largely producing for export; other employment in traditional and informal sectors.
Radical	(3) Considerable emphasis on automation as means of reducing differences between manual and mental work; technologies chosen to maximise worker control and choice. Fundamental change in nature of work, away from alienated form as wage-labour; but objective differences probably persisting between different countries, regions and types of work in extent to which this process has begun in R and P.	(6) R: work and leisure increasingly brutish and unsatisfying. Threatened by economic insecurity among plenty (especially through automation), and lacking perception of revolutionary alternatives, workers are deskilled and engage in monotonous production tasks. P: peasantry either pursues impoverished traditional way of life or coerced or bribed into plantations and work camps for luxury export production. Industrial labourers regulated to the utmost, with threat of deportation from cities for malcontents.

Low Growth, Inegalitarian	Low Growth, More Equal
(7) R: life reminiscent of Great Depression; perhaps wasteful public works to disguise unemployment; 'softness on unions' results in over-manning, under-productivity; capital machinery unproductive because of poor maintenance. Associated social problems might include competition for welfare resources, 'culture of poverty', malingering. P: as in (4), but successful industrialisation possibly less marked.	(10) R: probably similar to (7). P: massive growth in employment opportunities, and large expansion of secondary and tertiary sectors.
(8) R: despite technological innovations at work-place, labour productivity low as workers reject poor conditions and machines are idle in face of low levels of effective demand. Conflicts possible over 'scabbing' and plight of unemployed workers. P: work conditions vary enormously: many areas with large proportion of unemployed, subsistence farmers and workers in menial services; few areas with sizeable industrial labour force.	(11) R: product life lengthened as well as other strategies adopted to reduce energy and resource requirements. High unemployment in some R. P: labour-intensive appropriate technology as backbone of development, supported by local manufacture and imports of capital goods (particularly simple machine tools).
(9) R: probably closely resembling (6), with more automation and unemployment likely. P (including, possibly, declining industrial nations): totalitarianism attempting to revive production with forced labour gangs, conscription to necessary services, and the like.	(12) Some R like (9). Others: more socialist pattern of development, with moves towards worker control of industry and increasing production via selective automation. P: pattern tending to be communal self-reliance and hard work; expertise and labour-intensive technologies communicated among P.

TABLE 9.11: LEISURE

High Growth, More Equal	High Growth, Inegalitarian

Conservative

(1) R: people with free time (practically everyone) find 'cultural delicatessen' of crafts, hobbies, obscure areas of knowledge, available in heavily packaged and predigested form. Tourism important, and a justification for maintaining form of indigenous cultures, whose substance has long ago perished.
P: because of 'global village' media effects, fashions mirror R; 'crazes' for sports and popular entertainments, particularly film or pop stars.

(4) R: resource shortages might reinforce already passive, spectator activities, e.g. mass-televised, high-paid professional sportsmen, many alternative T.V. channels, new entertainments media (e.g. holography, 'personalised' T.V.), mild narcotics.
P: main respite from struggle for existence might merely be debilitating idleness. Possible access to communal T.V. set showing monotonous diet of canned, incongruous Western programmes and government propaganda; probable large-scale development of illegal skills and various vices.

Reformist

(2) In R and P serious attempts to reanimate traditional arts and local culture probably go hand in hand with cultural eclecticism, recognising validity of alternative cultures. Much international apolitical (Olympic Games) sporting and cultural contact. Contact with non-R culture might lead to inversion of cultural domination of mass media, and world-wide predominance of P philosophies and art. Probably major growth of mass media, with innovative and 'personalised' communications receivers.

(5) R: leisure probably oriented to achievement and (possibly ostentatious) creativity. Existence of colonial 'frontier' might encourage skilled games and physical activities.
P: might exploit picturesque local customs where possible, leading to cultural trivialisation on lines of current African tourist sculpture. Otherwise leisure in P would largely be shoddy version of activities available in R.

Radical

(3) R: leisure activities largely educational, linked to community needs, or oriented to improving mind and body (chess, gymnastics); functional values and realism set above abstract aestheticism. Social analysis might become an art form.
P: similar to above, more intermingling of leisure with education and work of development. In both R and P, distinction between work and leisure fading.

(6) R: leisure probably towards passive barbarism, violence and pornography taking various institutionalised and non-disruptive forms (e.g. Roller Derbies and other combat sports, contending fan-clubs) with night-life rowdy and sleazy except for very young, very old, or rich.
P: infrequent, less expensive version of R, as relief from culture of illicit bars (shebeens, speakeasies, etc.) Americanisation of world entertainment, local sports displaced by novel sensational spectator sports.

<table>
<tr><td>

Low Growth, Inegalitarian

(7) R: high or disguised unemployment in essentially pointless jobs engenders cultural poverty in R. Leisure stimulation-seeking and compensatory: gambling and bar-room sports (perhaps organised by quasi-criminal groups), perhaps tolerance of soft drugs.
P: probably similar to (4).

</td><td>

Low Growth, More Equal

(10) R: probably as in (7), and might even be importation of entertainment and fashions from P (at least by elites).
P: local entertainments industries boom, specialising in repackaging traditional performing arts for mass media; fashions and 'crazes' probably influential even on 'high' culture.

</td></tr>
</table>

(8) R: entertainment largely provided through backward-looking mass media, e.g. T.V. replaying films and series from past decades. Also, perhaps, growing enthusiasm for neighbourhood and town sports teams as way of attaining some cultural pride.
P: perhaps as in (5).

(11) R: for countries adapted to low growth, leisure activities probably often similar to (2). Possibly communications technologies developed more in direction of local networks (e.g. cable T.V. systems) rather than privatising gadgetry. For other R, as in (8).
P: conditions might resemble (2).

(9) In R and P alike dominant leisure activities might be similar to (6). Probably more regional diversity in culture, but only making it less professional and slick, not less heavily ideological. Sporting and social clubs possibly developed around para-political groups.

(12) R: leisure activities varying considerably with different socio-political circumstances of R, with extremes perhaps resembling (3) and (6).
P: strong encouragement for functional and educative leisure pursuits: sports, training in self-discipline and defence, public works, etc.

Text continues on page 316

Table 9.12: EDUCATION

	High Growth, More Equal	High Growth, Inegalitarian
Conservative	(1) R: education of children partly education for leisure, partly utilitarian and functionally oriented, probably using programmed computer learning techniques as supplement to conventional classroom. Adults frequently retrained according to demands of technological change. P: education largely based on R's systems, using imported packages of materials, satellite beaming of educational TV, and R-trained experts in colleges and universities.	(4) R: tendency to two-tier system with education for consumption and leisure, but rising technocracy are 'creamed off' early for education with different values, and more specialised goals. P: schooling probably sporadic and unfocused except for tiny elite; its function more custodial than anything else.
Reformist	(2) R: goal of education the creation of generalist, liberal intellectuals, creative artists and craftsmen. Intellectual pursuits highly valued. Education lifelong- some training in social skills provided. P: orientation probably more functionally oriented towards engineering, medicine, entrepreneurial skills.	(5) R: emphasis on technical expertise likely. Competition among industrial nations leading to heavy R & D expenditure requiring scientific skills, as would demands of the communications industry. P: education systems providing minimum required for slowly industrialising economy and neocolonial bureaucracy, laced with stress on cultural superiority of R.
Radical	(3) Education oriented to training of basic skills, but more overt emphasis on personal development- this aims at producing socialist consciousness. High value placed on productivity and labour, practical relevance, the goal being to assist people to be part of collectivity rather than train them to be rulers and ruled. P: might follow Chinese example, with experience of labour (e.g. actually working on the land) regarded as part of rounded education.	(6) R: education probably with custodial function for all but children of ruling class- somewhat larger fraction of children destined to become professional and technical workers. P: education indoctrinates children with sense of cultural or racial inferiority.

Low Growth, Inegalitarian	Low Growth, More Equal

(7) R: at best authoritarian, conventional systems, but school facilities ageing and battered. At worst, progressive education and impact of social decay lead to anarchic conditions in which only apathy can be learnt.

P: similar to (4), perhaps with more tendency for children of wealthy to be schooled at private institutions in R, or for best educationalists from R to migrate to elite schools and colleges in P.

(10) R: similar to (7), with possibly even less adequate facilities.

Private enterprise could possibly provide P with highly specialised training packages involving programmed learning, and powerful technology for efficient acquisition of skills. Might be facilitated by fairly widespread system for imparting basic literary and numerical skills. Company schools might go with company factories and houses.

(8) R: education one of social institutions desperately trying to help clear up cultural disasters of economic depression. Might attract many idealists, but would probably remain short of vital funds and thus alleviate only few of society's problems.

P: might pay considerable attention to primary schooling but only rudimentary higher education for elites.

(11) In some R education a prop to authoritarian political system. If some R adapted to resource shortages and low growth without great stress, education might be oriented toward training in crafts, appreciation of ecology, etc.

Education in P probably functionally oriented.

(9) R: probably similar to (6), but less money spent on educational system, so its repressive class nature might be more obvious. Possibly emphasis on militarism, discipline and combat training.

P: much variation, with dominant tendency
- custodial schooling and indoctrination for masses, technical training for elite
- resisted by radical groups (including some priests and educationalists as well as revolutionary movements).

(12) Socialist R and many P likely to have decidedly practical education, oriented towards tasks of reconstruction and in many ways following pattern in (3).
In other R, schooling might resemble (9).

Text continues on page 316.

Table 9.13: SHELTER

High Growth, More Equal	High Growth, Inegalitarian
(1) For wealthier groups in R housing might resemble high-technology U.K. 'stock-broker' belt/U.S. 'Westchester County'. Most people live as conventional nuclear families in highly automated, self-contained, inward-turning households in dense urban agglomerations. Mass-produced housing estates likely in P with high-density flats replacing squatments, and housing standards improving with economy.	(4) R: dominant urban form possibly the megalopolis - more dense than in (1) because of fuel and materials scarcity; to compensate, even greater emphasis on personal privacy. P: some cities might collapse into looted, half-habitable wrecks, because of growing anarchy, food riots, collapse of services, law and order.Rural re-population might lead to famine and brigandry. Possibly revival of gypsy-like nomadic groups, but likely to lack foraging and surviving skills in hostile, defensive society of scarcity.
(2) R: well-planned 'garden cities' (or suburbs) designed to maximise privacy, though concern for environment might lead to higher densities of living than now. Family structures probably remaining basically nuclear, though deviance (communal living etc.) tolerated. P using local materials and traditional building systems to upgrade and finally replace shanty-towns and build new urban centres.	(5) R: widespread public housing partly as form of macroeconomic demand management. Possibly second homes common, with immigrant domestic labour from P. In many ways similar to (2). P: strictly utilitarian housing for workers in industrial colonies. Otherwise traditional and low-grade mass-produced housing common.
(3) R: high-density, high-amenity, multi-occupancy apartment blocs in cultivated parkland. Implies high local living density, with workplaces near but ready access to country and parkland. P: emphasis on communal development, extended families provid ing social welfare/ security. In this case, housing substantial but with limited facilities and extensive communal facilities (e.g. cooking). But massive socialist aid might allow development of new cities along lines of R.	(6) Great disparities within nations mean upper classes in both P and R live in guarded sybaritic suburbs. In R worker housing probably provided as utilitarian housing estates. P: maintenance of growing shanty-towns might be best expectation for dispossessed masses.

Conservative

Reformist

Radical

Low Growth, Inegalitarian

(7) R: existing city structures probably
maintained but decaying and with
occasional breakdowns of sanitation or
power services heralding eventual
instability. Housing crowded and old,
buildings kept in use despite
deterioration.
P: conditions approach those in (4).

(8) Hearts of R cities gouged out by
'development' replacing living communities
with offices and high-rise apartments
made more unpleasant by vandalisation.
Some P possibly coping reasonably
well with urban problems, perhaps
achieving norm of (5); others with
permanent social crises in city fringes.

(9) R: similar to (6), but with serious
urban decay and abandonment of attempts
to patch up old structures leading to
housing shortages and overcrowding.
Possibly huge apartment blocks built to
house working-class families.
P: conditions might be similar to (6).

Low Growth, More Equal

(10) Housing in R might resemble (7).
Many P might have improving housing
stock, some private, some provided
by companies. Living styles tend
towards nuclear family; housing with
good facilities but based on cheap
materials and shortcuts, e.g. septic
tanks instead of main drains.

(11) R: housing conditioned by attempts to
conserve materials and energy. High
urban densities to reduce transport
requirements, emphasis on communal
facilities; innovative family structures
developed in some R. In others old
housing patched up, provision strictly
utilitarian except for elites.
P: drift to cities reduced by rural
development based on appropriate village
level technology. Gradual improvement
in villages. In cities, basic services
(drainage, electricity) provided for
shanty-towns and small-scale
industrial development encouraged near
by.

(12) In many R attempts to halt decline in
housing stock and quality, meeting
varying success. Possibly experiments
with different living forms in more
socialist R (e.g. communal households).
P also vary considerably, some adopting
approach similar to (3), some permitting
only barest minimum of public dormitory
facilities.

Text continues on page 316

Table 9.14   TRANSPORT

	High Growth, More Equal	High Growth, Inegalitarian
Conservative	(1) R: personal transport mainly privately owned and operated, though with high levels of state provision of roads and perhaps systems to aid automatic guidance. Public transport, if developed and modernised, follows dictates of profit and is oriented to needs of more affluent: we might find inter-city rapid transit, P.R.T., self-drive electric cars. Conventional public transport rudimentary and concentrated around low income areas in richest countries. P: moving along same line, substituting private for public. In all countries and internationally rapid efficient goods transport developed to facilitate trade.	(4) R: developments similar to (1) moderated by needs for fuel economy. Thus greater emphasis on collective mass transport might be expected. Technological advances devoted to fuel saving. P: only ramshackle public and private transport. Broken-down machinery left to rot because of lack of mechanics, or ancient cars, engines and boats from R extensively re-used.
Reformist	(2) R: emphasis on high-technology public transport - super jumbo jets, moving pavements, widespread P.R.T., dial-a-ride, subsidised shoppers' buses, etc., for poorer areas. Restriction on private access to cities - hence 'park and ride', 'kiss and ride' systems - likely. Advanced telecommunications probable. P: similar emphasis on public transport, bus services, jitneys. Local authorities would regulate privately operated trams, enforcing car sharing. Public expenditure on traditional technology, e.g. railways, likely.	(5) R: might resemble (2), possibly with emphasis on substituting communication for transport (e.g. computerised information processing and relay, 'packet switching'). Also production might be reorganised to reduce transport needs. P: efficient transport systems developed where instrumental to production or export. Otherwise rudimentary but functional roads and railways built for reasons of internal and external security. Long-distance goods/materials transport for export from P to R (e.g. supertankers) developed on large scale.
Radical	(3) Transport provided free or very cheaply, especially in cities. Private cars reserved exclusively for out-of-town holiday, leisure use. Because of town planning many journeys, particularly to work, achieved by walking. P: heavy emphasis on goods transport as instrumental to growth, with possibly some local environmental damage (e.g. by heavy lorries) in short term traded-off against long term development needs.	(6) R: striking contrasts between run-down, grimy, expensive public services and fast, impressive, semi-automatic (but also expensive) private transport systems (non-profitable infrastructure for latter might be installed at public expense, e.g. under-road guides). P: contrasts even more marked, with only tiny fraction of population using advanced transport technologies.

Low Growth, Inegalitarian

(7) R: due to subsidies and careless public
expenditure sprawling public transport
systems, but inefficient, expensive,
unpopular, vandalised and under-used.
Technological innovations have probably
been applied to only a limited extent.
P: similar to (4), but probably more
importation of vehicles from R.

(8) In both R and P goals of policy might have
turned to sorts of transport implied in
(3). But lack of finance and problems of
reconstructing over-developed systems
designed for private transport and
run-down public facilities probably very
difficult to overcome.

(9) R: similar to (6), but technological
innovation probably more towards introducing
gimmicky status symbols than increasing
mobility. Personal private transport
available, but expensive and relatively
inefficient; public transport probably
drably utilitarian with even city
services infrequent.
P: similar to (6) but more dilapidated
forms of transport even for elites.

Low Growth, More Equal

(10) R: probably similar to (9).
P: would have had rapid development
of road networks, air- and seaports,
etc., largely oriented to goods
transport but with efficient passenger
rail and air services between new
industrial centres.

(11) R: between the images in (2) and (8),
but with further constraints imposed
by needs for energy and resource
conservation (thus possible renaissance
of bicycle, airships and sailing ships
for long-distance goods). Innovation
more likely in operating systems than in
actual transport technologies (thus
dial-a-bus and similar systems
dominant in more affluent R.
P: as (2) but many vehicles and transport
technologies taken over from R.

(12) P: aiming at transport systems as in
(3).
Socialist R hindered by residues of
capitalist developments as in (6) and
(9), and facing considerable
redevelopment problems; other R's
might have conditions like (9), though
limited but fairly efficient transport in
totalitarian states.

Text continues on page 316

Table 9.15:   ENERGY ISSUES

	High Growth, More Equal	High Growth, Inegalitarian
Conservative	(1) High levels of consumption in R largely because of personal transport, heating, air conditioning. Energy-intensive agriculture. Oil exhausted rapidly, thermal nuclear energy insufficient, breeders required. Conservation only if commercially necessary. Potential for ecological problems. Not much attention to 'alternative' energy sources. Similar patterns in P: consumption geared initially to industrialisation rather than agriculture.	(4) High consumption in R; much lower in P. Rapid depletion and export of P reserves; attempts to preserve supplies for future in R. Exploitation of oil shale, tar sands, coal in R and attempts to use more efficiently, especially if costs increase. Strong nuclear lobby and sales of nuclear installations to P.
Reformist	(2) High consumption in R and P, but some attempt at energy conservation. Long-term planning of energy supply including attempts to 'stretch' lifetime of oil exports from P. Nuclear energy important (possibly including breeders) but encouragement for solar, hydro, wind power, etc. Lower heating and transport demands than (1). Smaller cars, insulated dwellings, compact cities, and less artificial fertiliser in agriculture. More attention in P to rural problems than in (1); requirement for smaller energy installations.	(5) R: lower energy consumption than in (4) but higher energy content in imported goods. Serious attempts by government to control demand for energy and possibly level of nuclear supply. Attempts to avoid localised thermal pollution. P: little serious energy or any other related planning.
Radical	(3) High consumption in R and P; oil depleted as in (2). Rapid increase in consumption in P with attention to local sources. Attempts to plan as in (2) but less attention to conservation and environment initially.	(6) Fossil fuels in P rapidly depleted – less attempt at conservation in R. Widespread use of breeders. High energy costs lead to commercial (but unplanned) conservation effort.

Low Growth, Inegalitarian

(7) Opec cartel continues; higher energy inputs needed in material and agriculture sectors. Overall possible failure in supply or technology, affecting overall growth. Too much government interference in market for energy (either over-priced, encouraging inefficient alternatives, or over-commitment to too few sources or vast expenditure in unneeded capacity). Very poor P suffer from high energy prices, but cannot avoid impact of continued recession in R.

(8) Failure in energy supply due to innovative failure or lack of attention by industry to social and environmental questions. Possibly nuclear disaster, oil spillage, etc., and strong public reaction, affecting economic growth as in (7). Failure to employ appropriate energy technology in P.

(9) Continued recession with sporadic attempts to formulate co-ordinated energy policy - little success. Some attempts at conservation. Similar to (8) in both R and P. Failure in R leads to exploitation of P as in (6).

Low Growth, More Equal

(10) Big increase in consumption in P. Possibly using nuclear power to fuel industrial development. R economies stagnant - little energy policy planning. Public opposition to nuclear power on environmental grounds.

(11) Low energy consumption. Deliberate but reluctant attempt to slow energy consumption in R as result of P solidarity. Oil remains expensive. Nuclear power option where possible. Use of manual labour, waste and vegetable crops in P initially, later wind power, etc. Wide variety of sources but little, if any, nuclear (possibly coinciding with slow-down in the arms race).

(12) Similar but worse than (9) and (11) in R, but less emphasis on conservation initially. Main purpose of energy policy in P to promote equitable growth. Wide variety of sources as in (11).

Text continues on page 316

Table 9.16: MATERIALS AND RESOURCES ISSUES

High Growth, More Equal

(1) High levels of consumption and trade in many materials- increased mining, especially in P (unless rising energy costs make recycling economically attractive, or new technologies for widespread conversion of currently unused, but accessible and widely distributed, materials into useful forms, such as ceramics). High energy requirements, relatively high environmental degradation in mining.

(2) Increased recycling of some materials stimulated partly by environmental concern, partly by increases in materials prices (possible form of indirect aid to P). Attempts to reconcile demands for increased energy with environmental impacts of many energy technologies, e.g. by improving efficiency of energy use in transport and heating, development of renewable power sources.

(3) High levels of resource consumption and extraction-; recycling developed for reasons of economy and environmental protection. Materials consumption levels rapidly increase in P; much reliance on developing local materials and industrial bases.

High Growth, Inegalitarian

(4) R: engaging in much mutual commerce but little with stagnant rest of world; expand production and efficiency of use of materials - both mining and recycling grow and technologies required to substitute for and/or conserve rarer materials. High world consumption of materials largely concentrated in R, probably calls for substantial energy inputs.
P: mining decays for lack of external or internal market.

(5) Much productive activity shifted to peripheral areas of each 'zone of influence', with both mining and processing at some remove from centres of 'post-industrial societies'. This imposes heavy environmental burdens on parts of periphery, and requires development of bulk carriers and other forms of transport; only moderate levels of recycling likely, possibly in 'peripheral' industrial areas, but development of technologies for separating waste products efficiently might encourage this.
P: similar to (4).

(6) High levels of materials consumption, especially in R and richer areas of P, but mining and processing bring little benefit to mass in P, work conditions often wretched, with large environmental damage. High levels of energy consumption needed; much waste of resources in conspicuous consumption and military apparatus.

Conservative

Reformist

Radical

Low Growth, Inegalitarian

(7) Commodity price increases make many
materials prohibitively expensive;
depressed trade leads to run-down
of many mines, reduced levels of resources
consumption. But technological developments
also limited: recycling remains
small-scale activity; efficiency of usage
does not develop due to no stimulus
for entrepreneurs.

(8) Materials aspects resemble (7) in many
ways, but resource shortages and commodity
price increases might here follow failures
in technological innovation, or belated
recognition of dangers of high technologies
(e.g. nuclear reactor disasters, spate of
accidents in bulk carriers, etc.).
Possession of materials resources possible
source of international tension and
conflict.

(9) Given cyclical economic activity and
uneven distribution, pockets of fairly
high levels of materials consumption
in overall context of general depression
or stagnation of trade likely. Probably
great emphasis on substituting and
recycling scarce materials, though not
in planned or just way - so business
would strive to displace cost of those
activities to its benefit on to the
public sector.

Low Growth, More Equal

(10) Materials consumption increases
dramatically in P; R remain fairly
stagnant. Both P and R benefit from
technological advances increasing
efficient use, but possibly R
struggling with unprofitable and
expensive systems of recycling and
pollution control.

(11) Materials consumption constrained by
attempts at conservation based on
recycling, appropriate labour-intensive
technologies in P, reliance on local
sources of energy and materials
(probable costs of imported fuel
high).
R: similar to (10)

(12) Fairly high levels of materials
consumption, especially in P, where
development varies between Chinese
style 'mass line' (with emphasis on
local production of essential resources,
labour-intensive technologies and
conservation) and orientation towards
regional 'socialist solidarity' with
interchange of materials and products;
environmental reclamation postponed until
higher living standards achieved.

Text continues on page 316

Table 9.17: ENVIRONMENT

	High Growth, More Equal	High Growth, Inegalitarian
Conservative	(1) Standards vary with local geography and level of development; protection is response to unwanted side effects. Commercialised beauty spots, landscaped high-income estates. 'Dustbin' areas from mining, etc., in R and P cleaned up. Wildlife and oceans selectively protected for tourism and fish farming. Pollution-emitting industry located in P where lower standards acceptable. Game reservations for tourists.	(4) Similar to (1) but exploitation of oceans for deep-sea mining and factory ships. P: poor-quality, squalid; industrial air and water pollution but especially 'poverty' pollution, soil erosion, loss of wildlife, etc. Some game parks and areas of natural beauty commercialised for tourism in a few areas.
Reformist	(2) Attempts to set up world-wide standards, with anticipatory and comprehensive evaluation. Attempts to preserve and restore wilderness and historic cities. Fair variety in appearance of artificial environment (e.g. agricultural landscape). International legislation on exploitation of oceans, etc. Perhaps attempt to restock oceans. P: attempts to apply international standards and develop non-polluting appropriate techniques. Spoliation arising from mining usually put right as soon as possible.	(5) Similar to (2) in R with possibly less conscientious attention to environment. Polluting activities located where possible in P, especially mining. Some attempts at control but P unable to meet international standards - which in effect are trade controls.
Radical	(3) In many ways mixture of (1) and (2). In R standards applied and 'upgrading' of landscape to improve on nature. Parkland for recreation, wildlife, parks, zoos. In P standards more selective, and refurbishing less priority. 'Clean up' campaigns conducted periodically; perhaps mobilisation of local environmental corps.	(6) R: factory ships, ocean mining, etc., may place oceans in danger. Local thermal pollution problems in some areas. P: a heavily polluted environment, with much poverty-caused pollution in urban and rural areas. Large areas of world devastated in search for cheap sources of materials.

Low Growth, Inegalitarian	Low Growth, More Equal

(7) Environment hardly a priority in R with serious economic difficulties; environmentalism may have contributed to decline of growth. Technological failures and inappropriate standards have led to dust-bowl conditions in some areas and to oceans fished out. Where applied, legislation is response to crisis. Vandalism and air pollution from badly maintained vehicles in urban areas.
P: squalor, soil erosion from subsistence farming, pollution serious at all levels, affecting air and water; much wildlife endangered.

(10) Similar to (7) in R. Controls too expensive to introduce except as luxury items in more affluent areas. In P: attempts to avoid worst abuses, through coercion where necessary.

(8) Insufficient controls result in poor environment; much need for improvement recognised but no economic means.
P: situation close to (7). Severe environmental damage in some localities, due to careless introduction of new technologies, may have contributed to indecisive economic policies.

(11) In some variants here environmental issues might be priority. Global threats have prompted action and led to 'conservationist ethic' in R.
P: traditional eco-system preserved as far as possible with ecologically sound technologies. In countries of half-hearted adaptation to new economic order, environmental issues recognised as important but remedies unreasonably costly; rather than repair of environmental damage controls to limit its extension.

(9) No effective controls in most R. Environmental issues mostly luxurious concern of wealthy. Some resorts and parks superficially preserved. Some attempts at ecological management in boom years, but many exotic and rare species lost. Seas may be 'fished out' and quality of natural environment   ended.
P: similar to (6)

(12) Environment low priority in some R as in (9); in others attempts to reclaim natural and artificial environments.
P: similar to (3) with effort put into clean-up campaigns and development of community-based environmental monitoring and standards-setting.

Text continues on page 316

Liberty and Equality

Obviously such a condensed presentation cannot do justice to many of the more subtle problems and we now turn to two of the most complex.

Among the most fundamental quality-of-life issues are those of liberty and equality. The difficulties of definition do not reduce their importance.

Conservatives often stress liberty as the central element of social welfare. Here they may draw on the arguments of some neoclassical economists about the impossibility of comparing different people's satisfactions; since they can only be privately experienced, individuals require liberty in order to pursue their own satisfactions. This is qualified by the need to restrict each individual's infringement of others' liberties; the only legitimate coercion is that vested in the state to prevent both rampant libertarianism and conspiracies against freedom.

Reformers, too, stress the value of liberty. But just as they argue that an unregulated economy will not make optimal use of resources and will be prone to slumps, so they argue that liberty is an insufficient value: a completely *laissez-faire*, unplanned society suffers disharmony due to conflicting goals. The freedom of some individuals is curtailed by the development of large inequalities. While reformists see grounds for some inequalities of status and wealth, they advocate equality of opportunity, with inequalities based only on meritocratic grounds. Poverty and hardship can often be reduced without disrupting society's smooth running. Indeed, public intervention in the structure of social opportunities can harmonise the goals of different groups and in fact safeguard liberty.

Radicals are often caricatured as stressing equality to the exclusion of liberty. Marxists, at least, would repudiate the charge of being naive egalitarians, perhaps citing Marx's dictum that under socialism individuals would be rewarded according to their efforts and in a later stage of social development – communism – according to their needs. In neither case is equal provision regardless of individual differences advocated. However, radicals would in general argue that inequalities represented by the existing power structure of society are critical impediments both to social progress and to individual freedom. The freedom advocated by conservatives who would not change this power structure become a justification for the domination of the many by the few. The individualistic equality of opportunity promoted by reformists disguises structural inequality and exploitation as a just allocation of rewards for effort and ability. While many radicals see the defence of civil liberties as a necessary part of the struggle against exploitation and oppression, it is the abolition of a society in which different classes have different access to economic power that they regard as a prerequisite for social justice and human fulfilment.

The Good Society in the Conservative Worldview

(i) *Sources of low growth and reduced liberty* Conservatives assert liberty as a central human value. The structural–functionalist school in contemporary sociology draws attention to the role played by 'norms' in maintaining the social order. Social norms are guidelines about the functions of different roles in society, and should protect liberty while preventing its degeneration into irresponsible libertarianism. Their purpose should be, according to conservatives, to limit the constraints that each person's actions might impose on the freedom of others. Within the framework of a shared 'normative order' (value system), the pursuance of self-interest is beneficial to all; consensus is paramount over conflict. Some norms are codified as laws, professional rules and the like, but many remain at the level of shared but largely unspoken expectations.

Some of the four 'conservative' scenarios in chapter 8 are more conflict-ridden and less beneficial than this ideal. Conservatives can well conceive of situations in which unscrupulous business practices are common, attempts to override democratic rules are made by government bureaucracies or trade unions, or nations become embroiled in economic or even military wars. How do such circumstances come about, and what would be their consequence for social welfare?

Underlying the specific imaginary circumstances depicted in the scenarios, conservatives would identify two factors as obstacles to progressive social change: atavism and faulty socialisation. These are essentially psychological concepts: atavism is a reversion to some earlier practices harmful to the present state of evolution of society; and faulty socialisation is a failure of the 'integrative sub-systems' of society (family, religion, education, etc.) to transmit the appropriate set of social norms, that is to communicate to individuals a proper sense of their expectations, rights and duties.

To be viable in the long run a social order must overcome such problems. Otherwise they may lead, for example, to the development of sub-cultures that attempt to impose their own ways of behaviour and political ideals on society at large. Such alienated groups may on occasion bring about a successful political revolution; but the new regime will have to reinstitute the same basic norms and adaptive structures: an example often cited is the re-establishment of support for the family in the Soviet Union as the Bolshevik regime consolidated its power. What is true for national societies also applies to the world. A prospering world economic system requires shared norms about the governance of international trade and investment.

Conservatives often see 'atavistic' behaviour as a source of trouble in international affairs. The governments of new nations may lack adequate experience in contemporary economic affairs and attempt to cope with them as if they were similar to colonial or tribal politics. Even the people of more advanced countries still retain residues of antiquated values and beliefs from earlier periods in their societies' histories. Nationalistic attitudes still carry over from the days of mercantilism and empire-building; socialistic ideas from the early period of industrialisation. Such values may inspire groups deviating from the core values of society. In some circumstances these groups may have a disproportionate effect on social affairs through their influence in schools, mass media and trade unions. They can contribute to, and derive strength from, faulty socialisation.

These pressures manifest themselves as strains in the moving equilibrium that normally characterises social order: political disruptions, restrictions on free speech, interest groups attempting to impose their will on society, and abuses of international institutions and arrangements. If integrative systems cannot contain such strains, consensus temporarily breaks down. This may be particularly likely to happen in the new nations, where integrative systems have often been only incompletely developed. Disorder may sometimes be advantageous to the general welfare, as in a successful mass uprising against a despotic regime that is inhibiting social modernisation. Even in such cases, the diffusion of more adaptive ideas will in the long run probably whittle away barriers to progress, perhaps with less cost to liberty and life. Increasing the freedom of individuals to pursue their own ends (in the knowledge that they will have to bear responsibility for the results, and in harmony with the norms of society as a whole) is the path to social improvement. Social movements that claim to be guided by a millennial vision of a more perfect society (e.g. unorthodox religions, Marxism the 'counter-culture') are particularly dangerous, for they may engage in utopian conspiracies. The Good Society is not likely to be advanced by forcing people to fit themselves into a blueprint for perfection. Conservatives dismiss reformist and radical policy prescriptions as likely to restrict liberty and inhibit economic growth.

It is argued, for instance, that some reformists' proposals for international action to maintain international liquidity and to direct more spending power to the poorer countries are unsound, since they would increase inflation in the world economy, thus contributing to financial instability, and ultimately would be counter-productive. Regulation of the activities of multinational corporations, even to help poorer countries acquire more control over their operations, would shackle business to bureaucracy, depressing its initiative and reducing its efficiency. These proposals could encourage 'creeping socialism' or substitute yet more intrigue for fair play, by concentrating coercive power in massive bureaucracies; they ring of jealousy or unrealistic idealism to conservative ears.

The radical vision of world revolution is regarded as more callous than naive. After all, the world is fairly well fed and free from the violence of earlier times. Political turmoil would disrupt this order, with no guarantee of a workable replacement. Fortunately, conservatives might argue, people in the richer countries by and large accept this fact and radicals have turned their hopes to poor countries. Their proposals for these countries to 'go it alone'

are seen as nothing new and nothing that has not been refuted as impracticable and undesirable many times before. The idea of groups of poorer
countries attempting autarkic strategies of development as regional blocs is
the old idea of import-substitution extended to a larger scale (but with the
added vulnerability of possible disagreements between bloc members). Some
development might be possible under autarky, at least for the better-endowed
and more technologically advanced areas of the world. But production could
not be as efficient as with an optimal international division of labour; goods
would be costlier and, at least in the poorer countries, inefficiently produced
and of lower quality. Strategies of increasing 'self-reliance' would be disastrous for some countries, leaving them short of earnings to finance the
imports of materials and components which they would still require. Such
strategies could instigate a round of retaliatory trade policies that would
further depress international economic growth. Trade wars could be sparked
off by a retreat into protectionism. The outcome would probably be a general
depression of the world economy.

Problems and solutions within nations tend to be described in similar
terms by conservatives. Governments have tried to expand their monopolistic social services and, in financing them, have imposed unduly high levels
of taxation depressing the economy, or have created inflation by running into
deficit or by printing too much money. Attempts to interfere in the operation
of private enterprise often limit the initiative of businessmen and lead to
industries stagnating or transferring overseas. Leading managers and
specialists in everything from health care to steel manufacture are likely to
depart from countries in which there are indications of a growing militancy in
politics and dissatisfaction with the reward structure of society.

Equalisation in practice means levelling: levelling the performance of
schoolchildren to that of the less able, culture to the poor taste of the mass,
and wealth to the low average of prosperity that would ensue if incentives,
namely income differentials, were removed. Abundant welfare services can
reward thriftlessness, scrounging and malingering. The more radical calls for
socialism or anarchy can lead to dictatorship. With both economic and
political power concentrated in the state, it is inevitable that an elite would
use this in its own interests, involving the suppression of opposition and loss
of liberty.

(ii) *Towards the Good Society*   Conservatives aim to increase welfare by
enabling the maximum total net output to be obtained from the economic
system. Those who contribute most to productivity will receive higher
rewards. Conservatives would expect the world to develop a more efficient
international distribution of labour if trade were thoroughly liberalised.
Wage levels for given occupations would become similar in different
countries; the contribution of poor countries to world output would grow as
modern ideas and institutions became widely diffused. This could favour

peace and prosperity: people and nations should realise that the benefits of
society depend upon the amount contributed, and ensure that individual
effort rather than unjustly held power is the basis of reward. All people
should be equal in law, having equal responsibility for their conduct as
guided by social norms. Conservatives would generally temper this rather
optimistic account, however, with warnings that progress is bound to be
uneven and that people and cultures may lag behind or oppose it.

This 'Good Society' is most nearly achieved in the conservative high
growth, more equal scenario. Although some areas of the world might secure
liberty and welfare in both the high growth, inegalitarian and the low growth,
more equal scenarios, there would in these cases, however, be sub-optimal
use of resources, more risk of international conflict, and possibly some resort
to repression even in the more prosperous parts of the world. Economically
stagnant parts of the world are liable to social decay and political corruption.

What of the domestic policy of the Good Society? *Laissez-faire* is not appropriate to all aspects of life: there are some services (e.g. law enforcement, basic
research) that can best be operated or financed by the state. But well-being
could be improved by decreasing much state interference in society. What
follows will deal more explicitly with the richer countries than with the
poorer, for it is admitted by some conservatives that a fairly high degree of
state involvement is needed if poor countries are to undergo rapid social and
economic change. Governments may facilitate the social changes involved in
the progress of the world towards an optimal international division of labour,
through, for example, offering assistance in physical relocation, retraining
workers or co-ordinating schemes of urban development.

In many other respects, governments would do better to reduce their (often
invisible) coercive roles in social life; this often involves positive steps that
restore liberty to the individual. Private choice should be protected as far as
possible in areas where bureaucracies have tended to strive for monopoly and
uniformity, such as health, education and housing. Conservatives argue that
such proposals are at the heart of a Good Society. Ideally, market
mechanisms should raise the standards and the efficiency of the services and
goods involved.

Where public provision is necessary, waste and abuse should be minimised
(e.g. with minimum charges for health care, no subsidies to those who can
afford to pay) and competitive private enterprise encouraged. More choice
should be allowed within the state systems (e.g. voucher schemes for
schooling). The cost of public services should be kept at a minimum with low
taxes allowing for more individual choice. The efficiency of such services as
education could be improved by a return to traditional methods, involving
tighter quality controls of pupils' learning or basic abilities. In the Good
Society there would be fewer hasty attempts at social innovation that might
prove to have long-term negative consequences. The quality of life for the
individual would be raised by a revival of principles eroded by the welfare

state, such as self-reliance, neighbourliness and family cohesion. There would be the reaffirmation of individual responsibility and autonomy. Problems would be seen as a challenge to personal strength rather than as the fault of society. Wrong-doing would meet with firm punishment, rather than with derisory yet costly attempts at 'rehabilitation'. The cultural degeneration of much present art and intellectual life, and even of sport (with displays of gratuitous violence on the playing field), would be replaced by a more affirmative approach. Conservatives argue that a society of this sort is quite practicable: what it depends upon in the first instance is the willingness of ordinary people and their representatives to speak out against vociferous and self-interested minorities.

Quality of Life and the Reformist Worldview

(i) *Inequality versus totalitarianism?* Reformists would not agree that social problems overwhelmingly result from individual wrong-doing or deviance from socially accepted norms. A whole host of problems, ranging from environmental degradation to crimes of violence, are very often the result of social structures. Society is composed of a multitude of different groups whose interests may be in conflict; there is no hidden hand ensuring that the self-interested actions of individuals will add up to a rational outcome for all. While reformists would not reject everything in the conservative view of social welfare, and indeed accept much of the social theory that conservatives draw upon, they would argue that blanket application of conservative policies often takes insufficient account of the dynamics of different cases. Intervention in the spontaneous operation of the social order is sometimes necessary. There is always a trade-off between freedom and equality. The quality of life in a grossly unequal society would be abysmal, no matter what liberties were available in theory. Indeed, a poorly managed and generally undirected *laissez-faire* system may limit individual opportunities far more than the 'coercion' of liberal governments; and it could cause festering social discontent that might bring a totalitarian regime to power. Careful balancing of the scales between too much and too little state intervention is required; decision-making must be pragmatic since in different circumstances a given policy may be more or less appropriate.

Reformists consider that conservatives overemphasise the rationality of the unguided social system and pay too little attention to desires for status and power that often tend to dominate *laissez-faire* domestic and international arrangements. Radicals are criticised for their reluctance to come to terms with the costs of life and liberty that so often accompany attempts to centralise social and economic planning. A more pluralistic view of social affairs is needed. Reformists advocate, for example, that both trade unions and large corporations should be regulated by the state in incomes policies. They do not side with one or the other, as conservatives and radicals are seen to do. It is possible to aim at a society in which some differentials remain and hardship is relieved. Total equality would involve coercion and be counter-productive but 'meritocratic' equality is possible with differentials serving to reward responsibility, effort and the mobilisation of skills. These inequalities should be less extreme than those resulting from 'conservative' prescriptions.

Conservative ideals of a world moving towards complete economic liber-alisation are criticised as producing neither economic optimums nor political stability. Under free-trade arrangements the world's resources of capital and labour would not be used to the full. Without deliberate government or inter-national efforts to limit unemployment, sinking employment levels are likely to depress the level of consumer demand and thus restrict economic growth. The existing structure of the world economy largely benefits the wealthier countries. Free trade would therefore breed suspicion and resentment else-where, which could lead to renewed international conflict. Mercantilist and protectionist policies have usually in the past been disguised under supposed free-trade conditions and there is little reason to expect events to take a different course in a world guided by basically self-interested competitive values.

Radicals are charged with another kind of utopianism. The idea of world revolution is horrific and the likelihood of its slipping into nuclear war cannot be discounted. Even if it were successful or if regional blocs could be formed as socialist alliances, the prospects would not be good. National self-interest can still emerge as in the Sino-Soviet conflict or the disputes between Vietnam and Cambodia. The repression of popular aspirations and the burgeoning of massive, unrepresentative bureaucracies in state socialist countries are further reasons for desiring a pluralist economy and govern-ment.

Reformists identify similar problems in the domestic policy prescriptions of the other two worldviews. Conservative policies might widen social gulfs to such an extent as to throw increasing numbers of people into absolute hard-ship or relative discontent, which could lead to political upheavals. The actual pattern of events would depend upon specific circumstances in the world economy, especially the general economic growth situation and the nature of international tensions. In terms of quality of life, however, things would be inequitable for much of the population. Serious hardships would afflict certain social groups (e.g. the old minorities) and places (e.g. city centres and already declining regions) and repressive measures might need to be employed against signs of local protest. If monetarist policies produced high levels of unemployment, these scenarios might resemble those of the Great Depression. If, somehow, a slump were avoided and growth continued, we would be faced with a world of jealousies: different sections of the work-force contending for privileges, ethnic antagonisms and strong chances of conflict between different blocs of countries.

Radical reforms are criticised in different terms. Left-wing radicalism is a possible form of totalitarianism that would be encouraged by an utter collapse of conservative policies. Whilst a socialist 'command economy' might ensure economic stability, various facets of the quality of life would be impaired. At the level of economic production the abolition or strict limitation of the market system would impair efficiency, encourage the growth of parasitism and waste and reduce the power of consumers over the manufacturer. Especially in the political sphere new elites would strive to perpetuate themselves and so prevent meritocracy. Income inequalities might thus be maintained in a disguised form. Despite the egalitarian claims of some socialists, their policies might develop a more unequal society. In the long term, especially in the absence of international conflicts, pluralism would probably re-emerge in response to the demands of the different interests and ideologies in industrial society. But for some time there could exist a more or less dictatorial regime whose possible benevolence in the sphere of social services would be unlikely to extend towards cultural or political self-expression on the part of the citizenry.

(ii) *Improving the quality of life*   Neither equality nor liberty are ultimate states that a changing society may attain permanently. Reformists see different groups in society as forever developing new aspirations, which lead them into conflict with one another. In one sense, maximisation of the quality of life can be described as a balance, calling for a coordination that can stand above the particular short-term interests of specific groups.

Both high and low growth options are in principle compatible with improved quality of life in more equal reformist futures. Status and power needs may be satisfied through cultural activity, concern with the environment and identification with a local community. The satisfaction of basic material needs and a sense of security and fairness may stimulate the emergence of 'higher needs', possibly involving concern with non-economic goals and the welfare of the less-powerful and inarticulate groups. Quality of life is not merely defined by the material goods available to the individual; it also depends upon social comparisons and the sense of community that may be established both in people's local environments and in the wider society. However, more economic growth is probably needed to achieve a levelling-off of 'materialistic' aspirations, as well as to provide an opportunity for moves towards greater equality to be made in a gradual way that does not penalise the already wealthy.

A steady movement towards more international equality requires world economic restructuring. While this could in principle enhance the quality of life in ways shortly to be detailed, reformists have often suggested that the impetus to such change might itself be somewhat unpleasant. Whether it be a limited war, ecological disturbance or natural disaster, major impairment of the well-being of some part of the world's population would seem likely. The only way to avoid this would be if advance warning signals were sufficiently visible for the major world powers to agree to prevent disaster.

Agreement between countries would have to overcome fears of loss of national sovereignty and the likelihood of some states attempting to expand their spheres of influence in the new international system. Political disturbances might occur as nationalists made stands against internationalism. The reformist ideal, however, would be for a broad consensus to emerge on the goals to be embodied in the new international order.

One problem in outlining a reformist perspective on social values should be acknowledged here. Whilst it is fairly easy to do so about both international and domestic affairs, many advocates of international reform are wedded to more conservative strategies where internal change in their own countries is involved. Thus the present account of the reformist worldview may suggest a more coherent set of values than often obtain in reality, perhaps especially as regards policy-makers in poor countries.

For industrial countries the high and low growth scenarios differ in the extent to which Keynes's vision of a society of abundance turning its concern increasingly towards non-material pursuits and to the material needs of others is to be realised in the near future. The likelihood of this is a matter of dispute among reformists, who disagree about the salience of 'higher needs' in the human psyche. Concretely it may depend on the vigour of ecological activism and the emergence of environmental threat of one sort or another, on the climate of international affairs and on the actual period of time in which the reorganisation of national economies must be carried out.

The implications for quality of life of reformist policies are many. Participation, stabilisation, enrichment, meritocracy and the abolition of hardship are complementary values embodied in these prescriptions. Welfare policies, for example, could provide means of economic stabilisation far more attractive than military expenditure. Ideally, economic growth can be guided so that inequalities can be reduced without lowering the circumstances of all but the most privileged minorities, and so that an eventual transition to low or even zero growth rates can be made with little trauma. Private enterprise should continue to play a major role in economic development, but its operation should be more closely scrutinised and regulated: the investment and financial practices of multinational enterprises and the social and environmental responsibility of corporations should be guided and monitored. Legislation should cover issues ranging from anti-pollution and the choice of technology through to the hiring of minorities and the provision of facilities (less restrictive working hours, child-care services) for working parents. Participation in industry should be organised around such arrangements as the enlisting of workers' representatives on boards of directors and the encouraging of workers to buy shares in their firms.

In a 'post-industrial society', often the desired image for the richer countries, social change could be effected through the actions of planners and expert managers. Recruited on a meritocratic basis they could retain good communication with the wider community through consultative councils, citizens' pressure groups and a modernised parliamentary system. The last could probably formulate social goals, set up commissions of inquiry and maintain international coordination.

Good, informed management could bring about social as well as economic stabilisation and thus improve the quality of life. Given such developments as technological progress, changing family patterns and growing urban centres, the state has a positive role to play in buttressing or reforming traditional institutions and values to reduce the stress of modernisation. This should be particularly important in poor countries, where technologies could be chosen so as to be least disruptive to cultural traditions other than those associated with systems of feudal oppression.

Some reformists consider that richer states might direct the development of the service economy in order to limit unemployment. As workers were displaced from industry by increasing automation, new jobs could be created in the services sector that looms so large in discussions of 'post-industrial society'. Other reformists, however, are less convinced by this thesis, taking a more pessimistic view of the supposed trends towards a service economy in contemporary industrial societies.

Many aspects of the quality of life could be improved. At work, reformists argue for job enrichment, with group technologies, job rotation, flexible working hours and the like, allowing workers more freedom and variety in the composition of their working time. More services should be available, and there could be the 'new liberty' in the market-place, with consumer goods more adaptable to individual requirements and better consumer education and information.

Social inequalities and people's subjective sense of inequity could be lessened if policy were directed more towards removing poverty and particular blemishes in society than to removing all inequalities and thereby penalising those who contribute more than the average. Thus progressive taxation should be complemented with health insurance, minimum wages and special aid to deprived areas and groups. Education should be made more accessible to the under-privileged, with recruitment to official positions made more dependent on merit, perhaps with a system of quotas for minorities and deprived groups.

Reformists have made many proposals for new or extended community organisations and services. These include child-care centres to let women develop their careers and to provide pre-school education, especially in terms of intervention programmes for the most deprived; community health centres with paramedical staff backing up experts in environmental and psychosomatic medicine, new systems of social service as a means of criminal rehabilitation, and the like. While the state should encourage such developments, innovations might often be pioneered under private or charitable auspices, to be adopted on a large scale only if the experiment proved successful.

The current economic and social state of poor countries leads reformists to make more modest proposals for them designed to ameliorate extreme material hardship. Often they argue that the most practicable course for the poor world is for local business elites to gain the support of other inhabitants in confronting foreign interests and traditional elite groups in order to push forward economic progress. Poor countries need not necessarily follow the experience of the industrial ones, whose development often polarised the interests of the bourgeoisie and the ordinary people.

Reformists see their proposals as more than a mere smoothing over of the problems of industrial and poor societies in the interdependent world economy; rather as an infusion of humanity and democracy into the pattern of social and technological change. The best features of traditional society would be protected and when necessary revitalised, while forces undermining social cohesion and ecological stability would be checked. Neither participation nor scientific rationality, neither equality nor liberty, should predominate; their balance lends variety and challenge to life.

Social Justice and the Radical Worldview

(i) *Ideology and exploitation*   Radicals admit the tension between liberty and equality, but dispute conservative and reformist concepts of freedom. To proclaim that human beings should develop in liberty is often rendered meaningless by an unhistorical use of the term 'liberty'. Institutions often held up as epitomising freedom – parliamentary systems, a relatively uncensored press, etc. – may indicate different forms of freedom and coercion at different times. Parliamentary forms often disguise the fact that crucial decision-making takes place in a private, undemocratic arena. 'Press freedom' may be of no real significance when the ownership of the mass media is virtually monopolised by one class. Given glaring social inequalities, the legal freedoms of individuals to engage in a wide variety of activities count for little when these activities are priced well beyond the average person's means. The freedom of one person to accumulate resources may well limit the freedom of others.

These radical criticisms are not meant to devalue the striving for a freer society, but to point out that conceptions of freedom are shaped by history; what characterises 'liberty' in concrete terms may be a quite different matter from the liberty to which people are entitled on paper. Freedoms are devalued by the existence of a class society with its consequent inequalities. Where one class has greater access to resources than another, even equality of opportunity is likely to prove a legal fiction. Class differences entail varying life chances, even when there is apparent eagerness to compensate for them, as in reformist prescriptions for education and welfare services. Rather than focus on trade-offs between liberty and equality, radicals will tend to point to the mutually supportive aspects of the two, when they are understood as historical concepts. The polemics between different groups (e.g. 'Leninists' versus 'libertarians') indicate that the exact nature of this mutual support is by no means resolved among radicals, at least not in their own practice.

The fundamental problem of capitalist society and in state socialism, according to many radicals, could be described as an amalgam of inequality and lack of freedom. While many people engage in routine or manual labour, only a few are involved in the crucial decisions about the ends to which labour-power will be put. In a market economy, even those with decision-making power are constrained by the demands of the competition of different firms. People lead limited lives under conditions and structures that they mostly feel powerless to change; they are cast in occupational and other roles by necessity rather than choice.

Alienation is the fundamental human condition produced by the capitalist system, to radical analysts. People face circumstances – at work, at home, in society at large – that are alien forms and forces rather than human constructions and social relations. Their own work and actions, sold as labour or assigned as duties, seem to be carried out at the behest of 'market forces', 'society' or even 'progress' (and, in poor countries, 'tradition'). Social processes, in fact, as the outcome of relationships developed throughout human history, are taken to be natural phenomena. Money, technology and the like appear to be autonomous forces. Material possessions are assigned progressively more worth, 'rationality' based on narrow economic criteria pervades more areas of life, and human lives and relationships are devalued. Individuals are privatised and attempt to cope with the consequent bordom and frustration through titillation, vicarious experiences and passivity.

This fundamental critique is often opposed on empirical grounds. It is said, for example, that improving working conditions, increasing civil liberties in the permissive society and the emergence of new elites and new forms of domination in socialist states constitute strong arguments against radical analyses and prescriptions. Radicals may reply that the economic and political fluctuations of capitalism make any gains of which its apologists may boast decidedly tenuous and that many of these gains are of dubious significance in the first place. The limitations of contemporary socialist regimes are often partly ascribed to the relatively under-developed state of most of their countries during the period of revolutionary struggle, which has meant that fairly severe restrictions on consumption have been the price of long-term gains in living standards. Also, these countries have generally been subjected to heavy pressure from external counter-revolutionary forces, and have been embroiled in imperialist wars despite their own pressing problems. Nevertheless, criticism of the abuses perpetrated by state socialist countries has come from many radicals; even the communist parties of Western Europe, traditionally aligned closely to Soviet interests, include such criticism in their 'Eurocommunism'.

Conservative and reformist policy proposals are seen to run up against the basic problem that business, multinational and otherwise, must act in a self-interested way to survive in the capitalist system. Simply allowing big business its head would lead to the continued polarisation of wealth and power in the world. The reformist ideal of national governments regulating private corporations fails to recognise the dominance over the state of the ruling class that owns these businesses. A restructuring of the world economy might well sound very progressive, but would probably develop its inter-nationalisation to the advantage of capital rather than of humane ends. In some cases the commitment to profit might coincide with humane goals, e.g. the prevention of nuclear war, although corporate interests have large stakes in armaments spending. Overwhelmingly, the capitalist system remains ex-ploitative, despite its appeals to the 'common interest'. Its historical task – the development of the forces of production – is complete and it now conflicts with social progress.

A clear echo of these analyses may be found in 'radical' evaluations of domestic policy proposals. The state in capitalist society is not some neutral entity standing above social conflict, but an agent of coercive and ideological domination acting largely for the ruling class. A small minority of the population (and in many cases, foreign imperialist interests) effectively controls much of the wealth produced by the working class. The state apparatus is one means whereby the power of this minority is exercised over the economy and polity. Thus, it is futile to expect significant steps towards social equality to be taken by non-revolutionary governments. While conservatives are at least frank about the unattainability of equality through their policies, reformists imply that their strategy could lead to a significant redistribution of power. The potential power of the working class is normally needed to gain significant social-reform concessions from capitalist states, but often these concessions are divisive for the interests of different groups of workers.

Radicals would not expect current reformist suggestions to be any more successful than similar policies tried in the past. State education, the welfare state, nationalisation of basic industries: except where the working class has been vigilant in defending its gains, none of these has led to more than marginal improvements in equality, security or democracy. Reformist good intentions tend to be diluted when they conflict with the interests of capital. Many reformist policies actually reinforce oppression: they may disguise the non-neutrality of the state, and direct attention away from exploitation and structural injustice to more secondary products of capitalism such as hard-ship. In practice, reforms have often instituted means tests and similar systems that stigmatise the poor and make social problems appear to be the result of individual failings.

One of the critical expressions of the contradictions of late capitalism from a radical perspective is the simultaneity of inflation and unemployment. Conservatives and reformists have in the past often sought to avoid one of these problems by worsening the other. Radicals argue that the existing organisation of society embodies and generates social conflicts that could be removed, but not by technocrats or the mythical soulful corporation. To build a society with broad participation in fundamental decisions requires the overthrow of the ideologies of consensus and conflict management, proposed by conservatives and reformists and supported by coercion and domination. While pursuit of the policies advocated by these two worldviews may well stave off or contain developing class-consciousness, the contradictions and instabilities of the capitalist system must either at last be resolved in a radical transformation or else plunge the world into barbarism.

(ii) *Social justice* Radicals are often accused of being more adept at criticising society and proposing strategies for its violent overthrow than at detailing their visions of the future. In this respect they actually resemble such conservative critics of utopian thought as Karl Popper. However, radicals would retort that to make blueprints for a future social order that should be democratically planned by those who live in it would be self-contradictory and utopian since the future will inevitably be produced by human action in particular real circumstances. Nevertheless, issues of welfare, justice and quality of life are apparent in radical thought about the future.

The form of the future society visualised by radicals can often be discerned in the apparently negative goals they set. Radicals seek to end alienation by destroying the social divisions of labour between manual and intellectual work, between production and planning, and by ending the subjection of individuals to market forces in their career choices. They aim for a creative labour process that allows for the many-sided development of the human personality, for the integration of work and leisure. These conditions have never been possible in the past, but radicals argue that the technological capacity to build such a society is now available. Only outmoded social relations stand in the way; to transform them is the most pressing, and most difficult, task of our times.

The terms 'classlessness' and 'social justice' have been used by some radicals as a better representation of their goals than 'welfare', 'fairness' or 'quality of life'. Social justice could be summed up as 'to each according to his/her needs'. Human needs, however, are not just physical requirements that can be technically determined, but are in part social products. Their evolution is inextricably linked to the growth of the personality in its social relationships. The radical goal would be for society so to develop that an increasing range of needs as defined in an on-going democratic process could be satisfied. No criterion of race, class or influence should produce inequalities among people with the same pattern of needs.

The two more equal scenarios based on the radical worldview represent different stages of progress toward this ideal, with the high growth, more equal scenario being somewhat more advanced. The task of constructing a truly liberated society will take generations. It must derive from the activities of a mobilised working class, since according to Marxist theory it is this class that creates wealth and is potentially the 'universal class' which can abolish class differences.

Socialist world development should be directed towards the equalisation of welfare and income levels across countries. A world planning agency might be the vehicle for these aspirations; its activities would for some considerable time be likely to reflect the different development paths adopted by socialist countries before and during the transition of the world economy away from capitalism. Since many revolutionary states will probably have pursued policies of diversification or 'self-reliance', it is to be expected that a socialist international division of labour would differ considerably from that proposed by orthodox economists. Large-scale socialist aid projects should enable the poorer countries to embark upon modernisation without impoverishing their agricultural sectors.

Radical views of domestic policy are influenced by the successes and failures of the Russian and Chinese revolutions, as well as being infused with commitments generated by the experience and analysis of capitalism and its 'welfare' systems. For radicals, direct democracy is both a means and an end. Its archetype is perhaps the workers' council with the power of decision-making on community needs and programmes. Regional and national congresses of such councils should adjudicate these issues at appropriate levels. Alternative plans and priorities should thus be decided by delegates (rather than representatives) of workers in different branches of the economy. The old state should wither away as self-management replaces it.

In a wealthy world, basic necessities such as food, clothing, shelter and access to information and knowledge should be provided free as a matter of priority; a longer-term aim would be to abolish the money economy altogether and have all social products assigned free of charge. This would call for radical changes in infant and adult socialisation, which would sweep away the egoistic and competitive personality characteristics reproduced by existing schools, sport, religion and entertainment (to mention only the least coercive institutions).

In the case of poor countries striving to move towards socialism in a world still dominated by waning capitalist power, as in the radical low growth, more equal scenario, the 'new person' to be sought might resemble the ideal held up in China and Cuba. The ideal is for workers to be motivated by community and national needs rather than personal material incentives. Indeed, given a commitment to classlessness and to investing much of the precious surplus wealth of a poor country to ensure future development, anti-consumerism is likely to be an important objective of social policy. The desire for luxury goods should be curtailed.

In societies progressing rapidly towards socialism, radicals would argue that social policy should be directed towards eroding the remaining vestiges of the market economy and its individualistic values. Social and moral incentives rather than legal and economic coercion would prevent waste and injustice. Welfare services would allow people to have increasing control of their own destiny: thus there would be neighbourhood crèches, readily available abortion, mass education in health and safety. Local media would be encouraged; courts would be operated by the local community. That such conditions have yet to be permanently established anywhere is proof not of their incompatibility with 'human nature', but of their limited practicability while capitalism remains the dominant social system in the world.

Although some radical goals resemble those of reformists, there are several fundamental differences. Most critically, radicals believe that without public ownership and democratic control of land and industry, liberal reforms are bound to be subverted by landowners and capitalists acting in their class interests. This democratic control is not to be understood as a mere rubber-stamping of the decisions of a technocratic elite, but as people collectively active in debating and determining the directions of social change. Social divisions of labour, especially those involving the allocation of responsibility and control, are not allowed to breed alienation and a class structure.

FUTURE SOCIAL ACTIVITIES

For an adequate appreciation of the daily experience of people in alternative futures one needs some view of the things they eat, their work and leisure, their transport and housing arrangements and their educational and health services. We now turn to these areas, which are admittedly just part of the fabric of social life. We can, of course, only speculate about the relation of some of their aspects to the twelve futures.

Nutrition and Health

Analysing world food prospects in chapter 4 we concluded that the world is capable of producing by conventional means sufficient food for many times its present population, but that such a growth in production requires changes in the directions of world growth. To develop an idea of the possible types, quantity and distribution of food in each of the twelve scenarios means taking into account such factors as: (i) cultural influences on diet and eating habits, (ii) forms of food production, which could range from fairly conventional farming methods, with or without substantial inputs from advanced technologies, to novel approaches such as industrial food production, (iii) sources of dietary proteins, which might be animal, vegetable or micro-organic in origin, (iv) adequacy and distribution of food supplies and the related questions of nutrition and health.

Some scenarios, most notably the high growth, more equal futures and perhaps some views of low growth, more equal futures, imply a fair degree of realisation of the optimistic physical and technological prospects described in chapter 4. A large increase in world food production is called for in the case of rapid economic growth in poor countries. These countries have experienced fairly dramatic changes in staple foods: wheat has increasingly replaced rice in Japan, while urban Chinese have adopted cornflakes instead of cassava and poor Indians millet instead of rice. In many of the inegalitarian scenarios the hunger of the poorer portions of the world's population is likely to continue.

The implications for the quality of life are fairly obvious. Severe and sustained hunger renders people listless, prone to incapacitating disease and to death through normally trivial infections. Infant mortality is greatly increased; there is evidence suggesting that not only is children's stature curtailed, but also their brain development. In futures in which famine or long-term food shortage are mainly confined to the poor world, the particularly susceptible groups are the landless labourers and the urban unemployed, the former often swelling the ranks of the latter. The accumulation of problems in agriculture in some countries might provide a crippling burden for regimes committed to social transformation.

Turning more specifically to questions of health, it seems obvious that improved water supplies and sewage disposal, vaccination against smallpox and other diseases, and the introduction of antibiotics and the like have played a significant part in curbing disease. But it is worth stressing that improved nutrition is an important determinant of resistance to infection. It has been a major factor behind the historical advances in longevity and disease-resistance seen in many regions of the world. In scenarios where nutrition is poor, influenza epidemics may cause many deaths.

Economic development and technical change in rich countries have led to a decline in infectious diseases and malnutrition; but they have also been associated with a rise to prominence of 'diseases of civilisation'. These diseases are associated with industrial lifestyles and are apparently non-infectious. They typically affect men more than women, manual and unskilled workers much more than those of higher social status; they appear mostly in middle and later life. Typical examples are degenerate heart disease, chronic bronchitis, most cancers and diabetes. The decline in death from infectious diseases (especially tuberculosis) has been partially offset by a rise in the diseases of civilisation.

Pollution is an important source of disease. Recent concern over asbestosis, silicosis and similar occupational hazards indicates just how little serious attention has been paid to airborne pollutants in the work-place. It is possible that lead and other pollutants from automobile exhausts may be involved in several widespread disease syndromes including damage to infant brains. Radiation can produce cancer. Diet is itself a major source of diseases of civilisation:foodstuffs are contaminated by additives and by the residues of high-technology agriculture (hormones from rearing of tender meat, nitrates from fertilizers). Furthermore, industrial civilisation has historically been associated with dietary changes and with sedentary living styles. Increased consumption of animal fats (meat and dairy products), stress and lack of exercise have all been linked to cardio-vascular disease; reduced consumption of roughage to digestive illnesses; consumption of alcohol and tobacco to cancer; and many more such cases.

So we can speculate on the incidence of diseases of poverty and diseases of civilisation in the scenarios. Where living standards remain poor or deteriorate, the former must be expected. While for poor countries the improvement of the living standards of the poorest is clearly the first priority, much of the disease load of early development might be eased by a more equitable distribution of health care. Where industrialisation proceeds or life-styles continue along the lines established in the richer countries, a high incidence of diseases of civilisation is probable. But this does not seem to be inevitable. The physical environment could be regulated in order to reduce or limit pollution, especially at the work-place. Diet, especially the consumption of additives and luxuries with little nutritional value, might be changed. So, too, might leisure activities, methods of transport, and the types of physical and mental demand imposed by the nature of working life.

Work, Leisure and Education

The costs and rewards of work are of such significance to human material and mental welfare that quite explicit analyses may readily be made in terms of the three worldviews, and images of alternative futures derived.

Several scenarios, for example, entail circumstances in which regions of the world are stagnant, thus implying both explicit and disguised unemployment. Other scenarios feature severe recessions or cycles of boom and slump; job security is here likely to be low, unemployment often high. In some scenarios workers have little or no chance of unemployment relief and are thus tied financially to particular jobs, while in others people might be pressed into service by the state and cannot choose their occupation. The type of work in which people are engaged varies across time and scenarios: in some cases agricultural work has been largely mechanised and industrialisation has proceeded apace, in others economic and labour-intensive systems have been developed, while in still others there has been a trend toward replacing many industrial processes by automation.

With rapid development and diffusion of technologies, expansion of production in poor countries could result in the transfer of many jobs from craftsmen's workshops to factories (as in the conservative, more equal scenarios, in which historical trends of technological change might largely continue). In contrast, the appropriate technology arguments of some reformists and radicals imply the redesign of jobs so that tasks performed in

Western factories might take place instead in workshops or cottage industries in poor countries. Some commentators have argued that the development of industry in the poor world might imply a major threat to industrial employment levels in the 'North'.

Changes in the nature of factories and workshops may well happen in the industrial countries, a possibility advanced particularly by reformist promoters of such innovations as 'group technologies'. Job rotation and job enrichment are related strategies for relieving boredom at work.

Changes in the labour force's composition would occur in several scenarios, with more women freed to participate in traditional male jobs and with a shift in industrial countries towards more tertiary (services) labour being possible in some high growth scenarios. Many white-collar jobs could be transferred from the office to people's homes, given high growth and cheap and better-quality telecommunications. This optimistic view of the impact of advances in communications technology in a high growth 'North', shared in a lot of ways by many conservative and reformist commentators, has been challenged by other reformists and radicals, who have sometimes pointed to a prospect of cybernation de-skilling and displacing many existing white-collar workers, creating unemployment and a wide gulf between higher-level technical posts and the manual labour force. Rather than increasing productivity leading to a 'civilisation of leisure', some commentators have raised the prospect of it leading to a 'civilisation of unemployment' with a possible return to Depression conditions.

Assuming employment is available, another change in working life would have more to do with the individual's work career. Some of the high growth scenarios allow for the possibility of careers changing in various ways: the frequency of change of jobs in a working life could increase or decrease, as could the range of occupations through which individuals might move. In high growth scenarios with good employment prospects high rates of technical change would call for frequent retraining. In some of these situations a large degree of occupational mobility and choice might be available, with special provisions to enable women to take on traditionally male occupations, to help the handicapped find rewarding employment, and to improve the conditions of unpleasant or boring jobs. In others there might be compulsory circulation of jobs, as when educational or other services are made contingent on completing a term in 'public service' or agricultural or industrial work.

Above and beyond these questions of job content and patterning stand questions about job control and industrial democracy, intrinsic and instrumental satisfactions obtained from work and 'alienation'. Radicals contend that alienation is a social problem and the result of treating human labour as a commodity to be bought and sold, when it could be treated as a part of the worker's life activities that could be integrated with individual and collective needs for personal and social growth. In the other worldviews 'alienation' refers to a psychological state of boredom or anomie, which is either an acceptable condition to which the worker willingly submits in order to earn higher wages or else a consequence of unfortunate but partly flexible technological arrangements. The latter perspectives are linked to ideals such as job enrichment and group technology. A more radical approach to work-place problems is to call for industrial democracy, as part of a more general process of socialist transformation in which decisions about the operation of each work-place may be made in coordination with decisions about overall social needs and directions. Radicals would argue that the reformist response to these demands – admitting union representatives to the boards of directors of companies – is inadequate, since it merely accepts the existing framework, which is, however, the ultimate source of the problem.

Leisure is not identical with free time. In some scenarios there would be much 'free time', simply through high rates of unemployment, yet it is unlikely that anyone would consider this desirable. In a very wealthy world with much structural unemployment produced by automation, considerable resources could be devoted to entertainment – the bread-and-circus scenario of many science-fiction novels – or people might amuse themselves by playing games with and against their technological environment. If people were to use this time to exercise some control over the course of social change, however, it becomes debatable whether one is dealing with 'leisure' or with political organisation.

Views of leisure, like those of work, differ. One view sees leisure as the goal of economic development and technological change. The goal is not merely to have maximum free time, but to achieve an optimum balance between available free time and earned income (or production), which will enable one to fill such time with agreeable (or fulfilling) activities. This suggests the image of a highly automated society in which jobs have been mechanised so that they make diminishing demands on time, skill or patience, and the major part of one's life is spent in intrinsically satisfying recreation. An alternative view, however, sees both work and leisure as having the potential to be intrinsically satisfying activities; both are possible routes to personal and social development, and mutually supportive. The political and economic circumstances constraining or contributing to the realisation of these potentials vary across the different scenarios and would, of course, be analysed differently in the three different worldviews.

Images of what education actually does at present and what it could and might do in future society are closely related to images of leisure. Education may be vocational training, socialisation of children into different roles or social classes, a child-minding service for rearing the unskilled workers of the future, a means of disguising unemployment and damping down social con-flicts, a system for the reproduction of ideologies, a form of conspicuous intellectual consumption for the middle classes or a medium for personal development and the expansion of people's aspirations, commitments and skills.

Techniques of education would differ across scenarios. In some futures life-long continuing education would probably be a concomitant of rapid growth in the industrial countries, introduced in some cases for necessary occupational retraining, in others for voluntary personal development. Mass education in poor countries might use high-technology communication systems (e.g. educational satellites) for large and scattered populations in a world of high economic growth. These latter circumstances might be associated with requirements for education about immediate practicalities of crop production, small-scale industrial development or the use of local fuels.

In a wealthy industrial society high technologies in education could include computer-assisted learning systems, videotaped recordings of classes, automatic devices to make learning to write (or type) and cope with arithmetic more enjoyable activities. A return to disciplines reminiscent of the traditional classroom, training children in values and competencies seen as necessary for industrial capitalism, might be advocated by conservatives. Reformists would incline more to experiment in education systems, with community-based schools and training in problem posing and solving. Radicals would argue that curricula should be harmonised with planned social development, but also that the education system should be responsive to the needs expressed by those engaged in learning.

Transport, the Built Environment and Living Patterns

Transport of goods, people and ideas span the primary, secondary and tertiary sectors of the economy. Technological innovation has been rapid in each of these spheres: super-tankers carry vast loads of petroleum, jumbo jets each ferry hundreds of passengers and communication satellites have been one link in the increased quantity and quality of world communication.

The dominant form of motorised transport in Western societies, the motor car, is typically privately owned and privately operated, although dependent on collective provision of roads and other infrastructures. Its enormous impact on living patterns is well documented. Collectively owned and operated transport is the usual pattern for mass public transport. Taxi systems in many countries (and the jitneys – shared taxis – of some Asian countries) are individually owned but collectively operated; collectively owned and individually operated transport has been experimented with in self-drive taxi 'clubs' in Europe. The coexistence of all these forms within industrial societies might suggest that any form could be projected for any scenario; however, some forms are actually dominant and others less important or even marginal in the real world and, presumably, in scenarios of the next century.

Privately owned, privately operated transport discriminates against large minorities in the present population of industrial countries, notably the old, the young, the poor and the infirm. Whilst advanced technologies may offer a remedy for such discrimination (e.g. cybernetic town cars with pro-grammed guidance routines), this would probably be very expensive and thus inaccessible to many of the population except in a scenario of extravagantly high growth and/or involve considerable collective provision of new types of roadway or track, proximity detection equipment, etc. These technologies could be developed in all high growth futures, but conservatives might recom-mend that the apparatus be owned and developed by private corporations to serve those areas with most demand and willingness to pay for it; while radicals might seek public ownership and provision based upon public decisions about the social need for transport in different areas.

Future transport options are constrained by the resource requirements and environmental impacts of the different technologies as well as by social considerations. For example, mass transport is more energy-efficient than individual transport, so energy prices would influence the range of transport alternatives in a given scenario. The motor car is a major consumer of many materials in most industrial countries; however, there are wide variations from country to country, suggesting that the materials-intensity of automo-biles could decline considerably – European cars typically weigh about half as much as cars from the U.S.A. Likewise, great savings are possible in the energy consumption of motor vehicles. A large growth in the world 'car population' would nevertheless involve consuming much material resources (and of course, energy).

Whilst one might imagine the multi-car household becoming common, there are suggestions that saturation point for car ownership is approaching in O.E.C.D. countries, which account for about 90 per cent of the total world car population. Since 1960, the growth rates of car numbers have declined steadily in almost all these countries. In a high growth scenario with a 'Western' pattern of consumer demand diffusing around the world, a rapid rise in car numbers would accompany the development of the poor world, perhaps with the evolving of 'appropriate' types of automobile such as the Asian car that Ford plans to manufacture in several countries of South East Asia. More egalitarian governments in the poor world might well be more concerned, however, to develop adequate public transport services and to limit the use of private cars.

In the choice between different transport systems, poor countries face various constraints. Roads and canals have the advantage over railways that they can be made from indigenous materials and do not necessarily call for steel mills and the like. Rail is relatively steel-intensive and may be less economic where low traffic densities are expected. Prospects for canals are much affected by the local terrain. Where a great deal of local self-sufficiency is possible and preferred, roads usually seem to be the best means of keeping open regional transport links. In the longer term, and given high growth rates, roads might be built that would require more 'industrial' inputs – overhead lighting, crash barriers, etc. – and would correspondingly need more materials. The need for goods transport could be reduced by the spatial reorganisation of production or by product redesign.

Long distance transport has long been a growth industry. Aircraft and freighters are becoming larger, carrying more passengers and freight per unit of material consumed. Other technologies for goods transport also operate on a fairly large scale; for example, we may find longer-distance applications of pipelines carrying solid goods (pneumatically, as with letters and parcels; or mixed with water, as with slurries in mining operations). These technologies would probably be developed to different extents in the twelve scenarios, according to the amount of world and regional trade and personal mobility projected and the availability of materials and energy. A world placing a high premium on environmental protection might make more use of technological options promoted by contemporary environmentalists: sailing craft and airships with their low energy and materials cost and low levels of pollution, for long distances; muscle-power and perhaps electric vehicles, for local travel and transport.

One of the issues in transport and communications most frequently raised in the futures literature is the possibility of transporting information instead of people: holding conferences through video-systems, the substitution of much direct person-to-person communication by computer-to-computer interactions, and so on. Whether the gains in information yielded by these possible new forms of technology will significantly reduce the amount of personal travel is debatable. Telephone calls seem to have displaced letters rather than business trips, and travel films are employed to whet people's appetites for tourism rather than to replace it; on the other hand television has to some degree replaced cinema and theatre in the richer countries. A more detailed study of the social functions of physical contiguity and of different media of communication than is possible here would be required for us to deal with this issue adequately. We may, however, point out that several technological advances in communications – e.g. holography, optical fibres, cybernetic systems for decentralised mass communications networks, video-cassettes, etc – would probably be developed in a world of high economic growth.

Almost half the world's present population lives in the few hundred biggest cities. Large-scale city life is, of course, a recent phenomenon – only a few per cent of the population of European countries lived in cities at the beginning of the nineteenth century – but the speed of the transition from rural to urban life is rapid, and is considerably more so in poor countries than in the European experience.

In all parts of the world, city populations have been swollen by workers and their families displaced by the technological and economic transformations in agricultural production. The failure of building programmes to keep up with this flood has led to many urban centres being surrounded by shanty-towns, lacking adequate sanitation or other public services, and with 'houses' often made from industrial or consumer discards, such as piping, automobiles, corrugated iron, etc.

Shanty-towns may simply continue to grow and, in many cases, fester, bringing risks of disease, fire and crime; this could happen with low growth in poor countries. Public authorities could make an effort to accommodate shanty-towns within planned socio-economic development, for example by laying down basic water supplies and facilities or even by erecting very cheap temporary housing (the materials needed for them would be relatively low). Or a massive development effort might be made to provide both jobs and shelter for urban populations, along the lines of the Maoist principle of replacing cities of consumers with cities of producers; if the trend towards urban migration were not halted under radical policies it might at least be slowed.

It seems likely, in low growth and inegalitarian scenarios at least, that poor countries would largely rely on traditional building methods and local materials, which for practical purposes are mostly inexhaustible. Rapid growth using appropriate technologies could likewise involve local materials and improved traditional building practices rather than imported approaches. However, we may expect that more and more construction will use current Western technologies and new ones of whatever origin. Western building styles might be promoted in these countries, however, by multi-national business interests. Rapid growth in the poorer countries might mean in other scenarios the development of indigenous cement, steel and associated industries.

Evidence suggests that construction industries in the industrial nations now use many metals and wood less intensively than in the past, though plastics intensity has been growing. High-rise buildings call for more iron, steel and concrete (but less brick) consumption, and poor countries have also shown greater demand for cement and reinforcing steel (and structural steel for large projects where traditional, labour-intensive materials are not appropriate). Construction industries account for a fairly large proportion of the GNP of most industrial nations – up to a tenth in fact – and if the poor countries were to follow their growth paths, materials consumption might well increase at a higher rate than that of GNP growth. While such high levels of materials requirements for these purposes are unlikely to strain the earth's resources, energy costs could be a problem and could stimulate new technological developments to reduce the materials requirements of building.

Future dwelling patterns would also influence, and be influenced by, changing family sizes and structures. Studying the 'family' is notoriously difficult. Definitional problems arise: is, for example, a family bonded by the physical dwelling unit that is common to its members? There are theoretical problems, too, such as: what effect has socialisation on individual character within different types of family? What is the role of social structures in these processes? A once-standard account of the historical development of the family from tribal, through extended, to nuclear forms has been increasingly questioned. One of the major challenges stems from data indicating that nuclear families (typically consisting of parents and their children, but no kin other than the occasional dependent relative) living as small households existed in the United Kingdom and other areas of Western Europe well before large-scale industrialisation or urbanisation. Functionalist sociologists have often argued that the modernisation of traditional societies in the present world tends to break up established systems of kinship, leading to the establishment of nuclear families as a newly dominant type. Research data are conflicting, and the policy prescriptions seem to be based more on value judgements about modernity and tradition than on scattered pieces of empirical evidence.

Still, the tripartite distinction of families into tribal kinship groupings, extended families and nuclear families does offer a preliminary basis for classification. To this may be added various proposals that have sometimes reached experimental forms in industrial societies: different types of commune, intimate networks and a host of minor modifications to the overt sexual activities of the nuclear family, such as 'swinging' and 'open marriage'. We would guess that, while substantial divergences from currently dominant family structures may be common in several scenarios – notably those in which high levels of income and thus of economic freedom have been attained, and those in which there is more emphasis on individual liberty – it is unlikely that any one other structure would become the norm in the timescales covered in the twelve scenarios. This does not preclude a deliberate effort by poor nations intent on pursuing their own distinctive path of development to preserve or attempt to revive particular family structures.

Government intervention to reduce individual dependence on contemporary householding arrangements is possible in the industrial nations. For example, recent Swedish party manifestos have tackled issues of the sexual division of domestic labour, which have also been a recurrent concern of women's liberation and other movements. Existing housekeeping tasks could be, as at present, distributed largely on sex and age bases, or be more symmetrically arranged; or existing activities could be collectivised, with or without continued identification of these tasks as 'women's work'. Thus, some feminist groups advocate payment for domestic labour; child-rearing could be transferred to state or private auspices. The potential abuses of such arrangements have restricted the interest in them; where less risk of bureaucracy is involved – as in the case of day care for the children of working or poor parents – there have been steps forward in industrial countries (especially the Soviet bloc). The pattern of domestic labour could also be changed by families sharing cooking and recreational activities; or domestic work could be further 'industrialised', with disposable utensils, highly mechanised cleaning, etc.

New living patterns call for new institutions. Recent examples include the 'singles bars', newspapers for isolated young adults and the formation of groups to fulfil the social needs and advance the political interests of single and separated parents and sexual minorities such as homosexuals. Not only this area but virtually all aspects of the quality of life need creative social inventions. Where they are forthcoming they should be systematically evaluated for their contribution to the quality of life.

CONCLUSIONS

In terms of the aspects of the quality of life considered in this chapter it is evident that forms of high growth, more equal profile, possible within each worldview, represent the most desirable future circumstances. This is almost a truism: these images of the future after all are the outcomes of the success- ful application of the prescriptions of each worldview. But this does not stand as an endorsement of growth *per se*. Inegalitarian high growth futures all appear as potentially unpleasant for many of the inhabitants of the poor world. Some visionary reformists believe that with adequate political will, low growth, more equal futures could be desirable, although other reformists suspect that this 'political will' would in fact have to be imposed by an un- democratic and even ruthless state authority. Many radicals, whilst accepting the long-run desirability of a high growth, more equal future, see a low growth world as a more practicable goal to aim for in the next few decades.

Low growth futures may have desirable aspects and it is certainly hard to imagine a planetary economy in which material demands expanded at rates similar to those in the high growth profile for long spans of time. However, in the periods considered in this study, even low growth, more equal scenarios may pose severe problems for some countries. If, for example, it became imperative to introduce conservation measures for energy and materials, would the financial resources and political will for such measures be forth- coming in time? All three worldviews suggest that a low growth future would involve hardship and suffering. There is, of course, hardship and suffering in the world today, and to remove such problems to a significant extent would probably involve changes that would at first only 'redistribute' the burdens. But our analyses indicate that there are no evident physical reasons why the pressing material problems of the world could not be resolved in decades rather than in centuries.

The three worldviews point to very different processes of attaining this goal and very different future patterns of social organisation. Earlier we argued that differences in political perspectives underlay many of the polemics of the world futures debate. Our images of the future, based on a mixture of speculation and systematic analysis of political orientations to world trends, suggest that the range of conceivable and plausible future patterns of life is considerably wider, nevertheless, than would be gathered from a reading of the world futures literature. The explanation for this probably lies in the national politics of much of the futures debate. Writers like Kahn and Modrzhinskaya give prescriptions for the future that echo the goals of ruling groups in the super-powers; their descriptions are limited by the need to present desirable images of the future and benevolent images of their own countries.

With a range of possible futures as wide as we have considered, the introduction of worldviews proved to be a useful tool for highlighting basic differences in values, mechanisms of change and patterns of living, even if there is some overlap between them particularly when it comes to speculating about various aspects of a future quality of life. Several scenarios imply international tensions that might shatter whatever quality of life had been achieved. War is the greatest threat to current and future generations, and the next chapter deals with this spectre.

CHAPTER 10

War

Mary Kaldor and Julian Perry Robinson*

Introduction and Summary

War is a subject often avoided in futures studies. With undue charity perhaps, Dror (1974) has suggested that this reflects a kind of tacit trust in the adjustment capacity of the human species: since war in the nuclear age may endanger the survival of whole societies, war will not happen. This wishful thinking is of course not surprising, for some such assumption is necessary for orderly speculation about other matters. Yet the fact remains that the possibility of a new world war is finite; and if it were to happen, the discontinuity it would create in the history of the human race would be of such a magnitude that tidy projections of the future would not fail to perish in it. It is therefore a problem with which futures studies must come to terms more realistically than by just referring to it as the ultimate danger or assuming it away. This chapter is a preliminary attempt at doing so.

One may avoid a subject in ways other than ignoring it. The potential destructiveness of large-scale war is recognised in most futures studies, but their tendency is to treat it in terms of such generality as to lift the subject away from the level of analysis being applied to the topics that are of direct concern. In effect, war then becomes a kind of independent variable, ready to be inserted if it suits a flow of argument or left out of account if it does not. There are exceptions. Kahn and Wiener (1967) offer a range of future scenarios that pay singularly detailed attention to war, though their utility – like that of the war-avoiding policy prescriptions developed from them by Kahn, Brown and Martel (1976) – is limited by the idiosyncratic projections of present world order in which implicitly they are rooted. The futures studies of King-Hele (1970) and Heilbroner (1974) are also exceptional, war being

*We are indebted to several people inside and outside SPRU for help with this chapter, and we would especially like to thank Ian Miles and Robert Neild (Faculty of Economics and Politics, University of Cambridge) for their particularly detailed and useful comments on a preliminary draft.

fully organic to the conceptions offered. King-Hele supposes that man is both innately aggressive and innately optimistic, the latter characteristic hindering the social development that could protect against disasters impending because of the former characteristic. Heilbroner sees war as a 'fundamental moulding element in the human prospect', its continuing likelihood preserving the nation-state as the dominant mode of social organisation: a mode that itself preserves the threat of war, thereby closing a vicious circle that severely restricts conceivable futures. Whatever else one may feel about the validity of the King-Hele and Heilbroner speculations, their attention to structural determinants of war seems to us an approach that is well worth developing further.

Accordingly, we define the problem before us in the following way. Preparedness for war, nowadays called 'defence', has long been an accepted and integral part of the functioning of modern society. Defence activities – which include the maintenance of peace-time armed forces, military trade and aid, defence industries, and military R & D programmes – have become deeply embedded in economic, political and social structures. This is a phenomenon that has grown in step with technological change and, within whatever worldview that progress is defined, it may well act to interweave defence activities still more closely into the fabric of society. Moreover, appearances suggest that war-preparedness serves deep-rooted social functions, at least within the industrialised countries, that are only partly related to the contingency of conflict. The basic dilemma facing studies is therefore this. War will remain a potential discontinuant for so long as states continue to prepare for it by equipping themselves with mass-destruction weapons; but a future in which war-preparedness is not embedded may also be discontinuous with the present. Does this mean, therefore, that we are obliged to anticipate discontinuity, in one form or another?

We do not attempt a firm answer to this question. Our purpose is instead to explore what the three worldviews we are using as perspectives on the future have to say about it within our alternative high-growth/low-growth more-equal/less-equal profiles.

We start with technological considerations. It is in the destructiveness of warfare that the possibility of discontinuity resides; with each successive development in weaponry the potential (and actual) destructiveness has increased. Its present magnitude is symbolised by nuclear weapons, though it is at the same time partly obscured by them, for nuclear weapons have tended to conceal the increases that have taken place over the past two decades in the power and applicability of 'conventional' weapons. Advances in weapons technology may or may not influence the likelihood of conflict degenerating into war: this is a matter we take up later. But if there is war, such advances must be expected to increase the likelihood of discontinuity.

Next we turn to war-preparedness, of which there are many variants around the world, ranging from a virtual absence of standing peace-time

armed forces (as in Costa Rica) to countries where extreme forms of militar-
isation prevail. This we illustrate with a compilation of statistical data on
trends in three particular features of war-preparedness: resources devoted to
military R & D, military procurement and military manpower. We note some
of the broader economic and social impacts of this resource consumption.

From this description of the present, we move on to consider alternative
futures, concentrating first on what the three worldviews teach about conflict
as the precursor of war and about the processes of war-preparedness. We
note that they concur in suggesting that a low growth, inegalitarian world will
be militaristic and conflict-ridden; for the other profiles the predictions
diverge.

We then use this analysis to probe the basic dilemma formulated above. To
anticipate that war-preparedness will continue is at variance with none of the
three worldviews; but none of them excludes the possibility of this continuity
carrying with it the seeds of its own discontinuity, which may be large-scale
war or comprehensive disarmament. The fundamental matter, therefore, is to
define the limits to the validity of the widely held assumption that large-scale
war may be prevented by commensurate war-preparedness. Since there *are*
limits, and since we would all (presumably) prefer to contemplate the discontinuity of disarmament rather than war, we end by identifying necessary
preconditions for it implicit in the three worldviews. We conclude that each
of them sees disarmament as an ineluctable concomitant of a high growth,
more equal world.

TECHNOLOGY AND MASS-DESTRUCTION

War and the expectation of war have always pervaded human society; but we
are now compelled to contemplate discontinuity. Essentially this is because
the development of technology over the past four decades has raised the
potential physical and social destructiveness of war to a point where victory
may no longer be clearly distinguishable from defeat. This means that war
between belligerents each possessing the most advanced weapons may now
end not in the capitulation of one or the other, but in a final suicidal
invocation of 'mutual assured destruction'. The basic preoccupation of
military strategists has thus largely become a search for ways of preserving
war as a non-suicidal foreign-policy choice. Hence the prevalent concepts of,
for example, 'limited war' and 'flexible response'; hence also the attempts to
redirect weapons technology, chiefly by 'arms control' negotiation, so as to
give some plausibility to these concepts.

The destructiveness of warfare has, of course, been increasing over a much
longer timespan than the past four decades. It has been a graduated process,
each step being definable (more or less credibly) in terms of a particular

development in weaponry. Since quantifications of destructiveness are possible, this process can be illustrated with numbers and, though they rest on weak assumptions and sparse data, it is useful to show one such illustration here. Table 10.1, taken from a study prepared under contract for an agency of the U.S. Army (Sunderland *et al.*, 1964), compares the lethalities of the more significant of the new weapons that have emerged since the bow and arrow, 'lethality' being taken to mean 'the inherent capability of a given weapon to kill personnel or to make material ineffective in a given period of time, where capability includes the factors of weapon range, rate of fire, accuracy, radius of effects, and battlefield mobility'.

For some novel weapons – notably the eighteenth-century artillery innovations of de Vallière and Gribeauval, the machine guns and high-explosives of the late nineteenth century, and the poison gas, bomber aircraft and nuclear explosives of the twentieth century – a common contemporary view has been that the development in question would make war so deadly as to be impossible. This notion received especial prominence in the pacifist literature of the 1920s and 1930s, for it then seemed that the most destructive weapons innovations of the First World War had not yet been developed to anything like their full power, even though the carnage of that war had been immense. The fact that war has none the less recurred – and there have been about a hundred over the past thirty years alone (Wood, 1968; Naidu, 1969; Kende, 1972) – does not completely vitiate this wishfulness. The advance of weapons technology may not have eliminated war, but with each step towards greater destructiveness, greater restraint in exploiting it to the full seems to have been engendered. We may see this in those lines of strategic thinking, alluded to above, in which deterrence is grounded in military capabilities for controlled

TABLE 10.1   *A comparison of the lethalities of successive major weapons*

Weapon	Lethality index*
Sword	20
Javelin	18
Bow and arrow	20
Longbow	34
Crossbow	32
Arquebus, 16th century	10
Musket, 17th century	19
Flintlock, 18th century	47
Rifle, Minié bullet, mid-19th century	150
Rifle, breechloading, late 19th century	230
Rifle, magazine, World War I	780
Machine gun, World War I	13,000
Machine gun, World War II	18,000
Tank, WWI (armament: two machine guns)	68,000
Tank, WWII (one 3-inch gun, one machine gun)	2,200,000

TABLE 10.1 *(continued)*

Weapon	Lethality index*
Field gun, 16th C, *c*. 12-lb cannon-ball	43
Field gun, 17th C, *c*. 12-lb cannon-ball	230
Field gun, 18th C, Gribeauval, 12-lb shell	4,000
Field gun, late 19th C, 75 mm high-explosive shell	34,000
Field gun, WW1, 155 mm HE shell	470,000
Howitzer, WWII, 155 mm HE shell with proximity fuse	660,000
Fighter-bomber, WWI (one machine gun, two 50-lb HE bombs)	230,000
Fighter-bomber, WWII (eight machine guns, two 100-lb HE bombs)	3,000,000
Ballistic missile, WWII, HE warhead (V-2)	860,000
Fission explosive, 20 Kt airburst	49,000,000†
Fusion explosive, 1 Mt airburst	660,000,000†

Notes: * The product of values, calculated from known or estimated performance, assigned to each of the following factors:

— Effective sustained rate of fire: largest feasible number of strikes per hour, but ignoring logistical constraints (e.g. on ammunition supply).

— Number of potential targets per strike: a target is taken to be one man, and for comparability it is assumed that the men against whom the weapon is used are standing unprotected in the open in massed formation, each man occupying four square feet of ground.

— Relative effect: a $0-1$ weighting reflecting the probability of a man affected by the weapon being incapacitated by it; the weightings assigned by Dupuy seem to be based on 50 per cent probability of death.

— Effective range (R): factored in as $(1 + R^{1/2})$, R in thousands of yards.

— Accuracy: a $0-1$ weighting reflecting the probability of a strike hitting its target.

— Reliability: a $0-1$ weighting reflecting the probability that misfires, etc., will not happen.

For the tanks and the aircraft the index is calculated as the product of:

— Armament lethality: the sum of the lethality indices for the armaments carried.

— Mobility: taken as the square root of the maximum speed, in miles per hour. An attempt is also made, for the tanks and aircraft, to reflect ability to withstand attacking fire, but in fact the method used for this affects the index significantly.

† Calculated without conderation of delivery means and for blast effects only, i.e. ignoring thermal and nuclear radiation effects (though as to the latter, the weapons are of large enough yields for blast to surpass. immediate nuclear radiation as casualty agent). It is also to be noted that the basis for the area-of-effectiveness figures that Dupuy uses to derive the number of potential targets per strike for the nuclear explosives does not seem to be strictly comparable with that used for the other weapons. A method that gives a better basis for comparison yields values for radii of effectiveness of 1800 metres (for the 20 Kt explosive) and 5900 metres (for the 1 Mt explosive) rather than the 2400 and 8900 which Dupuy uses. The lethality indices are then:

Fission explosive, 20 Kt airburst	27,000,000
Fusion explosive, 1 Mt airburst	290,000,000

Source: Colonel T. N. Dupuy 'Quantification of factors related to weapon lethality', annex III-H in Sunderland *et al.* (1964).

escalation, a concept that lies at the root of current Nato security policy. We may also see it in the development since about the middle of the nineteenth century of the international law of warfare so as to prohibit the use of particular weapons or particular ways of using them. And we may see it again in the inter-governmental disarmament negotiations that since 1959 have produced a succession of modest international treaties constraining certain types of military activity: the 1963 Nuclear Weapons Partial Test-Ban Treaty, the 1968 Nuclear Weapons Non-Proliferation Treaty, and the 1972 Biological Weapons Convention, have been the least insignificant of them.

It has to be observed, however, that weapons technology is advancing at a considerably faster rate than the negotiations for restraining it by formal treaty. With the social, economic and ecological consequences of the Vietnam War (for example) now before us, we may well doubt the efficacy of informal restraint, whether embodied in strategies of controlled escalation or anything else. We note that commentators within the military profession have rarely been among those who have suggested that advances in weapons technology may prevent war. For the military the necessity of continually reconciling organisation and doctrine with changing 'firepower' capacity has long been a fact of professional life. By altering the manner in which forces are protected and deployed and by exploiting developments in tactical mobility, a way has generally been found for mitigating the deadliness of enemy weapons to the point where concerted counterforce remains possible. Indeed, the evolution of military doctrine may be seen as an equilibration process in which acceptable balances are struck between the dominant variables of firepower, mobility and dispersion. Without such a balance new and more powerful weapons might indeed render war either fruitless or impracticable or intolerable.

This line of reasoning suggests merely that the military will always take time to adjust to advances in weapons technology, not that those advances necessarily engender restraint. We may see from history that there has always been a substantial time lag between the emergence of a major new weapon technology and its assimilation into military policy and doctrine (Holley, 1953; Sunderland *et al.*, 1964; Ellis, 1975; Robinson, 1977). During this period the military disfavour and moral opprobrium traditionally attached to new weapons may dominate attitudes, thus giving the appearance of restraint. The question we have to ask, then, is whether weapons technology may not advance to the point where a particular development cannot be assimilated within acceptable notions of military force structure. And we may well conclude that in nuclear weapons just such a discontinuity has been reached.

In the case of nuclear weapons, unlike earlier developments, military analysts have joined lay commentators in recognising an innovation that can scarcely fail to influence the probability of future war. Some analysts have perceived an increased probability, laying stress on those circumstances in which nuclear weapons may favour pre-emptive attack, or even demand it. Others have seen a reduced probability, since new and more compelling modes of deterrence may be grounded in a nuclear 'balance of terror'. There is a similar ambivalence at the tactical level as well as the strategic. Is it conceivable, for example, that land armies can exist at all, let alone fight, if the other side uses nuclear weapons on the battlefield? May not nuclear weapons represent a magnitude of firepower that no amount of elasticity in mobility and dispersion can accommodate?

We may doubt whether definitive answers to these questions have yet been found or whether they ever will be, short of the experience of nuclear war. Yet in the East–West confrontation area in Europe, to say nothing of other parts of the world, some 10,000 nuclear warheads are being held in readiness for battlefield operations (Leitenberg, 1971; Record and Anderson, 1974). Their presence, like that of the similar number of larger nuclear warheads assigned to strategic forces, can adequately be explained only in terms of a complicated interaction of military and political factors spread out over the past two decades; an interaction in which rational considerations of utility have been subordinated to organisational and doctrinal rigidities, themselves born out of perceptions that inevitably lag behind events (see, for example, Iklé, 1973; Allison and Morris, 1975). The principal consequences are twofold: military commanders in Europe are required to believe that their forces are capable of fighting a war using the battlefield nuclear weapons with which they have been supplied; and, at the strategic level, national security is committed to an arcane theology of nuclear deterrence.

The fact that no war has yet occurred in which nuclear weapons have been available to both sides is commonly taken to justify this situation and hence to consolidate the commitment to nuclear weapons. There has been a steady growth in the size and sophistication of the nuclear arsenals of the five known nuclear weapons states (the U.S.A., the U.S.S.R., the U.K., France and China). At the same time there has been an increasing flow of analysis serving to refute the proposition that nuclear weapons cannot be used in pursuit of tactical objectives. Dupuy (1968), for example, has made a statistical analysis of battle casualties during the Napoleonic War, the American Civil War and the two World Wars, which, he reports, shows that despite major increases in weapon lethality the casualty rates among combatants per day of intensive combat remained much the same (15–25 per cent); this he explained primarily in terms of increased dispersions of combat forces, and went on to conclude that the dispersion needed to keep combatant casualty rates at the same level if nuclear weapons were used, though considerably greater than the dispersions typical during the Second World War, would none the less be tactically feasible. Subsequent analysts (e.g. Gray, 1976; Cohen and Van Cleave, 1976), dealing with a matter that Dupuy so conspicuously ignored – namely con-combatant casualties and other aspects of what the military call 'collateral damage' – have seen realistic war-fighting possibilities in the use of nuclear warheads with yields in the sub-kiloton range. Others (e.g. Canby, 1975) have recommended solutions combining both approaches. This doctrinal debate is both reflected in and stimulated by the present state of nuclear-weapons technology, for procurement decisions are now imminent (if indeed they have not been taken already) on the new 'enhanced radiation' munitions. These are the 'neutron bombs' of popular parlance since the early 1960s: fusion weapons with blast effects corresponding to an explosive yield that may be very low by present nuclear-weapons standards, but radiation effects corresponding to a much higher yield. They are thus nuclear anti-personnel weapons.

It may be argued, no doubt with some validity, that it is necessary to show that nuclear weapons could be used in a rational scheme of things in order to ensure that they are not so used, for the prevailing logic of deterrence requires a convincing display of capability and resolve. Yet, on another line of logic, such signs of increased readiness to embark upon nuclear warfare may actually serve to promote it, for instance by loosening command-and-control of deployed nuclear weapons or by encouraging expectations of benefit in the minds of decision-makers. We shall return to this later. For the present we merely note that the prevailing view in the nuclear-weapons states is evidently that the weapons are more an asset than a liability.

The risks associated with this belief are, to say the least, large. The full extent of the devastation that nuclear warfare might bring (see Stonier, 1963; Hemingway, 1972) is poorly predictable, despite the experience of Hiroshima and Nagasaki, though the broad outline is clear. The death toll from even a limited 'nuclear exchange' is expected to number millions or tens of millions (e.g. Schmidt, 1962; Drell and von Hippel, 1976), and there will be a still greater number of people whose lives will depend on medical attention that few will be likely to receive. Damage may extend down the generations through genetic injury and far across national borders through atmospheric transport of radionuclides. Full-scale nuclear war will mean the unleashing of 'assured destruction capabilities' which, in the case of the U.S.A., embody the assumption that adequate deterrence necessitates an ability to kill at least a quarter of the Soviet population and to destroy at least half of the Soviet industrial capacity – a capability that the U.S. strategic arsenal in fact provides several times over (Carter, 1974) and with which the Soviet strategic arsenal is now thought to be in a state of rough parity. Destruction on this scale and the forms that recovery from it might take are virtually unimaginable. The intensely interdependent components that enable a modern society to function will be disrupted and may take decades to reassemble, if indeed this can happen at all. Patterns of international inter-course, built up around food, for example, or technologies, may be extinguished. The ultimate calamity of total destruction of the biosphere now appears improbable on the latest estimates (U.S. National Academy of Sciences, 1975), but there is little doubt that the enormity of the devastation in the immediately affected regions will be compounded by long-term world-wide physical effects of comparable gravity. In particular, there is the likelihood of a significant reduction in the stratospheric concentration of ozone, the resultant increase in ultraviolet irradiation having a global impact on, for example, climate and crop production.

A sombre parallel is to be found in the extrapolations that have been made of past trends in the scale of killing during war. Thus, working from the statistics on war deaths since 1815 collected by Richardson (1960b) and Singer and Small (1972), Stefflre (1974) has put forward the hypothesis that for each interval in which the human population doubles, there occur wars in which ten times as many people are killed as were killed by wars in the previous interval. He predicts that some 200 million people will die in war during the next twenty years.

Nuclear weapons have imposed and will continue to impose a sense of caution upon the mutual international behaviour of their possessors; this and the move from confrontation to détente, such as it is, may act to subvert Stefflre's grim march of statistics. But one may observe, first, that the risks of accidental or irrational nuclear war, discussed later, may already be irreducible and, second, that in U.S.–Soviet relations there is an evident separation between political détente and military competition.

Moreover, the technology of mass-destruction is neither static nor limited to nuclear weapons. In the super-power nuclear arsenals the possibility that war will impose discontinuity is already with us, and further technical change seems more likely to bring it closer than cause it to recede. The crucial question is perhaps this: can technological developments be expected that will upset the state of mutual deterrence that has so far served to reduce the likelihood of discontinuity? Note that this formulation contains two big assumptions: that deterrence is both necessary and works; and that technology is a major if not a determining factor in deterrence. These we discuss later. Such developments can indeed be envisaged, in one or more of five categories. The first two chiefly relate to the present super-power strategic nuclear arsenals; the other three to the more distant possibility of threats to continuity that are additional to these arsenals.

The first category comprises offensive developments that may allow the destruction of opposing retaliatory forces before they can be used, thereby preventing retaliation at an unacceptable level of damage. Such 'disarming first strike' weapons would have to be long-range missiles with warheads of such explosive power, deliverable with such accuracy and in such numbers as to be capable of destroying enemy missiles at launching sites. However, it can confidently be stated that these launching sites – which may be submarines, aircraft or other vehicles – will not be targetable in their entirety within the foreseeable future. The principal cause for concern lies in the rate of development of anti-submarine-warfare technique, since submarine-launched ballistic missiles are for the present essentially invulnerable.

The second category comprises developments that may afford a substantial measure of protection against retaliation, for example by reducing the penetration ability of opposing missile forces. In this example the development might take the form of a technique for interfering with missile guidance or with terminal guidance and fusing of missile warheads. It might also take the form of an anti-missile missile system capable of intercepting and destroying incoming warheads. Construction of such systems commenced during the 1960s, but a recognition of their destabilising propensity (a concept we discuss later) led to the 1972 U.S.-U.S.S.R. Treaty on the Limitation of Anti Ballistic Missile Systems, which precludes deployment of ground-based A.B.M.s on a scale that might threaten deterrence. In addition the treaty prohibits entirely the development, testing and deployment of sea-based, air-based or mobile land-based A.B.M. systems, a provision that, if duly observed, would exclude such things as satellite-mounted high-energy lasers being used for ballistic missile defence. Research into the feasibility of new A.B.M. concepts, such as this one, is not forbidden, however, and is apparently conducted on a substantial scale.

The third and fourth categories comprise mass-destruction weapons against the use of which nuclear retaliation may, for one reason or another, be discounted. For example, in a world of proliferating nuclear weapons, circumstances must be anticipated in which nuclear threats may not be neatly cancelled off by credible expectations of nuclear response. This is one possibility; as a potential discontinuant its principal risk is that a war in which nuclear weapons are actually used, however primitive or limited in numbers, may inevitably draw the super-powers into direct military confrontation. This factor alone may for the present act to minimise the risk; but futures are conceivable in which the world is characterised not by the self-balancing tendency of only two super-powers but by the inherent instabilities of a three-body (or more) dynamic system. Political more than technological factors will determine the rate of proliferation, but certain technical developments can be expected to be influential: wider accessibility of plutonium from nuclear-power programmes (see Jasani, 1974, and Wohlstetter, 1976), for example, or the discovery of a way of using plutonium or a non-fission device (on which see Brunelli, 1971) to trigger fusion bombs.

Another possibility, comprising our fourth category, is some new technique of mass-destruction in which it is the mode of action that may reduce the likelihood of nuclear retaliation. Current strategic nuclear forces are designed with hair-trigger controls ensuring very short response times: nuclear retaliation may be unleashed within minutes of nuclear attack, this capability being considered essential for deterrent preservation. But for a mode of attack in which neither the fact of attack nor the identity of the attacker are immediately obvious, this same capability may weaken deterrence. Here we may think, for example, of a form of biological warfare in which a large-scale outbreak of disease takes weeks or months to build up

TABLE 10.2   *Lethality indices of some modern weapons*

Type of weapon	Specific weapon* for which index is calculated	Lethality index†
Non-nuclear weapons		
Assault rifle	5.56 mm M16	4,200
Light machine gun	7.62 mm M60	21,000
Medium howitzer, HE shell	155 mm M109 with M107 HE projectiles	89,000
Shoulder-fired TPA flame-rocket launcher	66 mm M202 with 4-rocket M74 clip	1,200,000
Medium howitzer, nerve-gas shell	155 mm M109 with M121 GB projectiles	1,400,000
Automatic grenade launcher, HE/frag grenades	40 mm XM174 with M406 grenades	1,500,000
Fighter-bomber with napalm firebombs	Phantom with 19 × BLU-1 750-lb firebombs	1,900,000
Main battle tank	M60 with a 105 mm gun, a light MG and a heavy MG	3,200,000
Medium howitzer, HE/frag submunition shell	155 mm M109 with M449 'improved conventional munitions'	3,500,000
Multiple rocket launcher, nerve-gas rockets	115 mm M91 with 45 × M55 GB rockets	6,800,000
Tactical guided missile, HE/frag bomblet warhead	Lance with M251 warhead	7,200,000
Fighter-bomber with HE general-purpose bombs	Phantom with 19 × M117 750-lb bombs	9,600,000
Multiple rocket launcher, HE/frag rockets	140 mm RAP-14 (French) with 21 rockets	12,000,000
Fighter-bomber (1950s) with FAE cluster bombs	Skyraider with 14 × CBU-55 cluster bombs	20,000,000
Heavy bomber with HE general-purpose bombs	B52 with 108 × Mk82 500-lb bombs	23,000,000
Fighter-bomber with nerve-gas bombs	Phantom with 19 × MC-1 750-lb GB bombs	28,000,000
Bomber with blockbuster light-case HE bombs	Hercules with 2 × BLU-82 15,000-lb bombs	52,000,000
Tactical guided missile, nerve-gas warhead	Lance with E27 GB warhead	91,000,000
Fighter-bomber with HE/frag cluster bombs	Phantom with 19 × CBU-58 cluster bombs	150,000,000
Heavy bomber with HE/frag grenade clusters	B52 with 2 × SUU-24 dispensers for ADU-256 clusters	207,000,000
Nuclear weapons		
Tactical guided missile, 'mininuke' warhead	Lance with developmental 0.05 Kt whd, airburst	60,000,000
Tactical guided missile, 1 Kt warhead	Lance with M234 whd, airburst at middle yield option	170,000,000
Medium howitzer, 'mininuke' shell	155 mm M109 with 0.1 Kt shell, airburst	680,000,000
Tactical guided missile, 20 Kt warhead	Pluton (French) with AN-52 warhead, airburst	830,000,000
Fighter-bomber with 350 Kt bomb	Phantom with one B-61 bomb at highest yield option	6,200,000,000
Strategic guided missile, 1 Mt warhead	Submarine-launched M-20 missile (French)	18,000,000,000
Strategic guided missile, 25 Mt warhead	SS-18 (Soviet) intercontinental ballistic missile	210,000,000,000

Conventions: (FAE) fuel-air explosive; (frag) fragmentation; (HE) high-explosive; (LC) light case; (MG) machine gun; (TPA) thickened pyrophoric agent, a napalm follow-on.

Notes: *U.S. weapons unless otherwise indicated. †Calculated according to the method of Colonel Dupuy as in Table 10.1 (the nuclear-weapons indices being comparable with those in note† of Table 10.1 rather than those in the table itself). For further details of the method, see J. P. Perry Robinson 'Studies in qualitative arms limitation, 2: Trends in conventional munitions', Science Policy Research Unit, June 1977.

and may not at first appear unnatural. Or we may think of some other simulant of natural disaster, such as might be brought about by a geophysical manipulation that has yet to be developed. These are far-fetched possibilities, it has to be said, in terms both of the motivation they impute to the aggressor and of current scientific knowledge. We may also suppose that, should their development ultimately appear feasible, such actions would be possible only with the resources at the command of super-powers. It is true that biological weapons are often described as cheap and easy to acquire, even as the 'poor man's deterrent'; but this is nonsense. When the U.S.A. decided, in 1969, to renounce biological warfare, it had spent the better part of a billion dollars on their development, and, with the exception of a few small-scale covert-use devices, had still not come anywhere near B.W. weapon systems in which service chiefs were prepared to place confidence.

The fifth and last category is perhaps the most ominous of all the contingencies we are considering here. It is also the least appreciated, probably because it hinges on evolutionary not revolutionary change in weapons technology. The intensity of the R & D successive modernisations of conventional weapon systems since the Second World War has brought about such an increase in the destructiveness of the weapons that the gap between conventional and nuclear warfare is closing rapidly. We illustrate this in Table 10.2, which presents lethality indices for a range of modern nuclear and non-nuclear weapons calculated on the same basis as those in Table 10.1. Moreover, with the current pressure (at least in the West) to deploy very low yield battlefield nuclear weapons, the gap is closing from both sides. What this means is that the 'nuclear threshold', which many strategists conceive as the last dependable respite before general nuclear war, may soon come to be deprived of all but its symbolic significance. As Williams (1975) has suggested, conventional war may become as 'unthinkable' as nuclear war.

WAR-PREPAREDNESS: PATTERNS OF CONSUMPTION

At the height of the rearmament period immediately before the First World War, some 3–3½ per cent of total world output was given over to military uses. By 1968 the share had risen above 7 per cent; the amount of resources devoted to military purposes in that year exceeded the total world output of 1900 (Blackaby and Jämtin, 1969). At the growth rate in military spending then prevailing, resources exceeding the total world output of 1968 would be consumed annually by the military soon after the year 2000. In fact there was a slight decline in real-term world military expenditure during the late 1960s, though in the early 1970s expenditures rose again to a plateau from which a new ascent is now beginning. The spending is now equivalent to (a) the combined GNPs of the sixty-five countries of Latin America and Africa, (b) total world-wide governmental expenditures on education, (c) almost twice total governmental expenditures on health, (d) about fifteen times the value of total governmental aid to under-developed countries (Huisken and Booth, 1976).

In Table 10.3 we show global and regional trends in military expenditure during 1965–74. The rich countries dominate world military expenditure: in 1975 the U.S.A. and the U.S.S.R. accounted for about 60 per cent, and their allies in Nato and the Warsaw Treaty Organisation for a further 20 per cent (Huisken and Booth, 1976). Growth rates over the last decade have, however, been most pronounced within the poor world, though recently within the rich countries the rates have once more begun to increase markedly, even allowing for inflation (International Institute for Strategic Studies, 1976).

War-preparedness, like other services and products, can be viewed in three

TABLE 10.3   *Total military expenditure*
(constant 1973 U.S. dollars × 10⁹)

	1965	1970	1974	Average annual growth rate, 1965–74 (per cent)
World	222.36	268.16	285.50	2.5
Rich countries	197.83	231.64	235.33	1.8
Poor countries	24.53	36.52	50.17	7.5
Near East	2.54	5.37	13.93	18.5
Africa	1.30	2.30	3.40	10.0
Latin America	2.54	3.41	4.34	5.5
East Asia	13.74	20.52	22.99	4.3
South Asia	2.59	2.55	2.88	1.1
Oceania	1.76	1.94	1.69	−0.4
OPEC	2.50	4.89	11.79	16.8
Nato	110.06	127.30˙	122.89	1.2
Warsaw Pact*	83.39	99.24	107.27	2.5

*These figures are based on C.I.A. statistics, which value Soviet military output (hardware and manpower) at U.S. costs, a method that is open to serious criticism: Soviet military manpower – badly paid conscripts – is much cheaper and probably less efficient than U.S. military manpower, while Soviet military hardware is generally much less sophisticated. Alternative figures are available, for example those of SIPRI, which are based on official statistics but make allowances for undisclosed R & D expenditure and under-valued exchange rates. Here is a comparison (at *current* prices, U.S. dollars × 10⁹):

U.S.S.R. (SIPRI)	44.90	63.00	61.90	3.6	(Benoit-Lubell
U.S.S.R. (C.I.A./A.C.D.A.)	52.40	76.20	103.00	7.8	exchange rates)

Source: U.S. Arms Control and Disarmament Agency *World Military Expenditures and Arms Transfers 1965–1974* Washington, D.C., U.S. Government Printing Office (1976); and Stockholm International Peace Research Institute *World Armaments and Disarmament, SIPRI Yearbook 1976* Stockholm, Almqvist & Wiksell (1976).

different ways. It is an output consisting of weapons and soldiers, a capability for waging war; it is a type of expenditure, expressed in (say) dollars or pounds; and it is a type of production requiring a particular composition of specific inputs, i.e. plant, machinery and labour. If one makes the somewhat questionable assumption that military capability is proportionate to the resources devoted to war-preparedness and that these resources can be quantified in money terms, then figures of the kind shown in Table 10.3 tell us something about the composition and tendencies of military power, about war-preparedness as an output. They also tell us something about war-preparedness as an expenditure, which is to say the long-term cost to society of war-preparedness. It can be assumed that a given quantity of resources, expressed in money terms, can in the long term be shifted from one use to another and that, therefore, a given military budget represents, in the long term, a forgone opportunity for alternative social benefits.

In the short term, however, resources are not so versatile. There are technical and social constraints against the substitution of one type of expenditure for another. And these may have important long-term consequences that outweigh the simple form of opportunity cost described above. On the one hand, war-preparedness may absorb specific types of resources in scarce supply elsewhere in the economy and may consequently represent an obstacle to economic growth or to equitable distribution of income. On the other hand, war-preparedness may serve to mobilise resources and generate certain kinds of economic and social development in a way that could not otherwise have occurred within the existing form of social organisation. To explore these consequences, we need to look at war-preparedness as a type of production.

Broadly we can distinguish several categories of input, similar to those required by any system of production: research and development establishments (i.e. scientists, engineers, test equipment, etc.); fixed capital (weapons and military bases); intermediate products (fuel, ammunition, etc.); and production labour (soldiers). The equivalent expenditure categories are roughly but not exactly: R & D expenditure, procurement and military construction (representing additions to fixed capital), operations and maintenance, and pay and allowances. We find that, compared with other types of products and services, the military or war-preparedness sector is more science-intensive and more capital-intensive. The science-intensity of the military sector is shown in Table 10.4. Capital-intensity is more difficult to establish but it is worth noting that gross annual additions to fixed capital, measured as annual expenditure on weapons and military construction, represent between 25 and 30 per cent of the British military budget, and about half of the U.S. military budget, compared with less than 20 per cent spent on gross fixed investment as a proportion of GNP (Great Britain, Ministry of Defence; Rumsfeld, 1977). Further, a study undertaken by the U.S. Bureau of Labor Statistics in 1975 indicates that $1 billion spent on defence creates

TABLE 10.4 *A comparison of military and civil science-intensiveness for 16 countries in 1967*

Country	Military R & D spending as a percentage of total military spending	Non-military R & D spending, including non-governmental, as a percentage of GNP
U.S.A.	12.54	2.18
Sweden	10.85	1.25
France	10.60	1.74
U.K.	9.04	1.60
West Germany	4.57	1.66
Canada	4.34	1.18
Japan	2.26	1.84
Switzerland	2.06	2.17
Norway	1.57	0.79
India	1.29	0.34
Netherlands	1.27	2.49
Italy	0.74	0.62
Belgium	0.34	0.89
Austria	0.21	0.63
Denmark	0.16	0.75
Finland	0.06	0.63

Sources: These figures are calculated from data on civil and military R & D expenditures contained in Forsberg (1972), and on military expenditures, military manpower, GNP and population contained in U.S. Arms Control and Disarmament Agency, *World Military Expenditures and Arms Trade 1963–1973* Washington, D.C., U.S. Government Printing Office (1974).

directly 51,000 jobs compared with 60,000 jobs if it were spent on public housing, 88,000 jobs for Veterans Administration Health Care and 136,000 jobs for manpower training (Lewis, 1976). Hence it is not unreasonable to conclude that war-preparedness is likely to have a strong impact on the future of science and technology and on industrial investment.

To explore these and other patterns in more detail we concentrate in turn on military R & D and on military procurement and industrial investment, and then consider the impact of war-preparedness on economies that are neither science-intensive nor capital-intensive, namely the developing countries.

Military Research and Development

There is a widely quoted estimate to the effect that military-related R & D now engages about 25 per cent of all scientific manpower in the world and accounts for about 40 per cent of all R & D spending (Sivard, 1976). These, and higher percentages still for earlier years, may well be true; but the uncertainties attaching to the collection of comparable national R & D statistics, especially military ones, make substantiation difficult. The available information is highly regionalised. Thus, much can be said about levels and trends in military R & D expenditure within the O.E.C.D. area; for the socialist countries the outside observer can rely on little more than guesswork.

So far as we are aware, only one attempt has yet been made to collect, compare and contrast on a world-wide basis runs of annual national military R & D spending figures. This is the study done by Randall Forsberg (1972), for the Stockholm International Peace Research Institute, now in need of updating and further refinement. Data from this study are excerpted in Table 10.5. It will be seen that rather sharp categorisations of countries can be made according to the proportion of total military expenditure devoted to R & D. Apart from certain obvious exceptions where data are lacking, it can be assumed that this proportion is either very small or non-existent for countries not shown in the table.

Rather detailed statistics have been published by the O.E.C.D. on the distribution of R & D resources between military and non-military activities in many of its member states. Table 10.6 shows some of these, giving percentage distributions of governmental R & D expenditure for the years 1963 and 1971. The fall in the proportion of military R & D over this period should not be taken to indicate a decline in military R & D spending; instead it reflects the growth of governmental R & D spending in general.

Government-sponsored R & D in the military sector has been a significant factor in the growth of science and technology for most of this century. It has had the indirect effect of promoting the application of science in the civil sector. It did not begin to impose a substantial charge on public funds until the military in rich industrialised countries adopted the idea in the aftermath of the Second World War that a failure to have on hand in peace-time the most technologically advanced weapons would invite aggression. Military R & D in these countries was thus accorded a continuing high priority, with commensurate increases in the quality and quantity of the scientific and technical workforce. An East–West confrontation developed, and with it the competitive development of improved weaponry, the anticipated dangers of lagging technologically became a self-fulfilling prophecy (Huisken and Booth, 1976). If it persists, this powerful military drive to pre-empt 'technological surprise' – in sharp contrast with the traditional military conservatism of earlier times – will continue to have two major, and probably increasing, impacts on future economies. The first will be the continuing opportunity costs to the civil sector of allocating R & D resources elsewhere, costs against which military-to-civil spin-off in the sense of stimulating economic growth can provide only scant compensation. There is, furthermore, evidence to suggest that the pervasive influence of the military in all kinds of R & D spending has unduly oriented civilian development towards complex and hierarchical types of technology. The resources devoted to development of the Concorde supersonic transport aircraft or to nuclear energy – instead of

TABLE 10.5   *Some national military R & D expenditures*

| Country | Average annual military R & D expenditure (U.S. $ × 10⁶) | | | | Average annual percentage of total military expenditure devoted to R & D | | |
| | Current prices, R & D exchange rate* 1967–70 | Constant (1963) prices, official exchange rate | | | | | |
		1955–59	1960–64	1965–69	1955–59	1960–64	1965–69
U.S.A.	8700	4792	7608	7475	9.8	14.8	11.5
U.S.S.R.	(4600–6000)						
U.K.	860	681	761	609	13.0	14.4	11.3
France	770	253	329	546	5.9	7.1	10.8
West Germany	350	19	123	206	0.9	2.9	4.5
China	(150)	..	..	..	..	..	..
Sweden	110	..	67	81	..	9.2	10.9
Canada	89	70	52	72	3.8	3.2	4.8
India	62	3.7	12	17	0.5	1.0	1.2
Japan	53	6.0	8.2	16	1.2	1.3	1.7
Australia	51	38	37	40	7.7	7.0	4.1
Israel	(50)	..	(5–10)	..	..	(2.5)	(5.0)
Italy	53	7.7	10	17	0.6	0.7	1.2
Yugoslavia	(20)	..	(12)	..	..	(3.0)	..
Netherlands	17	2.1	3.8	8.0	0.4	0.7	1.2
Switzerland	(9.8)	..	..	..	..	..	1.7
Norway	7.3	..	3.2	3.8	..	1.6	1.5
Belgium	3.9	..	2.1	1.8	..	0.5	0.4
Spain	(2.4)	..	..	..	..	..	..
Greece	(1.2)	..	..	..	..	..	..
Denmark	0.7	..	0.2	0.4	..	0.1	0.1
Austria	0.5	..	..	0.2	..	..	0.2
Turkey	(0.3)	..	..	..	..	..	..
Finland	(0.1)	..	..	0.1	..	..	0.1

Note: Parentheses denote figures of much lower reliability.
*The exchange rates used here were developed in an attempt to reflect international differences in the costs of R & D input. For details, see the original source.

Source: Forsberg (1972).

Prospects for Social Change

TABLE 10.6   *Distributions of governmental R & D expenditure*

		Defence	Civil space	Civil nuclear	Agric. forestry & fishing	Mining & manufact.	Economic services
U.S.A.	70/71	52.7	19.9	5.7	2.0	3.3	1.7
	63/64	55.4	27.9	5.9	1.4	0.9	0.7
France	1971	28.4	7.1	15.5	3.2	12.0	2.9
	1963	38 9	2.7	24.0	2.7	4.0	3.0
U.K.*	70/71	41.0	1.1	7.0	2.2	17.2	2.2
	63/64	59.4	2.5	11.1	1.3	7.3	0.7
Germany	1971	14.3	6.6	14.2	2.1	5.8	1.0
	1963	20.8	1.9	15.3	–	–	–
Japan	69/70	2.2	0.7	7.5	14.0	7.0	2.2
	63/64	2.2	–	5.1	14.9	9.6	3.7
Sweden	69/70	30.8	1.4	10.1	7.9	4.4	4.4
	63/64	45.4	0.7	23.6	4.9	2.6	1.8
Netherlands	1971	4.7	3.7	9.0	7:3	7.6	2.1
	1963	4.8	0.8	13.0	9.7	7.6	1.1
Italy	1971	4.4	5.8	22.8	1.3	14.4	0.9
	1963	6.8	2.7	43.0	0.8	0.5	0.7
Canada	70/71	9.3	1.4	18.0	17.7	27.7	5.0
	63/64	19.9	0.7	16.2	24.2	20.6	3.3
Belgium	1971	1.0	4.2	14.6	6.3	14.3	3.2
	1965	2.1	4.6	20.0	8.4	12.3	3.6
Norway	1971	8.2	1.3	6.0	13.2	12.7	6.6
	1963	7.1	0.5	13.2	20.1	8.7	2.0
Spain	1969	8.1	7.2	16.9	20.2	29.7	4.3
	1963	3.8	4.1	17.6	12.2	40.2	4.2

*Excluding social sciences.
Source: Organisation for Economic Co-operation and Development, *Patterns of Resources Devoted* (1975) p. 42.

to cheaper forms of public transport or to energy-saving devices – might be good examples. The second impact manifests itself in growing military budgets, for the prevailing state of military technology is such that small amounts of current R & D inevitably lead to bigger amounts of procurement: the well-known 'acorn effect' with consequences for civil investment and the economy as a whole.

Military Procurement and Industrial Investment

The term military procurement has widely differing connotations. Its meaning can vary according to the range of material items it includes, e.g. food, *by objective for 12 countries, 1963 and 1971 (percentages)*

Health	Pollution	Public welfare	Other comm. serv.	Advance-ment of R & D	Adv. of sci. via general univ. funds	Developing countries	Misc.	Total
8.0	0.7	2.2	1.0	2.4	–	0.2	–	100
5.2	0.2	0.4	0.5	1.4	–	–	–	100
1.8	–	0.6	0.7	14.7	11.1	1.8	0.3	100
0.7	–	0.3	0.6	12.2	9.0	1.7	0.2	100
1.1	–	0.2	0.5	15.9	10.2	0.5	1.0	100
0.1	–	–	0.2	8.1	7.4	0.5	1.4	100
2.3	1.1	3.9		45.6		3.2		100
–	–	–	–	3.6	34.0	–	–	100
1.8	–	1.7	0.7	0.2	61.2	–	0.9	100
2.5	–	0.8	0.6	0.2	59.5	–	0.8	100
7.5	1.1	2.8	1.2	5.5	22.9	–	–	100
4.0	–	0.8	0.7	1.8	13.7	–	–	100
4.3	2.2	5.3	1.8	6.6	43.8	0.7	0.9	100
3.6	2.2	3.9	1.4	5.9	45.4	0.1	0.4	100
2.3	–	0.1	0.6	18.4	28.6	–	0.3	100
1.2	–	0.8		14.3	27.7	–	1.4	100
10.0	1.6	–	0.7	8.2	–	0.2	0.2	100
6.3	–	–	0.6	8.0	–	0.1	–	100
15.5	1.2	5.0	3.6	30.8	–	0.3	–	100
13.7	0.7	2.6	2.9	28.8	–	0.3	–	100
4.4	–	3.6	1.3	8.0	34.6	–	–	100
4.3	–	1.9	1.2	7.4	33.6	–	–	100
–	–	0.2	–	12.5	0.9	–	–	100
–	–	0.3	–	17.2	0.4	–	–	100

to Research and Experimental Development in the O.E.C.D. Area, 1963–1971 Paris, O.E.C.D.

clothes, fuel etc., and according to the definition of procurement: whether it includes R & D and operations and maintenance, as well as production. As we are using it here, the term is taken to mean the production of weapons and equipment and spares. However, any conclusions reached must be treated cautiously since data on military procurement or production are less accessible even than data on military R & D, though case-study information about particular Western countries is now becoming available.

Just as military R & D represents resources for non-military innovation forgone, so too does military procurement represent capital investment forgone. The industries that produce new military equipment are, for the most part, the capital-goods industries; we find, for example, that in the U.K.

during 1971 arms accounted for some 20 per cent of mechanical engineering, 30 per cent of telecommunications and electronic equipment, half of ship-building, and three-quarters of aerospace output. In theory, of course, society can choose to allocate increased resources to the capital-goods sector so that investment is unaffected by the size of military spending. In practice, however, the diversion of capital-goods output to the military is not offset by an overall expansion of the sector. There are two reasons for this. First of all, military spending can create short-run bottlenecks for civilian investment that might set in motion a negative momentum that is hard to arrest. Failure to invest sufficiently, in a given period, might slow down productivity growth, reducing the competitiveness of civilian products and consequently blunting the incentive and financial ability to invest in the future. Equally, the production of arms may generate its own positive momentum (Kaldor, 1972; Kurth, 1973), which exceeds or is equal to the expansion of the capital-goods industry as a whole. A number of theories have recently suggested that the impact of military spending on the capital-goods industries in Britain and the United States during the 1950s and 1960s has contributed to the relative decline of these economies vis-à-vis West Germany and Japan (Rothschild, 1973; Melman, 1974). A second reason for the constraint on the total size of the capital-goods sector is, in rich countries, the relative stability of consumption as a share of output. This is the outcome of a given social organisation, and it is lower in socialist countries than capitalist ones. Table 10.7 (capitalist countries) and Table 10.8 (socialist countries) display striking inverse correlations between investment and military spending. For the U.K. this inverse correlation has been shown to hold over time (Smith, 1977).

In the United States military procurement accounts for somewhat more than a quarter of present military expenditure, a proportion that over time, has been growing faster than total spending (Rumsfeld, 1977). A similar situation prevails in other rich countries for which data are available. Just as investment represents additions to the stock of capital and hence increases in output, so military procurement means expansion of the stock of military equipment and hence further increases in overall military expenditure, since it necessitates more spending on operations and maintenance.

Since investment and military expenditure are so directly competitive, any increase in procurement, and hence military expenditure, can be treated as a decrease in civil investment and hence economic growth. Thus, in terms of conceivable futures, one can expect that a highly militarised world will, at least among the rich countries, be a low-growth world. There are, of course, the under-consumptionist theories, discussed later, which hold that military expenditure is a response to low investment rather than the other way around. Because military spending stimulates demand, it is argued that invest-ment and hence growth would have been even lower without it. This would suggest that a massive increase in military spending, as in the Second World

TABLE 10.7   *Investment and military expenditure in rich capitalist countries, 1974*

Country	Military expenditure* (U.S. $ x 10⁶)	Mil. exp. as percentage of G.N.P.*	Investment as percentage of G.D.P.†	Average annual growth rate in G.N.P. 1963–73 (per cent)‡
U.S.A.	85,900	6.15	18	3.9
U.K.	10,100	5.24	20	2.7
France	10,600	3.63	25	5.7
West Germany	13,800	3.58	22	4.7
Netherlands	2,320	3.45	22	5.4
Sweden	1,780	3.10	22	3.4
Norway	671	3.13	32	4.7
Italy	4,630	2.93	23	4.8
Belgium	1,460	2.77	22	4.8
Denmark	728	2.37	22	4.5
Canada	2,790	2.05	23	5.2
Switzerland	856	1.91	27	4.0
New Zealand	237	1.75	26	3.4
Finland	255	1.31	29	4.9
Austria	292	0.91	28	5.2
Luxembourg	18	0.87	26	3.4
Japan	3,670	0.83	34	10.5

Sources: *U.S. Arms Control and Disarmament Agency *World Military Expenditures and Arms Transfers 1965–1974* Washington D.C., U.S. Government Printing Office (1976).
†United Nations Department of Economic and Social Affairs, Statistical Office *Statistical Yearbook, 1975* New York, U.N. (1976).
‡U.S. Arms Control and Disarmament Agency *World Military Expenditures and Arms Transfers 1963–1973* Washington, D.C., U.S. Government Printing Office (1974).

TABLE 10.8   *Investment and military expenditure in centrally-planned economies, 1973*

Country	Military expenditure† (U.S. $* x 10⁶)	Mil. exp. as percentage of net material product†	Investment as percentage of net material product‡	Average annual growth rate in N.M.P., 1970–74‡ (per cent)
East Germany	2,457	(6.5)	19	5.5
Soviet Union	63,000	5.3	18	4.8
Czechoslovakia	1,876	4.7	19	4.6
Yugoslavia	700	4.6	28	5.4
Poland	2,538	3.8	28	9.8
Bulgaria	364	3.5	16 (1972)	7.1
Hungary	547	2.7	21	6.2

*Benoit-Lubell exchange rates.

Sources: †Stockholm International Peace Research Institute, *World Armaments and Disarmament, SIPRI Yearbook 1976* Stockholm, Almqvist & Wicksell (1976).
‡United Nations Department of Economic and Social Affairs, Statistical Office, *Statistical Yearbook, 1975* New York, U.N. (1976).

War, would stimulate growth. Even if this argument could be established, it would – like the argument about spin-off from military R & D – hold only on limiting assumptions about the social system. There is evidently something peculiar about a system, so conceived, that requires massive wastage in order to mobilise resources.

War-Preparedness in Poor Countries

The impact of military spending on poor countries is likely to be very different from its impact on rich countries. This is for two reasons. First, the indigenous science and capital-goods base is extremely small or non-existent. Therefore weapons and equipment are, for the most part, imported. Secondly, poor-country military spending is much more manpower intensive than rich-country military spending. Table 10.9 compares the military manpowers and military expenditures of rich and poor countries in 1965 and 1973. Rich-country expenditure per soldier is greater than poor-country expenditure per soldier by almost an order of magnitude, and the poor country growth rate in military manpower is substantially the larger.

From this one might infer that, in general, there is less competition between military spending and investment in the poor countries (although the absorption of scarce foreign exchange may act against this conclusion). Expenditure comparisons suggest the same thing. Countries with high levels of military expenditure tend also to have high levels of other forms of public expenditure and, in peace-time, high investment, indicating that consumption may vary. It has been shown that high levels of military spending are associated with high levels of foreign dependence, i.e. foreign aid and investment (Benoit, 1973; Schmitter, 1971) and, less convincingly, with high growth rates (Benoit, 1973). As we shall see below, it is widely argued that this association can be explained by the 'modernising' and 'Westernising' impact of armed forces. An alternative explanation might turn on the relationship

TABLE 10.9   *Military manpower comparisons*

	Number of people in armed forces			Military spending (constant 1973 U.S. $) per person in armed forces		
	1965	1973	Average annual growth rate, 1965–73 (per cent)	1965	1973	Average annual growth rate, 1965–73 (per cent)
Total world	20,763,000	25,740,000	2.8	10,709	11,092	0.4
Rich countries	9,536,000	10,140,000	0.8	20,746	23,208	1.4
Poor countries	11,227,000	15,600,000	4.2	2,185	3,216	4.4

Source: U.S. Arms Control and Disarmament Agency *World Military Expenditures and Arms Transfers 1965–1974* Washington, D.C., U.S. Government Printing Office (1976).

between the level of military spending and the degree of inequality. Domestic inequality tends to be associated with economic growth both as cause and consequence. On the one hand, inequality tends to be positively related to the level of savings since richer people save more. On the other hand, the benefits of economic growth are unevenly distributed. (For further exploration of this argument, see Kaldor, 1976.)

In Table 10.10, poor-country military and other public expenditure is related to a social indicator that, in default of anything better, may serve as a rough measure of the standard of living, namely infant mortality. This particular indicator is chosen because it does not seem to vary much with total population and because it seems, from country-to-country comparisons, to be related to social equality levels. Infant mortality can, of course, be expected to be sensitive to other factors, notably environmental ones; and it is likely to be understated in countries where birth/death registration systems are not fully effective. Be that as it may, Table 10.10 shows some association between military expenditure and infant mortality at given levels of income and given environmental conditions. Hence, to the prediction that a militarised world is likely to be a low-growth world, we may also have some justification for adding the prediction that, domestically at least, it is also likely to be an inegalitarian world.

CONFLICT AND WAR-PREPAREDNESS IN ALTERNATIVE FUTURES

We have shown that war-preparedness in the world is increasing and, with it, technology is developing in ways that will determine whether the wars for which this preparation is being made are likely to impose discontinuity. We have not yet looked at the fundamental matter of the causes of war – the factors that may transform intra- and inter-state rivalries into large-scale armed conflicts from which discontinuity could result. Nor shall we in any great detail, for this is a major field of enquiry – Bramson and Goethals (1968) and Singer (1976) provide a convenient entry – in which there is a large literature pitched at many different levels of analysis, lacking much consensus. We shall look instead at the differences and similarities in the perspectives on conflict provided by the three worldviews in order to see what they teach us about war-preparedness in conceivable futures. Since our primary concern is the possibility of discontinuity, our focus will be on armament.

Two aspects of armament must be differentiated. On the one hand arms are instruments of violence representing a response to conflict situations – external threat or domestic unrest – in which force might be used. On the other hand arms are an embodiment of resources: people, plant, machinery and money. Thus, decisions about the response to conflict situations are also

TABLE 10.10 *Comparisons of military and social expenditures, GNP per head and infant mortality, 1973*

	Per head expenditure (U.S. $)			Gross national product		Rate of infant mortality (per 1000)	As percentage of GNP:	
	Mil.	Educ.	Health	Per head (U.S. $)	Growth, 1963–73		Mil. exp.	Social exp.
World	64	66	37	1271	2.9	88	5.0	8.1
Rich countries	206	223	134	3968	3.9	20	5.2	9.0
Poor countries	13	10	3	306	3.2	101	4.2	4.2
Latin America	14	22	7	724		50	1.8	6.2
Argentina	26	28	12	1287	3.3	93	2.0	3.1
Bolivia	4	8	3	193	2.0	108	2.1	5.7
Brazil	15	20	2	622	4.7	94	2.4	3.5
Chile	22	28	22	872	1.9	71	2.5	4.8
Cuba	34	31	15	617	0	25	5.5	7.6
Mexico	6	23	5	892	3.1	61	0.6	3.1
Peru	23	24	7	613	1.3	110	3.8	5.1
Venezuela	27	63	38	1468	1.8	50	1.8	6.2
Middle East	94	25	8	657		112	14.3	5.0
Egypt	48	11	6	258	0.9	103	18.6	6.6
Iran	75	29	9	781	7.6	139	9.6	5.6
Iraq	79	27	6	598	5.6	99	13.2	5.5
Israel	1137	110	16	3023	5.0	21	37.6	4.2
Saudi Arabia	139	56	15	1037	6.5	152	13.4	6.8
Syria	56	14	2	359	2.9	93	15.6	4.5
South Asia	4	2	1	120		138	3.3	2.5
Bangladesh	1	1	–	79		132	1.3	1.3
India	4	2	1	128	0.9	139	3.1	2.3
Pakistan	6	2	–	96	(4.2)	132	4.4	2.1
Sri Lanka	2	7	4	198	2.1	45	1.0	5.6

East Asia (incl. Japan)	15	21	13	523		64	2.9	6.5
Burma	5	3	1	81	1.0	126	6.2	4.9
China	15	9	2	221	3.5	55	6.8	5.0
Indonesia	3	3	—	90	3.0	125	3.3	3.3
Khmer	14	4	1	92	−2.5	127	15.2	5.4
N. Korea	41	10	1	364	3.2	110	11.3	3.0
S. Korea	14	10	1	374	7.9	60	3.7	2.9
Laos	7	1	—	80	3.1	123	8.8	1.3
Philippines	4	7	1	262	2.1	78	1.5	3.1
Taiwan	49	23	17	601	7.6	18	8.2	6.7
Thailand	7	7	1	242	4.5	65	2.9	3.3
N. Vietnam	13	3	1	80	−5.7	150	16.3	5.0
S. Vietnam	25	6	1	156	0.2	150	16.0	4.5
Africa	7	11	3	284		156	2.5	4.9
Algeria	9	43	7	519	3.8	128	6.0	9.6
Chad	5	3	1	84	0.6	160	1.1	4.8
Ethiopia	2	2	1	89	1.8	181	1.6	3.4
Ghana	5	10	3	309	−0.1	156	3.7	4.2
Guinea	5	7	2	134	1.2	216	1.7	6.7
Kenya	3	10	1	181	3.8	135	1.6	6.1
Libya	46	186	60	2747	10.2	130	3.0	9.0
Morocco	10	19	5	328	1.1	149	5.1	7.3
Nigeria	9	3	1	177	3.7	180	5.7	2.3
Somalia	5	2	1	87	0.6	177	18.3	3.4
Sudan	25	6	1	136	−0.9	141	2.4	5.1
Tanzania	3	4	2	123	3.0	162	1.5	4.9
Tunisia	7	28	10	464	3.4	128	3.2	8.2
Uganda	5	5	2	158	2.0	160	3.8	4.4
Zaire	5	6	2	133	3.4	157	5.4	6.0
Zambia	15	28	11	418	0.1			9.3

Source: R. L. Sivard (1976).

decisions about the social allocation of resources. Both aspects involve wider social considerations, which means that attempts to conceive war-preparedness futures cannot be isolated from more general conceptions of the future. We proceed, therefore, by taking the two aspects in turn, identifying the manner in which they are perceived in the three worldviews – conservative, reformist and radical – and suiting these perceptions to our different profiles of economic growth and equality.

Arms as a Response to Conflict

To neoclassical economists, on whose work conservatives tend to draw, the very concepts of conflict and war are alien in a pure capitalist world order in which goods, money, people and speech are fully mobile and in which the harmony of the market place prevails. Powerful states, armies or revolutionary groups are viewed as remnants of the feudal order or as some new type of cancerous growth; in Schumpeter's words (1919) 'an atavism in the social structure', obstacles to the full development of capitalism. Such obstacles are treated as exogenous factors and are, strictly speaking, external to the neoclassical system of thought. Naturally, some conservatives have developed theories to explain such exogenous factors and some of these have been used in chapter 3. The most important conservative theory of conflict is the balance of power approach: the idea that every nation state has a natural subjective impulse for aggression and aggrandisement and that only an international system of checks and balances prevents inter-state conflict from taking place (cf. Buchan, 1966).

The reformist worldview admits of conflicts arising out of the economic and social system. Such conflicts might be international wars arising from national economic warfare – competition for scarce resources, competitive protection, competitive fishing limits, dumping, etc.; domestic instability arising from unemployment and stagnation; Weberian bureaucratic conflicts; or structural–social conflicts like those described by Galtung (1975), which stem from what he calls 'rank disequilibrium'. But, in one sense, these conflicts are also due to exogenous factors since they result from the irrationality of the participants. This is because conflicts are in principle amenable to mutually beneficent solutions; the failure of these solutions in practice has to be ascribed to inexplicable prejudices such as racialism or extreme ideologies or, alternatively, to lack of information or communication. Indeed, there is a strong school of thought in peace research that explains aggressive or irrational human behaviour in terms of the structure of a conflictual relationship: once the abstract elements of this structure are elucidated – the dynamics of crisis, escalation, repression and so on – it ought to be possible to locate the points at which and the methods by which a non-violent solution can be negotiated. In the reformist utopia such a theory could provide an important tool of management, a potential instrument for international institutions, operating in conjunction with effective national governments and a rational education system. Underlying the theory are the assumptions that there are no human interests more important than non-violence, that the dynamics of a conflict are somehow unrelated to the real interests of the participants and that violence stems from lack of understanding.

The reformist solutions to conflict are largely ruled out in the radical view, which perceives conflict as the fundamental relation in capitalism. Class-divided social systems are seen as based on force – the subordination of one class to another and the competition between ruling classes. Correspondingly, all conflicts fall into two broad types: the struggle between different classes, categorised as revolutionary struggle; and the rivalry within the ruling classes, categorised as inter-imperial rivalry, e.g. Germany and Britain before the world wars. The complexity of class structure is apparent in the numerous variants of conflict and the mediation of class conflict through racial or ethnic conflicts. Conflict and war can only be avoided through the abolition of the class system that most radicals expect to follow the overthrow of capitalism.

As to the East–West confrontation, there are varying radical interpretations. Some argue that it is a form of revolutionary class struggle, with the Soviet state representing the international working class. Some argue that it is a form of inter-imperial rivalry on the grounds that the Soviet system is a mutation of capitalism. Others, viewing the Soviet Union as a bureaucratised non-capitalist state, would claim that there has been no real conflict between East and West since the Second World War when the Soviet system became a closed system with minimal links to the capitalist world, therefore reducing causes of conflict: the U.S.A. and U.S.S.R. have an interest in maintaining the perception of conflict in order to hold together respective spheres of influence. Similar interpretations might be applied to the Sino-Soviet conflict, depending on whether the Chinese system is viewed as revolutionary, state–capitalist or bureaucratised non-capitalist.

Setting aside the 'solutions' that emerge from the three worldviews – pure capitalism, reform or revolution – it is possible to outline the potential conflict situations that arise from the twelve scenarios. In a low growth world, unless it is the 'ecological' reformist world of stability and equality, one can expect greater international instability among rich countries, or, in marxist terms, inter-imperial rivalry. This stems from economic nationalism, the cause or the consequence of low growth. In an inegalitarian world one can also expect increased conflict – revolution and war among poorer countries and, additionally in the radical worldview, increased repression. Thus, there seems to be general consensus that a low growth, inegalitarian world would be an unstable world characterised by war, revolution and repression, and that a high growth, more equal world would be relatively harmonious. The conservatives and perhaps also the reformists would be a bit vague about the nature and extent of conflict in alternative scenarios; radicals would see conflict, or more specifically revolution, as a necessary precondition for the more equal scenarios.

Arms and Resource Allocation

Among both conservative and radical thinkers there are two important groups who maintain that armaments are entirely conflict-determined. The one would argue that capitalism responds to external aggression by the most efficient method available, the professional army, representing a 'natural' consequence of the division of labour (e.g. Huntington, 1957). The other would argue that the response to conflict is the most efficient allocation of resources possible, given social constraints: the more 'advanced' the society, the more efficient the response (e.g. Liebknecht, 1907; Engels, 1894). Thus, among the first group would be those who consider that American defence policy is the most efficient response to the Soviet threat, an atavism. And among the second group would be those who view the Soviet state as the spearhead of socialist revolution and regard the Soviet arsenal as an efficient response to the hegemony of capital. Both would probably put forward an 'action–reaction' theory of the armament process, perceiving it as an 'arms race' (cf. Richardson, 1960a).

As to the effects of armament on the economy, both groups would accept that military spending is a waste of resources, a tax on the funds available for investment and future growth, but might argue that the absorption of resources would be insignificant compared with the reallocation of resources resulting from the *use* of armaments. This might simply mean physical destruction, as in war. But such pro-armament views might also be defended on the grounds of establishing conditions under which economies can operate effectively. Hence, conservative thinkers talk about the importance of armaments in establishing the necessary degree of 'stability' for the free functioning of capitalism (e.g. McNamara, 1968). Thus, with regard to poor countries, they often argue that the army, as a 'modern' institution, helps to overcome traditional barriers to development, e.g. deviant or backward cultures, etc., and that it induces 'nation-building' or other 'modern' attitudes and skills (e.g. Pye, 1962; Halpern, 1962). For radicals, this concept of 'stability' (in capitalist countries) means the hegemony of capital. The military may therefore be seen as key agents in the spread of capitalism. Under capitalist relations of production, accumulation is linked with exploitation, and repression (i.e. armament) is necessary to maintain or increase the degree of exploitation (Albrecht *et al.*, 1976). Hence the finding, mentioned above, which is consistent with both interpretations, that in some poor countries high growth is often associated with high levels of military spending.

Any historical or geographical survey of armaments, however brief, would suggest that conflict and war are the most important determinants. Nevertheless, a theory of armament that rests entirely on assumptions about the nature and level of conflicts must come to terms with a vexing difficulty. This is the simple fact that the only test of military efficiency is war. There is no competitive market for armaments, unless the politically dominated arms trade is treated as such. In peace-time wide areas of disagreement can persist, for there can be no *a priori* reason why any decision-maker (unless he be the perfectly informed rational manager of the less-credible 'policy science' literature) would adopt the particular set of strategic decisions that the subsequent eventuality of war shows to be efficient. This difficulty has given rise to a number of theories of the armament process that are based on allocative considerations.

Most of these theories centre round the idea that powerful vested interests, known as the military–industrial complex (MIC), determine the outcome of the debate about military efficiency (see Rosen, 1973). In the conservative view, shared by some reformists, the MIC is an exogenous factor, a cancer in society, stifling the prospects for harmony and the free operation of capitalism. Armaments can be expected to increase or breed conflict, irrespective of other trends in the world economy; the abolition of the MIC would probably be seen as the necessary condition for achieving a high growth world (e.g. Melman, 1970). For radicals and for structuralists the MIC is the dependent variable arising out of broader social developments. An important school of radicals would argue that military expenditure is an essential capitalist tool for overcoming the tendency of the rate of profit to fall. Those who interpret the falling rate of profit as the consequence of under-consumption – i.e. an imbalance between the wage-goods and capital-goods sectors resulting from the low level of wages – would argue that military spending can correct this imbalance because armaments are, par excellence, waste products, being neither objects of consumption nor investment (e.g. Baran and Sweezy, 1968; Kidron, 1968). Some of those who view the falling rate of profit as the consequence of declining technological progress argue that military spending boosts innovation and inventiveness through the concentration of scientific and technical personnel (e.g. Annerstaedt, 1972). These arguments are roughly the same as those of the structuralists, with the difference that the latter would argue that the functions of demand management or scientific mobilisation could be undertaken by other more peaceable forms of government spending, and that only such matters as lack of information, misguided greed, institutional inertia or irrationality stand in the way of such a solution. This structural interpretation of the MIC suggests than an increase in armaments can be expected to take place in a low growth world and that high, and in the long term increased, levels of military spending are a necessary condition for a high growth, inegalitarian world economy.

Most MIC theorists would argue that the MIC is a dynamic phenomenon. It involves perpetual development of more expensive, more sophisticated, more harmful military technologies and the acquisition of these technologies by leading military powers. It promotes wars and conflicts as the market and testing-ground for new weapons. It leads to the geographical spread of armaments through exports and foreign adventures, and it is primarily responsible for the unsavoury underworld of international relations: the mercenaries, private armies, bribery and corruption. The MIC is generally considered to characterise the Soviet Union as well as the West. For some, it is a central aspect of the Soviet state, itself an aggressive nationalistic and inexplicable exogenous phenomenon; for others, it is the structural consequence of Stalinist development policies, which arose from the historical conditions of the Russian revolution, with their emphasis on heavy industry and the safety of the infant Soviet state.

All these various theories of armament concur in the view that war-preparedness and conflict are inextricably associated. For MIC theorists, war-preparedness is the independent variable. It is associated with conflict because of underlying social and economic conditions that are the cause or consequences of the MIC. And it can produce conflict through self-interested manipulation and through generating suspicion and mistrust. In conflict-determined theories, the relationship self-evidently works in the opposite direction. In the one case, war-preparedness is the cause or consequence of a slow growth or inegalitarian world, which is linked, in turn, to conflict. In the other case, conflict is the cause or consequence of a slow growth or inegalitarian world and it leads to war-preparedness.

ALTERNATIVE DISCONTINUITIES: WAR OR DISARMAMENT?

We may now return to the basic dilemma of alternative discontinuities. We have shown in very general terms how the principal worldviews differ in explaining causes of conflict and what they suggest about relative likelihoods of conflict in our different profiles of conceivable futures. We have shown that although the expectation of future conflict is seen in each of the worldviews as a major stimulus to war-preparedness, the worldviews differ as to the extent to which such expectation determines levels of war-preparedness. Since we cannot anticipate a conflict-free future, we now need to look more closely at the relationship between war-preparedness and the probability of war, especially large-scale war from which discontinuity could result: how reasonable is it to envisage the coexistence of conflict and war-preparedness on a long-term basis? We must then think about futures in which levels of war-preparedness are such that it is no longer possible to conceive of war as a potential discontinuant; and we must try to describe the types of linkage that could exist between these disarmed futures and the armed present.

War-Preparedness and War

The notion that a high level of war-preparedness may prevent war by dis-couraging aggression has a history long enough to inspire credence. Yet if we are to continue to believe, with Vegetius, that he who desires peace must prepare for war, we have to discount the risk of that preparation provoking war. For both theorists and practitioners of international relations (at least in Europe), the classical concept for accommodating this problem is that of the 'balance of power', through the stability of which peace is preserved. Clauses in war-preparedness may be assessed for their 'stabilising' or 'destabilising' propensity. The power of a state, in this concept, resides in such factors as military potential, diplomatic weight, cultural affinities and economic strength, all of which contribute to overall capacity for influencing others. An effect of accelerating military–technological change has been the attachment of greater importance to the factor of military potential, so much so that balances of power are now commonly equated with 'military balances'. Since nuclear weapons, by their sheer destructiveness, may be perceived to con-tribute overwhelmingly to military strength, it is widely believed that their symmetrical possession by opposing states creates a balance that is peculiarly stable in situations of conflict. The belief has thus grown up that nuclear weapons have greatly increased the security of their possessors against coercion and, by the same token, have greatly diminished the likelihood of a future world war.

Yet this comfortable belief in nuclear deterrence rests on an uncertain foundation. The fact of the Eastern and Western blocs having survived nearly three decades of intense war-prepared confrontation may be taken as evidence justifying the belief. But other explanations are also tenable. We have alluded to one already, based on the proposition that there has in fact been no real conflict of interest between the United States and the Soviet Union, the Cold War rhetoric and the 'intelligence wars' instead serving a shared interest in maintaining perceptions of external threat in order to con-solidate spheres of influence. Since neither side has had anything to gain from war, nuclear weapons have not, on this line of reasoning, been a major influence in preventing it. Be that as it may, it is clear that the true test of nuclear deterrence must be success in preventing genuine conflict situations between nuclear powers from degenerating into war. We have already seen that such situations cannot be excluded from conceivable futures, especially in a low growth, inegalitarian profile; and when we look in more detail at the functioning of deterrence, we see a number of potential shortcomings.

The first has to do with credibility. Despite the concepts of limited re-sponse that now imbue official Western thinking about deterrence (see, for example, Davis, 1976), there has for many years been a strong line of reasoning that holds that once nuclear warfare has commenced, even on the most limited scale, it will inevitably be pressed to the limits of available capability. For the super-powers this means in theory, and probably in practice, the ultimate catastrophe of mutual destruction. The greater the credence attached to this reasoning, the less plausible will seem the possibility of nuclear retaliation against anything other than nuclear attack. Yet it does not follow from this that opposing nuclear forces in effect cancel one another out. In the event of conventional war between nuclear powers, the initial reluctance of either side to use its nuclear forces would undoubtedly diminish the closer it approached defeat. Equally, the closer it approached victory, the stronger would be its temptation to pre-empt with nuclear weapons the nuclear counter-attack that its opponent would be under increasing pressure to mount. The chance of either side capitulating with its nuclear arsenal intact would surely be small. Hence, as Howard (1973) has rightly observed, the nuclear element can neither be left out of account altogether nor postponed to the latter stage of hostilities. However incredible it may seem in the abstract, the possibility of a nuclear strike is present from the very beginning as an inescapable parameter affecting the calculations of both sides. These are calculations whose complexity must increase with the growing complexity of modern weapons systems. We thus have to recognise one major shortcoming in reliance on nuclear deterrence: the risk of miscalculation. This risk will increase with the narrowing of that gap to which we have already referred between the destructive potentials of conventional and nuclear forces. And we may also judge that any disjunction between war-preparedness levels and expectations of conflict will have a significant bearing on the possibility of unsuccessful deterrence, for a plethora of armaments is likely to create exaggerated perceptions of their value: the more weapons there are around, the more likely they are to be used.

Then we must recognise that successful deterrence and the prevention of nuclear war are not necessarily the same thing. Nuclear retaliation capabilities are structured according to preconceptions of what potential aggressors might otherwise do in the absence of a deterrent: they postulate for the aggressor a particular type of rationality that will lead him to decide on one course of action in preference to another. But there can be no assurance that the rationality will in fact prevail; in a case where it did not, the nature of the available retaliatory capability might prove quite unsuited to influencing what would appear as an 'irrational' decision. The extreme example was given by Churchill in the original 'balance of terror' speech in 1955: 'The deterrent does not cover the case of lunatics or dictators in the mood of Hitler when he found himself in his final dugout.' Iklé (1973), then at the RAND Corporation, has written as follows about the thinking that underlies U.S. deterrence doctrine:

On the long slope descending from rationality to irrationality, it postulates that only a short stretch needs to be considered. We must prepare – it is argued – for the possibility that Soviet leaders might move so far down this slope as to be tempted to decide on a surprise attack, provided the calculations that we impute to their military staff indicate that the attack would 'succeed'. That is, we prepare for the event that Soviet leaders might judge how a global nuclear war would turn out by relying on such largely untested calculations, trusting their military advisers to have used unbiased estimates and avoided gross mistakes. But we need not prepare for the possibility that Soviet leaders might be somewhat less 'rational' and let a cabal of officers mislead them by twisting the enormously complicated data to show that a surprise attack could 'succeed' even where our own analysis clearly indicated it would fail.

Nor is this the only lacuna in the nuclear-war-preventing capacity of nuclear deterrence, for, besides irrational war, there is also the possibility of accidental war. Situations can be envisaged in which a technical failure or a misinterpretation of events sets in motion established procedures for nuclear retaliation, which national authorities may then find themselves incapable of stopping. Above all there are the possibilities of false alarm of attack, such as might result from a defective or inadequate early-warning communication system, and of accidents with actual nuclear weapons. The open literature contains a disturbing record of such happenings (Dumas, 1976); if similar events were to recur against a background of heightened international tension, conditions in which military forces were held in just that state of nervous alert most likely to exacerbate the risks, who can say with confidence that all would end well? Both Russian and American strategic nuclear forces are designed to provide retaliation within a matter of minutes, for this is conceived as a necessary safeguard against the disarming first strike. With so little time available for deciding whether an alarm is true or false, the only real choice may be whether to verify or to attack, since doing one may preclude the other.

What, then, can be said about the likelihood of war-preparedness preventing war? We have to acknowledge grave uncertainty. We note that there are military concepts in wide currency that foster belief in the feasibility of designing defensive or deterrent forces that stand a good chance of dissuading calculated attack. But we also have to recognise that postures of war-preparedness that are built up to maximise this benefit may increase the likelihood of miscalculated or accidental nuclear war and be powerless to prevent irrational war.

War-Preparedness and Disarmament

If war-preparedness cannot be relied upon to prevent the wars of mass destruction for which some of its instrumentalities provide, we cannot doubt that its continuation jeopardises currently conceivable futures. They are, in effect, held hostage by the war-preparedness of the small number of states capable of waging such wars. We therefore have to ask whether scenarios are conceivable in which this hostage situation no longer exists and, if so, whether they are to be seen as continuous or discontinuous with the present. In short, we must think about the prospects for disarmament.

The hostage situation can be seen as one facet of the distribution of power among states. In pursuit of that military strength wherein power may reside, the leading states have developed mass-destruction technologies as a means for preserving a balance of power among themselves. The resultant mass-destruction capabilities have also come to serve another function, more shadowy and more pervasive, in the underpinning of present world order. It is evident from their foreign policies that the two super-powers perceive a common interest in avoiding direct confrontations that might lead to general nuclear war. They act upon it. Since this is an objective in which few states are not also compelled to acknowledge an interest, it enables the super-powers to exert an indirect form of nuclear coercion upon third parties. This becomes most obvious during the resolution of local conflicts that could involve the super-powers on opposite sides of a war. It is not, however, limited to this, for it is also one of the means whereby spheres of influence are built up within which the super-powers can intervene without fear of counter-intervention by the other. Though we cannot reasonably question the merits of a situation in which states adjust their foreign policies so as to reduce the risk of general nuclear war, we must nevertheless recognise that these same risks serve to promote a world political structure in which the super-powers can maintain their ascendancy. From the privileged position that is thus partly provided by their war preparations, the super-powers can cooperate, as Hedley Bull (1976) has put it,

> to frustrate the objectives of others: of allied states which seek to divest themselves of great power restraints, of client states which seek to engage great power support for their private goals, of fettered states which seek to break free of the spheres of influence to which they have been assigned, and of aspirant great powers which seek to stake out new spheres of influence of their own.

This is a part of the Realpolitik backcloth against which disarmament must be viewed. It suggests that measures of disarmament extensive enough to reduce the present likelihood of cataclysmic war would, for that very reason, profoundly affect the world political structure and therefore be resisted by states whose position in the hierarchy of power might then become threatened. Yet this is to conceive the matter much too narrowly. If we accept that we cannot judge the prospects for disarmament without having some conception of a future world order, we must also take into account those other factors besides war-preparedness that contribute to the ordering of power. In peace-time, when military strength remains unproven, the power it confers is a matter solely of perception. But perceptions change; and what constancy may be anticipated for perceptions of the power afforded by a strength so great that it could prove suicidal? May not military strength, as opposed to economic strength, say, or societal cohesion, come to seem greatly over-rated as a source of power? The disturbing effect that approaching super-power strategic parity has had on the Nato alliance may be cited in support of this view; so may the failure of the U.S. intervention in Indo-China; so may the growing acquisition of power by the South at the expense of the North symbolised in the rise of OPEC. What this broadened perspective admits is the possibility of a future in which mass-destruction weapons have become sufficiently insignificant in the shaping of world order for the states concerned to accept that their capacity for destroying the world is a liability unmixed with any overriding asset, and therefore best abandoned.

With this line of reasoning we are moving towards a definition of necessary preconditions for disarmament. To go a stage further we may differentiate between degrees of disarmament – quantitative or qualitative, regional or global, partial or complete, etc. – for the preconditions may vary. Since our concern is with war as a potential discontinuant, we need not look beyond mass-destruction weapons. By so narrowing our focus we can at once discern one aspect of a general problem that faces any measure of disarmament. Mass-destruction weapons, in the war-preparedness of the major powers, lie at one end of several inter-related continua. We have seen that weapons technology is closing the gap between nuclear and non-nuclear destructiveness. The more deeply nuclear and other mass-destruction weapons come to be assimilated into military force-structure and doctrine, the less feasible will it become for disarmament purposes to isolate mass-destruction components of war-preparedness from other components. This much we may learn (Robinson, 1975) from the past fifteen years of inter-governmental negotiations on partial measures of disarmament (for comprehensive reviews of which see United Nations, 1971 and 1976; Myrdal, 1976; Epstein, 1976). The obstacles exist primarily at the level of domestic politics. Here it is difficult to question the value of maintaining so conspicuous a component of war-preparedness without at the same time casting doubt on the value of other components: the attempt may then appear as a direct assault on the psychological, and hence political, underpinning of the war-preparedness of the state. War-preparedness activities may, as we have noted, be deeply embedded in the national economic, political and social structure, to a degree that is only partly determined by expectations of conflict; resistance to the curtailment of war-preparedness may be correspondingly deep-rooted and strong. Hence, in defining the necessary preconditions for disarmament, we have to have some conception of future domestic orders as well as future world order.

Above all we shall need a much clearer idea than research has so far provided of the range of functions that war-preparedness serves in international relations and in social structure at the national level. It is one thing to recognise that reductions in war-preparedness may be predicted on reorderings of power at both national and international levels. It is quite another thing to describe that reordering. Yet until we can do it, we shall not be able to make any serious judgements about the prospects for disarmament, still less prescribe possible routes to it. For all we know, a disarmed future might be as discontinuous with the present as a world that had suffered the ravages of that cataclysmic war that disarmament could preclude. In the absence of detailed guidance, we have only the general frames of reference provided by the major worldviews. But though we have identified something of what they teach about war-preparedness and conflict in our profiles of conceivable futures, their teaching on disarmament is less visible.

Analytical approaches to disarmament are most difficult to deduce from conservative thought. This is primarily because subjects become compartmentalised in conservative thinking, so that any one theory necessarily contains a central element that is exogenously determined and consequently inaccessible to explanation. As we have observed, nationalism and militarism embodied in the nation state are seen as the main causes of conflict and war-preparedness and as important obstacles to economic growth. Conservative thinkers have devoted much attention to the ways in which these phenomena may be controlled through various more or less sophisticated international systems of checks and balances. Yet the fundamental problem of the long-term instability of such systems, as discussed above, tends to have been neglected. While most conservatives would probably agree that the goals of disarmament and growth would ultimately necessitate the elimination of offending phenomena such as the more aggressive forms of the nation state, their framework of thought by its very nature tells us little about how this could be achieved.

The reformist worldview takes us rather further. Much of what we have already said about the prospects for disarmament is located within it, notably the use we have made of concepts of order. It suggests that political will is the determinant, progress towards disarmament requiring a fundamental shift in attitudes and beliefs about the relative importance of military strength and, say, international cooperation in assuring the security of individual states against the coercion of others. It would relate the chances of such a shift to dominant perceptions of the types of conflict situation intrinsic to whatever world order was likely to prevail in the near future. At the same time it would place value on the continuation of the present inter-governmental disarmament negotiations as a means for keeping the disarmament option firmly in the consciousness of policy-makers and public opinion. MIC theorists within this worldview would, in addition, place value on unilateral reductions in war-preparedness since this would weaken domestic obstacles to the necessary shift in attitudes. Expectations of conflict would remain the key. They would be highest in low growth or inegalitarian futures, which would therefore be the least conducive to disarmament.

The radical worldview potentially has more to offer still, primarily because holistic theories operate at a deep enough level to capture more of the social, political and economic factors that determine war-preparedness. The most relevant difference about disarmament between reformists and radicals concerns their view of the primary motive force in society. For reformists, this is an institution – the nation state, the corporation, an ethnic community or even a social class – which is analytically static, although in practice subject to various kinds of influence or persuasion; hence, pluralistic politics. For radicals, it is a dynamic relationship, generally the relationship between social classes, defined by their role in the production process, which involves a complex exchange of ideas, resources and physical force, incorporated in a changing process of perpetual suppression and rebellion. While radicals and reformists concur in the view that disarmament is linked to alterations in the structure of power, radicals would identify those alterations as being ones that effect underlying social relationships as opposed to particular institutions. Hence radicals would go further in postulating radical social change as a prerequisite, though one from which disarmament would flow automatically.

While the generality of the three worldviews gives us little purchase on the specifics of disarmament, we may nevertheless observe that all three converge in seeing disarmament as a necessary condition and consequence of a high growth, more equal world.

CONCLUSION

We close this chapter with a plea for the future. We have managed little more than a statement of the obvious. Conflict situations carrying risks of war exist in most conceivable futures. War will be bad for us all and could be unimaginably bad. Some types of war may possibly be prevented by war-preparedness, but others no less bad may be promoted by it. Current war-preparedness represents massive and growing opportunity costs for both rich and poor countries, especially taxing to the latter. Disarmament is a conceivable way out, possibly the only one, but existing knowledge is inadequate to show us how. The key, we believe, lies in a deeper understanding of war-preparedness: its roots, its components and, above all, its dynamics. A concerted attack on this ignorance is now needed, by means of policy-oriented research preferably drawing from each of the major worldviews. Elsewhere we have suggested a possible research methodology for so complex a study (Curnow *et al.*, 1976). We do not pretend that it is the best; but, one way or another, the task is certainly the most urgent now facing futures studies.

CHAPTER 11

Conclusions

Marie Jahoda

Three aims have guided the production of this book: we wanted to make a contribution to forecasting methodology, that rapidly proliferating art of anticipation; we wanted to take a substantive position in the world futures debate by examining whether a future we consider desirable has any chance of realisation within the next half century or so; and, as all forecasters, we wanted to offer some ideas for considering deliberate actions and choices in the less distant future that could affect the fate of the next two or three generations. It is appropriate now to review what we think we have achieved with regard to these aims.

FORECASTING METHODOLOGY

We began our exploration of what the future may hold for humanity with an exposition of what some other participants in this great debate have contributed to it. In the process of reviewing the literature we have learned much about the manner in which others have approached the same task, even if in the end it was to some extent negative learning, that is, the confirmation of our suspicion that no one has so far demonstrated *one* best method of forecasting. As a result, a major attribute of our methods is eclecticism, with all the assets and liabilities this usually involves. Outstanding among the advantages is the possibility of combining quantitative and qualitative approaches, a possibility we have amply used, guided by Aristotle's principle that the educated mind will insist on precision to the extent that a subject matter warrants it.

It would indeed be an intellectual help for forecasting if existing degrees of liberty, equality and justice could be numerically expressed. But it is not possible to do so. Even beyond the unmeasurable, however, a purely quantitative approach to forecasting has as many faults as a purely qualitative one.

380

The former tends to hide both the qualitative assumptions that underlie the selection of data, and the woeful inadequacy of quantitative information about the current world situation, let alone its projection into the future. The latter approach, of which Heilbroner is an example, eschews to a dangerous degree the necessary testing of the realism of quantitative propositions. We believe that quantitative data must be used even if qualified where their uncertain base requires it, and in the recognition that this often means restricting quantitative aspects in long-term forecasting to orders of magnitude rather than precise numerical predictions.

We have, inevitably, also demonstrated the weaknesses of eclecticism, perhaps particularly in the different methodological choices that the various authors have made from the repertoire of available techniques in the discussion of the three resource sectors of the world economy. The inherent characteristics of each sector we wished to highlight made it impossible to adopt a generalised method of forecasting. Food, energy and materials differ in their present pattern of final demand, in the degree of substitutability, in the institutional arrangements that surround them, in the degree to which their future use is sensitive to changes in income distribution and in the nature of their underlying technologies. Even if it is debatable whether this concern with inherent problems in each sector is necessarily a disadvantage of our approach, we cannot accord ourselves the benefit of such doubt in another methodological aspect of our work. Under the umbrella of eclecticism it proved impossible to integrate what we have to say about quality of life with production and consumption patterns as they are mediated by international trade in these basic resources. This decidedly is a shortcoming; we are beginning to see some possibilities of improving our approach in this respect.

But there is more to this approach than the issues of eclecticism. The combination of two rates of growth with two levels of equality, yielding four profiles, proved to be a useful framework for analysis, and provided a link between all the different issues considered in this book. The establishment of these four profiles constitutes a distinctive approach to forecasting beyond its analyticial utility; it permits us to be explicit about basic values in thinking about the future. Such explicitness is often missing from the work of other forecasters, including all the neo-Malthusians and also Kahn, to the extent that he has permitted a simple-minded optimistic public image to be associated with his name that does little justice to the many caveats in his published work.

All forecasting is done with a purpose in mind and based on fundamental assumptions; these remain, however, as a rule implicit, even though they determine to a large extent the nature of the forecast. As a result the debate is often sidetracked away from these significant tacit assumptions to questions of data adequacy and methods of analysis, issues whose importance in their own right is best discussed after achieving clarity about the way in which the tacit assumptions influence results.

The current debate is 'great' because it deals with great issues rather than because it has achieved such clarity. This is why we have tried to identify the positions of major forecasters by trying to show with what goals, interests and aims their ideas are compatible, and how their inferred outlook influences, sometimes subtly, their choice of assumptions, notwithstanding many interesting by-products. Since neither values nor assumptions can be excluded from the study of human affairs, and certainly not from analyses of possible futures, they should be made explicit in the futures debate. Merely asserting that one's own assumptions are superior will not change this fact of life but only confuse the debate. We consider that some of the global forecasters have created confusion in this way.

There is one major goal on which all contributors to this volume agree: we regard it as desirable to strive for a world in which the current extreme inequalities between rich and poor countries are significantly reduced not by a world-wide return to primitive living, but by increasing the standard of living in the poor world much more rapidly than in the rich world. In other words, our preferred profile incorporates growth and reduced inequality. But just because we know that such preferences can affect assumptions and methods and because we wanted a fuller understanding of difficulties and alternatives, we have simultaneously examined three other profiles, contrasting in level of growth or inequality. Our conclusions about the possibility of world development in our preferred direction will be summarised below.

In clarifying our approach to forecasting another basic assumption needs to be made explicit: we believe that the future is not irrevocably determined by past and present trends, but that choices exist which when implemented in policy and action can modify trends, sometimes slightly and at other times profoundly. Only a fool would ignore the existence of such trends, but only a defeatist would submit to their apparently inexorable dictatorship. Even if contemporary action can modify a trend only slightly, if other steps in the same direction are taken subsequently, such modifications may have far-reaching consequences in half a century or so.

There is one further feature of our approach that we regard as a contribution to the manner in which thinking about the future could be improved: the identification of 'worldviews' – conservative, reformist and radical – and the utilisation of economic and social theories that are often but by no means invariably associated with these views. Reading through the contributions to the great debate about the future it is a useful ordering principle to try and assign contributors to a worldview; their taciturnity on this matter as well as on their use of one of the other related economic theories may be a result of their being as eclectic as we are, but leaving their stand implicit prevents a summary of where the debate now stands, unless some such ordering principle is introduced.

However, we do not want to overstate the advantages of 'classification'. We are as aware as anyone of the inherent limitations involved. We used the worldviews and economic theories not only to make inferences about the stance of other forecasters, but also for the construction of our own scenarios. The four basic profiles of world futures leave room for wide-ranging alternatives, depending on values and worldviews. Social and economic theories offer many important insights into mechanisms for development and change, even if none of them provides complete answers.

But in developing our own ideas we have realised that we would find it hard to 'classify' ourselves. The analytical tools of neoclassical economics may not be very useful for some of the problems we have examined but they are useful, for example, in exploring pricing and taxation policies for the type of world energy future that we have prescribed. Similarly, dependency theories offer, we believe, valuable insights into the international politics and economics of the oil industry. But mainstream Marxist theory cannot tell us why the U.S.S.R., together with France and the U.K., has committed enormous resources for the development of the sodium-cooled fast breeder reactor, and – until recently – planned to reach levels of energy consumption per head approaching those of the U.S.A. We suspect that both neoclassical analysis and the libertarian variants of marxism can offer more useful insights into these phenomena.

Given what we have said in the energy chapter, we could be labelled as 'conservatives', 'Malthusians', 'extreme environmentalists', 'anti-nuclear', 'radicals', technological determinists', or 'advocates of the convergence of social systems'. Nevertheless, ideology certainly informs analysis, and we hope that we have demonstrated this as well as trying to make our ideological preferences clear when they have influenced our analysis and interpretation.

In the light of our own analysis we conclude that few futurologists consider a sufficiently wide range of possible futures. On some issues Kahn does take into account a range of variables and alternatives and, in spite of differences in tone and style, we find ourselves in agreement with him on some points: for example, the feasibility of largely non-nuclear futures for the next hundred years and the considerable potentialities for energy conservation.

We have not developed a more elaborate analytical framework because we think that neither our theoretical understanding nor the available empirical evidence allow this to be done meaningfully. Our 'profile' approach is crude rather than sophisticated, simple rather than elaborate, and it leads to a very wide range of future possibilities depending on assumptions about the pattern of economic development.

It has been pointed out to us that a forecast, say, of energy consumption in the industrialised countries in the year 2000 of between 8 and 16×10^9 tce in a high growth, unequal world is not much guidance to the policy-maker. Perhaps the policy-makers like precision from experts, and perhaps experts are tempted to provide it, even when it is not justified. We think that better policies are likely to emerge if the wider uncertainties about the future are recognised, be they about the size of oil and gas resources, the eventual development of thermonuclear fusion, or the future consumption of copper. We also think that the existence of some of the long-term uncertainties in fact means that conscious action today can influence what will happen tomorrow, be it on prices, conservation, technology, investment or international trade.

For all these reasons, long-term forecasting should be a continuous activity, incorporating changing circumstances and reduced – or increasing – uncertainties. Open and informed public debate about forecasts and scenarios, and their implications for policy and R & D are a necessary condition for their improvement. There is always the danger in public debate of over-simplification and exaggeration, by experts as well as by politicians. However, in public debate they are more likely to be found out than in a system of closed and monolithic decision-taking. With apologies to Churchill, we would say that public debate about forecasts – like democracy – may be a pretty bad system, but all the others are worse.

We have ourselves tried to avoid identification with either a particular worldview or a particular theory. This is in part the result of the fact that the several authors of this volume take different stands on these issues and some of them would not wish to be committed or classified in any category; in part it is due to our realisation that the distinction between dogma and theory becomes uncomfortably hazy in these matters. In the conviction, however, that available theories are a precious tool for sharpening thought, we have attempted to learn from all of them, even though none is sufficiently elaborated and coherent to explain all the social and economic complexities of the current world situation, let alone of conceivable futures. It would advance the entire debate considerably if forecasters who fully espouse one or the other worldview and economic theory were to elaborate not only the assets of their stance, but also the problems that would have to be faced were their views to prevail, which are so often left implicit. For there surely is no paradise ahead, either in a conservative or reformist or radical development of the world. There is only one aspect of the future which can be predicted with certainty: that it will present problems and conflicts on substantive issues.

Is a Desirable Future Possible?

Our contribution differs from other global forecasts not in the subject with which it deals; every single issue we raise has been raised elsewhere before. While we have cast our net perhaps more widely than some others, we have caught no new fish. Indeed many issues have been omitted here that require, or have already received, examination, and every single one with which we have dealt has been explored in greater depth by others. The width of the net is inevitably partly determined by limits in our capacities. But not entirely.

We did aim at including what we consider the most crucial subjects in the futures debate.

We now turn to the all-important question of whether what we consider a desirable future is within the realm of the possible in the light of our analysis. For almost two centuries one debate about the future has been conducted within a Malthusian framework: will the carrying capacity of this planet suffice to support its growing population at decent standards of living? The question cannot be pushed aside and we have dealt with it sector by sector. But there is a danger in letting this one question about physical limits monopolise the entire debate; not only because Malthusian pessimism may tend to create fatalistic despair, but because the concentration on this one major issue blinds some participants in the debate, so that they ignore the social, political and military problems that may arise in the less distant future and that contain comparable dangers.

Our own analysis of the agricultural sector shows clearly that world-wide physical limits in the provision of food are not the main problem now, and need not be in the future, even with a greater increase in population than is now generally assumed will occur within the next half-century. Given favourable international distribution arrangements, world food production could suffice to provide an adequate diet for everybody. If people are starving or malnourished in some parts of the world, it is because they cannot pay for the food they need. The problem is one of income distribution, rather than of physical shortage. In future, food production could keep pace with population growth, if unused land were brought into production, soil fertility preserved, wastage reduced, land reforms instituted and feasible technologies appropriately developed and applied.

At present many poor countries are dependent on food imported from the rich world. But in contrast to some other forecasters, our analysis suggests that most of these regions could eventually become self-sufficient in food production. Not that the transition to such a state of affairs will be easy. Fundamental social, political, economic and technological changes will be required. But the fact remains that a high growth, more equal world is physically and technically possible as far as food production is concerned, and that the required knowledge of how to prevent starvation and malnutrition is already available, even in the unlikely event that no radically new technological developments occur.

Food production will, however, require increased energy inputs. It is true that at this moment there is a huge unused reservoir of energy in the many millions of unemployed or underemployed people of the poor world. But this will not suffice. The supply of nutrients to the soil through the use of fertilizers can increase the productivity of land, particularly where marginal acreage is being brought into production. Energy inputs may also be essential for improvements in the quality of irrigation. Even if mechanisation is only gradually introduced, taking care that it does not create new masses of unemployed who lack the income to buy the fruits of mechanisation, it would require additional inputs of both energy and materials.

It is indeed in the energy sector where the problems are most severe for the future: once again not because of identifiable physical limits, even if certain traditional fuel sources may be exhausted in the not too distant future. The central questions about energy in the future involves the dilemmas inherent in the use of nuclear energy, which could temporarily solve the world's energy problem, but which could also lead to major dangers, and may leave to the technological ingenuity of future generations the problem of dealing with radioactive waste for tens of thousands of years. Whether the problem of waste disposal, or the proliferation of nuclear weapons, or the possibility of major accidents or of sabotage constitutes the greatest danger of nuclear energy is a moot question. What is clear is that the knowledge of nuclear fission as a source of energy is irreversible knowledge. Only a major catastrophe could eliminate it – and everything else too. Thus an energy-hungry world must learn to live with this knowledge and establish controls and alternative sources of energy that will reduce the danger, even if it cannot be fully eliminated.

Accordingly we have taken a cautious position vis-à-vis this all-important sector. The needs are enormous. The possibility of meeting them without an immediate and massive extension in the use of nuclear power does, however, exist. An all-out effort is required in research and development of traditional sources of energy such as coal, of less conventional sources such as geothermal, solar or wind energy, and a radical improvement in policies designed to adopt energy-saving methods. Research on nuclear fusion does and must continue, even though many experts do not expect a solution of its problems within the time horizons we are considering in this book.

Our calculations demonstrate that a pattern of energy consumption consistent with the high living standard of Western Europe could be shared the world over, without relying heavily on nuclear sources, if these policies are instituted. Even here, in the most difficult sector, the desirable future is not beyond our reach.

In some ways the conclusions drawn from the analysis of the materials sector parallel those of the agricultural sector. There are virtually infinite quantities of most materials in the earth's crust, sufficient to support very high levels of consumption for an indefinite period of time. The question thus becomes not a matter of physical constraints but rather of the technologies to exploit these resources, and the economic, political and environmental constraints on their use.

The future of individual materials varies greatly, depending on the pattern of end-uses, possibilities for substitution and the current distribution of production and consumption. Systematic efforts to improve the efficiency of use of raw materials could save on consumption; the rates of discovery and extraction of primary materials required by our preferred profile seem feasible in the light of historical and geological evidence. For individual materials there could be severe limits and for others there could be temporary barriers to expanded production arising from failures in technology or institutional arrangements. But the possibilities of substitution and alternative use-patterns are very great. In contrast to the agricultural sector, where redistribution·alone could prevent malnutrition, let alone starvation, a very considerable increase in materials production is called for if the poorer countries of the world are to develop the industries necessary for economic growth and improved living standards. Raw materials production again demands energy inputs: and if we were to make use of the vast quantities of resources contained in low-grade ores and move toward more sophisticated materials we would require a great deal of energy.

Thus we return to energy, the one resource where efforts to transcend physical constraints might involve ecological damage of an intolerable degree. But it need not, if appropriate policies are implemented to remain within these limits. According to our analysis the dominant world-wide problems are not those of Malthusian physical limits. The difficulties ahead stem from other sources. Different regions of the world are differently equipped with essential resources. The U.S.A. and U.S.S.R. are well-endowed with coal, oil and gas resources; the U.S.A. leads in food production; South East Asia and to some extent Latin America are badly placed for both. The regional distribution of resources is likely to cause more problems than overall world-wide shortages.

Notwithstanding these difficulties, we conclude from the analysis of three important sectors of the world economy that our *a priori* preference for a world that grows so that existing international inequalities can be significantly reduced is not utopian. Our analysis confirms this, while it also shows that some of the other profiles present fewer problems for, say, energy or other non-renewable materials, taken in isolation. But an inegalitarian or a zero growth profile would have to be paid for by international conflicts and human misery on an increasing scale. As long as there is some rational basis for thinking that the world's population could have enough to eat, an adequate material base, a satisfactory quality of life and less fear of war, it would be irresponsible to strive for less.

THE CHOICES AHEAD

As has been made abundantly clear, there is one choice that we have ourselves made from the outset and that we urge others to accept: we have opted for the reduction of inequalities as a world-wide goal. Even though this choice originally rested on a moral decision, the analysis of critical issues in the world economy and of the danger of war has lent a rational justification to it, which may persuade those who share our commitment to a reduction of inequalities but have considered it impracticable. But the idea of equality has recently come under attack not as an impossible but as an undesirable aim. Some of these attacks rest on a vulgarised version of equality, implying a drab uniform levelling of all individual, social and cultural differences in the world or in a country. Once such a straw man is erected, it is indeed easy to knock him down. The reduction of inequalities we have in mind has nothing to do with such over-simplification. The diet of people in the South will probably always be different from that in the North, as will the requirements for heat and for materials. Social and cultural differences will continue to exist. One hopes at least that the pattern of industrialisation in the rich world with all the disastrous mistakes it contained will not be slavishly imitated by countries now entering on industrialisation. A reduction of inequalities between the rich and the poor world would enhance rather than prevent diversity in patterns of development.

Even though we have not in this book dealt in detail with the existing inequalities in the rich world, where attacks on equality are usually most vociferous, the idea applies to them too. It is not a demand for equalising everybody's income, independent of skill and effort. What is required is the introduction of compensatory measures so that the good things in life – work satisfaction, income, leisure, respect, education and so on – are not given all together to some and withheld from others, but are equitably distributed. Such policies for compensatory equalities will obviously meet with opposition. But the concern with inter- and intra-national equalities cannot be wiped from the agenda of the futures debate.

Choices about the reduction of inequalities, as much as choices about other matters raised in the book, are now largely but not exclusively in the hands of national governments. We live in a world in which governments are so organised that they must give highest priority to national interests while simultaneously recognising their growing dependence on the fate of others; where governments must deal with relatively short-term problems as best they can, even when such policies conflict with long-term objectives. But a loosening process began long ago, of which the League of Nations was an early example, followed by the U.N. with its many specialist international organisations, and by organisations of world regions across national boundaries. The European Community and OPEC are cases in point, however dissimilar their function and organisation.

The point of referring to existing international institutions of varying scope is not to extol their functioning, which in every single case leaves much to be desired, but to show that it is not impossible to achieve compromise with national interests in some areas, that conflict management rather than provocation of violent conflict between nations is being practised. Current efforts fit a reformist outlook. Conservatives might well believe that less interference might be in the better interest of the world; radicals that only revolutionary changes could produce the required effect. But whatever worldview one adopts, some conflicting interests cannot be eliminated. Even if there were a world-wide revolution it would be necessary to arrange that fertile lands helped to feed those in less fertile areas, that minerals available in one part of the globe could be used in another, that the world stock of coal be available to all regions that need it.

Whatever worldview one adopts, whichever scenario one prefers, problems will have to be faced in the here and now, and the manner in which they are dealt with will to some extent shape the future. An enormous amount of work remains to be done in transforming our analyses into policy recommendations. Only in two areas have we been able to make some suggestions in this direction: in policies for technology and technology transfer, and in matters of war and peace.

The world futures debate abounds with mutual accusations of 'technological optimism' and 'technological pessimism'. If technological optimism implies the belief that there is a technological fix for every ill that besets the world, we do not belong in that category; if technological pessimism implies the belief that technology cannot make a major contribution to tackling these ills, we equally dissent. Such over-simplifications do not advance the debate. On a more realistic level, the debate has in part been about whether it is possible to maintain technological advance on the level of the last century or so, or whether we are approaching diminishing returns from research and development.

The answer to this question will vary somewhat from one technology to another. But pending much detailed analysis that remains to be done we have approached the issue first in terms of the impact that could be achieved if no further technological development occurred, unlikely though this may be. We have concluded that a spread of currently available best technological practice could transform productivity in manufacturing. But continuing technical change will be required to meet the needs of the future, as we have seen, for example, in relation to energy. Investment now in basic research and in the training of scientists and technologists is therefore a global insurance policy against the possibility of sudden barriers to production processes and of resource shortages. The mechanical transfer of advanced technologies to the developing world could be counterproductive to the extent that such technologies are often dependent on technical personnel from the rich world, inappropriate for the conditions and needs of a poor country, and cause adverse social consequences. Deliberate action now could prevent such damage. The design of appropriate technologies that use the best available knowledge and adapt it to the specific conditions of specific countries, particularly to their need for employment opportunities, is an essential though undoubtedly long-drawn-out process for the improvement of the standard of living.

We have tried to deal with the possibility of war in a dispassionate manner. But such effort need not be maintained here. It is impossible to survey this field without being thunderstruck by its inherent lunacy: the over-kill potential of nuclear weapons in the two dominant powers, their proliferation, the power of modern conventional weapons, obsolete while still in production, the amount of financial and natural resources devoted to military purposes, the investment of the highest technological inventiveness – so badly needed elsewhere – in objects that everyone professes are created only in order not to be used – all this would defy imagination, were we not so used to it in everyday life. So entrenched is the arms race in the economy of the great powers that a discontinuity here in favour of disarmament would create problems of its own in the allocation of resources and manpower. Confronted with the choice between discontinuity due to war or discontinuity due to disarmament, few, even in the armaments industry, would opt for war. It is in this overwhelmingly important area where current decisions can have a major impact on the fate of the world.

So far, the possible choices we have identified as following from the preceding analysis require implementation by national and international policy-makers. But this is not enough. The future we are envisaging is the future of our children and grandchildren. It is the people of the world, not their governments, who will suffer or benefit, as the case may be, by the consequences of the choices made now.

During this century there has developed in many parts of the world, in 'democratic' and in 'totalitarian' regimes, a sense of frustration about the powerlessness of individuals in shaping their own fate and that of their children; the gulf between us and them, the powerful, appeared to be growing. However well one understands such feelings, just to bewail the state of affairs will not do. In any case, it must be recognised that such a widespread sense of frustration is in itself a sign of development in a promising direction.

Many wish to participate, first of all in the day-to-day regulations that govern their lives. But matters never stand still; wider horizons open with every step taken. As we all have learned more about the intolerable misery in some poor countries, about the dangers ahead for all of us unless choices are made with a view to the future, the possibility opens for much more widespread participation in shaping events to come. Such participation requires informed imagination. This is why we have tried to develop as best we could some images of the future in the scenarios. Their function is to indicate directions in which the world may go and to illustrate that there is more to the quality of life than growth and reduced inequalities, important though they are. The narrow decisions of each individual have not magically assured that everything is for the best of all. The type of forecasting we have attempted in this book is designed to help extend our collective knowledge and vision.

Bibliographies

CHAPTERS 1-3

I. ADELMAN and C. T. MORRIS *Economic Growth and Social Equity in Developing Countries* Stanford, Ca., Stanford University Press (1973)

E. ARAB-OGLY *In the Forecasters' Maze* Moscow, Progress Publishers (1975)

G. BARRACLOUGH The Battle for the New Economic Order *Sunday Times* London (16 May 1976) p. 63 Originally published in *New York Review of Books*

W. BECKERMAN Economists, Scientists and Environmental Catastrophe *Oxford Economic Papers* London (1972) p. 327

D. BELL *The Coming of Post Industrial Society* London, Heinemann (1974)

Blueprint for Survival, *The Ecologist* Wadebridge, (January 1972)

L. BROWN *World Population Trends: Signs of Hope, Signs of Stress* (Worldwatch Paper 8) Washington, D.C. Worldwatch Institute (1976)

R. H. CASSON Population and Development: A Survey *World Development* Oxford (October / November 1976) p. 785

G. CHICHILNISKY Economic Development and Efficiency Criterion in the Satisfaction of Basic Needs *Applied Mathematical Modelling* Guildford (1977) To be published

C. CLARK *Starvation or Plenty?* London, Secker and Warburg (1970)

A. C. CLARKE *Profiles of the Future* London, Pan (1964)

R. CODONI *The International Division of Labour in View of the Second Development Decade* Zurich, Center for Economic Research, Swiss Federal Institute of Technology (1974) (Research monographs new series Vol. 10)

H. S. D. COLE et al. *Thinking About the Future* London, Chatto and Windus (1973) Also published in U.S.A. *Models of Doom* New York, Universe Books (1973)

H. S. D. COLE and R. C. CURNOW An Evaluation of the World Models in H. S. D. COLE et al. (1973)

H. S. D. COLE *Global Models and the New International Economic Order* Brighton, Science Policy Research Unit, for UNITAR project on the future (1976) mimeo

R. DUMONT *Utopia or Else . . .* London, Deutsch (1974) New York, Universe Books (1975)

A. and P. R. EHRLICH *Population, Resources, Environment — Issues in Human Ecology* San Francisco, Freeman (1970)

P. R. EHRLICH and R. HARRIMAN *How to be a Survivor* London, Pan / Ballantine (1971)

P. R. EHRLICH *The Population Bomb* London, Pan (1971)

S. ENCEL et al *The Art of Anticipation: Values and Methods in Forecasting* London, Martin Robertson (1975) New York, Pica Press (1976)

J. W. FORRESTER *Urban Dynamics* Cambridge, Mass., M.I.T. (1969)

J. W. FORRESTER *World Dynamics* Cambridge, Mass., Wright-Allen (1971)

J. W. FORRESTER Population vs. Standard of Living — The Trade-off that Nations Must Decide *Futurist* Vol. X, No. 5, October 1976.

T. FREJKA *The Future of Population Growth: Alternative Paths to Equilibrium* New York, John Wiley (1973)

R. BUCKMINSTER FULLER *Utopia or Oblivion: the Prospect for Humanity* Harmondsworth, Penguin Books (1972)

C. FURTADO Development and Underdevelopment. Berkeley, Ca., University of California Press (1964)

J. GALTUNG On the Future of the International System R. JUNGK and J. GALTUNG (eds.) *Mankind 2000* London, Allen and Unwin (1969) p. 12

J. GALTUNG *The Politics of Self-Reliance* Oslo, University of Oslo (1976) Paper no. 44
J. GALTUNG *Self-Reliance: Concepts, Theory and Rationale* Oslo, University of Oslo (1977) Paper no. 35
R. GILLETTE The Limits to Growth: Hard Sell for a Computer View of Doomsday *Science* Washington, D.C. (March 1972) p. 1088
R. GOLUB and J. F. TOWNSEND *Malthus, Multinationals and the Club of Rome* Brighton, Science Policy Research Unit (1975) mimeo
R. L. HEILBRONER *An Inquiry into the Human Prospect* New York Review of Books (24 January 1974) p. 21 and New York, Norton (1974)
R. L. HEILBRONER *The Great Ascent* New York, Harper (1963)
R. L. HEILBRONER Growth and Survival *Foreign Affairs* New York (1972) p. 139
R. L. HEILBRONER *An Inquiry into the Human Prospect* New York Review of Books (24 January 1974) p. 21 and New York, Norton (1974)
R. L. HEILBRONER *Business Civilisation in Decline* London, Boyars (1976)
A. HERRERA *et al. Catastrophe or New Society?* Ottawa, I.D.R.C. (1976)
M. HOPKINS *et al. Basic Needs, Growth and Redistribution* Geneva, I.L.O. (1975)
J. HUXLEY Annual Report to the General Conference of UNESCO in *Planet in Peril* by R. F. DASMANN A UNESCO book, New York, World Publishing Co. (1972)
I.L.O. *Meeting Basic Needs* International Labour Office, Geneva, (1977)
H. KAHN *On Thermonuclear War* Princeton N.J., Princeton U.P. (1960)
H. KAHN A Way Beyond Our Resources / Pollution Problem *PHP* Tokyo (April 1973)
H. KAHN Things are Going Rather Well *Futurist* Washington, D.C. (December 1975) p. 290.
H. KAHN and A. J. WIENER *The Year 2000* London, Macmillan (1967)
H. KAHN and B. BRUCE-BRIGGS *Things to Come* New York, Macmillan (1972)
H. KAHN, W. BROWN and L. MARTEL *The Next 200 Years* New York, Morrow (1976)
Y. KAYA and Y. SUZUKI Global Constraints and a New Vision for Development *Technological Forecasting and Social Change* (1974) Vol. 6, Nos. 3 and 4, p. 277 and p. 371
Y. KAYA *et al. On the Future Japan and the World — A Model Approach* Tokyo, Japan Techno-Economics Society (1973)
A. KING The Club of Rome Today *Simulation in the Service of Society* August 1974
V. KOSOLAPOV *Mankind and the Year 2000* Moscow, Progress Publishers (1976)
S. KUZNETS 'The Gap: Concept Measurement Trends' in G. RANIS (ed.) (1972) p. 3
E. LASZLO (ed.) *The World System, Models, Norms, Applications* New York, Brazillier (1973)
W. LEONTIEF *et al. The Future of the World Economy* Preliminary Report, New York, United Nations (1976)
I. M. D. LITTLE, T. SCITOWSKY and M. SCOTT *Industry and Trade in Some Developing Countries* London, Oxford University Press (1970)
M. MARIEN 'Herman Kahn's "Things to Come"' *Futurist*, Washington D.C. (February 1973) p. 7
P. MAXWELL The Shape of Things to Come? Interview with J. Forrester and D. Meadows *Internationalist* Wallingford (May / June 1972) p. 6
D. MEADOWS *et al. The Limits to Growth* New York, Universe Books (1972) and London, Pan Books (1974)
M. MESAROVIC and E. PESTEL *Mankind at the Turning Point* New York, Dutton / Readers Digest Press (1974a)
M. MESAROVIC and E. PESTEL *Multilevel Computer Model of World Development System* 6 vols. Laxenburg, Austria, International Institute for Applied Systems Analysis (I.I.A.S.A.) 1974b
Y. MODRZHINSKAYA and C. STEPHANYAN *The Future of Society* Moscow, Progress Publishers (1973)
D. MORAWETZ Employment Implications of Industrialisation in Developing Countries: a survey *The Economic Journal* London (September 1974) p. 491
M. NICOLESCU *et al. The Revolution in Science and Technology and Contemporary Social Development* Bucharest, Academy of the Socialist Republic of Rumania (1974)
W. D. NORDHAUS World Dynamics: Measurement Without Data *Economic Journal* London (December 1973) p. 1156
A. PECCEI *The Chasm Ahead* London, Macmillan (1969)
A. PECCEI The Club of Rome — The New Threshold *Simulation* La Jolla, Ca. (1973) p. 199.

E. POHLMAN (ed.) *Population — A Clash of Prophets* New York, Mentor (1973)

G. RANIS *The Gap Between Rich and Poor Nations* London, Macmillan (1972)

E. ROTHSCHILD How Doomed Are We? *New York Review of Books* (26 June 1975) p. 31

J. G. RUGGIE and B. GOSOVIC The Catalyst *Ceres* Rome (January/February 1976) p. 28

E. F. SCHUMACHER *Small is Beautiful — A Study of Economics as if People Mattered* London, Blond and Briggs (1973) New York, Harper & Row (1973)

E. F. SCHUMACHER Economics should Begin with People not Goods *Futurist* Washington, D.C. (December 1974) p. 274

J. SPENGLER The Economist and the Population Question *American Economic Review* Providence, R.I. (March 1966) p. 1

J. SPENGLER *Population Change, Modernization and Welfare* Englewood Cliffs, N.J., Prentice Hall (1974)

J. TINBERGEN Report on the 6th Session (Committee for Development Planning) New York, United Nations (1970) United Nations Document E/4776

J. TINBERGEN *Reshaping the International Order — A Report to the Club of Rome* New York, Dutton (1976)

B. WARD et al. *The Widening Gap: Development in the 1970s* New York, Columbia University Press (1971)

S. WEISSMAN in R. MEEK *Marx and Engels on the Population Bomb* 2nd ed. Berkeley, Ca., Ramparts Press (1971)

World Bank *Report on 'The Limits to Growth'* Washington D.C., World Bank (1972) mimeo

CHAPTER 4

P. ABELSON *Food: Politics, Economics, Nutrition and Research* Washington, D.C., American Association for the Advancement of Science (1975)

I. ADELMAN, C. T. MORRIS and S. ROBINSON Policies for Equitable Growth *World Development* Oxford (July 1976) p. 561

C. ARROYO *Institutional Constraints to Policies for Achieving Increased Food Production in Selected Countries* Paper presented at International Peace Research Association's Food Seminar (January 1977)

J. E. AUSTIN *Agribusiness in Latin America* New York, Praeger (1974)

S. AZIZ (ed.) *Hunger, Politics and Markets* N.Y.U. Press (1975)

J. BARDACH *Harvest of the Sea* London, Allen and Unwin (1969)

C. BLYTHE Problems of Diet and Affluence *Food Policy* Vol. 1, no. 1, Guildford (February 1976) p. 91

W. S. BROECKER Climatic Change: Are we on the Brink of a Pronounced Global Warning? *Science* Vol. 189 (1975) p. 460

L BROWN *By Bread Alone* New York, Praeger (1974)

R. A. BRYSON A Perspective on Climatic Change *Science* Washington D.C., (17 May 1974) p. 753

P. BURINGH, H. D. J. VAN HEEMST and G. J. STARING *Computation of the Absolute Maximum Food Production of the World* Wageningen, Netherlands, Agricultural University (1975)

C. D. CARRUTHERS *Water Control, Irrigation and Hydrological Research* Paper presented at the Institute of Development Studies Conference on 'Food Problems in South Asia, 1975-1990', Brighton, Sussex (16 November 1974)

C. CLARK *Population Growth and Land Use* New York, St. Martins Press (1967)

H. S. D. COLE et al. (eds.) *Thinking About the Future* London, Chatto and Windus (1973). Also published in U.S.A. Models of Doom New York, Universe Books (1973)

D. L. DAWSON *Communist China's Agriculture: its Development and Future Potential* New York, Praeger (1970)

R. DUMONT *Utopia or Else....* London, Deutsch (1974) New York, Universe Books (1975)

J. DUNMAN *Agriculture: Capitalist and Socialist* London, Lawrence and Wishart (1975)

N. EBERSTADT Myths of the Food Crisis *New York Review of Books* New York (19 February 1976) p. 32

P. R. and A. H. EHRLICH *Population, Resources, Environment* San Francisco, Freeman (1970)

S. ENCEL *et al.* (eds.) *The Art of Anticipation* London, Martin Robertson (1975)

F.A.O. *Food and Agricultural Commodity Projections, 1970-80; and . . . . 1975-85* Rome, F.A.O. (1971 and 1975)

F.A.O. *Assessment of the World Food Situation* World Food Conference, Rome (1974)

F.A.O. *Food and Nutrition* Rome (1975) Vol. 1, nos. 1 and 2

F.A.O. *The State of Food and Agriculture* Rome, F.A.O. (annually)

F.A.O. / W.H.O. Informal Gathering of Experts on Energy and Protein Requirements (summarised) *Food and Nutrition* Rome (1975) Vol. 1, no. 2, p. 11

E. FEDER How Agribusiness Operates in Underdeveloped Agricultures *Development and Change* London (October 1976) p. 413

D. W. FINFROCK and A. R. THODAY 'Multicropping in Northern Thailand' Chieng Mai, Thailand, University of Chieng Mai, Faculty of Agriculture (1973) working papers

G.B. Select Committee on Overseas Development, Session 1975-76 *The World Food Crisis and Third World Development: Implications for U.K. Policy* London, H.M.S.O. (1976) Evidence from Science Policy Research Unit, p. 351

G.B. Select Committee on Overseas Development, *Minutes of Evidence on 17 July 1976,* H.M.S.O.

S. GEORGE *How the Other Half Dies* Harmondsworth, Penguin (1976) Montclair, N.J., Allanheld, Osmun (1977)

J. GRIBBIN Aerosol and Climate: Hotter or Cooler? *Nature* London (17 January 1975) p. 162

J. GRIBBIN (ed.) *Climatic Change* London, Cambridge University Press (1978) to be published

K. GRIFFIN *The Political Economy of Agrarian Change* London, Macmillan (1974)

K. GRIFFIN Multinational Corporations and Basic Needs Development *Development and Change* London (January 1977) p. 61

F. HAQUE (1974) see C. D. CARRUTHERS

R. HEILBRONER *An Inquiry into the Human Prospect* New York, Norton (1974)

M. HOPKINS, H. SCOLNIK and J. M. McLEAN *Basic Needs, Growth and Redistribution: a Quantitative Approach* Geneva, I.L.O. (1975) World Employment Programme, Population and Employment Working Paper no. 29

A. VAN ITTERSUM A Calculation of Potential Rice Yields *Netherlands Journal of Agricultural Science* Wageningen (1971) Vol. 19, p. 10

International Development Centre *Facts About Development — 3* London (1975)

E. H. JACOBY Transnational Corporations in Third World Agriculture *Development and Change* London (July 1975) p. 90

D. G. JOHNSON *World Food Problems and Prospects* Washington D.C., American Enterprise Institute for Public Policy Research (1975) Foreign Affairs Study, 20

L. JOY *Food and Nutrition Planning* Brighton, Institute of Development Studies (1973) I.D.S. reprint 107

H. KAHN, W. BROWN and L. MARTEL *The Next 200 Years* New York, Morrow (1976)

H. KAHN and A. J. WIENER *The Year 2000* New York, Macmillan (1967)

R. KAPLINSKY, K. HOFFMANN and A. BARNETT *Technical Change and British Multinationals in Kenya: Some Global Considerations* Paper presented at International Meeting of Researchers on the Transfer of Technology by Multinational Firms, Paris, 24-28 November 1975, Paris, O.E.C.D. (1975) mimeo

R. N. B. KAY Meat Production from Wild Herbivores *Proceedings of the Nutrition Society* London (1970) Vol. 29, p. 271

V. KOSOLAPOV *Mankind and the Year 2000* Moscow, Progress Publishers (1976)

V. A. KOVDA *Biosphere Soils and their Utilisation* Moscow, Academy of Sciences (1974)

D. LAL and DUANE (1973) cited in C. D. CARRUTHERS (1974)

H. H. LAMB *Climate — Present, Past and Future* London, Methuen (1972)

M. LIPTON *Why Poor People Stay Poor* London, Temple Smith (1977)

J. M. McLEAN and M. HOPKINS Problems of World Food and Agriculture — Projections Models and Possible Approaches *Futures* Guildford (August 1974) p. 309

A. MAKHIJANI and A. POOLE *Energy and Agriculture in the Third World* Cambridge, Mass., Ballinger (1975)

M. MANDAMI *The Myth of Population Control* New York Monthly Review Press (1972) p. 173

P. MARSTRAND and K. PAVITT 'The Agricultural Subsystem' in H. S. D. COLE *et al. Models of Doom* New York, Universe Books (1973) p. 56

D. MEADOWS *et al. The Limits to Growth* New York, Universe Books (1972) and London, Pan Books (1974)

K. MELLANBY *Can Britain Feed Itself?* London, Merlin Press (1975)

M. MESAROVIC and E. PESTEL *Mankind at the Turning Point* New York, Dutton / Readers Digest Press (1974)

C. A. MICHALET The International Transfer of Technology and the Multi-National Enterprise *Development and Change* London (April 1976) p. 157

D. MIR *The Semi-arid World* Longman (1974)

Y. D. MODRZHINSKAYA and C. A. STEPHANYAN *The Future of Society* Moscow, Progress Publishers (1973)

F. PAUKERT Income Distribution at Different Levels of Development *International Labour Review* Geneva (1973) p. 97

P. R. PAYNE 'Are World Protein Supplies Adequate? Some Observations on the Use of Protein Foods in Nutrition' in J. W. G. PORTER AND B. A. ROLLS (eds.) *Protein in Human Nutrition* London, Academic Press (1973) p. 119

N. PIRIE (ed.) *Food Protein Sources* Cambridge, Cambridge University Press (1975) International Biological Programme 4

T. T. POLEMAN and D. K. FREEBAIRN (eds.) *Food, Population and Employment: the Impact of the Green Revolution* New York, Praeger (1973)

R. REVELLE Resources Available for Agriculture *Scientific American* Vol. 235, no. 3 (September 1976) pp. 164-80

W. C. ROBINSON 'Fertility Patterns and the Green Revolution' in T. T. POLEMAN and D. K. FREEBAIRN (eds.) *Food, Population and Employment: the Impact of the Green Revolution* New York, Praeger (1973) p. 53

J. SIGURDSON Resources and the Environment in China *Ambio* Oslo (1975) Vol. 4 no. 3, p. 112

A. SIMONTOV World Food Consumption *Food Policy* Vol. 1, no. 3 (May 1976) pp. 232-8

R. SINHA *Food and Poverty* London, Croom Helm (1976)

J. SKINNER The Springbok: a Farm Animal of the Future *African Wildlife* Natal, South Africa (1973) Vol. 26, no 3, p. 114

B. R. STILLINGS 'World Supplies of Animal Proteins' in J. W. G. PORTER and B. A. ROLLS (eds.) *Protein in Human Nutrition* London, Academic Press (1973) p. 11

L TALBOT *et al. The Meat Production Potential of Wild Animals in Africa* Oxford, Commonwealth Agricultural Bureau (1966) C.A.B. technical communication no. 16

C. R. TAYLOR Ranching Arid Lands: Botswana Notes and Records No. 1 *American Journal of Physiology* Bethesda, Md., Vol. 219, p. 1136

M. K. THOMAS 'Changes in the Climate of Ontario' in *Changes in the Fauna of Ontario* University of Toronto Press (1957)

L. M. Thompson Weather, Variability, Climatic Change and Grain Production *Science* Vol. 188 (1975) p. 353

U.S. President's Science Advisory Committee *The World Food Problem, Report of the Panel on World Food Supply* Washington, D.C., U.S. Government Printing Office (1967)

J. T. WORGAN 'World Supplies of Protein from Unconventional Sources' in J. W. G. PORTER and B. A. ROLLS (eds.) *Protein in Human Nutrition* London, Academic Press (1973) p. 47

CHAPTER 5

P. H. ABELSON *Energy: Use, Conservation and Supply* Washington D.C., American Association for the Advancement of Science (1974)

J. P. ALBERS *et al. Summary of Petroleum and Selected Mineral Statistics for 120 Countries Including Offshore Areas* Washington, D.C., U.S. Government Printing Office (1973) U.S. Geological Survey professional paper 817

P. AVERITT Coal Resources of the United States, 1st January 1967 *Geological Survey Bulletin* Washington, D.C. (no. 1275, 1969)

P. S. BASILE *et al. Energy Demand Studies: Major Consuming Countries* First Technical Report of the Workshop on Alternative Energy Strategies Cambridge, Mass., M.I.T. Press (1976)

British Petroleum *Statistical Review of the World Oil Industry* London, British Petroleum Co. Ltd. (1976)

L. G. BROOKES More on the Output Elasticity of Energy Consumption *Journal of Industrial Economics* Oxford (November 1972) p. 83

I. C. BUPP and J.-C. DERIAN The Economics of Nuclear Power *Technoology Review* Cambridge, Mass. (February 1975) p. 14

Business Week New York (20 December 1976) How OPEC's High Prices Strangle World Growth p. 44

W. B. CASHION 'Bitumen-Bearing Rocks' in U.S. Geological Survey *United States Mineral Resources* Washington, D.C., U.S. Government Printing Office (1973) p. 99 (U.S. Geological Survey professional paper 820)

P. CHAPMAN *Fuel's Paradise* Harmondsworth, Penguin (1976)

C. CHENG *China's Petroleum Industry: Output, Growth and Export Potential* New York, Praeger (1976)

J. H. CHESSHIRE and C. M. BUCKLEY Energy Use in U.K. Industry *Energy Policy* Guildford (September 1976) p. 237

J. H. CHESSHIRE and C. HUGGETT Primary Energy Production in the Soviet Union — Problems and Prospects *Energy Policy* Guildford (September 1975) p. 223

B. COMMONER *The Poverty of Power: Energy and the Economic Crisis* New York, Knopf (1976)

J. DARMSTADTER *Energy in the World Economy* Baltimore, The Johns Hopkins Press (1971)

A. V. DESAI *Development and Energy Requirements* Brighton, Sussex, Science Policy Research Unit (1977) mimeo

R. DUMONT *Utopia or Else . . .* London, Deutsch (1974), New York Universe Books (1975)

G. EADS and R. R. NELSON Governmental Support of Advanced Civilian Technology Power Reactors and Supersonic Transport *Public Policy* Cambridge, Mass. (Summer 1971) p. 405

Economic Commission for Europe *Study on Measures Taken, or Which Might be Taken, to Achieve Increased Economy and Efficiency in the Extraction, Conversion, Transport and Use of Energy in the E.C.E. Region* United Nations Economic and Social Council, Geneva, Economic Commission for Europe (1976) (E / ECE 883 Rev. 1)

A. and P. EHRLICH *Population, Resources, Environment* San Francisco, Freeman (1970)

I. F. ELLIOT *The Soviet Energy Balance: Natural Gas, Other Fossil Fuels and Alternative Power Sources* New York, Praeger (1974)

E. W. ERICKSON and L. WAVERMAN (eds.) *The Energy Question: An International Failure of Policy* Toronto, University of Toronto Press (1974)

O. B. FALLS A Survey of the Market for Nuclear Power in Developing Countries *Energy Policy* Guildford (December 1973) p. 225

SIR B. FLOWERS (Chairman) Royal Commission on Environmental Pollution: 6th Report *Nuclear Power and the Environment* London, H.M.S.O. (1976) Cmnd. 6618

G. FOLEY *The Energy Question* Harmondsworth, Penguin (1976)

FOSTER ASSOCIATES *Energy Prices 1960-73* A Report to the Energy Policy Project of the Ford Foundation, Cambridge, Mass., Ballinger (1974)

D. S. FREEMAN *et al. A Time to Choose: America's Energy Future* Final Report by the Energy Policy Project of the Ford Foundation, Cambridge, Mass., Ballinger (1974)

J. D. GARNISH Geothermal Energy as an Alternative Source *Energy Policy* Guildford (June 1976) p. 130

G.B. Cabinet Office *Future World Trends: a Discussion Paper on World Trends in Population, Resources, Pollution etc. and their Implications* London, H.M.S.O. (1976)

G.B. Central Policy Review Staff *Energy Conservation* London, H.M.S.O. (1974)

G.B. Department of Energy (ACORD) *Energy R & D in the United Kingdom: a Discussion Document* London, Department of Energy (1976)

M. GRENON (ed.) *First I.I.A.S.A. Conference on Energy Resources* Laxenburg, Austria, International Institute for Applied Systems Analysis (1975) (CP-76-4)

E. P. GYFTOPOULOS *et al. Potential Fuel Effectiveness in Industry* A Report to the Energy Policy Project of the Ford Foundation Cambridge, Mass., Ballinger (1975)

W. HÄFELE *et al. Second Status Report on the I.I.A.S.A. Project on Energy Systems* Laxenburg, Austria, International Institute for Applied Systems Analysis (1975)

J. R. HAMMARLUND and L. L. LINDBERG (eds.) *The Political Economy of Energy Policy: a Projection for Capitalist Society* Madison, Institute for Environmental Studies, University of Wisconsin — Madison (1976)

M. HANSEN Trends in Uranium Supply *International Atomic Energy Agency Bulletin* Vienna (no. 5/6, 1976) p. 16

D. HAYES *Energy: the Case for Conservation* Washington, D.C., Worldwatch Institute (1976) Worldwatch Paper 4

R. HEILBRONER *An Inquiry into the Human Prospect* New York, Norton (1974)

A. O. HERRERA *et al. Catastrophe or New Society? A Latin American World Model* Ottawa, International Development Research Centre for the Fundacion Bariloche (1976)

J. M. HOLLANDER and M. K. SIMMONS *Annual Review of Energy* Palo Alto, Ca., Annual Review Inc. (1976)

J. H. HOLLOMAN *et al. Energy Research and Development* Papers prepared for the Energy Policy Project of the Ford Foundation, Cambridge, Mass., Ballinger (1975)

M. K. HUBBERT 'Energy Resources' in *Resources and Man* p. 157 by Committee of Resources and Man, National Academy of Sciences / National Research Council, San Francisco, Freeman (1968)

I. D. ILLICH *Energy and Equity* London, Calder and Boyars (1974)

Institute of Fuel *Energy for the Future* London, Institute of Fuel (1973)

J. JEWKES *et al. The Sources of Invention* 2nd edn, London, Macmillan (1969)

H. KAHN *et al. The Next 200 Years — a Scenario for America and the World* New York, Morrow (1976)

O. KECK *The Fast Breeder Reactor Programme in the Federal Republic of Germany* D.Phil. thesis, Brighton, University of Sussex (1977)

M. KENWARD *Potential Energy: an Analysis of World Energy Technology* London, Cambridge University Press (1976)

R. KRYMM A New Look at Nuclear Power Costs *International Atomic Energy Agency Bulletin* Vienna (1975) Vol. 18, no. 2, p. 2

R. KRYMM and G. WOITE Estimates of Future Demand for Uranium and Nuclear Fuel Cycle Services *International Atomic Energy Agency Bulletin* Vienna (no. 5/6, 1976) p. 6

G. L. KULCINSKI Fusion Power — an Assessment of its Potential Impact in the U.S.A. *Energy Policy* Guildford (June 1974) p. 104

H. H. LANDSBERG *et al. Resources in America's Future* Baltimore, Johns Hopkins Press (1963)

G. LEACH *The Motor Car and Natural Resources* Paris, O.E.C.D. (1972)

G. LEACH The Impact of the Motor Car on Oil Reserves *Energy Policy* Guildford (December 1973) p. 195

W. LEONTIEF *et al. The Future of the World Economy* Preliminary Report, New York, United Nations (1976)

H. R. LINDEN *The Future Development of Energy Supply Systems* Paper prepared for the Fuel Society of Japan's Conference (October / November 1972)

A. B. LOVINS *Soft Energy Paths: Towards a Durable Peace* Cambridge, Mass., Ballinger (1977)

A. B. LOVINS and J. H. PRICE *Non-Nuclear Futures: the Case for an Ethical Energy Strategy* Cambridge, Mass., Ballinger (1975)

A. MAKHIJANI *Energy Policy for the Rural Third World* London, International Institute for Environment and Development (1975)

A. MAKHIJANI and A. D. POOLE *Energy and Agriculture in the Third World* Cambridge, Mass., Ballinger (1975)

T. R. MALTHUS *An Essay in the Principle of Population; and Summary View of the Principle of Population* Harmondsworth, Penguin (1970)

D. MEADOWS *et al. The Limits to Growth* New York, Universe Books and London, Pan Books (1974)

M. MESAROVIC and E. PESTEL *Mankind at the Turning Point* New York, Dutton / Readers Digest (1974)

J. G. MYERS *et al. Energy Consumption in Manufacturing* A Report to the Energy Policy Project of the Ford Foundation, Cambridge, Mass., Ballinger (1974)

National Academy of Sciences *Energy for Rural Development: Renewable Resources and*

Alternative Technologies for Developing Countries Report of an Ad Hoc Panel of the Advisory Committee on Technology Innovation Board on Science and Technology for International Development Commission on International Relations, Washington, D.C., N.S.A. (1976)

National Petroleum Council *U.S. Energy Outlook — Coal Availability* Washington, D.C., National Petroleum Council (1973)

W. D. NORDHAUS (ed.) *Proceedings of the Workshop on Energy Demand* Laxenburg, Austria, International Institute for Applied Systems Analysis (1976) CP-76-1

P. R. ODELL *Oil and World Power: Background to the Oil Crisis* Harmondsworth, Penguin (1974)

O.E.C.D. *Oil: the Present Situation and Future Prospects* Paris, O.E.C.D. (1973a)

O.E.C.D. *Uranium: Resources, Production and Demand* A Joint Report by the O.E.C.D. Nuclear Energy Agency and the International Atomic Energy Authority Paris, O.E.C.D. (1973b)

O.E.C.D. *Energy Prospects to 1985* Paris, O.E.C.D. (1974a)

O.E.C.D. *Statistics of Energy 1959-1973* Paris, O.E.C.D. (1974b)

J. A. OVER and A. C. SJOERDSMA *Energy Conservation: Ways and Means* The Hague, Future Shape of Technology Foundation (1974)

W. C. PATTERSON *Nuclear Power* Harmondsworth, Penguin (1976)

R. S. PINDYCK *International Comparisons of the Residential Demand for Energy: a Preliminary Analysis* Cambridge, Mass., Massachusetts Institute of Technology (1976) Working Paper M.I.T. EL 76-023 WP

D. RICARDO *The Principles of Political Economy and Taxation* Harmondsworth, Penguin (1971)

J. RUSSELL *Energy as a Factor in Soviet Foreign Policy* Farnborough, Hants and Lexington, Mass., Saxon House / Lexington Books (1976)

RYMAN (1967) see H. R. WARMAN (1973)

L. SCHIPPER and A. J. LICHTENBERG Efficient Energy Use and Well-Being: the Swedish Example *Science* Washington D.C. (3 December 1976) p. 1001

Statistical Office of the European Communities *The Evolution of Prices of Oil Fuels in the Nine Countries of the European Community from 1960 to 1974* Luxembourg, EUROSTAT (1974) no. 2

S.C.E.P. (Study of Critical Environmental Problems) *Man's Impact on the Global Environment — Assessment and Recommendations for Action* Cambridge, Mass., The M.I.T. Press (1970)

A. J. SURREY and C. HUGGETT Opposition to Nuclear Power — a Review of International Experience *Energy Policy* Guildford (December 1976) p. 286

U.N. World Energy Requirements and Resources in the Year 2000 *Peaceful Uses of Atomic Power* Vol. 1, p. 303, Vienna, International Atomic Energy Agency (1971)

U.N. *World Energy Supplies 1950-1974* New York, U.N. (1976) Statistical Papers Series J, No. 19

U.N. Economic Commission for Europe *The Coal Situation in Europe in 1973 and its Prospects* New York, U.N. (1975) ECE / COAL / 9

U.N. Economic Commission for Europe *Report to a Symposium on the Future Role of Coal in the National and World Economies, Warsaw 1969* Geneva, E.C.E. (1970) ST / ECE / COAL / 47

U.S. Bureau of Mines *Mineral Yearbook, 1971* (1973)

U.S. Energy Research and Development Administration *A National Plan for Energy Research, Development and Demonstration: Creating Energy Choices for the Future* Washington, D.C., ERDA (1976)

U.S. Federal Energy Administration *Project Independence Report* Washington, D.C., U.S. Government Printing Office (1974)

H. R. WARMAN *The Future Availability of Oil* London, World Energy Supplies Conference (1973) (organised by *The Financial Times*)

WEEKS (1962) see WARMAN (1973)

A. M. WEINBERG AND R. P. HAMMOND Global Effects of Increased Use of Energy *Peaceful Uses of Atomic Power* Vol. 1. Vienna, International Atomic Energy Agency (1971)

S. WILDHORN *et al. How to Save Gasoline: Public Policy Alternatives for the Automobile* Cambridge, Mass., Ballinger (1975)

R. H. WILLIAMS (ed.) *The Energy Conservation Papers* Reports Prepared for the Energy Policy Project of the Ford Foundation, Cambridge, Mass., Ballinger (1975)

World Energy Conference *Survey of Energy Resources* London, World Energy Conference (1974)

The following journals were also widely used:

Energy Policy
International Atomic Energy Agency Bulletin
Petroleum Economist
Petroleum Times
Technology Review

CHAPTER 6

C. BARKER and W. PAGE OPEC as a Model for Other Mineral Exporters *Bulletin of the Institute of Development Studies* Brighton Sussex (October 1974) p. 81

H. J. BARNETT and C. MORSE *Scarcity and Growth* Baltimore, Johns Hopkins University Press for Resources for the Future, Inc. (1963)

Battelle Columbus Laboratories *Energy Use Patterns in Metallurgical and Non-metallic Mineral Processing* Springfield, Va. National Technical Information Service (1975) (PB245, 759AS, PB246, 357AS)

C. F. BERGSTEN The Threat from the Third World *Foreign Policy* New York (Summer 1973) p. 102

C. F. BERGSTEN A New OPEC in Bauxite *Challenge* White Plains, N.Y. (July / August 1976) p. 12

British-North American Committee *Mineral Developments in the Eighties: Prospects and Problems* London, Montreal, Washington, D.C. British North American Committee (1976)

P. F. CHAPMAN The Energy Costs of Materials *Energy Policy* Guildford (March 1975) p. 47

P. F. CHAPMAN *The Energy Costs of Producing Copper and Aluminium from Primary Sources* Milton Keynes, Open University Energy Research Group (1973) (Report ERG 001) and *Metals and Materials* London (February and June 1974)

A. and P. EHRLICH *Population, Resources, Environment — Issues in Human Ecology* San Francisco, Freeman (1970)

J. W. FORRESTER *World Dynamics* Cambridge, Mass., Wright-Allen (1971)

H. E. GOELLER and A. M. WEINBERG The Age of Substitutability *Science* Washington, D.C. (20 February 1976) p. 683

M. H. GOVETT The Geographic Concentration of World Mineral Supplies *Resources Policy* Guildford (December 1975) p. 357

Harwell (U.K.A.E.A.) *Proceedings of the Conference on Conservation of Materials, Harwell, 26-27 March 1974* Chilton, Harwell (1974)

E. T. HAYES Energy Implications of Materials Processing *Science* Washington, D.C. (20 February 1976) p. 661

R. HEILBRONER *An Inquiry into the Human Prospect* New York, Norton (1974)

J. HEMMING *The Conquest of the Incas* New York, Harcourt Brace (1970)

A. HERRERA et al *Catastrophe or New Society?* Ottawa, I.D.R.C. (1976)

Institute of Development Studies UNCTAD — A Fourth Chance? *Bulletin of the I.D.S.* Brighton, Sussex (April 1976)

H. KAHN, W. BROWN and L. MARTEL *The Next 200 Years* New York, Morrow (1976)

W. LEONTIEF et al. *The Future of the World Economy* Preliminary Report, New York, United Nations (1976)

J. W. LLOYD Importance of Water Resources in the Development of the Chilean Copper Industry *Institution of Mining and Metallurgy Bulletin and Transactions* London (April 1974) p. A63-66 (Bulletin 809)

D. MEADOWS et al. *The Limits to Growth* New York, Universe Books (1972) and London, Pan Books (1974)

J. MERO Oceanic Mineral Resources *Futures* Guildford (December 1968) p. 125

M. MESARORIC and E. PESTEL *Mankind at the Turning Point* New York, Dutton / Readers Digest Press (1974)

Metallgesellschaft *Metal Statistics* Frankfurt-am-Main, Metallgesellschaft A.G. (annually)

Y. MODRZHINSKAYA and C. STEPHANYAN *The Future of Society* Moscow, Progress Publishers (1973)

NATO Science Committee Study Group *Rational Use of Potentially Scarce Metals* Brussels, NATO Science Affairs Division (1976)

National Materials Advisory Board *Trends in the Usage of Silver* Washington, D.C. (1968) NMAB Report no. 241

W. D. NORDHAUS Resources as a Constraint on Growth *American Economic Review* Providence, R.I. (May 1974) p. 22

O.E.C.D. *Science, Technology and Material Resources Policies* Paris, OECD (1977) SPT (77)3

W. PAGE Mining and Development: are they Compatible in South America? *Resources Policy* Guildford (December 1976) p. 235

W. PAGE The Non-Renewable Resources Subsystem in H. S. D. COLE *et al.* (eds.) *Thinking About the Future: A Critique of 'The Limits to Growth'* London, Chatto and Windus Also published in the U.S.A. *Models of Doom* New York, Universe Books (1973)

Paley Commission (U.S. President's Materials Policy Commision) *Resources for Freedom* Washington, D.C., U.S. Government Printing Office (1952)

Sir R. PRAIN *Copper: The Anatomy of an Industry* London, Mining Journal Books (1975)

G. F. RAY Raw Materials, Shortages and Producer Power *Long Range Planning* Oxford (August 1975) p. 2

R. J. SMITH Medium-Term Forecasts Re-assessed: IV: Domestic Appliances *National Institute Economic Review* (n.d.) pp. 68—83

J. SPENGLER *Population Change, Modernisation and Welfare* Englewood Cliffs, N.J., Prentice Hall (1974)

A. SUTULOV *Minerals in World Affairs* Salt Lake City, University of Utah Printing Service (1972)

U.N. *Statistical Yearbook* New York (various years)

F. J. WELLS *The Long-Run Availability of Phosphorus* Baltimore, Johns Hopkins University Press for Resources for the Future, Inc. (1975)

World Bank *World Bank Atlas* 9th edn, Washington, D.C. (1974)

World Bureau of Metal Statistics *World Metal Statistics* Birmingham, U.K., W.B.M.S. (monthly)

Zinc Development Association *Zinc: Current Trends in Zinc Coatings and Castings* London, ZDA (1975)

CHAPTER 7

C. M. COOPER (ed.) *Technology and Development* Chichester, John Wiley (forthcoming in 1978)

C. M. COOPER and F. SERCOVICH *Mechanisms for the Transer of Technology from Advanced to Developing Countries* Geneva, UNCTAD (1971)

C. FREEMAN *The Economics of Industrial Innovation* Harmondsworth, Penguin (1974)

C. FREEMAN *et al* The Goals of R and D in the 1970s *Science Studies* London (October 1971) p. 357

C. FURNAS *The Next Hundred Years: the Unfinished Business of Science* London, Cassell (1936)

C. FURNAS The Next Hundred Years — Thirty Years Later. Paper presented at a General Session of the 45th Annual Meeting of the American Petroleum Institute, Chicago, 9 November 1965, Washington, D.C., American Petroleum Institute (1965)

R. GILPIN *Technology, Economic Growth and International Competitiveness* Washington, D.C., Government Printing Office (1975)

G.B. Monopolies Commission *Report on Chlordiazepoxide and Diazepam* London, H.M.S.O. (1974) H.C. 197

S. HOLLANDER *The Sources of Increased Efficiency: A Study of Du Pont Rayon Plants* Cambridge, Mass., M.I.T. Press (1965)

R. JUNGK *Brighter than a Thousand Suns* New York, Harcourt (1958)

H. KAHN and A. J. WIENER *The Year 2000* New York, Macmillan (1967)

V. KOSOLAPOV *Mankind and the Year 2000* Moscow, Progress Publishers (1976)

D. MEADOWS *et al. The Limits to Growth* New York, Universe Books (1972)

G. MYRDAL *Economic Theory and Underdeveloped Regions* London, Duckworth (1957)

National Resources Committee *Technological Trends and National Policy* including social implications of new inventions. Report of the Sub-Committee on Technology, Washington, D.C., Government Printing Office (1937)

W. E. G. SALTER *Productivity and Technical Change* Cambridge, Cambridge University Press (1961)

E. F. SCHUMACHER *Small is Beautiful — A Study of Economics as if People Mattered* London, Blond and Briggs (1973) New York, Harper & Row (1973)

J. -J. SERVAN-SCHREIBER *The American Challenge* London, Hamish Hamilton (1968)

I. SPIEGEL-ROSING and D. DE SOLLA PRICE (eds.) *Science, Technology and Society: a Cross Disciplinary Perspective* London, Sage (1977)

A. C. SUTTON *Western Technology and Soviet Economic Development: 1917 to 1930* Stanford, Ca., Stanford University, Hoover Institute on War, Revolution and Peace (1968)

C. VAITSOS *Intercountry Income Distribution and Transnational Enterprises* Oxford, Clarendon Press (1974)

CHAPTERS 8 AND 9

We cannot here give a comprehensive bibliography of writings relevant to our notion of three worldviews. The following references should provide an initial guide to the works of those authors cited in the text as representative of the worldviews, as well as detailing those sources to which direct reference has been made.

S. AMIN *Accumulation on a World Scale* New York, Monthly Review Press (1974)

P. ANDERSON *Considerations on Western Marxism* London, New Left Books (1976)

P. ANDERSON 'Origins of the Present Crisis' in P. ANDERSON and R. BLACKBURN (eds) *Towards Socialism* London, Fontana (1965)

M. BARRATT-BROWN *The Economics of Imperialism* Harmondsworth, Penguin (1974)

P. T. BAUER *Dissent on Development* London, Weidenfeld (1972)

D. BELL *The End of Ideology* New York, Free Press (1960)

D. BELL *The Coming of the Post-Industrial Society* New York, Basic Books (1973)

W. J. CHAMBLISS Introduction to *Sociological Readings in the Conflict Perspective* Reading, Mass., Addison-Wesley (1973)

R. H. CHILCOTE and J. C. EDELSTEIN Introduction to *Latin America: the Struggle with Dependency and Beyond* Cambridge, Mass., Schenkman Publishing Co., Halstead Press (1974)

R. A. DAHL *Modern Political Analysis* Englewood Cliffs, N.J., Prentice-Hall (1963)

R. DAHRENDORF *Class and Class Conflict in Industrial Society* Stanford University Press (1959)

E. DURKHEIM *The Division of Labour in Society* Glencoe, Ill., Free Press (1960)

A. EMMANUEL The Multinational Corporations and Inequality of Development *International Social Science Journal* Paris (1976) Vol. 28, no. 4, p. 754

A. FOSTER-CARDER From Rostow to Gunder Frank: Conflicting Paradigms in the Analysis of Underdevelopment *World Development* Oxford (Vol. 4, no. 3, 1976), p. 167

M. FRIEDMAN *Capitalism and Freedom* University of Chicago Press (1962)

C. Furtado *Development and Underdevelopment* Berkeley, University of California Press (1964)

J. K. Galbraith *The New Industrial State* Boston, Houghton Mifflin (1967)

V. George and P. Wilding *Ideology and Social Welfare* London, Routledge (1976)

R. Gilpin Three Models of the Future *International Organization* Madison, Wis. (1975a) p. 37

R. Gilpin *U.S. Power and the Multinational Corporation* London, Macmillan (1975b)

M. Hechter *Internal Colonialism: the Celtic Fringe in British National Development, 1536—1966* London, Routledge (1975)

R. Heilbroner *An Inquiry into the Human Prospect* New York, Norton (1974)

J. Horton Order and Conflict Theories of Social Problems as Competing Ideologies *American Journal of Sociology* Chicago (May 1966) p. 701; reprinted in J. E. Curtis and J. W. Petras *The Sociology of Knowledge* London, Duckworth (1970)

H. G. Johnson *Technology and Economic Interdependence* London, Macmillan (1975)

P. J. Katzenstein International Relations and Domestic Structures *International Organization* Madison, Wis. (1976) p. 1

J. M. Keynes *The General Theory of Employment, Interest and Money* London, Macmillan (1936)

P. F. Lazarsfeld *Main Trends in Sociology* New York, Harper & Row (1973)

V. I. Lenin *Imperialism: the Highest Stage of Capitalism* Peking, Foreign Language Press (1975; 1st ed. 1917)

I. M. D. Little, T. Scitowsky and M. Scott *Industry and Trade in Some Developing Countries* Oxford University Press (1970)

E. Mandel *Late Capitalism* London, New Left Books (1975)

E. Mandel *Marxist Economic Theory* London, Merlin Books (1969)

H. Marcuse *One-Dimensional Man* Boston, Beacon Press (1964)

K. Marx *Capital* (in English). London, Lawrence & Wishart (3 vols: 1954, 1957, 1960); also Penguin Books translation available

R. Miliband *The State in Capitalist Society* London, Weidenfeld (1969)

G. Myrdal *The Challenge of World Poverty* Harmondsworth, Penguin (1970)

M. Olson *The Logic of Collective Action* Cambridge, Mass., Harvard University Press (1965)

V. Pareto *The Mind and Society* New York, Harcourt Brace (1935)

T. Parsons *The Social System* Glencoe, Ill., Free Press (1951)

T. Parsons *Societies: Evolutionary and Comparative Perspectives* Englewood Cliffs, N. J., Prentice-Hall (1966)

K. Popper *The Open Society and Its Enemies* London, Routledge (4th ed., 1962)

K. Popper *The Poverty of Historicism* London, Routledge (2nd ed., 1960)

A. B. Shostak *Modern Social Reforms* New York, Macmillan (1974)

A. Smith *An Inquiry into the Nature and Causes of the Wealth of Nations* Harmondsworth, Penguin (1974)

Chapters 8 and 9: additional references.

R. Dumont *Utopia or Else . . .* London, Deutsch (1974) New York, Universe Books (1975)

A. and P. Ehrlich *Population, Resources, Environment — Issues in Human Ecology* San Francisco, Freeman (1970)

S. Encel, P. K. Marstrand and W. Page (eds.) *The Art of Anticipation* London, Martin Robertson (1975) New York, Pica Press (1976)

J. W. Forrester *World Dynamics* Cambridge, Mass., Wright-Allen (1971)

A. G. Frank *Capitalism and Underdevelopment in Latin America* Harmondsworth, Penguin (1971)

J. Galtung *Self-Reliance: Concepts, Theory and Rationale* Oslo, University of Oslo (1977) Paper no. 35 (As in chapters 2 and 3, our commentary is based on a draft:)

R. HEILBRONER *An Inquiry into the Human Prospect* New York Review of Books (24 January 1974) p. 21 and New York, Norton (1974)
A. HERRERA *et al. Catastrophe or New Society?* Ottawa, I. D. R. C. (1976)
W. S. JEVONS *The Theory of Political Economy* (1871). Harmondsworth, Penguin (1970)
H. KAHN, W. BROWN and L. MARTEL *The Next 200 Years* New York, Morrow (1976)
V. KOSOLAPOV *Mankind and the Year 2000* Moscow, Progress Publishers (1976)
W. LEONTIEF *et al The Future of the World Economy* Preliminary Report, New York, United Nations (1976)
F. LIST *National System of Political Economy* (1841). London, Longmans (1904)
A. MARSHALL *Principles of Economics* (1890) London, Macmillan (1961)
D. MEADOWS *et al The Limits to Growth* New York, Universe Books (1972) and London, Pan Books (1974)
M. MESAROVIC and E. PESTEL *Mankind at the Turning Point* New York, Dutton/Readers Digest Press (1974)
Y. MODRZHINSKAYA and C. STEPHANYAN *The Future of Society* Moscow, Progress Publishers (1973)
D. RICARDO *On the Principles of Political Economy and Taxation* (1817) Harmondsworth, Penguin (1971)
E. F. SCHUMACHER *Small is Beautiful — a Study of Economics as if People Mattered* London, Blond and Briggs (1973) and New York, Harper & Row (1973)
J. TINBERGEN *Reshaping the International Order — A Report to the Club of Rome* New York, Dutton (1976)
L. WALRAS *Elements of Pure Economics* (1894) London, Allen and Unwin (1954)

CHAPTER 10

U. ALBRECHT *et al Rüstungs und Unterentwicklung* Hamburg, Rowohlt (1976)
G. T. ALLISON and F. A. MORRIS Armaments and Arms Control: Exploring the Determinants of Military Weapons *Daedalus* Boston, Mass. (Summer 1975) p. 99
J. ANNERSTAEDT *Makten over Forskningen om Statling Forskningsorganisation och Forskningplanering: Dagens Sverige* Lund, Cavefors (1972)
P. A. BARAN and P. M. SWEEZY *Monopoly Capital* Harmondsworth, Penguin (1968)
E. BENOIT *Defense and Economic Growth in Developing Countries* Lexington, Mass., D. C. Heath (1973)
F. BLACKABY and C. JÄMTIN 'World Military Expenditure' in Stockholm International Peace Research Institute *SIPRI Yearbook of World Armaments and Disarmaments 1968/69* Stockholm, Almqvist and Wiksell (1969) ch. 1
L. BRAMSON and G. W. GOETHALS (eds) *War: Studies from Psychology, Sociology, Anthropology* New York, Basic Books (rev. ed., 1968)
B. BRUNELLI 'High Energy-Density Plasmas and Pure Fusion Triggers' in B. T. FIELD *et al.* (eds) *Impact of New Technologies on the Arms Race* (Proceedings of 10th Pugwash Symposium, Racine, June 1970) Cambridge, Mass., M.I.T. Press (1971) p. 140
A. BUCHAN *War in Modern Society* London, Watts (1966)
H. BULL Arms Control and World Order *International Security* Cambridge, Mass. (Summer 1976) p. 3
S. CANBY *The Alliance and Europe: Part IV. Military Doctrine and Technology* London, International Institute for Strategic Studies (Adelphi papers no. 109, 1975)
B. CARTER Nuclear Strategy and Nuclear Weapons *Scientific American* New York (May 1974) p. 20
S. T. COHEN and W. R. VAN CLEAVE Western European Collateral Damage from Tactical Nuclear Weapons *Journal of the Royal United Services Institute* London (1976) Vol. 121, p. 32
R. CURNOW *et al.* General and Complete Disarmament: a Systems-Analysis Approach *Futures* Guildford (October 1976) p. 384

L. E. DAVIS *Limited Nuclear Options: Deterrence and the New American Doctrine* London, International Institute for Strategic Studies (Adelphi papers no. 121, 1976)

S. D. DRELL and F. VON HIPPEL Limited Nuclear War *Scientific American* New York (November 1976) p. 27

Y. DROR War, Violence and Futures Studies *Futures* Guildford (February 1974) p. 2

L. J. DUMAS National Insecurity in the Nuclear Age *Bulletin of the Atomic Scientists* Chicago (May 1976) p. 24

T. N. DUPUY Tactical Nuclear Combat *Ordnance* Washington, D.C. (November-December 1968) p. 292

J. ELLIS *The Social History of the Machine Gun* London, Croom Helm (1975)

F. ENGELS *Anti-Dühring: Herr Eugen Dühring's Revolution in Science* Translated from the 3rd German ed., 1894) Moscow, Foreign Languages Publishing House (1962)

W. EPSTEIN *The Last Chance: Nuclear Proliferation and Arms Control* New York, Free Press (1976)

R. FORSBERG *Resources Devoted to Military Research and Development* Stockholm, Almqvist and Wiksell for Stockholm International Peace Research Institute (1972)

G. B. Ministry of Defence *Defence Accounts together with the Report of the Comptroller and the Auditor General* London, H.M.S.O. (annually)

J. GALTUNG *Essays in Peace Research, Vol. 2 Peace, War and Defence* New York, Humanities Press (1975)

C. S. GRAY Theater Nuclear Weapons: Doctrines and Postures *World Politics* PRINCETON, N. J. (January 1976) p. 300

M. HALPERN 'Middle Eastern Armies and the New Middle Class' in J. J. JOHNSON (ed.) *The Role of the Military in Underdeveloped Countries* Princeton University Press (1962) p. 277

R. L. HEILBRONER *An Inquiry into the Human Prospect* New York, Norton (1974)

H. R. HEMINGWAY The Interactive Dynamics of Nuclear Destruction *Stanford Journal of International Studies* Stanford, Ca. (Spring 1972) p. 173

I. B. HOLLEY *Ideas and Weapons: Exploitation of the Aerial Weapon by the United States During World War I* New Haven, Conn., Yale University Press (1953)

M. HOWARD The Relevance of Traditional Strategy *Foreign Affairs* New York (January 1973) p. 253

R. HUISKEN and R. BOOTH 'World Armaments 1975' in Stockholm International Peace Research Institute *World Armaments and Disarmaments SIPRI Yearbook 1976* Stockholm, Almqvist and Wiksell (1976) ch. 6

S. HUNTINGTON *The Soldier and the State* New York, Vintage Books (1957)

F. IKLÉ 'Can Nuclear Deterrence Last Out the Century?' *Foreign Affairs* New York (January 1973) p. 267

International Institute for Strategic Studies *The Military Balance 1976-1977* London, I.I.S.S. (1976)

B. JASANI (ed.) *Nuclear Proliferation Problems* Stockholm, Almqvist and Wicksell for Stockholm International Peace Research Institute (1974)

H. KAHN, W. BROWN and L. MARTEL *The Next 200 Years* New York, Morrow (1976)

H. KAHN and A. WIENER *The Year 2000* New York, Macmillan (1967)

M. KALDOR *European Defence Industries — National and International Implications* Brighton, University of Sussex Institute for the Study of International Organisation (ISIO monograph no. 8, 1972)

M. KALDOR The Military and Development *World Development* Oxford (June 1976) p. 459

I. KENDE *Local Wars in Asia, Africa and Latin America 1945-1969* Budapest, Center for Afro-Asian Research of the Hungarian Academy of Sciences (Studies on developing countries no. 60, 1972)

M. KIDRON *Western Capitalism Since the War* London, Weidenfeld (1968)

D. KING-HELE *The End of the Twentieth Century?* London, Macmillan (1970)

J. R. KURTH Why We Buy the Weapons We Do *Foreign Policy* New York (1973) no. 11

M. LEITENBERG *Background Material on Nuclear Weapons in Europe* a paper prepared for the 15th Pugwash Symposium, Finland, August 1971 'On Tactical Arms Limitation in Europe', mimeo. (1971)

P. LEWIS Defense Costs and the Economy *New York Times* (19 December 1976)

K. LIEBKNECHT *Militarism and Anti-Militarism* Cambridge, Rivers Press (1973; 1st ed. 1907)

R. S. MCNAMARA *The Essence of Security: Reflections in Office* New York, Harper (1968)

S. MELMAN *Pentagon Capitalism: the Political Economy of War* New York, McGraw-Hill (1970)

S. MELMAN *The Permanent War Economy: American Capitalism in Decline* New York, Simon and Schuster (1974)

A. MYRDAL *The Game of Disarmament* New York, Pantheon (1976)

H. NAIDU Conflicts in Stockholm International Peace Research Institute *SIPRI Yearbook of World Armaments and Disarmaments 1968/69* Stockholm, Almqvist and Wiksell (1969) p. 359

P. L. PYE 'Armies in the Process of Political Modernization' in J. J. JOHNSON (ed.) *The Role of the Miliary in Underdeveloped Countries* Princeton University Press (1962) p. 69

J. RECORD and T. I. ANDERSON *U.S. Nuclear Weapons in Europe: Issues and Alternatives* Washington, D.C., Brookings Institution (1974)

L. F. RICHARDSON *Arms and Insecurity: A Mathematical Study of the Causes and Origins of War* London, Stevens (1960a)

L. F. RICHARDSON *Statistics of Deadly Quarrels* Pittsburgh, Boxwood Press (1960b)

J. P. P. ROBINSON The Special Case of Chemical and Biological Weapons *Bulletin of the Atomic Scientists* Chicago (May 1975) p. 17

J. P. P. ROBINSON 'Should NATO have Chemical Weapons? A Framework for Considering Policy Alternatives' in M. S. MESELSON (ed.) *Policies for Chemical Weapons and Chemical Arms Control*, Boston, American Academy of Arts and Sciences (1977)

S. ROSEN (ed.) *Testing the Theory of the Military-Industrial Complex* Lexington, Mass., Lexington Books (1973)

K. W. ROTHSCHILD Military Expenditure, Exports and Growth *Kyklos* Basle (1973) p. 804

D. H. RUMSFELD *Annual Defense Department Report f.y. 1978* Washington, D.C., U.S. Department of Defense (1977)

H. SCHMIDT *Defense or Retaliation: a German View* New York, Praeger (1962)

P. C. SCHMITTER 'Military Intervention, Political Competitiveness and Public Policy in Latin America 1950-67 in M. JANOWITZ and J. VON DOORN (eds) *On Military Intervention* Rotterdam University Press (1971)

J. A. SCHUMPETER *Imperialism* [and] *Social Classes: Two Essays* New York, Meridian (1955; 1st ed. 1919)

J. D. SINGER 'An Assessment of Peace Research' *International Security* Cambridge, Mass. (Summer 1976) p. 118

J. D. SINGER and M. SMALL *The Wages of War 1816-1965: a Statistical Handbook* New York, Wiley (1972)

R. L. SIVARD *World Military and Social Expenditures 1976* Leesburg, Va., W.M.S.E. Publications (1976)

R. P. SMITH Military Expenditure and Capitalism *Cambridge Journal of Economics* (1977) no. 1, p. 61

V. STEFFLRE Long-term Forecasting and the Problem of Large-scale Wars *Futures* Guildford (August 1974) p. 302

T. T. STONIER *Nuclear Disaster* Cleveland, Ohio, Meridian (1963)

R. (SUNDERLAND *et al.* *Historical Trends Related to Weapon Lethality* (Report Prepared under Contract for the Advanced Tactics Project of the Combat Developments Command H.Q. U.S. Army) Washington, D.C., Historical Evaluation and Research Organization (1964) (A.D. 458, 760-3)

United Nations Department of Political and Security Council Affairs *The United Nations and Disarmament 1945-1970* New York, U.N. (1971)

United Nations Department of Political and Security Council Affairs *The United Nations and Disarmament 1970-1975* New York, U.N. (1976)

United States National Academy of Sciences *Long-Term Worldwide Effects of Multiple Nuclear Weapons Detonations* Washington, D.C., N.A.S. (1975)

R. WILLIAMS 'Science, Technology and the Future of Warfare' in R. A. BEAUMONT and M. EDMONDS (eds) *War in the Next Decade* London, Macmillan (1975) ch. 9

A. WOHLSTETTER Spreading the Bomb Without Breaking the Rules *Foreign Policy* New York (Winter 1976-77) p. 88

D. WOOD *Conflict in the Twentieth Century* London, Institute for Strategic Studies (Adelphi papers no. 48, June 1968)

Name Index

410

412

Subject Index

416